AF806415

Pandemics and Ethics

Andreas Reis · Martina Schmidhuber ·
Andreas Frewer
Editors

Pandemics and Ethics

Development – Problems – Solutions

Springer

Editors
Andreas Reis
Health Ethics and Governance Unit
Department of Research for Health
World Health Organization
Geneva, Switzerland

Martina Schmidhuber
Professorship for Health Care Ethics
Karl Franzens University Graz
Graz, Austria

Andreas Frewer
Professorship for Ethics in Medicine
Erlangen-Nürnberg University
Erlangen, Germany

ISBN 978-3-662-66871-9 ISBN 978-3-662-66872-6 (eBook)
https://doi.org/10.1007/978-3-662-66872-6

This book is a translation of the original German „Pandemien und Ethik" by Reis, Andreas/Schmidhuber, Martina/Frewer, Andreas (Eds.), published by Springer-Verlag GmbH, DE in 2021. The translation was done with the help of an artificial intelligence machine translation tool. A subsequent human revision was done primarily in terms of content, so that the book will read stylistically differently from a conventional translation. Springer Nature works continuously to further the development of tools for the production of books and on the related technologies to support the authors.

© The Editor(s) (if applicable) and The Author(s), under exclusive license to Springer-Verlag GmbH, DE, part of Springer Nature 2023
This work is subject to copyright. All rights are solely and exclusively licensed by the Publisher, whether the whole or part of the material is concerned, specifically the rights of translation, reprinting, reuse of illustrations, recitation, broadcasting, reproduction on microfilms or in any other physical way, and transmission or information storage and retrieval, electronic adaptation, computer software, or by similar or dissimilar methodology now known or hereafter developed.
The use of general descriptive names, registered names, trademarks, service marks, etc. in this publication does not imply, even in the absence of a specific statement, that such names are exempt from the relevant protective laws and regulations and therefore free for general use.
The publisher, the authors, and the editors are safe to assume that the advice and information in this book are believed to be true and accurate at the date of publication. Neither the publisher nor the authors or the editors give a warranty, expressed or implied, with respect to the material contained herein or for any errors or omissions that may have been made. The publisher remains neutral with regard to jurisdictional claims in published maps and institutional affiliations.

This Springer imprint is published by the registered company Springer-Verlag GmbH, DE, part of Springer Nature.
The registered company address is: Heidelberger Platz 3, 14197 Berlin, Germany

Contents

Ethical Challenges in Pandemics. Introduction 1
Martina Schmidhuber, Andreas Reis and Andreas Frewer

Pandemics and the Dignity of Man. Reflections on the History of Disease 7
Klaus Bergdolt

Solidarity in Times of a Pandemic: Everyday Practices and Prioritization Decisions in Light of the Solidarity Concept 25
Katharina Kieslich and Barbara Prainsack

Human Rights and International Obligations in Pandemic Times—More than Health Protection 39
Walter Bruchhausen and Eva Kuhn

Duties and Rights of Health Professionals During a Pandemic 53
Annabel Seebohm and Otmar Kloiber

Restrictions on Fundamental Rights in the Name of Public Health. Fundamental Rights as an Regulative Elements of Proportionate Pandemic Management 69
Stephan Rixen

Ethical Challenges of Resource Allocation in Pandemics 83
Georg Marckmann

Ventilator Triage and Vaccine Rationing in Covid-19: A New Paradigm for Promoting Social Justice in Allocation with Disadvantage Indices 97
Harald Schmidt

Vaccination Against Infectious Diseases—A Bioethical Debate in the Pandemic 121
Christiane Druml

Immunity and Vaccination Certificates in the Covid-19 Crisis 137
Steffen Augsberg

Pandemics and Research Ethics. An Overview of Central Challenges ... 149
Alice Faust, Lana Saksone, Stefanie Weigold, Lena Woydack and Daniel Strech

Ethical and Legal Challenges of Digital Medicine in Pandemics 165
Timo Minssen and Sara Gerke

'Infodemics': Dealing with Information in Pandemic Times from an Ethical Perspective 203
Sebastian Wäscher, Tim Nguyen and Nikola Biller-Andorno

Ethics and Old Age in the Covid-19 Pandemic 223
Hans-Jörg Ehni and Hans-Werner Wahl

Covid-19 Pandemic and the Protection of Older People in International Comparison. Results of Comparative Research from an Ethical Perspective 239
Sophia Forster and Andreas Frewer

Pandemics and Gender—The Unequal Effects of a Pandemic on Gender Equality 269
Elena Jirovsky-Platter and Anita Rieder

The Roles of National Ethics Committees in Pandemics. Orientation in Times of Crisis 281
Patrik Hummel and Andreas Reis

Clinical Ethics Consultation in the Covid-19 Pandemic. Practical Challenges for Safety and Quality 303
Andreas Frewer

Religion, Pandemics and Ethics. A Diaconal-Ethical Perspective on the Covid-19 Pandemic 325
Ulrich H.J. Körtner

Pandemics, Medicine and Ethics. An Outlook 341
Andreas Reis, Martina Schmidhuber and Andreas Frewer

List of Authors

Univ.-Prof. Dr. jur. Steffen Augsberg University of Giessen, Giessen, Germany

Univ.-Prof. Dr. med. Dr. phil. Klaus Bergdolt (1947–2023) Institute for the History and Ethics of Medicine, University of Cologne, Cologne, Germany

Prof. Dr. med. Dr. phil. Nikola Biller-Andorno Institute for Biomedical Ethics and History of Medicine, University of Zurich, Zurich, Switzerland

Univ.-Prof. Dr. med. Walter Bruchhausen Section Global Health, Institute for Hygiene and Public Health, University Hospital Bonn, Bonn, Germany

Prof. Dr. Christiane Druml Medical University of Vienna, Vienna, Austria

Prof. Dr. phil. Hans-Jörg Ehni University of Tübingen, Tübingen, Germany

Alice Faust Berlin Institute of Health at Charité – Universitätsmedizin Berlin, QUEST Center for Transforming Biomedical Research, Berlin, Germany

Sophia Forster Professorship for Ethics in Medicine, Erlangen-Nürnberg University, Erlangen, Germany

Univ.-Prof. Dr. med. Andreas Frewer Professorship for Ethics in Medicine, Erlangen-Nürnberg University, Erlangen, Germany

Sara Gerke Assistant Professor of Law, Penn State Dickinson Law, Carlisle, PA, USA

Dr. Patrik Hummel Eindhoven University of Technology, Philosophy & Ethics Group, DeZaale, Eindhoven, Netherlands

Dr. phil. Elena Jirovsky-Platter Medical University of Vienna, Center for Public Health, Department of Social- and Preventive Medicine, Unit Medical Anthropology and Global Health, Vienna, Austria

Dr. phil. Katharina Kieslich University of Vienna, Vienna, Austria

Dr. med. Otmar Kloiber World Medical Association (WMA), Ferney-Voltaire, France

Univ.-Prof. Dr. theol. DDr. h.c. Ulrich H. J. Körtner University of Vienna, Vienna, Austria

Eva Kuhn Section Global Health, University Hospital Bonn, Bonn, Germany

Univ.-Prof. Dr. med. Georg Marckmann Ludwig Maximilian University of Munich, Munich, Germany

Prof. Jur. Dr. Timo Minssen, LL.Lic., LLM., Center for Advanced Studies in Biomedical Innovation Law (CeBIL), Faculty of Law, University of Copenhagen, Copenhagen, Denmark; Research Affiliate, Centre for Law, Medicine and Life Sciences (LML), University of Cambridge, Cambridge, UK

Tim Nguyen Health Ethics and Governance Unit, Department of Research for Health, WHO Health Emergencies Programme (WHE), Geneva, Switzerland

Univ.-Prof. Dr. phil. Barbara Prainsack University of Vienna, Vienna, Austria

PD Dr. med. Andreas Reis Health Ethics and Governance Unit, Department of Research for Health, World Health Organization, Geneva, Switzerland

Univ.-Prof.in Dr.in phil. Anita Rieder Chair Center for Public Health and Vice Rector, Medical University of Vienna, Vienna, Austria

Prof. Dr. jur. Stephan Rixen Faculty of Law, University of Cologne, Cologne, Germany

Lana Saksone Berlin Institute of Health at Charité – Universitätsmedizin Berlin, QUEST Center for Transforming Biomedical Research, Berlin, Germany

Univ.-Prof. Dr. phil. fac. theol. Martina Schmidhuber Professorship for Health Care Ethics, Karl Franzens University Graz, Graz, Austria

Prof. Harald Schmidt University of Pennsylvania, Philadelphia, USA

Annabel Seebohm Lawyer, Wachtberg, Germany

Prof. Dr. Dr. Daniel Strech Berlin Institute of Health at Charité – Universitätsmedizin Berlin, QUEST Center for Transforming Biomedical Research, Berlin, Germany

Sebastian Wäscher Institute of Biomedical Ethics and History of Medicine, University of Zurich, Zurich, Switzerland

Prof. Dr. Hans-Werner Wahl Heidelberg University, Heidelberg, Germany

Stefanie Weigold Berlin Institute of Health at Charité – Universitätsmedizin Berlin, QUEST Center for Transforming Biomedical Research, Berlin, Germany

Dr. med. Lena Woydack Berlin Institute of Health at Charité – Universitätsmedizin Berlin, QUEST Center for Transforming Biomedical Research, Berlin, Germany

Ethical Challenges in Pandemics. Introduction

Martina Schmidhuber, Andreas Reis and Andreas Frewer

"Unwilling to face the present, hostile to the past and future deprived, we really resembled those who let the justice or hatred of men behind bars."

(Camus 1998, p. 84)

Contents

References 6

Many people could probably endorse this sentence from Albert Camus' novel "The Plague" (1947) after many months of the Covid-19 pandemic. In addition to the health concerns and fears, the Corona crisis causes many uncertainties: far-reaching restrictions in the private sector, existential fears that arise for many due to the economic situation—both for private individuals and for (smaller and larger) companies, lack of personal contacts, young people who wonder whether they will find work after their vocational training. And the one open question that nobody can answer: When will life finally be "like before" again? This shows how

M. Schmidhuber (✉)
Professorship for Health Care Ethics, Karl Franzens University, Graz, Austria
e-mail: martina.schmidhuber@uni-graz.at

A. Reis
Health Ethics and Governance Unit, Department of Research for Health, World Health Organization, Geneva, Switzerland
e-mail: reisa@who.int

A. Frewer
Professorship for Ethics in Medicine, Erlangen-Nürnberg University, Erlangen, Germany
e-mail: andreas.frewer@fau.de

© The Author(s), under exclusive license to Springer-Verlag GmbH, DE, part of Springer Nature 2023

A. Reis et al. (eds.), *Pandemics and Ethics*,
https://doi.org/10.1007/978-3-662-66872-6_1

vulnerable human beings are per se. Of course, some are more affected than others. Here a gap opens up between those who were better and worse off socio-economically before the pandemic. Social inequalities that already existed became even more apparent during the pandemic. For those who had to fight the everyday challenges of life before the pandemic—single parents, people in precarious employment relationships, people with a migrant background or pre-existing conditions, etc.—the situation has worsened even further. Nevertheless, the pandemic seems to affect everyone in some way and to make everyone aware of their vulnerability.

The three philosophers Catriona Mackenzie, Wendy Rogers and Susan Dodds (2014) show in their taxonomy that vulnerability is a part of the human condition and that every person can very quickly find themselves in a situation of particular vulnerability. In principle, three forms of vulnerability can be distinguished, which also apply in a special way in the Covid-19 pandemic: inherent, situational and pathogenic. (1) People are inherently vulnerable per se. Hunger, thirst, sleep, social contacts—these basic human needs refer to the inherent vulnerability of human beings. (2) Situational vulnerability can affect people in certain contexts, for personal, social or political reasons. Both a natural disaster that can make people homeless overnight, as well as diseases that can turn the apparently strong subject into a needy patient, or sudden unemployment—these are forms of situational vulnerability. (3) Pathogenic vulnerability arises from asymmetrical interpersonal relationships and institutional structures. This includes, for example, the abuse of a child by an adult. This taxonomy shows that all three forms of vulnerability can play a role in crises (see also Schmidhuber 2020; Bergemann and Frewer 2018).

At the same time, the gap between rich and poor is widening in this current pandemic: those who had to struggle with many challenges of life before the crisis—for example, a precarious employment relationship, unemployment, chronic or mental illness or single parenting—are particularly affected by the crisis (see Rümmele and Sprenger 2020). Those who are in a good employment relationship, have the opportunity to work from home and live spaciously, of course, experience the pandemic less dramatically, but social isolation can also be very stressful for them. Here a wealth of moral problems arise. This was also relevant in epidemics such as SARS, influenza and Ebola before Covid-19. The necessary measures for their research, prevention and treatment raise a number of ethical issues with which science, medicine and health policy are confronted. While individual aspects have already been discussed in various articles, there is no overview in German to date [editorial note: i.e. in 2021] that covers all important ethical topics. The present volume is intended to fill this gap and provide valuable hints to policy-makers, physicians and nursing staff as well as other professionals and interested laymen on how to deal with the difficult ethical questions in pandemics.

Against this background, it is our task as editors of this volume to show different perspectives on pandemics and important ways of coping with the problems. For this purpose, we were able to gather a number of renowned international scientists who agreed to present the state of the art of their discipline in the field of “pandemics and ethics”. The volume begins with a contribution by Klaus

Bergdolt, who uses the historical example of the plague to show that much that we experience in the Corona pandemic since the beginning of 2020was already there in history and that the role of the medical profession was existentially difficult in many ways in times of epidemics in the 14th century. The worries, fears and needs of people in the current pandemic can also be seen in other epochs and to varying degrees, as Bergdolt impressively demonstrates in his reflections on the history of epidemics. Solidarity is a central keyword that is often mentioned in pandemics. Katharina Kieslich and Barbara Prainsack show the diverse roles and meanings that solidarity can take on in a pandemic. Almost always, according to the authors, these are pro-social practices that strengthen cohesion within groups and societies. A study from Austria with nine participating countries provides interesting insights into the current understanding of solidarity among the population. Walter Bruchhausen and Eva Kuhn argue in their article on human rights that the right to health must not be considered in isolation from other human rights even in times of pandemics. Rather, the protection of other important rights, such as freedom of expression and a minimum standard of living, is still required. Annabel Seebohm and Otmar Kloiber deal with the special rights and duties of health professionals during a pandemic. They argue that, from an ethical point of view, there is no absolute duty of care for the medical profession and other health professions, even if a moral obligation is assumed. In practice, it often turns out that people in health professions are often willing to do considerable overtime work without any material compensation. In addition to human rights, the fundamental rights are also frequently invoked in public debates during a pandemic. Stephan Rixen discusses that, from a legal point of view, fundamental rights are not absolute, static quantities, but regulative elements, which grant more or less protection. However, restrictions on fundamental rights must be in accordance with the principle of proportionality in a pandemic. Ethical questions of resource allocation and prioritization are often in the foreground in times of crisis, as tests, drugs and hospital capacity are scarce at least in the initial phase. Georg Marckmann discusses ethical principles and practical applications using the example of the prioritization of therapies and vaccines. In the subsequent article, Harald Schmidt deals with the triage of patients with regard to the prioritization of ventilators in intensive care units and the preferred access to vaccines. Central questions of social justice in the US-American context are discussed, with special consideration of indices of disadvantage.

For more than 200 years, vaccinations have been a proven means of combating infectious diseases and epidemics. Christiane Druml spans a wide range of topics in her chapter, from questions of compulsory vaccination to placebo control in clinical trials to "Human Challenge Trials". Immunization certificates have been common practice for diseases such as yellow fever and polio in international travel under the International Health Regulations (IHR) for some time now. Covid-19 has raised new questions about the need for and usefulness of immunity and vaccination certificates, both nationally and globally. Steffen Augsberg addresses relevant ethical and legal issues. Of course, pandemics trigger urgent research needs on many levels in terms of preventive and therapeutic measures. However, ethical standards must still be taken into account for clinical trials to be conducted under great time pressure. This topic is addressed by Alice Faust, Lana Saksone, Stefanie Weigold, Lena Woydack and Daniel Strech. Based on an internationally recognized framework for research ethics (see, inter alia, Emanuel et al. 2011), the authors describe central ethical aspects such as social value, scientific validity and the fair selection of study participants in the Corona crisis. Covid-19 is the first pandemic to make widespread use of digital medicine, for example Corona "warning-apps". The ethical and legal aspects that arise from this, from data protection to fair access to these technologies, are examined by Timo Minssen and Sara Gerke in the following article. The discourse in the pandemic is characterized by information that people receive from (social) media. Sebastian Wäscher, Tim Nguyen and Nikola Biller-Andorno therefore examine the handling of information in pandemic times from an ethical perspective. Half-truths and false information can cause a lot of harm; in this context, the terminology of the WHO is used to speak of an "infodemic". It is essential, as the authors point out, that in communications ways be found to prepare highly complex information in such a way that citizens are very well informed but not overwhelmed. In the pandemic, solidarity with older people is of paramount importance, and this is also emphasized by politicians (Frewer et al. 2020a). In their contribution to the book, the two authors Hans-Jörg Ehni and Hans-Werner Wahl deal with the situation of older people in the pandemic. They critically examine both the often precarious situation of people in nursing homes and the question of age limits in intensive care as well as the possibility of [human] contacts in the context of digitalization. They plead for stronger intergenerational solidarity and against "ageism". In their comparative study, Sophia Forster and Andreas Frewer dealt with how the protection of older people in the Corona pandemic is handled in various countries around the world. In addition to Germany, they take four other countries with similar population numbers and development stages as examples—Spain, Canada, Australia and South Korea. In this context, they examine, inter alia, special measures in clinics and homes, vaccinations, lockdowns and mortality in senior citizen facilities. Another "group of people" particularly affected by the pandemic are women. Anita Rieder and Elena Jirovsky-Platter show on the basis of several countries that the Covid-19 pandemic has a significant negative impact on gender equality: domestic violence, socio-economic disadvantages and health impairments affect women in particular. In order to counteract this, special measures must be designed and implemented to promote equality between the sexes, otherwise these inequalities will be further reinforced, as the authors point out. National Ethics Committees have been playing an increasingly important role in policy advice and public discourse since the HIV epidemic. Through the Covid-19 pandemic, they have gained even more prominence and importance in many countries. However, their function could be extended or strengthened in some states, argue Patrik Hummel and Andreas Reis in their chapter with the presentation of numerous international examples of the work of National Ethics Committees. Andreas Frewer spans the bridge from the national level to clinical practice in the treatment of Covid-19 patients in the hospital. In the context of the Corona pandemic, numerous problems have also arisen for Clinical Ethics Committees and the ethical advice they offer. The chapter illuminates the current challenges for safety and quality in the mirror of the consulting cases from practice; in this way, in addition to the global macro level and the National Ethics Committees, the micro level of Clinical Ethics is also presented. In the final chapter, Ulrich Körtner looks at the role of religion in the pandemic. He shows that and how religious communities are important as part of civil society in coping with the crisis. Religious groups have several tasks: They shape the religious life of their members even in these difficult times, defend religious freedom and, in particular, have the task of actively participating in social and political debates on how to deal with the Corona pandemic.

Despite the variety of contributions, it is of course not possible to cover all relevant topics; some of them should therefore be mentioned briefly in this introductory chapter and in the afterword. Both the view of older people and of women are covered in this volume by specific chapters. Many aspects and the mentioned forms of vulnerability can also be transferred to children and adolescents (Ahadzada 2020; Platz 2020; Anonymus 2021), people with a migrant background (Giesing and Hofbauer 2020) and the socioeconomically disadvantaged (Döring 2003). The exemplary chapters in this volume offer numerous possibilities for transfer to other areas. The challenges exist at all levels: at the individual, political, scientific, economic, as well as at the health and social system level (Frewer et al. 2020b; Heinemann et al. 2020)—we are, according to some voices, becoming a "Corona society" (Keitel et al. 2020). It is difficult to find the right balance between lockdown and loosening, protection and hygiene measures, as well as individual rights of freedom and collective discipline. Regular surveys are used to examine which pandemic strategies are considered appropriate by the population. In spring and summer 2020, often still large parts of the population considered the measures taken to be in order (ZDF 2020). Opinion polls and political barometers have become even more sensitive instruments with numerous ethical implications in the pandemic. The present volume would like to point the way to appropriate medical and moral measures on the basis of the latest scientific research and expert knowledge. The problems of individual moderation and the political-legal proportionality have hardly ever been so important in the development of mankind. A culture of ethical reflection of the numerous fields of application of fundamental solidarity to the fair distribution of resources in extreme cases can bring our (world) society decisively forward.

Acknowledgements We would like to thank all the authors in this volume for their excellent cooperation during a difficult phase of work and life. Together we were able to develop the present handbook on the topic of pandemics and ethics in what was ultimately an astonishingly short time, especially in order to make it practically usable during the crisis phase. Dr Brigitte Reschke (Heidelberg) and Charu Pancholi as well as Sayantika Chakraborty (Chennai/India) from the Springer publishing house have supported this in a competent and committed manner. We thank the whole publishing team for their quick and smooth cooperation.

Disclaimer The authors are solely responsible for the opinions expressed in this book, and these do not necessarily represent the views, decisions or policies of the institutions with which they are affiliated.

References

Ahadzada A (2020) Coronapandemie: Psychische Gesundheit von Kindern verschlechtert. Dtsch Ärztebl Int 8:340

Anonymus (2021) Coronapandemie: Psychische Gesundheit von Kindern hat sich weiter verschlechtert. In: Deutsches Ärzteblatt. https://www.aerzteblatt.de/nachrichten/121027/Coronapandemie-Psychis. Accessed 28 Feb 2020

Bergemann L, Frewer A (eds) (2018) Autonomie und Vulnerabilität in der Medizin. Menschenrechte – Ethik – Empowerment. transcript, Bielefeld

Camus A (1998) Die Pest. Rowohlt, Reinbek

Döring D (2003) Armut: Begriffliche Unterscheidungen. In: Böhm R, Buggler R, Mautner J (eds) Arbeit am Begriff der Armut. Working Papers. Salzburg, pp 26–30

Emanuel EJ, Grady C, Crouch RA, Lie RK, Miller FG, Wendler D (eds) (2011) The Oxford textbook of clinical research ethics, 2nd edn. Oxford University Press, Oxford

Frewer A, Klotz S, Herrler C, Bielefeldt H (eds) (2020a) Gute Behandlung im Alter? Menschenrechte und Ethik zwischen Ideal und Realität. transcript, Bielefeld

Frewer A, Bergemann L, Langmann E (eds) (2020b) Unsicherheit in der Medizin. Zum Umgang mit Ungewissheit im Gesundheitswesen. Jahrbuch Ethik in der Klinik 13 (2020). Königshausen & Neumann, Würzburg

Giesing Y, Hofbauer M (2020) Wie wirkt sich Covid-19 auf Migration und Integration aus? In: ifo Schnelldienst, ifo Institut – Leibniz-Institut für Wirtschaftsforschung an der Universität München 73/07, pp 41–46

Heinemann T, Proft I, Sahm S, Schockenhoff E (2020) Covid-19. Ethische Empfehlungen über Beginn und Fortführung einer intensivmedizinischen Behandlung bei nicht ausreichenden Behandlungskapazitäten. BoD, Norderstedt

Keitel C, Volkmer M, Werner K (eds) (2020) Die Corona-Gesellschaft. Analysen zur Lage und Perspektiven für die Zukunft. Transcript, Bielefeld

Mackenzie C, Rogers W, Dodds S (2014) Introduction: what is vunerability and why does it matter for moral theory? In: Mackenzie C, Rogers W, Dodds S (eds) Vulnerability. New essays in ethics and feminist philosophy. Oxford University Press, Oxford, pp 1–29

Platz M (2020) Wohlergehensverluste bei Kleinkindern durch den coronabedingten Wegfall der außerhäuslichen Betreuung. Eine kritische kinderethische Analyse der Betreuungsverbote und -einschränkungen. Z Prakt Philos 7(2):359–384

Rümmele M, Sprenger M (2020) Wir denken Gesundheit neu! Corona als Chance für eine Zeitenwende im Gesundheitswesen. Ampuls, Unteraichwald

Schmidhuber M (2020) Vulnerabilität in der Krise. In: Kröll W, Platzer J, Ruckenbauer HW, Schaupp W (eds) Die Corona-Pandemie. Ethische, gesellschaftliche und theologische Reflexionen einer Krise. Nomos, Baden-Baden, pp 273–281

Zweites Deutsches Fernsehen (ZDF) (2020) Corona: Drei Viertel finden Maßnahmen richtig. In: ZDF-Politbarometer. https://www.zdf.de/nachrichten/politik/politbarometer-corona-massnahmen-100.html. Accessed 08 Nov 2020

Pandemics and the Dignity of Man. Reflections on the History of Disease

Klaus Bergdolt

Contents

1 Doctors, Clergy and the Management of Authorities—the Challenge of Society 7
2 Plague Epidemics as Crises in Medicine 9
3 Clergy at the Plague Front—the Importance of the Religious 12
4 Flight and Crime 14
5 The Atrocities of Everyday Life with the Plague—the Sick and Foreigners as Objects of Hatred 15
6 Plague Hospitals 17
7 The Question of Human Dignity 17
8 The Black Death, a Phenomenon Over Centuries 18
9 Brave and Less Brave Doctors 20
10 Thucydides at the Beginning... 21
11 Summary 22
References 22

1 Doctors, Clergy and the Management of Authorities—the Challenge of Society

Epidemics and diseases, especially pandemics, raise—as Covid-19 has been proving for months—a wealth of questions that touch on fundamental aspects of the *conditio humana*. Since antiquity, when the everyday life of epidemics was first addressed (Herodotus, Thucydides, Diodorus Siculus), the political, legal, organizational and ethical problems associated with them were considered highly

K. Bergdolt (✉)
University of Cologne, Cologne, Germany
e-mail: Bergdolt@uni-koeln.de

© The Author(s), under exclusive license to Springer-Verlag GmbH, DE, part of Springer Nature 2023
A. Reis et al. (eds.), *Pandemics and Ethics*,
https://doi.org/10.1007/978-3-662-66872-6_2

complex; contradictions, trade-offs, corrections and compromises determined the medical, but also the social debates. The struggle for moral interpretive sovereignty was already influenced by science *and* religion in ancient Greece—it shaped the behavior of the authorities as well as the medical profession (Schmitz 2005). Together with nursing staff, non-academically trained healers and—in Europe since the High Middle Ages first in Italy—local health authorities, doctors were in the forefront of everyday life in epidemics since antiquity. In the 14th century, the task of *government advice* was added to the individual care of patients, its "classical" task, which was increasingly institutionalized over the centuries, first in Italy and France, by guild regulations and (in the academic field) collegia. "Health authorities" played a particularly important role in the 16th and 17th centuries, for example in Milan, Venice, Florence or Lucca, only to be copied in numerous northern cities, even in Berlin in 1576, then a small town (Eikermann and Kaiser 2012, pp. 55 ff.). In the 17th century there were even plans for an "international cooperation" between Genoa, Florence, Rome and Naples, which looked far into the future despite initial problems (Naphy and Spicer 2003, pp. 85 ff.).

Disease, suffering, death, loneliness, friendship, neighborhood and family—phenomena that, at least until the 18th century, gained particular importance in times of epidemics—had, at least until the 18th century, other psychological, religious and philosophical connotations than today. They were anything but constants, but subject to changing discourses. This also applied to medical ethics. However, there were considerable exceptions. Above all, the mentioned religious dimension of disease and health played a central role in the history of epidemics for centuries. In the numerous *pest reports* that have been written by medical authors since 1348, the possibility of a divine punishment or test as the cause of epidemics was certainly considered (Esser 1997, pp. 38 f.). "The doctor should not attribute the brought about health to his learning or his cleverness, but to God, the creator of all health," emphasized the Italian doctor Gabriele Zerbi in 1495 in his ethical treatise *De cautelis medicorum* (Zerbi 2019, p. 61). The thesis of the French surgeon Ambroise Paré (1510–1590), that the doctor treats, but God heals (the healing of a seriously injured person he commented with the words "Je le pansay, Dieu le guarist"/I bandaged him, but God healed him), reflected a basic attitude of doctors that was already detectable in the Middle Ages (Paré 1963, pp. 35 f.). Nevertheless, therapy plans were designed, in which, as in the case of the medical humanist Josef Grünpeck (1497), astrological constellations were taken into account (Esser 1997, pp. 38 f.). The thesis of the "divine character" of medicine lost its importance only from the 17th century, although important natural scientists such as Johannes Kepler saw confirmation of creation in their research results (Boas 1988, p. 337). For the doctor Giovanni Borelli (1608–1679) medicine and natural science "deciphered the signs with which the creator of all things speaks from his works" (Rossi 1997, pp. 202 f.). In times of epidemics, this even seemed to be an important approach to salvation. No wonder that in Catholic areas some priests were said to have healing powers (Bergdolt 2004, p. 176). Already Pope Gregory the Great, witness to a great plague, had composed a "Pestilence Litany" for Rome around 590. Processions of prayers have been part of everyday life during epidemics since then (Leppin 2005). Not only notorious critics of medicine like the Italian humanist Francesco Petrarca (1304–1374) saw effective measures against the plague in such prayers. The role of the "Pest Saints", the *sancti protectores,* who prayed to God for mercy, above all Sebastian and Rochus, was of central importance, which was reflected not least in the fine arts (Bergdolt 2005).

As early as the 14th century, the disease, which was introduced to Europe from Asia—probably via the Crimea—and which was to flare up again at irregular intervals, was associated not only with the fear of infection, but also with existential fears. It is no coincidence that it is not medical but rather aesthetic literature that provides information on this subject. Petrarch, Boccaccio, Machiavelli, Pepys, Defoe, Manzoni, Jakobsen, Camus, Szcypiorski and others created great works of world literature, the theme of which revolved around the everyday life of the plague (Paulsen and Schulze 2005). Ethical and religious questions played an outstanding role in this. Even in historical research on epidemics, it is the effects on society that are the real fascination—associations with the current situation arise of their own accord. Doubts about God, fellow human beings, family, community, charitable institutions, whose representatives failed in the face of the threat no less than the individual, often led to resignation and despair. In the 20th century, Camus once again masterfully portrayed the "psychology of the plague", i.e. the feeling of existential threat in everyday life during an epidemic (Camus 1998).

2 Plague Epidemics as Crises in Medicine

From the perspective of doctors, the history of epidemics, which is at the center of the following considerations, represented a kind of "eternal return" of deadly threats until the 20th century. The modern research is rather pessimistic here—epidemics, the danger of which goes far beyond Covid-19, will probably also determine the future (Schadewaldt 1994). For a long time, historians of culture and medicine were also convinced that the social reactions to epidemics in the Middle Ages and Early Modern times had been characterized by a certain constancy, whereby the Hippocratic ethos, as it was believed, served as a moral guideline (Deichgräber 1983). Human behavior seemed to have changed little during times of real deadly threats in comparison to Antiquity. The metaphor of the beam, which can only hold *one* shipwrecked person, but which *two* desperate people fight for ("plank of Carneades"), which was already commented on by Cicero (De officiis 3,89), seemed to confirm such continuity, although the problem of *triage* mentioned here initially played a role more in times of war than in times of epidemics (Eckart 2005). Contrary to the popular catchphrase of the *breaks and discontinuities* (from Bruch et al. 2006), which are not quite assumed dogmatically in historical sciences, the encounter between a sick person seeking help and a competent healer was assigned an almost archetypal importance (among others Geisler2008). Wasn't the longing for "rescue" or "healing" in great need the origin of the entire history of medicine, from ancient Babylon to today? Nevertheless, as already indicated, there were considerable differences in the ethical questions depending on the century and zeitgeist. Already in the surprisingly large number of contemporary sources, which discuss the "plague of 1348" (it swept across Europe from 1347 to 1352 successively from Southeast to Northwest), the behavior of the physicians, which was observed in the everyday life of the pandemic hardly less sharply than today, was an important topic. Their challenge was considerable. Was it, in view of the increasing number of victims among the physicians now praiseworthy or blameworthy, if, as the Florentine chronicler Marchionne di Coppo reported, quite a few felt the pulse "only with averted face" and judged the urine "only from afar"? (Bergdolt 1989, p. 67). Was it defensible, to risk one's life for *an* individual in danger of life and thus to risk that hundreds of other infected people had to forego medical treatment? Was the motivation behind the apparent cowardice maybe evenresponsibility, as paradoxical as it seemed? Luther, who had survived the plague in Wittenberg in 1527, saw medical assistance in the highest danger as a Christian duty, while Theodor Beza, a student of Calvin, put the interest of the community in the foreground, as an surviving physician was indeed more useful than a dead one (Jonsen 2000, p. 46). It is obvious that the doctrine of grace of the Geneva reformer formed the background for this. Should one, and this was not only asked in Switzerland, leave the time of death simply to God? In 1687 the theologian Christian Scriver, whose father and siblings were victims of the plague, disputed that the question of the alleviation of agonizing pain was of importance. At least among the God-fearing he had seen only a few die, where one "of such natural means would have been needed" (Benzenhöfer 1999, pp. 70 f.). The pietistic author turned against alleviating the suffering of the dying with drugs, as the manner of death was ultimately predetermined. In the 17th century *one* problem, which is today the concern of the ethics committees, however, was still unimaginable: that complicated late stages of diseases, which raise related medical ethical questions, could be made possible by life-prolonging therapies, indeed the "progress of medicine". Montaigne (1533–1592) had propagated a secularized *ars moriendi,* which can include the alleviation of pain and a shortened life in the case of severe illness and unbearable pain. In the 16th and 17th centuries, however, this position was the exception (Amstutz 1974).

Even if one takes into account that treatments for the plague were virtually ineffective up until the late 19th century and that a reduction in the number of physicians could hardly have an effect on the spread of the disease (an argumentation that of course presupposes our knowledge and therefore could not play a role at the time of Luther and Calvin), the question of medical care during times of epidemics always represented a massive *psychological* problem: How desperate must have been the patients for whom the physician, on whom one had pinned all hopes, failed to appear! The fact that up until the early modern period only a small percentage of the population ever got to see academically educated physicians, does not change anything about this—the problem just as much concerned surgeons, barbers and countless alternative healers. That in addition, despite all precautions, every medical visit represented an additional infection risk for the relatives, without any benefit resulting from it, could at best be guessed by contemporary critics. In this context, Welborn referred to the ancient deontological tradition not to treat incurably ill people with the plague, just as incurably ill patients in general (Welborn 1996). Approximately since the 70s of the 14th century, a minimal ethos crystallized in the Western countries: The physician should under all circumstances visit new patients who wished for his visit—the right to diagnosis and prognosis was to be respected. If it really was the plague, it was up to the medical doctor to attempt a therapy. The principle "selfless first aid with maximum self-protection" hardly aroused any sympathies in this context, since it in fact made physicians judges over life and death. The mentioned principle of triage, that is an *a priori* separation of patients to whom one attributed chances of survival from those for whom treatment seemed to be futile, added an additional cruelty to the everyday life during epidemics.

Many humanists of this time, such as Petrarch, Boccaccio, Bruni and Salutati, despised the doctors because of their obvious incompetence in the everyday life of the plague, but also because of their moral failure. "In this disease, neither the advice of a doctor nor a medicine was obviously of any use," Boccaccio noted in his famous description of Florentine conditions (Bergdolt 1989, pp. 140 f.). But their alleged arrogance and moral degeneration were also denounced. Petrarch in particular ridiculed doctors and philosophers, indeed the entire scholastic academic community as pompous: "Consult the doctors: they only wonder. What is to be said of the philosophers? They shrug their shoulders, frown, put their finger on their lips and ask for silence" (Bergdolt 1989, pp. 140 f.). To this day it remained a mystery whether the representatives of the Hippocratic guild really believed in the effectiveness of traditional medicine, which was based on the *Doctrine of Four Humours* . According to this, plague sufferers had an excess of heat and moisture in their bodies, which was favored by youthful age and the summer season, according to Galen. They had, Galen believed, inhaled or swallowed humid, foul air (miasma), which caused decay in the organism, indeed the plague. It must be remembered here that medicine had been an authoritative science since antiquity. Until the late 16th century it was considered certain that the ancient and Arab authorities were always right with their theses. If their doctrine did not prove to be effective, other reasons, such as the mistakes of the translators or the deficient copies, were suspected. Paracelsus, whose fame was exalted by some and condemned by others, delivered harsh criticism, but hardly more effective healing suggestions (Schipperges 1998).

In any case, medicine also remained credulous of authority during times of plague. On a medieval fresco in Anagni (around 1100), we see Hippocrates and Galen, the highest authorities in medicine, in a solemn conversation. One is even reminded of a *sacra conversazione* after the model of Christian saints, which of course was intentional. Galen reaffirms: "Mundi praesentis series manet ex elementis" ("The order of the existing world consists of the elements"), while Hippocrates assures "Ex his formantur quae sunt quaecumque creantur" ("From these [elements] everything is formed that exists and that is created"). So the world consists of four elements—just like every human being, whose health is determined by the eucrasia of the four humours and elements (Bergdolt 2001;

Schöner 1964). Whatever was created, nature presented a harmonious principle of order. Thus, on the basis of theology, as the explanatory scroll of the fresco shows, the *dogma salutatis* is proclaimed. The image of the divine order, which until then had also been a central concept of medicine and conveyed security and comfort, now began to waver in the face of the experience of the plague. Hippocrates and Galen could not give any information whatsoever about how the plague actually originated. "Everything was shaking"—the word coined by Ernst Troeltsch for the crisis of theological historicism can also be applied to the time of catastrophe around 1348 (Dahm 2000).

3 Clergy at the Plague Front—the Importance of the Religious

Until the early 19th century, the ideal was that the dying would be cared for by their relatives and, of course, in old tradition, by the clergy. The "psychotherapeutic" accompaniment remained the task of the family, although their bonds often could not withstand the pressure and fear of death. Doctors had nothing to do at the deathbed, in contrast to today! Exceptions were prominent patients, such as monarchs, bishops or popes, whose court staff also included personal physicians. However, suspicion was often the order of the day here (Bergdolt 1992, pp. 38 ff.). The dignity of the plague victims could only be saved from a Christian perspective by loving and caring for them at the risk of one's own life. The nursing orders often appeared as the last hope—they were therefore, to use the current term, "systemically relevant" for centuries. Religious brotherhoods also proved themselves—in 1348 the Scuola della Carità in Venice lost about 300 members who had cared for the sick and dying. In the sick person (in the New Testament it was still the leper), the *Christus patiens* (Bergdolt 2004, pp. 64 and 72) appeared to the healthy person as he had revealed himself in Matthew 25, 31–40 ("What you have done to the least of my brothers, you have done to me"). The sick person thus gained an almost divine aura. Of course, theory and practice often differed—many clergy, monks as well as secular priests, were seized by panic: "Priests and notaries refused to enter the houses [of the plague victims]. If one of them nevertheless entered a house to draw up a will or the like, he too could not escape the imminent death. The Franciscans, Dominicans and other members of religious orders who wanted to enter the houses of the sick so that they could confess their sins and become partakers of divine justice through repentance, were suddenly swept away by death," noted the Sicilian Franciscan Michele da Piazza (Bergdolt 1989, p. 34). Courage and cowardice therefore also went hand in hand in the clergy. However, one can only note with admiration how clergymen in the countryside bravely gave their lives in England, to be replaced almost immediately by others (Ziegler 1972, pp. 188 ff.). The Welsh poet Jeuan Gethin and the Scottish historian

John of Fordun described pictures of everyday life in England that are reminiscent of Boccaccio. There were dioceses where almost every second clergyman died. Also across the Channel, countless people put their hope in pilgrimages and prayers. Here too, society's reaction was irrational and desperate. In Ireland, the Black Death struck almost as harshly as in England, although the Archbishop of Dublin, Richard Fitzralph, had informed the Pope in August 1349 that "two thirds of the English people" had died, but only few inhabitants of Ireland and Scotland. Already one year later, John of Fordun made it clear that also in Scotland one third of the population had died (Ziegler 1972, p. 196).

When it came to deciding between individual and society's interests, a person with the plague had little chance. People avoided his company—a behavior that remained characteristic of plague situations right up to the present day. Anyone who showed symptoms was, in contravention of all Christian principles, ruthlessly confined to a lazaretto, where he rarely survived. In 1349, the Florentine poet Antonio Pucci noted: "Today one man leaves his own flesh and blood brother, a father his child, if he sees them in danger, so that he himself will not be infected with the disease. Thus many people, abandoned by advice and help, die—Saracens, Jews, and heretics. They must not all be abandoned! O you doctors, for God's sake, and you priests and begging brothers, visit out of love for your neighbor those who are calling for you. Show them your kindness. Think of your own souls and do not look to profit. And you, relatives, neighbors, and friends, when you see that someone is complaining to you, by God, do not hesitate. Be magnanimous and comfort him!" (Bergdolt 1989, p. 148). Pucci's poem is an appeal to Christian conscience! The author had recognized with horror that the moral principles taught could quickly lose their effect under threat of death.

For centuries, and during times of plague as well, physicians liked to appeal to the famous Hippocratic Oath, which had the advantage of appearing compatible with central principles of Christian morality. But in this oath there was no direct reference to the plague problem. What was admonished was always an "honorable" behavior as well as an action "for the benefit of the sick" to the best of one's ability and judgment. In the few copies of this oath that have been preserved from the early and high Middle Ages (the actual heyday of the later so revered ancient text only began in the 16th century), Apollo, before whom the ancient physician had to swear, was replaced by Christ. The label "Christian" appeared somewhat problematic in this context, because *medical* help was offered for money (Lichtenthaeler 1984). The classical medical saints, such as Cosmas and Damian, but also Saint Pantaleon, were considered *anargyroi,* healers who did not demand money, but who acted out of love for their neighbor. During times of plague, those who actually took care of the infected and dying were understandably paid handsomely for the risk they were taking, while many nuns and monks, brothers and sisters, and even whole convents died because they selflessly and out of purely Christian conviction nursed and comforted the highly infectious sick and dying.

4 Flight and Crime

Today, one aspect of medical ethics that was also upheld by medical faculties seems particularly strange, namely the recommendation to flee from a "infected" city, namely "quickly and as far away as possible". It was at least attributed to Galen, the great authority next to Hippocrates. "The doctor felt the pulse and disappeared, the servant prepared a meal for the lord and sought his fortune", it was said—by no means an exception—in a Neapolitan chronicle from 1656 (de Renzi 1968, pp. 72 ff.). The phenomenon appeared everyday, but of course it did not exclude that physicians who fled or harbored thoughts of flight—here even Koryphaei like Guy de Chauliac in the 14th or Thomas Sydenham in the 17th century would have to be mentioned—were severely criticized. However, Jonathan Goddard justified his departure from the infected London (1665) with the argument that most of his patients had also left the city. In fact, also judges, scholars and high clergymen had made themselves scarce, not least the members of the *College of Surgeons*. The roads leading out of town and the boats on the Thames were overcrowded with refugees. Crime flourished, fake health certificates were in great demand. In 1720, the flight of about 10,000 people from Marseille led to the spread of the epidemic in cities such as Aix, Arles and Avignon (Mauelshagen 2005, pp. 244 ff.). If universities or faculties were relocated to other cities during plague times (as in the 16th and 17th centuries from Heidelberg to Dilsberg, from Marburg to Frankenberg or from Freiburg to Constance), a fleeing medical professor could of course refer to this. In Venice and Florence, a kind of health emergency legislation had already been passed in the 14th century, which assigned specific tasks to doctors and officials in the event of an epidemic. Flight was strictly prohibited. As in the case of judges, notaries and officials, the citizenship was also withdrawn from physicians in the event of an escape attempt. To be fair, one must say that the local elites, above all the rulers with their court, when the danger increased, often fled themselves. Charles II, who withdrew from London to Oxford in 1665, was just one example among many (Mauelshagen 2005, p. 241). Leopold I. fled in 1679 from Vienna via the pilgrimage site of Mariazell to Prague, in order to settle further in Linz when the plague had also broken out there (Schmölzer 1988, pp. 94 ff.). In the countryside as well, the peasants and craftsmen often left their villages, which contributed to the decline of agriculture, even to famines (Zinn 1989, pp. 188 ff.). In some places, people who looked sick were simply driven away, which of course contributed to the further spread of infections.

Quite a few doctors simply disappeared from public view, overwhelmed by fear. They fled with their families, supplied with food, into their houses. Jacme d'Agremont, a doctor from Lerida in Spain, already recommended in 1348 that his colleagues not think about profit at times of disease, as the danger to life was too great. All the treasures of the world had not saved countless doctors from a shameful and painful end. In the same year, Chalin de Vinario, one of the papal physicians in Avignon, bluntly explained: "We doctors are closest to ourselves.

None of us is so blinded by madness that he cares more about the salvation of others than his own, especially in such a rapid and contagious disease" (Rath 1957). There is no question that such statements contradicted the traditional medical ethic. However, the situation was not easy. If doctors refused treatment or fled, they risked being considered cowards. If they helped under life-threatening or hopeless conditions, they were often accused, especially among colleagues, of greed (Amundsen 1977, p. 415). After all, it was considered a medical duty to encourage the sick to confess at the right moment—and thus to transfer the care to others. The call for the priest seemed in extremis more important than the inspection of urine or the feeling of pulse! The personal risk of the doctors depended, if the plague broke out, on many factors. In particular, surgeons were considered to be at risk because they had to cut the plague buboes and had direct contact with the blood and excretions of the sick (Rodenwaldt 1953, p. 102). In early modern times, they were therefore, for example in London in 1665, even externally marked, indeed almost stigmatized and were—like the executioners—avoided by many. However, for prominent patients, academically trained physicians also carried out bloodletting and cupping—they wrote, paradoxically often with little practical experience, the relevant textbooks (which revealed subtle knowledge of ancient and Arabic medicine).

5 The Atrocities of Everyday Life with the Plague—the Sick and Foreigners as Objects of Hatred

In many cities, since the 14th century, the transport of the plague-ridden had been the task of prisoners and delinquents, often even, as in Venice, of those condemned to death, who had nothing more to expect from life. During the plague that decimated Naples in 1656, the *Beccamorti* (undertakers), who had come to new freedom, committed serious crimes. That they neglected their duties was to be expected—in some churches one could see open family graves in which thrown-in corpses spread an unbearable smell (de Renzi 1968, pp. 126 and 73). Almost everywhere, the executive was too weak to resist. Also in Vienna, robbery and murder increased in 1679, since the collection of corpses was "left to released criminals" (Schmölzer 1988, p. 99). In view of the risks of their work, they considered themselves justified in robbing plague victims. The governments were hardly able to allow a dignified treatment of the sick. In Venice it was forbidden for the *Picegamorti* (undertakers) and *Nettezini* (street cleaners) to carry weapons (Rodenwaldt 1953, pp. 137 f.). Already Boccaccio, who in the *Decameron* delivered the most famous report on the plague of 1348 in literature, had complained: "With such a terrible and miserable state of our city, the venerable reputation of our laws, both divine and human, had almost completely been sunk and destroyed, because their administrators and executors, like the others, were dead or sick and they lacked assistants to take any official action. So everyone was allowed to do what they wanted" (quoted from Bergdolt 1989, p. 43).

Pandemics were, morally speaking, bad times. The autonomy of the individual was sacrificed to the interests of the utilitarian-thinking public. Ethical principles were set aside by the paralyzing fear. The guilty were usually seen in foreigners or believers of other faiths. According to Matteo Villani, the Florentine chronicler, inhumanity first broke out among the unbelievers, so "that father and mother left their children and the children their parents and siblings to each other, and the other relatives, a cruel, wonderful appearance, which is completely contrary to human nature and is abhorrent forbelieving Christians. But even among these, this heartless behavior was found, since they imitated the barbaric and godless peoples" (Bergdolt1989, p. 61). Many died alone and helpless. In a chronicle from Piacenza it said: "A sick man lay in his house. No relative came near him. Those who were closest to him wept, but they lay down in a remote corner of the house. No doctor came in. The priest was full of fear and only timidly administered the church's sacraments. Ah, and then the sick man's plaintive voice sounded: Pity me, pity me […], as the hand of the Lord has touched me! Another called out: O my father, why have you abandoned me? Remember that you fathered me. Another: O mother, where are you? Why are you so cruel, when only yesterday you were so loving to me? When you nursed me with your breasts' milk and carried me for nine months? Another: O my sons, whom I raised under sweat and many hardships, why are you fleeing? And man and wife accused each other in turn: Woe to us, who rejoiced peacefully in our marriage and are now, o pain, divorced and separated in mourning! And while one sick person suffered terribly in this way, he cried out in lament: Come, my relatives and neighbors, give me a drop of water, I am thirsty! I am still alive! Do not be afraid. Perhaps I will live on! Take hold of me, touch my wretched body! You must touch me now!" (Bergdolt 1989, pp. 28 ff.). That the plague had been brought in from Asia fanned xenophobia early on. It was obviously travelers who spread it in Europe as well. The accusation, persecution, and murder of many Jews was a well-known and scandalous accompanying chapter of everyday life during the plague (Haverkamp 1981). Only a few personalities of rank, including Pope Clement VI in Avignon, protested. There were almost no pogroms in Italy in 1348 either. Beggars, flagellants, pilgrims, and merchants were almost automatically suspect (Graus 1987; Erkens 1999). An illustration in the *Schedel World Chronicle* (1493) showed, as did a 14th century manuscript from Tournai, the burning of Jews at the stake, which had a dark tradition in the Upper Rhine region since the 11th century. The treatment of refugees who had come to the city because of an earthquake was hardly any less cruel in Venice. They were captured and, if they showed symptoms, thrown into mass graves even while still breathing. The conviction of many was that the survival of the city was at stake. If trade came to a standstill and the harbor was closed, hunger and more epidemics threatened. Social coldness spread. The *Bocche della Sanità* were letter boxes of denunciation, where one could and should anonymously report fellow citizens or people who looked bad and sick! (Venezia e la Peste 1980, p. 113)

6 Plague Hospitals

Hospices and hospitals were also a genuinely Christian legacy and played a particularly important role during times of plague. In Venice, the first plague hospitals were set up on islands in the lagoon that were managed by Christian orders. In the Tuscan cities, they initially used former leper hospitals that were located outside the walls to care for plague victims. In 1423, the first permanent plague hospital was established in Venice—significantly on an island which was easy to isolate *(Santa Maria di Nazareth)* that was also managed by an order. As early as the fourteenth century, they had also set up quarantine stations where people, such as merchants or sailors from trading ships, who wanted to enter from supposedly infected areas, were kept under observation for a certain period of time. The first such facility is documented in 1374 in Reggio d'Emilia (10 days), then in 1377 in Ragusa/Dubrovnik (30 days), and finally in 1383 in Marseille, where isolation lasted 40 days, from which the today common word *quarantine* is derived. By the sixteenth century, almost all European port cities had strictly controlled quarantine stations (de Lannoy 2016, pp. 51 ff.). The violation of the ordered isolation often led to disasters. The plague of Marseille (1720) was caused by sailors from the ship *Grand St. Antoine* which during their quarantine secretly smuggled ship's goods into the city. No favours were granted to individual travelers. Montaigne complained in 1585, to cite a prominent example, on the occasion of a plague in the Périgord, that he had had to wait forty days "in suspense and trepidation", "whether the evil actually breaks out, while the imagination by its nature is torturing each [isolated] individual and even the health begins to fever" (Mauelshagen 2005, p. 253). Certainly, Europe's plague and disease history would have been different if one had always adhered to the quarantine regulations. Carelessness, hubris, boredom, greed, and mental alteration cost the lives of hundreds of thousands of people over the centuries.

7 The Question of Human Dignity

The violation of *dignitas humana* by government measures was not only commonplace in Venice. Cicero had once founded the concept of dignity on human *auctoritas,* which he derived from the reasonableness of man (Cicero, De inv. II, 166). But in the everyday life of the 14th century, which was still shaped by the hierarchical structures of the Middle Ages, it was also connected with the social status of the individual—the king had a different rank and thus more "dignity" than a craftsman or peasant. Many intellectuals, but also simple believers were therefore shaken by a phenomenon that seems strange today. In a letter to his brother Gerardo, a Carthusian, who was the only monk of his monastery to survive the plague, Petrarch complained: "The honorable lie next to the common people in dishonor" (Bergdolt 1989, p. 146). This seemed scandalous. In Venice, Lorenzo de

Monacis (1354) reported that "the moderate, restrained, chaste, sober" were just as much carried away as "the drunk, gluttonous, drunkards and gourmets, the frugal and spendthrifts, the cheerful and sad, the bold and shy, those who fled, as well as those who remained, without confession and the sacraments of the church" (Bergdolt 1989, p. 120). An illustration from the chronicle of the pharmacist *Sercambi* from Lucca (1423) (Sercambi 1892) showed the social destruction very clearly. Princes, kings, bishops and cardinals lie dead here next to peasants and the poor, a state that must have reminded contemporaries of the chaos of hell, which also swallowed representatives of all classes, while—as can be seen on Orcagna's frescoes in the Strozzi Chapel of Santa Maria Novella in Florence (around 1350) or Stefan Lochners Cologne *Weltgericht* (1432)—an heavenly order prevailed in paradise. The plague had such demonstrably infernal features. With the "divine order", the *Ordo medievalis,* the guarantee of a virtuous life seemed to have faltered in 1348. The "external" social hierarchy had hitherto been regarded as a reflection of the divine, which is why it offered many people security and comfort. Suddenly questions were asked which revealed the new insecurity. The *subjective* became more important. Autobiographies, letters, short stories and the now flourishing aesthetic literature thematized this mentality, which ultimately, at least in Italy, initiated the Renaissance (Friedell 1989, p. 6).

It was thus not only the encounter with death, which shocked the contemporaries of 1348 and later plague epidemics—death was much more present in everyday life in the late Middle Ages than today. Rather, the mass death raised the question of whether God wanted to let humanity perish. Where was his justice when the good and the bad died together? The nightmare of Augustine's doctrine of predestination seemed to become reality. The coping strategies that were used were initially conservative. On the basis of a medieval-theological foundation, a new *ars moriendi* was developed. Whoever thought about death every day lost his fear of it—so the theory went. Death and dying became popular topics of literature and art (Ariès 1984; Bergdolt 1996). Penitential sermons, mirrors of confession, dances macabres and the motif of the *Triumph of Death* came into fashion around 1400. A constant *Memento mori*—for example, in the classical motif of the "Meeting of the Three Living with the Three Dead" ("quod estis fuimus, quod sumus, eritis"—"What you are, we were, what we are now, you will be") (Comoli 2002)—was supposed to neutralize the fear. But the disturbing question remained: Is God just? Or even more disillusioning: "Does he care about humanity at all?" But the question of theodicy, why God allowed all this, only came up in the 18th century.

8 The Black Death, a Phenomenon Over Centuries

Later, the mortality of the plague, considered Europe-wide, was never as high as in the 14th century. In cities such as Florence, Venice, Genoa, Tournai or Paris, about a third of the population is estimated to have died at that time (de Lannoy 2016,

p. 30). Retrospective projections are characterized by uncertainties, but appear to confirm, with regard to 1348, a loss rate of between 30% and 40% of the population at that time. In Central Europe, about 15 to 20 million people lost their lives in a painful way, a number that was "unheard of" in the truest sense of the word (Bergdolt 2011, p. 50). Later, corresponding mortality figures were "only" achieved in individual cities, such as Venice (1576 and 1631/1632), Milan (1576), Naples (1656), London (1665/1666) or Marseille (1720). In London, the *bills of mortality* confirmed that at least 40% of the population had died (Naphy and Spicer 2003, pp. 107 ff.). In contrast to the Italian and French tradition, the houses of plague victims were sealed on the Thames, even if healthy relatives lived there. Infected and non-infected, sick and their relatives formed a quarantined community of fate in such cases. Others starved or showed secondary infections that also led to death. An important role was played by the immunization through previous epidemics. From about 1480, the intervals between epidemics became larger, which facilitated preventive measures (Naphy and Spicer 2003, pp. 83 ff.). As early as the 14th century, society seems to have arranged itself in a admirable, sometimes even uncanny way with the phenomenon of everyday death. Many people seemed to develop supernatural powers. That a father, like the Sienese chronicler Agnolo di Tura, had to bury all his children, was by no means a unique tragedy (Bergdolt 2003, p. 46). The Nuremberg councillor Ulmann Stromer lost eight sons, his wife and his brother during the plague in 1406. He remarried and fathered another son who ensured the survival of the family before he himself fell victim to the disease (Stromer 1961). The everyday life of the plague created—also later in Milan, Naples or London—dramas that would have been worthy of any theatre. In 1656, the *Via Toledo,* one of the main streets of Naples, is said to have been "paved" with corpses to such an extent that the coaches could only drive "over baptized flesh" (Bergdolt 2011, p. 81). The evangelical pastor Wolfgang Ammon saw three children, his wife and his brother die during various epidemics between 1611 and 1617 before he himself, although much later (1634), fell victim to the "plague" (Bergdolt 2011, pp. 46 f.).

The fact that, as can be seen particularly in Italy since the 16th century, *public* rather than *medical* measures were more successful explains why the successful, toughly implemented policy on epidemics in the 18th century finally contributed to the development of the "strong state" favored by the Enlightenment (Dinges 2005, pp. 296 ff.). One can ask why, in view of the clearly visible tradition of medical helplessness, city governments had repeatedly consulted medical celebrities up to then. There were several reasons for this. Increasingly personally and professionally connected with the upper class, quite a few physicians tried to share the concerns and views of their clients in times of danger and at least initially to disguise a state crisis threatened by the epidemic through harmless diagnoses. This psychological moment made them—in the sense of their clients—more likely to tend to optimistic assessments. Like them, they despised unrest and panic and discussed the pros and cons of the epidemic emergency and the diagnosis "plague" with representatives of the authorities without bias. Some doctors and some laymen may have suspected the contagiousness of the plague—but the doctrine in any case insisted on the miasma theory. In this situation, the state, as the example of Venice in 1576 shows, simply could not afford to bypass the medical celebrities, even if they were wrong and the subject of general ridicule (Venezia e la Peste 1980, p. 123; Preti 1984, p. 50; Rodenwaldt 1953, pp. 180 ff.). Above all, the universities were dear to the municipalities. They quickly recognized the advantages and the image gain of a local university and cultivated its aura. After all, it was in the municipal interest that the responsible university always knew what to do, even if it was overwhelmed by it (Bergdolt 2011, pp. 75 ff.). The tendency of medical experts to downplay was probably also promoted by *deontologies* (books on ethics) in which radical enlightenment of the patient was condemned as downright immoral. The truth should—as was already the medieval tradition—only be spoken if death was imminent and the sick person was to be exhorted to confession. At first, however, "therapeutic lies" seemed justified, even ethically required. The *medicus prudens* always had to take into account the psychological effect of telling the truth, as the Hamburg doctor Roderich Castro (1614) put it. What applied to individuals also seemed advisable for the masses, especially since public order seemed to be at risk.

9 Brave and Less Brave Doctors

The doctors' reputation was of highest ambivalence during times of plague—just think of Boccaccio's novellas or Petrarca's caricaturising criticism. Nevertheless, if one were to take a diachronic summary, many people probably kept some sort of primal trust in the healing arts, which were also practiced by herbalists, barbers, monks (rural monasteries' medical care was in their hands), astrologers, dentists, and surgeons. A special situation crystallized in Vienna, where, since 1551, the *Magistri sanitatis* represented a sort of medical corps of officials, whom the medical faculty of the university, however, refused to cooperate with. Poorly paid and despised by their colleagues, they were only allowed to treat those with the plague. No wonder that "only the most destitute of physicians", often poor students (Schmölzer 1988, pp. 158 ff.) took on this task. These assistant physicians were controversial up until the 18th century, but revered by the people. For many established physicians of the Danube town, however, the plague remained a disgusting, dangerous phenomenon, which they did not want to deal with. There was, however, one outstanding and effective health authority, which, after much time had already been lost (as was almost everywhere, where the situation was initially downplayed), fought the crisis very successfully. The imperial sanitary councilor Paul de Sorbait, professor and rector of the university (1668), banned the usual "controlled fires" in the city (whose smoke, according to the doctrine of the four humors, was supposed to neutralize the miasmas) and organized the isolation of the sick. At his side was Prince Ferdinand Schwarzenberg, the "Pestkönig", who—partly from his private purse, partly from the state treasury's funds (both of which was unusual)—simultaneously fought the famine and strictly went against crime and corruption (Mauelshagen 2005, p. 243).

In many places of course academic doctors also bravely treated plague victims at the risk of their lives. They bled them, anointed their wounds, cauterized skin bleeding, and also advised them on dietary matters. In 1354, an Italian chronicler confessed that his doctor had bled him when he was acutely ill with the disease: "The blood that flowed out spurted into his face. And on the same day he became ill and died the following day." While the Swiss doctor Felix Platter (1536–1614) survived nine epidemics, his contemporary, the naturalist Conrad Gesner, succumbed to the disease at the age of 49 (1565). Gentle da Foligno died during the Black Death in 1348, as his son reports, in the Florentine plague everyday life. "In the month of June, the venerable Magister put together recipes for pills that should be taken three times a week. Thereupon Gentile himself fell ill because he had taken care of the plague patients too much. This happened on June 12. He lived for another six days and then died. May his soul rest in peace. This happened in 1348. And I, Francesco from Foligno, was present when he was sick and did not leave him anymore, until he died and was buried in Foligno at the hermitage church." (Bergdolt 1989, pp. 150 ff.) In Trento, as the cleric Johannes von Parma reports, countless doctors also died in the same year, "and especially the better ones". In Venice, the master Francesco from Rome, who had lost a son himself during the plague, was promised an increase in his salary by the government because he had bravely treated plague victims and, "although he recognized the so dangerous situation, did not want to give way on his own decision and said that he would rather die here than live elsewhere and that, as it were, the grace of the Almighty had to judge on his fate" (Bergdolt 2003, pp. 55 ff.).

10 Thucydides at the Beginning...

The story of the plague is, like the history of epidemics in general, a comprehensive cultural history topic. It could only be treated in an exemplary way here. Already Thucydides (ca. 460–400 BC) had depicted the cruelty of epidemics with a sharp look:

> Some died due to lack of care, others despite self-sacrificing care. It was also found that there was not a single remedy whose application would have promised safe help. What had helped one, harmed the other. With regard to physical constitution, the strong differed in nothing from the weak in this disease. It swept away all of them, also those who were taken care of with great diligence. The most terrible feature in the malady was the despair as soon as one felt sick. For one immediately abandoned oneself to despair, completely gave up and did not resist. That one infected the other in the care of the other and all died like the livestock was the cause of the mass death (Thucydides 2,51).

Thucydides' report on the "Plague of Athens" (429 BC) was often received by later writers. In Athens, however, taking into account all the historical hints available to us today, it was not the *plague,* i.e. the disease caused by *Yersinia pestis,* but this is ultimately of secondary importance (Schmitz 2005; Thucydides 2002). The representation of the "psychology of everyday life in the plague" is decisive. Precisely because basic thoughts on the history of epidemics always have to be limited to the essentials, the report of the Athenian author is highly informative. In the end, the question arises whether the behavior of man in existential need and fear of death has changed at all in the last two and a half thousand years. Also in Athens the plague came from the east (Ethiopia), already then the accusation of poisoning the wells circulated on the Peloponnese, and finally countless patients died lonely in their homes, anticipating countless later plague scenarios. The relatives fled, friendships dissolved, the good died like the bad. Religion, law and tradition lost their influence temporarily. But the Athenians also drew lessons from the catastrophe. And after the plague, societies quickly returned to normality.

11 Summary

The plague story is of astonishing intensity. It shows, based on numerous sources, in an exemplary way how people deal with the deadly danger. It is anything but reassuring. Although the behaviour of city societies and state authorities depended on the cultural or spiritual contexts of the respective epoch, there seem to have been considerable constants as well. In the event of extreme danger, individuals apparently resort to certain, almost archetypal, patterns of reaction. The flight of the elites, especially of the doctors, the suspicion of the environment, the hatred of foreigners, religious explanatory patterns, the loss of authority of orthodox medicine, crime and moral decline, but also the desperate experience of loneliness can be demonstrated for the "Black Death" of the 14th to the 18th century. Of course, during each epidemic, to quote Schiller, "the saving power also grew". Heroism was observed during each catastrophe. However, in case of doubt, the authorities intervened harshly. Their intentions were utilitarian—the interests of the community always took precedence. Until the 19th century, only the idea of Christian mercy was opposed to this, which often enough found its limits in deadly danger. At first, pesthouses were formed on the basis of this thought. After shorter economic and supply crises, the societies visited by epidemics consolidated surprisingly quickly.

References

Amstutz J (1974) Montaignes Begriff der Gesundheit. Heidelb Jahrb XVIII:101–122
Amundsen DW (1977) Medical deontology and pestilential disease in the Late Middle Ages. J Hist Med 23:403–421
Ariès P (1984) Bilder zur Geschichte des Todes. Dtv, München/Wien
Benzenhöfer U (1999) Der gute Tod? Euthanasie und Sterbehilfe in Geschichte und Gegenwart. C. H. Beck, München

Bergdolt K (1989) Die Pest 1348 in Italien. Fünfzig zeitgenössische Quellen. Manutius, Heidelberg
Bergdolt K (1992) Arzt, Krankheit und Therapie bei Petrarca. Die Kritik an Naturwissenschaft und Medizin im italienischen Frühhumanismus. Wiley-VCH, Weinheim
Bergdolt K (1996) Totentanz und Ars moriendi im Spätmittelalter. Forum MUL (Medizinische Universität zu Lübeck) 1996(3):3–16
Bergdolt K (2001) Hippokrates, Galen und das medizinisch-naturwissenschaftliche Programm der Kryptafresken von Anagni. In: Bergdolt K, Bonsanti G (eds) Opere e Giorni. Studi su mille anni di arte europea. Marsilio Editori, Venezia, pp 51–58
Bergdolt K (2003) Der Schwarze Tod in Europa. Die große Pest und das Ende des Mittelalters, 5th edn. C. H. Beck, München
Bergdolt K (2004) Das Gewissen der Medizin. Ärztliche Moral von der Antike bis heute. C. H. Beck, München
Bergdolt K (2005) Das Pestmotiv in der bildenden Kunst. In: Meier M (ed) Pest. Die Geschichte eines Menschheitstraumas. Klett-Cotta, Stuttgart, pp 317–327
Bergdolt K (2011) Die Pest. Geschichte des Schwarzen Todes, 2nd edn. C. H. Beck, München
Boas M (1988) Die Renaissance der Naturwissenschaften 1450–1630. Übersetzt von Trier M und Knust T A. Dtv, Nördlingen
Bongi S (Hrsg) (1892) Le Croniche di Giovanni Sercambi Lucchese. vol 3. Istituto Storico Italiano, Roma
Camus A (1998) La peste – Die Pest. Deutsch von Aumüller U. Rowohlt, Reinbek
Comoli P (2002) Il tema dell'incontro dei tre vivi e dei tre morti nella letteratura e nell'arte medievale: le testimonianze italiane. Universita degli studi, Torino
Dahm KW (2000) Rechtfertigungslehre und kirchliche Religiosität. J Relig Cult 38:1–5
Deichgräber K (1983) Der hippokratische Eid, 4th edn. Hippokrates, Stuttgart
Dinges, Martin (2005) Pest und Politik in der europäischen Neuzeit. In: Meier M (ed) Pest. Die Geschichte eines Menschheitstraumas. Klett-Kotta, Stuttgart, pp 282–313.
Eckart WU (2005) Triage. In: Gerabek W, Haage WD, Keil G, Wegner W (eds) Enzyklopädie Medizingeschichte. de Gruyter, Berlin/New York, pp 1419–1420
Eikermann D, Kaiser S (2012) Die Pest in Berlin 1576. Basilisken Presse, Rangsdorf
Erkens FR (1999) Buße in Zeiten des Schwarzen Todes. Die Züge der Geissler. Z historische Forschung 26:483–513
Esser T (1997) Die Pest – Strafe Gottes oder Naturphänomen? Eine frömmigkeitsgeschichtliche Untersuchung zu Pesttraktaten des 15. Jahrhunderts. Z Kirchengesch 108:32–57
Friedell E (1989) Kulturgeschichte der Neuzeit. Die Krise der europäischen Seele von der Schwarzen Pest bis zum ersten Weltkrieg. Dtv, München
Geisler L (2008) Arzt und Patient, Begegnung im Gespräch, 5th edn. pmi Verlag AG, Frankfurt am Main
Graus F (1987) Pest – Geißler – Judenmorde. Das 14. Jahrhundert als Krisenzeit. Vandenhoeck & Ruprecht, Göttingen
Haverkamp A (1981) Die Judenverfolgungen zur Zeit des Schwarzen Todes im Gesellschaftsgefüge deutscher Städte. In: Haverkamp A (ed) Zur Geschichte der Juden im Deutschland des späten Mittelalters und der frühen Neuzeit. Hiersemann, Stuttgart, pp 27–93
Jonsen AR (2000) A short history of medical ethics. Oxford University Press, New York/Oxford
Lannoy F de (2016) Pestes et Épidémies au Moyen Age (VIe-XVe siècles). Ouest France, Rennes
Leppin H (2005) Gregor der Große und die heilsame Seuche. In: Meier M (ed) Pest. Die Geschichte eines Menschheitstraumas. Klett-Cotta, Stuttgart, pp 108–116
Lichtenthaeler C (1984) Der Eid des Hippokrates. Ursprung und Bedeutung. Deutscher Ärzteverlag, Köln
Mauelshagen F (2005) Pestepidemien im Europa der frühen Neuzeit. In: Meier M (ed) pp 237–265
Naphy W, Spicer A (2003) Der Schwarze Tod. Die Pest in Europa (The Black Death, A History of plagues 1345–1730. Stroud 2000). Magnus, Essen

Paré A (1963) Rechtfertigung und Bericht über meine Reisen in verschiedene Orte. Huber, Bern
Paulsen T, Schulze C (2005) Das Motiv der Pest in der Literatur. In: Meier M (ed) Pest. Die Geschichte eines Menschheitstraumas. Klett-Cotta, Stuttgart, pp 328–357
Preti P (1984) Peste e Società a Venezia 1576 (=Studi e testi Veneziani 7), 2nd edn. Neri Pozza, Vicenza
Rath G (1957) Ärztliche Ethik in Pestzeiten. MMW 99:158–160
Renzi S de (1968) Napoli nell' anno 1656. Documenti della pestilenza che desolò Napoli nell'anno 1656. Reprint of 2019. Forgotten Books, Napoli
Rodenwaldt E (1953) Die Pest in Venedig 1576/77. Ein Beitrag zur Frage der Infektionskette bei den Pestepidemien West-Europas. Springer, Heidelberg
Rossi P (1997) Die Geburt der modernen Wissenschaft in Europa. Deutsch von Sattler Charnitzky M und Büchel G. C. H. Beck, München
Schadewaldt H (ed) (1994) Die Rückkehr der Seuchen. Ist die Medizin machtlos? Bastei-Verlag Lübbe, Bergisch Gladbach
Schipperges H (1998) Die Entienlehre des Paracelsus. Aufbau und Umriß seiner theoretischen Pathologie. Springer, Berlin/Heidelberg
Schmölzer H (1988) Die Pest in Wien. Verlag der Nation, Berlin
Schmitz W (2005) Göttliche Strafe oder medizinisches Geschehen. Deutungen und Diagnosen der „Pest" in Athen (430–426 v. Chr.). In: Mischa M (ed) Pest. Die Geschichte eines Menschheitstraumas. Klett-Cotta, Stuttgart, pp 44–65
Schöner E (1964) Das Viererschema in der antiken Humoralpathologie. Mit einem Vorwort von Herrlinger R (=Sudhoffs Archiv Beiheft 4). Franz Steiner Verlag, Wiesbaden
Stromer U (1961) Püchel von meim geslecht und von abentewr 1349 bis 1407. In: Hegel K (ed) Die Chroniken der fränkischen Städte. Nürnberg. Bd. 1: Die Chroniken der deutschen Städte vom 14. bis ins 16. Jahrhundert. Leipzig 1862. Neudruck, Göttingen
Thukydides (2002) Der Peloponnesische Krieg. Übersetzt von Georg Peter Landmann. Artemis und Winkler, Düsseldorf/Zürich
Venezia e la Peste (1980) Ausstellungskatalog 1348–1797 (eds. vom Assessorato alla cultura e alle belle arti). Venedig, Marsilio
Welborn MC (1996) The long tradition: a study in fourteenth century medical deontology. In: Cate JL, Anderson E (eds) Medieval and historiographical Essays in honour of James W. Thompson. University of Chicago Press, Chicago. Chicago 1938 (Reprint 1996)
Zerbi G (2019) Über die Kautelen der Ärzte. De cautelis medicorum (ca. 1495). In: Gadebusch Bondio M, Förg M, Kaiser C (eds) Edition und Übersetzung. Franz Steiner, Stuttgart
Ziegler P (1972) The black death. Penguin, London
Zinn KG (1989) Kanonen und Pest. Über die Ursprünge der Neuzeit im 14. und 15. Jahrhundert. Westdeutscher Verlag, Opladen

Solidarity in Times of a Pandemic: Everyday Practices and Prioritization Decisions in Light of the Solidarity Concept

Katharina Kieslich and Barbara Prainsack

Contents

1 Introduction 25
2 Scholarly Approaches to the Concept of Solidarity 26
3 Solidarity in Times of Pandemic 28
3.1 State of Research 28
3.2 The SolPan Study on Solidarity in Times of Pandemics 30
4 Solidarity and Prioritization 33
5 Conclusion and Outlook 35
References 36

1 Introduction

Since the beginning of the COVID-19 pandemic, appeals for solidarity within society and the international community of states have been ubiquitous. The diversity of these calls suggests that solidarity, as a guiding principle for the management of the pandemic, plays an important role and assumes different functions in this context. Politicians appeal to people to comply with measures such as wearing masks or maintaining distance and justify these appeals by reference to solidarity. For example, the Director-General of the World Health Organization, Tedros Adhanom, declared that the COVID-19 pandemic was a test for global solidarity (The Guardian 2020). The concept of solidarity thus appears, on the one hand, to function as a principle for justifying measures to contain the spread of infection

K. Kieslich (✉) · B. Prainsack
University of Vienna, Vienna, Austria
e-mail: katharina.kieslich@univie.ac.at

B. Prainsack
e-mail: barbara.prainsack@univie.ac.at

© The Author(s), under exclusive license to Springer-Verlag GmbH, DE, part of Springer Nature 2023
A. Reis et al. (eds.), *Pandemics and Ethics*,
https://doi.org/10.1007/978-3-662-66872-6_3

and calling on people to comply with them, and on the other hand as a fundamental principle of social and international coexistence, which is endangered by challenging developments in the pandemic.

The different uses of the concept of solidarity are contradictory only at first glance. They can be explained in particular by the fact that solidarity is a much-used but often not (or not sufficiently) defined concept. Through a systematic consideration of the concept, which we undertake in this article, it is possible to distinguish solidaristic practices from other prosocial actions. This makes it possible to distinguish situations in which solidarity is used merely as a rhetorical device from genuine instances of solidaristic practice—including some new forms of solidarity emerging in the pandemic.

This article begins with an overview of different approaches to the concept of solidarity (Sect. 2), followed by an introduction to the definition of solidarity as developed by Prainsack and Buyx (see 2011, 2017), which is used in the article (Sect. 3). We then sketch the research and theoretical approaches that deal with solidarity in pandemics, highlighting that extant knowledge about the role of solidarity in pandemics has gaps despite the diverse applications of the term (Sect. 3.1). The multinational comparative study "Solidarity in Times of a Pandemic" (SolPan) attempts to address some of these gaps. It is was initiated and led by the authors of this article. Some of its results are reported in this article (Sect. 3.2). In addition to first empirical findings from the Austrian part of the SolPan study, we also reflect on how the principle of solidarity relates to other guiding principles for setting priorities in times of scarce resources, such as justice in priority setting, (Sect. 4) before offering some concluding remarks in the last section (Sect. 5).

2 Scholarly Approaches to the Concept of Solidarity

The concept of solidarity was much used and strongly criticized in the COVID-19 crisis. Because it was used at the beginning of the crisis to celebrate very heterogeneous forms of prosocial practice—from neighborhood assistance to support within families to global research cooperation—criticism of its inflationary use soon started to emerge (see Gaztambide-Fernández 2020). Some argued that the concept of solidarity obscured the increasing polarization within the crisis-ridden societies (ibid.). Criticism of the undifferentiated use of the concept in the context of the coronavirus crisis reflects a problem that the scientific literature knows well: Here, the term has also been applied in very different ways to legitimize different—and sometimes even diametrically opposed—goals: from the need for solidaristic health insurance for all to the exclusion of those people who have "chosen" an unhealthy lifestyle from certain health services (see Buyx and Prainsack 2012 for a critical discussion). For this reason, it is important to define solidarity in a manner that is analytically specific enough to distinguish solidarity from other forms of prosocial practice.

This is possible: Almost all conceptualizations of solidarity describe prosocial practices and phenomena that strengthen the cohesion within groups or societies. Most conceptualizations of solidarity have three things in common (for an overview see Prainsack and Buyx 2011, 2017): First, they refer to one (or more) form(s) of mutual support. Secondly, the people who provide support have something in common with those who receive support: this can be a common goal (e.g. averting the climate catastrophe), a common characteristic (e.g. working under precarious conditions) or an experience that one shares (for example, if one has experienced a certain illness oneself or within one's family or circle of friends). Despite the numerous differences that exist between people, it is the similarities and not the differences that become action-guiding for solidaritistic practices (see Prainsack and Buyx 2011, 2017). Thirdly, solidarity is not an isolated, purely individual act, but it is part of a social or political fabric, of social and political institutions. As such, it requires a certain degree of (indirect) reciprocity (see, for example, Sternø 2005; Molm et al. 2007). Solidarity practices and solidaristic institutions in a society are more stable when the people who practice solidarity in the present know that they will also receive support if they need it in the future. Jürgen Habermas' famous description of solidarity as "the other side of justice" captures the essence of solidarity as "putty" between the building blocks that make up the architecture of our political and social institutions (Habermas 1991, p. 70; see also Scholz 2008). Within this architecture, solidarity is to a large extent that which cannot be prescribed, but what people do of their own initiative and their own free will.

Based on these elements, which can be found in many conceptualizations of solidarity, we understand solidarity as a practice that expresses the willingness of people to support others with whom they recognize similarity in a relevant respect (see Prainsack and Buyx 2011, 2017). The "relevant respect" is determined by the specific situations in which solidarity takes place. In the context of discrimination at work, for example, we could recognize similarity with someone who is currently the target of discrimination if I—or someone close to me—have made or are making similar experiences. Recognizing similarity in a relevant respect is therefore not just a matter of recognizing "objectively" existing properties or ethnic, religious or gender attributions. It is an active process in which we see (or do not see) in others what we recognize in ourselves. If we learned to see people with a different religion, a different gender or different political values as "the others" and to exclude them from the concept of "we", then it is more difficult for us to see ourselves in these people than if we had learned to always see what unites us as and with people.

In summary, it can be said that solidarity is characterized by symmetry between people *in the moment of mutual support*. This symmetry is not an ontological statement about the overall configuration of our societies or the denial of differences and structural inequalities. Solidarity takes place when the similarities in a concrete situation of action or in a specific context of institutional practice are seen by the acting persons as more important than the differences that exist between people (solidaristic health systems are an example of this).

This definition makes it possible to distinguish solidarity from other forms of support or prosocial practice, such as empathy, collegiality and friendship or love. Solidarity differs from empathy in that it requires an external expression; the mere feeling of connectedness—or compassion—with someone else is not enough for solidarity to exist. Although empathy is regularly an element of solidaristic practice, it is not a sufficient condition for solidarity. Solidarity differs from charity in that, with the latter, differences between people are regularly decisive for action, rather than (naturally existing) commonalities: because we have more than you, we give you something. In addition, charity is also a religious duty in many religions; if charity is primarily motivated in this way, it can only be qualified as a form of institutional, but never interpersonal solidarity (we will return to the difference between these levels below). Finally, solidarity differs from the support between lovers or friends in that love or friendship are much stronger bonds. Persons who are connected by love or friendship do not need solidarity to support each other. Solidarity is subsidiary to these stronger bonds: it is particularly relevant in situations where there are no other bonds that hold people together (see in particular Dean 1996).

Solidarity can manifest itself at different levels (see Prainsack and Buyx 2011, 2017): at the interpersonal level (level 1), at the group level (level 2) and at the level of formal institutions and norms (level 3). If actions of mutual support become so common at the interpersonal level—that is, from person to person—that they become "normal" expected behaviour in some groups, then we see solidarity at level 2. If solidarity is expressed in legal, administrative and bureaucratic norms, regulations and designs, we speak of a solidarity at level 3. Solidarity typically occurs at this third, "highest" (i.e. most stable) level when the practices at the interpersonal or group level have solidified into "harder", more structural forms of solidarity (see Prainsack and Buyx 2017). This distinction between different levels of solidarity can help clarify apparently contradictory developments in solidaristic practice during the coronavirus crisis (see Prainsack 2020). Previous results from our own research show that while some forms of interpersonal solidarity shift with the progression of the crisis, the importance of institutional solidarity is also coming to the fore.

3 Solidarity in Times of a Pandemic

3.1 State of Research

Despite the inflationary use of the term solidarity during COVID-19 and also in previous pandemics, research on the role of solidarity in health crises exhibits gaps. In particular, how people understand and practice solidarity, as well as the question of whether prosocial practices strengthen or change in pandemics, is currently under-researched. This is surprising because solidarity seems to play a role on several levels in pandemics. On the interpersonal level, people support each other, even though they are often in challenging situations caused by the pandemic. On the relationship level between state and society as well as between social actors, most people are willing to accept the costs associated with temporary restrictions on their usual freedoms in order to protect themselves and others. And finally, solidarity plays a role on a global level, in international cooperation and support, and in the actions of global institutions such as the World Health Organization, the success of which depends to a large extent on whether individual countries show solidarity with each other by, for example, allowing WHO experts into their country. The latter is often associated in global health policy with an (necessary) interference in the national sovereignty of individual states (see, for example, Frenk and Moon 2013). Prainsack and Buyx's (2011, 2017) approach allows us to see these interventions into their national sovereignty as necessary costs that states accept in order to show solidarity with others and contribute to containing the pandemic.

A large part of the scientific work that is concerned with the role of solidarity in pandemics refers to the global arena (cf. Pang 2016; De Grandis and Littmann 2011, for example). For example, de Campos (2020) argues that solidarity can be understood as a principle of justice which can contribute to global resources for health promotion and pandemic containment being distributed in a solidaristic manner. West-Oram and Buyx (2017) take a similar view, arguing that solidarity at the global level can lead states and people to recognize their own vulnerability to threats such as climate change, antimicrobial resistance, and pandemics, and to be moved to act in solidarity as a result. The fact that the motivation for any given solidarity-based action is also based on self-interest is, according to West-Oram and Buyx, no reason not to recognize the solidarity that arises from the recognition of similar vulnerabilities as such. In contrast to other approaches that represent self-interest as the opposite of solidaristic behavior (cf. Karlsson et al. 2020; Gelissen 2000, for example), this is therefore a pragmatic approach in which (initial) self-interest can lead to solidarity because, firstly, similarities with others are recognized and, secondly, the costs incurred in solving problems are not inconsiberable.

The role of solidarity on a societal level or in individual countries is occasionally addressed in conceptual and empirical literature. In a discussion of the Canadian government's failures to adequately protect Indigenous peoples during the H1N1 pandemic, Krishnamurthy (2013) refers to the concept of political solidarity, in which solidarity is associated with the rights and responsibilities of a democratic and rule-of-law government. In connection with vaccination plans to combat pandemics, Lundgren (2016) explains that during the H1N1 pandemic, the Swedish government tried to increase vaccination rates in the population through appeals to solidarity. However, this was only successful to a limited extent due to the side effects of the Pandremix vaccine. With regard to the Covid-19 pandemic, Cheng et al. (2020) explain that wearing a face mask is a measure whose normative and practical justification is anchored at the interface between altruism and solidarity. Recognizing the need to wear a mask as an expression of altruism, and not for self-protection, is an important symbol of global social solidarity here (cf. Cheng et al. 2020, p. 2). In summary, the concept of solidarity often appears in pandemics in the context of explaining and justifying government measures, or as an appeal to comply with them, or as a conceptual approach to improving global health initiatives.

Prainsack and Buyx (2011) also consider how solidarity and measures to contain and prevent pandemics relate to each other. They conclude that this relationship is complicated because the recognition of similarity with other people in a relevant respect cannot be assumed in a pandemic. The risks and burdens within the relatively short timeframe of a pandemic are very unevenly distributed; most people either feel part of a risk group that needs the protection of others, or as a "net payer". Given the prominence of such differences in the public discourse, it is difficult to recognize similarities with others, which would justify solidarity practices across group boundaries. The mere recognition that we are all affected by the pandemic is therefore not a sufficient condition to see certain actions or measures as expressions of solidarity. Rather, state measures to protect health are to be seen as an expression of the state's responsibility to protect vulnerable groups.

On the other hand, in a crisis—as is also the case with the Covid-19 crisis—new forms of solidarity can emerge. Measures such as school or business closures entail significant costs for those affected; in the first case through the loss of educational and childcare opportunities for children and in the second case through financial damage due to loss of income. It is important to distinguish between costs incurred through voluntary action and those that must be accepted as a result of government regulations. Government measures create situations in which people recognize similarities with others, either on an interpersonal level or on a group level. Parents recognize similarities with families from their social environment because they suddenly have to organize home office and homeschooling. The owners of two businesses that are normally in economic competition with each other recognize a similarity with their competitor because they are also struggling with loss of income. This recognition of similarities can lead to a willingness to "accept costs" to support others with whom one was not previously connected by any ties such as friendship or collegiality. However, it is still unclear to what extent examples of solidarity on an interpersonal level actually occur in pandemics and how these examples are practised despite restrictions on public and private life (see Brendebach et al. 2020). This is where the SolPan study comes in, which we will report on in the following section.

3.2 *The SolPan Study on Solidarity in Times of a Pandemic*

The SolPan project is a multinational, qualitative research project led by the authors of this article. Together with partners in a total of nine European countries, it was conceived and launched at the beginning of the Corona pandemic in March 2020 in order to investigate how people in these countries see the Covid-19 crisis, how they react to it and how it has changed their daily lives. This was done against the background of different developments in infection rates and different crisis management strategies in Belgium, Germany, France, Ireland, Italy, the Netherlands, Austria, the German-speaking part of Switzerland and the United Kingdom (and later on also Portugal). Our goal was to find out how people react to the crisis, to learn more about new behaviours that they adopt in the context of the crisis (e.g. new work practices, new technological practices), to explore the reference points and values that underlie people's practices (why people do or do not do certain things). Ultimately, we wanted to analyze how the actions and views of people contradict or contribute to ideas of solidarity and mutual support.

The study employed qualitative in-depth interviews as the data collection instrument. The interviews were carried out simultaneously in all participating countries in three time periods (T1=April/May 2020, T2=October/November 2020, and T3=October/November 2021). Data from the transcribed interviews were analyzed according to the principles of constructivist grounded theory (cf. Charmaz 2006) and with the help of computer-assisted qualitative data analysis software (Nvivo, Atlas.ti). The opportunities that arise from this comparative study are manifold and range from the comparison between two countries to the reactions of the public to government measures against the background of national peculiarities to the comparison between two or more countries in a certain policy field (cf. van der Heijden 2014). Another level of comparability is added by the longitudinal design of the study, which means that the results are not only spatially (i.e. in different geographical regions), but also temporally (i.e. in different phases of the pandemic) comparable. The longitudinal design of the study allows an insight into the reactions and behavior of people at different times of the pandemic.

What results have arisen from this study, in particular with regard to the forms of solidarity that are promoted or hindered by crises? In what follows, we refer to the data from Austria, the analysis of which we are directly involved in, from the first two data collection periods (T1 and T2). Here we have found the following things with regard to solidaristic practices: Even if the public debate became increasingly polarized in the second half of the first year of the pandemic, and was often only presented as a debate between people who follow pandemic containment measures and those who do not (see Ciesek et al. 2021), this characterization does not apply to the behavior of the whole population. Compliance or non-compliance with the measures prescribed by governments or other authorities is not binary. It makes no sense to divide the population into those who follow the measures and those who do not. The overwhelming majority of the interviewees in our study reported that they generally complied with the given measures even if they did not agree with specific parts of it, as long as the set of measures was overall seen as effective, consistent, and fair. In addition, there were some among our study participants who broke one or more small rules in order to either get through the crisis better or also support others. For example, some single parents reported that they met with other parents and their children in the neighborhood during the lockdown in order to have contact and support each other, for example by looking after the children of other parents so that they could go shopping in peace. According to the definition by Prainsack and Buyx (2011, 2017), the similarity that leads to solidarity in this example is the challenging and specific situation that arises for single parents in a lockdown. The costs that people take on arise on the one hand from the time and the responsibility that looking after other people's children requires, and on the other hand from the possibility of being punished by the state for meeting with people from another household. This example illustrates how much nuance and information is lost when the behavior of people is simply characterized as "compliant" or "non-compliant".

Secondly, in contrast to what the media reported in particular at the time of the first lockdown in March/April 2020, we did not find any "herd" mentality in the Austrian population. Most people did not simply do what they were told, but rather critically questioned the measures, even if they followed them. A further finding is that almost all participants in the Austrian part of our interview study—in the first as well as in the second interview phase—named the protection of other people as the main reason for the observance (or non-observance) of rules and compliance with the measures. Even those who are themselves vulnerable usually stated that they adhere to many measures not only out of concern for their own health, but—often even primarily—out of concern for others. For example, people said that they wanted to be vaccinated in order to care for older family members or neighbours. This consideration of the interests and needs of other people in one's own decision-making process was also reflected with regard to economic and social aspects: In the second interview phase in October 2020, the interview participants reflected on their concerns and fears about the effects of the pandemic on certain groups. Concerns about the psychological and social stress on children who have not been able to go to school or kindergarten for a long time, as well as concerns about the isolation and loneliness of older, single and vulnerable people were expressed as examples. During the first wave of infection, this concern led to people contacting family members and acquaintances more often to find out how they were doing or to organize virtual meetings together. Despite personal challenges, this concern led to people finding creative ways to take care of each other and support each other despite the restrictions. Solidarity was particularly pronounced at the interpersonal, person-to-person level.

In the second interview phase in October 2020, we were able to determine that the feeling of togetherness and solidarity, which was still so strong in spring 2020, had given way to a feeling of exhaustion (cf. Kieslich et al. 2020). In autumn, people were increasingly worn out in the face of the ongoing challenges and frustrated due to unclear or incomprehensible government measures. Here, two results are particularly worth mentioning. In this second interview phase, we increasingly heard appeals to the government to take into account the negative effects of the pandemic and its containment, especially for socio-economically disadvantaged population groups. In other words, the desire for and expression of solidarity seemed to be shifting from the interpersonal level to the level of formal institutions and norms (level 3). For example, some interviewees wished for the introduction of a universal basic income without conditions in view of the fact that socio-economically disadvantaged population groups are disproportionately affected by the negative consequences of the pandemic. However, the desire that the government take the issue of the impact of the pandemic on vulnerable groups into account did not seem to be reflected in an individual willingness to stimulate the economy now or after the pandemic, for example by increasing consumption. These findings correspond to data from a representative survey of the Austrian population, which found that people in Austria generally want to reduce their consumption and are not willing to stimulate the economy through increased individual consumption (cf. Riefler 2020; Kittel et al. 2020). However, we believe that this result is not necessarily to be interpreted as a lack of willingness to show solidarity, but rather is due to the fact that many people reported that they have realized during the crisis how well they can live without excessive consumption. Here it becomes clear that patterns of behaviour that appear to be unsolidaristic at first glance are actually rooted in a range of motivations upon closer inspection, some of which come from the same place as solidarity.

4 Solidarity and Prioritization

The medium- and long-term effects of the COVID-19 crisis will continue to occupy politics, society and science in the coming years. In this section, we therefore reflect on a question that we believe has received too little attention so far. How does the principle of solidarity relate to the ethical criteria according to which medical services are prioritized in times of scarce resources and what consequences does this have for future prioritization debates?

We address these two questions by considering the formal level of institutions and norms of health systems, and ethical criteria for fair prioritization in times of scarce resources. The limited resources during a pandemic are due to the fact that resources such as intensive care beds, personnel capacities and materials such as protective equipment or ventilators experience excessive demand. As a result, political interventions such as restrictions on movement are necessary in order to contain the spread of infection and protect health systems from collapse. The scientific literature on prioritization in such situations particularly emphasizes the principle of justice, which urges clinical and political decision-makers to prioritize therapeutic care for those groups that are most affected—in terms of a serious course of illness—as well as for those people who belong to vulnerable groups, such as people with pre-existing conditions. However, in pandemic times, many health systems face the problem that this principle of justice can no longer be maintained due to the system being overwhelmed and clinical staff having to apply additional criteria in triage scenarios in order to decide, for example, which patients should be treated in intensive care units. In the best case, the chances of recovery for individual patients are included in the decision-making process. In the worst case, such triage decisions are made arbitrarily, intransparently and randomly due to the severe overload of staff and the system—a situation that must be avoided from an ethical, clinical and political perspective.

From our point of view, a solidarity-based perspective is helpful in order to illustrate why the opportunity costs of exceptional situations that can arise in the context of a pandemic are problematic. Opportunity costs are those costs that arise, for example, from the fact that people who need treatment or diagnosis for health problems either do not use or do not receive these offers during a pandemic because there are no more resources for this in the overstretched health system (see, for example, Maringe et al. 2020). In the first of these possible cases, that is, if people do not use a necessary health service even though it would be possible, the reason for this can either be that they are afraid of becoming infected or that they feel obliged out of a sense of solidarity not to visit health facilities in order to avoid overloading the system even further. This was described by some of the participants in the SolPan study in Austria and they described this as a contribution to protecting themselves and others during the pandemic. For this very reason, in the second wave of the survey in October, some of our study participants also said that they did not want to be vaccinated immediately. These people, who would be rated as vaccine skeptics in online surveys (!), are actually motivated by the opposite: They consider the vaccination to be so important that they do not want to take the vaccine away from anyone who looks after children or older people or who needs the vaccination for other reasons more urgently than they do themselves.

In this context, people seem to recognize a similarity with their fellow human beings, namely the risk of becoming infected with the virus. This may result in people taking on costs (i.e. sacrifices) that arise from the fact that necessary health services are not used. Such opportunity costs which arise from solidarity-motivated action have negative ramifications from a societal point of view, because the potentially negative health-related consequences are ethically and politically difficult to justify, even in pandemic times. In other words, without systematic counter-measures aimed at supporting people, costs are sometimes incurred that cannot be ethically justified. On the formal level of institutions and norms, this results in a requirement for state action on the one hand and a conceptual refinement of the understanding of solidarity on the other hand. Such solidaritstic practices of individual people reinforce the state's duty to develop strategies and measures to ensure the access to necessary psychological, social, and economic support for all patients in pandemic times. This duty can be justified, ironically, by the fact that there are situations in which people must not be left alone with the consequences of their solidaristic action. Based on our empirical data, it is clear that solidarity at the institutional level is particularly relevant in pandemic times. For example, a health system that functions on the principle of solidarity must be able to ensure that people do not have to forego treatment—also if this means that extra capacities need to be built and maintained in times when there is no crisis.

5 Conclusion and Outlook

This article has illustrated the diverse meanings and roles that solidarity can take during a pandemic. An overview of some important conceptual approaches to solidarity shows that it almost always includes prosocial practices that strengthen cohesion within groups or societies. The approach of Prainsack and Buyx (2011, 2017) allows such practices to be examined on the basis of concrete properties (recognition of a commonality; emergence of costs) at different levels of solidarity. Solidarity, as defined by Prainsack and Buyx, can thus help to better understand central challenges and serious problems in pandemics. This results in arguments that, for example, underline the state's duty to ensure healthcare for all patients during pandemics. Recommendations for action can also be derived, such as that people with chronic illnesses or multimorbidity should be contacted and supported proactively during pandemics, and not only by letter or general campaigns. In order to protect people from the possibly negative consequences of their solidaristic action, they must be given the opportunity to have regular, safe check-up appointments. Similarly, good reasons for solidaristic action at the global level can be derived from the consideration of solidarity sketched in this chapter, for example in view of the calls for a fairer distribution of available vaccines between rich and poor countries. Even if a fair distribution of vaccines between countries would initially lead to shortages for their own population, the willingness of some—otherwise rich—countries to accept these "costs" of shortages for the sake of supporting less wealthy countries would be a practice of genuine solidarity—and would help protect vulnerable people worldwide.

The approach of Prainsack and Buyx (2011, 2017) also opens up the possibility of empirically investigating the concept of solidarity, as we do in the SolPan study. The first findings of the study in Austria provide interesting insights into the understanding and practices of solidarity in the Covid-19 pandemic. The results show that solidaristic practices in times of pandemics are very nuanced. While many people's willingness to comply with measures that they experience as onerous or otherwise negative was motivated by solidarity, they also considered the behaviour of other people who did not comply with the same measures as unsolidaristic. We were able to determine that the first phase of the pandemic in spring 2020 was characterized by high levels of solidaristic practices at the interpersonal level, in the second phase of interviews (October 2020), calls and wishes for solidaristic action at the institutional level became louder. Interview participants desired that the government would offset the negative, and to a large extent unequal, effects of the pandemic more proactively. It is important that this support for solidarity reaches decision-makers to ensure that the same mistakes are avoided in the next crisis.

Acknowledgements This chapter draws on data collected in the context of the multinational study "Solidarity in Times of a Pandemic: What do people do, and why?" (SolPan). The study is led by the authors of this paper. A full list of participants and partner organisations can be found on our website: https://digigov.univie.ac.at/solidarity-in-times-of-a-pandemic-solpan/solpan/team-solpan/. We would like to thank all members of the SolPan Research Commons for the fruitful collaboration and discussions, and all interview partners for their time to talk to us.

References

Brendebach J, Poiares Pessoa Maduro LM, Tassinari F (2020) The EU response to the COVID-19 pandemic: achieving relevance, mobilising solidarity und preparing for the future. STG Policy Briefs, 2020/01. http://hdl.handle.net/1814/66789. Accessed 14 Dec 2020

Buyx A, Prainsack B (2012) Lifestyle-related diseases und individual responsibility through the prism of solidarity. Clin Ethics 7(2):79–85

Charmaz K (2006) Constructing grounded theory: a practical guide through qualitative analysis. Sage Publications, London

Cheng KK, Lam TH, Leung CC (2020) Wearing face masks in the community during the COVID-19 pandemic: altruism und solidarity. Lancet. https://doi.org/10.1016/S0140-6736(20)30918-1

Ciesek S, Nassehi A, Priesemann V, Pigeot I, Prainsack B, Czypionka T, Schöbel A (2021) Corona-Strategie. Eine Perspektive ohne Auf und Ab. Die Zeit 8/2021. https://www.zeit.de/2021/08/corona-strategie-lockdown-stufenplan-wissenschaftler-lockerungen. Accessed 08 June 2021

De Campos TC (2020) Guiding principles of global health governance in times of pandemics: solidarity, subsidiarity, und stewardship in COVID-19. Am J Bioeth 20(7):212–214. https://doi.org/10.1080/15265161.2020.1779862

De Grandis G, Littmann J (2011) Pandemics: background paper in the context of the Nuffield Council on bioethics forward look. https://www.nuffieldbioethics.org/wp-content/uploads/Pandemics_background_paper.pdf. Accessed 14 Jan 2021

Dean J (1996) Solidarity of strangers: feminism after identity politics. University of California Press, Berkeley

Frenk J, Moon S (2013) Governance challenges in global health. N Engl J Med 368:936–942. https://doi.org/10.1056/NEJMra1109339

Gaztambide-Fernández RA (2020) What is solidarity? During coronavirus und always, it's more than ‚we're all in this together'. The conversation. https://theconversation.com/what-is-solidarity-during-coronavirus-and-always-its-more-than-were-all-in-this-together-135002. Accessed 14 Jan 2021

Gelissen J (2000) Popular support for institutionalised solidarity: a comparison between European welfare states. Int J Soc Welf 9(4):285–300

Habermas J (1991) Erläuterungen zur Diskursethik. Suhrkamp, Frankfurt am Main

Heijden van der K, Olsen S.H., Scott A (2014) From Solidarity to Universality: How global interdependence impacts the post- 2105 development agenda. Independent Research Forum. https://pubs.iied.org/sites/default/files/pdfs/migrate/G04355.pdf. Accessed 08 June 2021

Karlsson D, Holmberg S, Weibull L (2020) Solidarity or self-interest? Public opinion in relation to alcohol policies in Sweden. Nordic Stud Alcohol Drugs 37(2):105–121

Kieslich K, El-Sayed S, Haddad C, Paul KT, Pot M, Prainsack B, Radhuber I, Schlögl L, Spahl W, Weiss E (2020) Vom neuen Miteinander bis zur Erschöpfung: Wie sich der Corona Diskurs wandelte. https://digigov.univie.ac.at/solidarity-in-times-of-a-pandemic-solpan/solpan-blog-deutsch/blogbeitraege/news/vom-neuen-miteinander-bis-zur-erschoepfung-wie-sich-der-corona-diskurs-wandelte/?cHash=b87084c24846033f0f622053c34d92da&tx_news_pi1%5Baction%5D=detail&tx_news_pi1%5Bcontroller%5D=News. Accessed 14 Jan 2021

Kittel B, Kritzinger S, Boomgaarden H, Prainsack B, Eberl JM, Kalleitner F, Lebernegg NS, Partheymüller J, Plescia C, Schiestl DW, Schlogl L (2020) The Austrian Corona Panel Project: monitoring individual und societal dynamics amidst the COVID-19 crisis. Eur Polit Sci. https://doi.org/10.1057/s41304-020-00294-7
Krishnamurthy M (2013) Political solidarity, justice und public health. Public Health Ethics 6(2):129–141. https://doi.org/10.1093/phe/pht017
Lundgren B (2016) Solidarity at the needle point: the intersection of compassion und containment during the A (H1N1) pandemic in Sweden 2009. Sociol Anthropol 4(12):1108–1116. https://doi.org/10.13189/sa.2016.041210
Maringe C, Spicer J, Morris M, Purushotham A, Nolte E, Sullivan R, Rachet B, Aggarwal A (2020) The impact of the COVID-19 pandemic on cancer deaths due to delays in diagnosis in England, UK: a national, population-based, modelling study. Lancet Oncol 21(8):1023–1034. https://doi.org/10.1016/S1470-2045(20)30388-0
Molm L, Collett JL, Schaefer DR (2007) Building solidarity through generalized exchange: a theory of reciprocity. Am J Sociol 113(1):205–242. https://doi.org/10.1086/517900
Pang T (2016) Is the global health community prepared for future pandemics? A need for solidarity, resources und strong governance. EMBO Mol Med 8(6):587–588. https://doi.org/10.15252/emmm.201606337
Prainsack B (2020) Solidarity in times of pandemics. Democr Theory 7(2):124–133
Prainsack B, Buyx A (2011) Solidarity: reflections on an emerging concept in bioethics. Nuffield Council on Bioethics, London
Prainsack B, Buyx A (2017) Solidarity in biomedicine und beyond. Cambridge University Press, Cambridge
Riefler P (2020) Die Pandemie könnte den privaten Konsum langfristig reduzieren. Vienna Center for Electoral Research. https://viecer.univie.ac.at/corona-blog/corona-blog-beitraege/blog83/. Accessed 14 Jan 2021
Scholz S (2008) Political solidarity. University of Pennsylvania Press, University Park
Sternø S (2005) Solidarity in Europe. The history of an idea. Cambridge University Press, Cambridge
The Guardian (2020) Coronavirus a test of global solidarity, says WHO director. The Guardian. https://www.theguardian.com/world/video/2020/feb/11/coronavirus-test-global-solidarity-who-director-video. Accessed 25 May 2020
West-Oram P, Buyx A (2017) Global health solidarity. Public Health Ethics 10(2):212–224

Human Rights and International Obligations in Pandemic Times—More than Health Protection

Walter Bruchhausen and Eva Kuhn

Contents

1 Introduction 39
2 Threatened Human Rights 40
2.1 Social Participation 41
2.2 Economic Cutbacks 42
2.3 Freedom of Opinion and Expression 43
2.4 Mobility 44
3 Human Rights-Based Public Health and Health Systems 45
3.1 (Inter-)National Health Equity 46
3.2 Global Health Governance 47
4 Outlook 49
References 50

1 Introduction

A pandemic not only crosses national or other political borders through its pathogen and countermeasures, but also through the emergence and disappearance of obligations. Some of them are largely codified in law, such as in the International Health Regulations (IHR; WHO 2005), others are highly open to interpretation, especially in the case of conflicts between different obligations. The latter include international human rights covenants.

In October 2020, D'Cruz and Banerjee (2020) referred to the COVID-19 pandemic as an "invisible human rights crisis". Regardless of whether one can speak

W. Bruchhausen (✉) · E. Kuhn
Section Global Health, University Hospital Bonn, Bonn, Germany
e-mail: walter.bruchhausen@ukbonn.de

E. Kuhn
e-mail: Eva.Kuhn@ukbonn.de

© The Author(s), under exclusive license to Springer-Verlag GmbH, DE, part of Springer Nature 2023

A. Reis et al. (eds.), *Pandemics and Ethics*,
https://doi.org/10.1007/978-3-662-66872-6_4

of such a crisis, which the two authors exemplify with the marginalization of older persons, human rights are to be given more attention, especially in the context of an ethical guidance.

Human rights have a legal-moral dual nature. On the one hand, they are guaranteed by international law on a universal and regional level, such as in the Charter of the United Nations and the Universal Declaration of Human Rights (UDHR; UN 1948), the European Convention on Human Rights or the African Charter on Human and Peoples' Rights. The addressees of human *rights* are states and their governments as well as legislatures. They have the legal *obligation* to protect human rights to the best of their ability (Sekalala et al. 2020). [1] On the other hand and due to their universal and egalitarian nature, human rights have increasingly become an "ethical lingua franca" (Tasioulas 2007, p. 75). Accordingly, they are increasingly being used not only in social ethics, but also in the Global Health debate as basic norms. In contrast to moral-philosophical, not least bioethical approaches, whose national dominance or regional origin is obvious—such as the biomedical principle-based ethics in the USA, utilitarianism in Great Britain or Kantian-deontological ethics on the European continent (cf. Hübner 2018; Jonsen 2003; Wolff 2018), human rights are—despite their rather European history and massive criticism from the elites of some world regions (e.g. by Mutua 2009; cf. Nooke et al. 2008)—much more universally accepted due to their long global consensus through politically legitimate representatives.

This article focuses on the moral nature of human rights. It shows by way of example which human rights, from an international perspective, are threatened by state regulations for containment of the COVID-19 pandemic. Building on this, solutions that are inherent in a human rights-based approach to Public Health are outlined with a focus on (inter)national health equity and Global Health governance, and their weaknesses are pointed out. Although the measures examined were all implemented in response to the COVID-19 pandemic, the conclusions drawn from them can be applied to other situations of a pandemic nature.

2 Threatened Human Rights

The UDHR itself explicitly recognises the unavoidable problem that the exercise of certain rights can endanger other rights. Therefore, Article 30 UDHR, as a general saving clause, stipulates: "Nothing in this Declaration may be interpreted as implying for any State, group or person any right to engage in any activity or to perform any act aimed at the destruction of any of the rights and freedoms set forth herein." Even linguistically, a ban on "destruction" does not categorically exclude the temporary suspension or partial restriction of rights. According to the

[1] For legal questions of human rights protection in connection with the Covid-19 pandemic, see, inter alia, Bennoune (2020), Lebret (2020).

'Siracusa Principles', even a restriction of civil and political rights in favour of Public Health is acceptable under certain conditions (UN 1984). But which rights from the international codifications are endangered by state measures in the event of a pandemic under the banner of the right to health? Due to the scope of the contribution, the following is an exemplary consideration.

2.1 Social Participation

Classic restrictions in the event of a pandemic concern freedom of movement and privacy (Art. 12 UDHR) (WHO 2007). However, in many parts of the world, the extent and duration of the measures, in particular of mobility and contact restrictions, are new in the current COVID-19 pandemic. In their intensity, the restrictions may threaten the right to social participation.[2] This is not only he marginalization of older people mentioned above. The participation of digitally illiterate members of society and of people with low socio-economic status who, for example, cannot afford digital communication is also restricted. In part, they are even completely excluded from social and cultural life. Since social isolation has an effect on psychosocial health, such regulations strengthen the human right to health by providing infection control, but also threaten it at the same time (Roy et al. 2020). Art. 4 UN Convention on the Rights of Persons with Disabilities (UN CRPD) (UN 2006) sets out comprehensive general obligations for the States Parties in this regard. Among other things, they have to ensure support services that are "necessary to support living and inclusion in the community, and to prevent isolation or segregation from the community" (Art. 19 lit. b UN CRPD). This also makes it clear where the state's duty to respect and promote participation in accordance with the human right to social participation reaches its limits. The provision of support services is not the same as actual support. To respect and promote social participation at the state level does not mean that someone actually participates in the lives of others and takes part. Accordingly, the preamble (lit. w UN CRPD) explicitly states that "the individual has duties to his fellow human beings and the community to which he belongs and is obliged to work for the promotion and respect of the rights recognized in the International Covenant on Human Rights". In political philosophy, this idea is pursued above all by Sikkink. She argues that "human rights" can only be fully respected, protected and fulfilled if the "human responsibilities" associated with them are also recognized and, above all, assumed (Sikkink 2020). Regardless of whether Sikkink's approach is followed, the right to social participation exemplifies that human rights, as a universal point of reference for a (Public Health) ethical framework, can indeed highlight problematic situations. However, as part of a weighing up and solution, they

[2] See Art. 27 para. 1 UDHR and Art. 15 para. 1 International Covenant on Economic, Social and Cultural Rights.

need to be supplemented by other aspects, in the case of social participation, for example, relationality and solidarity (see, for example, Baylis et al. 2008).

2.2 Economic Cutbacks

So far, restrictions in the sense of the human right to health, which entail considerable, sometimes livelihood-threatening (national) economic losses, have been rarely applied and thus reflected.

For most states, the order to close educational institutions, places of worship, event venues, catering businesses and shops that have not violated hygiene regulations for reasons of infection control is new. Already the reduction of use through prescribed distancing and maximum numbers of users represents a new kind of intervention with foreseeable economic losses. Already in the Ebola epidemic of 2014, such closures were widespread in the affected West African countries; the complete lockdown in Wuhan and other regions made this a global phenomenon in 2020 (Gostin and Friedman 2015; Lau et al. 2020).

Against the background of the new extent of income losses and other financial damage to individuals, the right to property (Art. 17 UDHR) raises new questions about short-term aid and long-term compensation. From the perspective of human rights and the principles of social justice and subsidiarity, there are good reasons to target state aid specifically to those who have been particularly damaged and endangered, rather than—as in Germany—to set general incentives for purchase through value-added tax cuts or additional child benefit for everyone (NN 2020a). Reasons for such a focus of measures can be found, parallel to corresponding discussions of the (global) allocation of resources in the health sector, in philosophy as "priority to the worse off" (Brock 2012). The UN resolution underlying the Sustainable Development Goals (SDGs) also requires "to reach the furthest behind first" (UN 2015, No. 4).

Economic considerations also have to be taken into account regarding health professionals. For it is not only the IHR that give them opportunities and obligations to participate in advice-giving and decision-making at the political level, which must be exercised appropriately. The difference of this situation in decision-making to that in ordinary health care becomes particularly apparent in countries like Germany. There external economic mechanisms such as the Medical Service of the Health Insurance Funds that assesses the required economic efficiency in individual cases of treatment, similar rules for private health insurance or the Joint Federal Committee (*Gemeinsamer Bundesausschuss*) exist. The latter is comprised of physicians and Health Insurance Funds that decide on medical necessity and public funding for treatment options at a superordinate level. Medical and nursing staff, however, should (be able to) act without day-to-day consideration of costs, within a framework defined for the micro level of individual patient care. Ideally they should be able to leave economic considerations to the upstream and downstream institutions. In contrast, in local and (inter-)national policy counselling, that is, at the meso- and macrolevel of Public Health, the respective health professions must take into account the proportionality vis-à-vis other health services, other infectious, non-infectious and further determinants of health, including but not limited to economics and individual incomes, as well as aspects that are not directly related to health (WHO 2016).

2.3 *Freedom of Opinion and Expression*

In addition to informational self-determination concerning communication of private data, which is not discussed in more detail here, the freedom of opinion and expression (Art. 19 UDHR) is currently a controversial and threatened good (Gasser et al. 2020). Irresponsible statements about the alleged non-existence or harmlessness of pathogens and the ineffectiveness of measures against them have a tradition of more than one hundred years (Regin 1995). Even then, they were often closely linked to general anti-scientific and anti-progressive, anti-Semitic and nationalist tendencies (Maehle 1996). In dealing with them, the neutrality obligation of the state must not be interpreted too broadly: Governments and administrations must bear the accusation of not having an equidistant position between science and anti-science in the ideological dispute. Because binding documents such as General Comment No. 14 (CESCR 2000) on the human right to health provide criteria such as "epidemiological evidence", "medically appropriate" and "scientifically approved" which must be taken into account in the selection and application of measures. However, the line between exclusion from scientific, political and journalistic discourse on the one side and restriction of freedom of opinion and expression on the other is extremely narrow.

In particular, the shift of public discourse into social media shows a need that could be filled by human rights as an international framework. In the meantime, the amount of digitally available (mis-)information has become so enormous that the Director-General of WHO speaks of an "infodemic" (Department of Global Communications 2020). If large amounts of false information ('fake news') are disseminated and rumors are spread, this can hinder or even counteract the efforts of states and the international community to protect or restore health. Regardless of the question of the narrow limits of a possible restriction of freedom of opinion and expression, an effective procedure against, for example, health-endangering misinformation would only be possible at national level or, at most, within a community of states such as the EU. Outside the legal sphere, however, international actors have taken various initiatives in the context of the COVID-19 pandemic to also contain the "infodemic" (see the article on infodemics in this volume). Such counter-action is hindered by the fact that many social media channels can now be accessed in large parts of the world and that the companies behind them act transnationally. In addition to various philosophical approaches such as 'Corporate Citizenship' or 'Corporate Digital Responsibility', the 'Guiding Principles on Business and Human Rights' also identify companies as responsibility bearers for human rights. This responsibility includes that companies strive to "prevent or mitigate adverse human rights impacts that are directly linked to their operations, products or services by their business relationships" (UN 2011, No. 13 lit. b).

Conversely, healthcare professionals are affected by questions of freedom of opinion and expression. Since the beginning of the pandemic and in several cases, they have been subject to repression for expressing what is right from the perspective of science and law. This already applies to the first reports in social media at the end of December 2019 from China, especially to the case of the young ophthalmologist Li Wenliang with his experiences of intimidation and his sensational death circumstances, but also for members of the press or bloggers who report about the true extent and the inadequate countermeasures in various authoritarian regimes (Green 2020; UN 2020). It is idle to speculate today how differently the Spanish flu of 1918, which is named that way because there was no censorship of press reports in Spain as a non-belligerent country, would have turned out if everyone in the world had had public access to information. But even in supposedly free societies, reports revealed that staff had been threatened with consequences up to dismissal if they had published shortcomings in the health system (NN 2020b).

These examples once again show a possible positive interaction between human rights: Although not necessarily in every single situation, freedom of opinion and expression usually protects health more than repression.

2.4 Mobility

Finally, for such pathogens that can only be transmitted directly from human to human, international mobility of people plays a central role, as this is the only way pandemics are practically possible. Therefore, their restriction is also in the focus of pandemic control. Restrictions on mobility in terms of emigration and immigration, which concern one's own country, and in the case of asylum seekers, are in tension with Art. 13 & 14 UDHR.

In addition to the information obligations, the IHR of 2005 are therefore mainly concerned with travel. The possible conflict between the application of the IHR and human rights is so obvious that it is mentioned right at the beginning: "The implementation of these Regulations shall be with full respect for the dignity, human rights and fundamental freedoms of persons." (Art. 3 para. 1 IHR)[3] Accordingly, in the current COVID-19 pandemic, one of the first internationally published protests from a human rights perspective was directed at the allegedly abusive application of the IHR against travelers from China (Habibi et al. 2020).

[3] Usually, as in the UDHR of 1948 or in the Universal Declaration on Bioethics and Human Rights of 2005, this inviolable priority of dignity, rights and freedoms is confirmed in the last article.

In the following articles of the IHR, human rights and other protective provisions that arise outside the right to health are only mentioned in relation to the treatment of travelers. Measures that affect the local population are not covered by these regulations. For example, it is required that "travellers who are quarantined, isolated or subject to medical examinations or other procedures for public health purposes" be provided with or have access to, inter alia, "appropriate medical treatment" (Art. 32 IHR).

The documents of the Review Committee on the Application of the IHR, which was commissioned during the pandemic of H1N1 ('swine flu'), do not contain any reference to General Comment No. 14 (WHO 2011), although it is the most important binding interpretation of the human right to the highest attainable standard of health. Moreover, the interpretation is undertaken in a consistent manner with other rights. In addition to the provisions mentioned in the IHR, aspects such as non-discriminatory access to health services, including diagnostics, vaccinations or infection therapies, which are particularly important in pandemic times and regardless of age, gender or social characteristics, are not specifically highlighted. The only rights mentioned explicitly are those well established in biomedical ethics, namely informed consent, but with the restriction of impending dangers, and confidentiality (WHO 2011, Appendix III No. 20). In addition, the detention of travellers as a possible violation of human rights is mentioned (WHO 2011, A No. 92 & 93). Interference with economic and personal livelihoods is not addressed. As in the IHR itself, there is no reference to the rights of local populations. Further development of the IHR in this direction is not envisaged there, but should definitely be carried out. The concern that such issues, which fall or appear to fall within national sovereignty, could jeopardise the success of the IHR by impairing its acceptance, can be assumed.

3 Human Rights-Based Public Health and Health Systems

In this exemplary discussion of threatened human rights it should be noted that these threats and risks are not solely the result of governmental measures in the context of the COVID-19 pandemic. Rather, pre-COVID-19 tendencies and existing trends are condensed as if in a burning glass and thus make latent moral dilemmas apparent. However, the question of what can follow from the identification of threatened human rights and how these can be made fruitful for Public Health and health systems becomes all the more urgent.

3.1 (Inter-)National Health Equity

The interpretation and application of human rights are shaped by changing systematisations, which affect the health sector in a particularly characteristic way. In contrast to historically based one-sided attributions, it must be noted that the right to the highest attainable standard of health includes both negative and positive rights. This means not only that health should not be impaired by measures, for example in environmental, agricultural, social or transport policy, but also that state-secured medical services are provided for the individual in order to maintain or restore health (Wolff 2012).

In order to replace a problematic opposition between positive and negative rights with a continuum of aspects, the framework of "respect-protect-fulfill" (Karp 2020) was introduced in several international human rights documents at the end of the 1990s, also as the basis for the right to health. This creates a clear connection between the various obligations to implement the right to health which is decisive not least for pandemics. Differing from the IHR, it is not only about people not being exposed to an infection risk, but also about active protection measures, access to health, survival-critical prevention and treatment measures (General Comment No. 14, No. 33; CESCR 2000). By signing and ratifying the corresponding covenant, most countries of the world have committed themselves to ensuring the necessary measures on their territory. A comprehensive human rights-based approach to issues of a pandemic therefore also has the question of access to health services in the sense of "fulfillment" in mind. The national and international differences between social groups are still much more pronounced in this respect than with regard to mere protection; health equity as equality of opportunity with regard to socially caused and remediable inequalities in health status is missed by far more here. But since during pandemics these differences can decide between life and death in the event of illness, the much-discussed question of (clinical) triage is not the only one at stake from a global perspective. With a view to the "fulfillment" level of the right to health, at least two conclusions must be drawn for health equity:

1. Hard lockdown measures that are primarily intended to ensure the availability of ventilation options by flattening the curve of infections would be cynical if those groups for whom lockdown means hunger would not have access to the medical equipment if they needed to be ventilated. This applies to the vast majority of the population of sub-Saharan Africa, but also generally non-insured, socio-economically marginalized people, for example in the USA.
2. If the comparatively very high costs for the acquisition of additional ventilators out of public funds would reduce the availability of more cost-effective treatment and protection forms for poor and rural populations, this would be contrary to international standards: "investments should not disproportionately favour expensive curative health services which are often accessible only to a small, privileged fraction of the population, rather than primary and preventive

health care benefiting a far larger part of the population." (General Comment No. 14, No. 19; CESCR 2000)[4]

3.2 Global Health Governance

Most prioritization decisions have to be made at the national or regional level, even though the COVID-19 pandemic makes global economic and epidemiological interconnections more apparent than ever. This problem is addressed, among others, in political philosophy with reference to cosmopolitanism in various forms. The approach is based on the premise that all human beings not only have the same human rights, but also deserve justice as "world citizens", regardless of their nationality. In the sense of a moral and/or political cosmopolitanism, this results in a duty of citizens and—depending on the theory—of state and global actors to cooperate and collaborate in order to establish global justice (Brock 2009; O'Neill 2005). A similar, if more moderate, approach is pursued by the idea of "global solidarity". This has been discussed in the literature in various ways since mid-2020 as a way of addressing problems associated with the COVID-19 pandemic, such as equitable access to healthcare (Ho and Dascalu 2020). In addition, a "reimagining" of the IHR as an "instrument for global solidarity" has been suggested (Taylor et al. 2020). Even if such proposals resonate with the Universal Declaration on Bioethics and Human Rights, which explicitly speaks of "solidarity", not only their concrete material content, but also their operability remain questionable (UNESCO 2005, Art. 13).

Among other things for this reason, state commitments and solidarity actions are currently primarily based on self-commitments and appeals to responsibility or enlightened self-interest. Global prioritization and allocation responsibilities remain very limited. Apart from expertise, even WHO or UN have no significant own resources for the prevention or control of diseases, but would be dependent on appeals to their member states or other donors. Their documents on international support for countries in need and on national or local action in sometimes tough prioritization and allocation decisions therefore only have the character of recommendations, but do not constitute enforceable obligations.

As already mentioned as a shortcoming in the IHR, General Comment No. 14 is the most important explanation of the (inter)national obligations arising from the right to health and which are to be considered in its implementation. Here, with reference to the resolution of the General Assemblies of UN and WHO, joint and individual responsibilities of states are set out in "times of emergency" (General Comment No. 14, No. 40; CESCR 2000), which, according to the definition of the IHR 2005, includes a pandemic—declared by WHO as a "public health

[4] A corresponding formulation outside of the human right to health can be found in *General Comment No. 3,* CESCR, 5th Sess, E/1991/23 (1990), No. 12.

emergency of international concern". In the prioritization, inter alia, of medical assistance, the most vulnerable and marginalized population groups are to be given priority. In the case of cross-border transmission of diseases, the joint responsibility of the international community and the special responsibility and interest of the "economically developed States Parties" in supporting the "poorer developing States" are emphasized.

The obligations formulated for signatory states also include the participation of the population in decision-making processes: "A further important aspect is the improvement and furtherance of participation of the population [...], in particular, participation in political decisions relating to the right to health taken at both the community and national levels." (General Comment No. 14, No. 17; CESCR 2000) The time required for such participation processes largely excludes them 'in the hour of the executive', but the provision refers to the great need for acceptance in the population, which can at least be improved by mutual communication.

The leading role in the implementation of human rights in the field of health should be taken by the WHO. It first formulated the "right to the highest attainable standard of health" in the preamble to its constitution 1946/1948 and continues to see itself—also after the inclusion of this right in various human rights catalogues and covenants—as a "champion of health as a human right" (WHO 2011, No. 13). In particular, when revising the IHR of 1969 in the year 2005, it also increasingly incorporated other human rights considerations (WHO 2011, I A No. 18). However, the expectation and hope for the WHO to play a pioneering role are met with various shortcomings.

In practical terms, it is regrettable that the WHO lacks its own means of investigating human rights violations by measures derived from the IHR. It is even more serious that the human rights discourse is not systematically reflected in relevant documents of the WHO and its committees. For example, the recommendations of the Policy Brief of the WHO Working Group on Ethics and COVID-19 (WHO 2020) lack any reference to human rights, e.g. in terms of a tension between different human rights or the human rights of different people. Instead, here and also in a relevant training manual on ethics in epidemics—despite a commitment to the human rights in the introduction (WHO 2015)—the principle-based biomedical ethics is applied. This is remarkable since, with the exception of the Universal Declaration on Bioethics and Human Rights, which focuses more on research and new technologies than on Public Health and clinical care, principlism hardly appears in high-level documents of the UN system and is particularly often criticized in the international discussion for its regional 'centrism' (Sanders 1994). Human rights other than health appear in WHO texts mostly as a rigid framework that is to be adhered to unreflectively, rather than as claims arising from basic human realities that have to be implemented in a dynamic way.

Instead of a correspondingly consistent line of argument, which only allows restrictions of human rights in the case of a possible violation of other human rights, various WHO publications mentioning human rights tend to work with the not always unproblematic opposition between public goods and individual rights (WHO 2015). Here it should be made even clearer that it is about general rights of individuals to this public good and not about aggregated benefits and their assessment.

A tendency towards a procedural approach rather than a norm-based discourse is also paradigmatic in the work of WHO committees. Thus—similar to committees in sports—a key point at the first meeting of the Committee on the COVID-19 Pandemic on 23 September 2020 was that the WHO official responsible for ethics explained conflicts of interest and confidentiality, and the corresponding documents were signed. This approach is therefore more oriented towards procedural ethics, where it is not so much the interpretation of given norms, but the self-responsible decision-making that is in the foreground.

At least from the self-understanding of human rights work, it should be questioned whether approaches of principle- and goods-weighing as well as procedural ethics are the best way to enforce the human right to health as well as all other human rights. In any case, it is striking how much WHO publications are more oriented towards the models of ethical counselling prevailing in medical care or research than towards UN system scalings.

4 Outlook

The contribution has shown that the individual human rights are complementary to each other, according to the "indivisibility, interdependence and interrelatedness of all human rights and fundamental freedoms" (preamble lit. c UN-CRPD). The right to health, which is in the foreground of pandemics (such as the COVID-19 pandemic), must not be considered in isolation. Rather, the realization of other rights, such as the freedom of opinion and expression or a minimum standard of living, must not be lost sight of—not least in order to protect them. Another limitation is that provisions of human rights do not replace the necessary individual decisions that often have to be made under time pressure and with uncertain knowledge. Deliberations on human rights can, however, ensure that the inclusion of additional claims in decisions on health interventions does not take place randomly, but systematically. They can help to correct national or other socio-cultural biases. Even if human rights address states and primarily oblige them, they can exert their moral power far beyond that. For example, they can serve health professionals active in Public Health, but also the WHO, to broaden the view beyond the human right to health to the entire 'crisis of human rights' and to constantly redefine the relationship between particular human rights.

References

Baylis F, Kenny NP, Sherwin S (2008) A relational account of public health ethics. Public Health Eth 1:196–209. https://doi.org/10.1093/phe/phn025

Bennoune K (2020) „Lest we should sleep“: COVID-19 and human rights. Am J Int Law 114:666–676. https://doi.org/10.1017/ajil.2020.68

Brock DW (2012) Priority to the worse off in health care resource prioritization. In: Rhodes R, Battin M, Silvers A (eds) Medicine and social justice. Essays on the distribution of health care. Oxford University Press, Oxford, pp 155–164

Brock G (2009) Global justice: a cosmopolitan account. Oxford University Press, Oxford

CESCR (2000) General Comment No. 14 The Right to the Highest Attainable Standard of Health (Art. 12) : https://www.refworld.org/pdfid/4538838d0.pdf. Accessed 03 Feb 2023

D'Cruz M, Banerjee D (2020) ‚An invisible human rights crisis‘: the marginalization of older adults during the COVID-19 pandemic – an advocacy review. Psychiatry Res 292:113369. https://doi.org/10.1016/j.psychres.2020.113369

Department of Global Communications (2020) UN tackles ‚infodemic‘ of misinformation and cybercrime in COVID-19 crisis. https://www.un.org/en/un-coronavirus-communications-team/un-tackling-%E2%80%98infodemic%E2%80%99-misinformation-and-cybercrime-covid-19. Accessed 29 Oct 2020

Gasser U, Ienca M, Scheibner J, Sleigh J, Vayena E (2020) Digital tools against COVID-19: taxonomy, ethical challenges, and navigation aid. Lancet Digit Health 2:e425–e434. https://doi.org/10.1016/S2589-7500(20)30137-0

Gostin LO, Friedman EA (2015) A retrospective and prospective analysis of the west African Ebola virus disease epidemic: robust national health systems at the foundation and an empowered WHO at the apex. Lancet 385:1902–1909. https://doi.org/10.1016/S0140-6736(15)60644-4

Green A (2020) Li Wenliang. Lancet 395:682. https://doi.org/10.1016/S0140-6736(20)30382-2

Habibi R, Burci GL, de Campos TC, Chirwa D, Cinà M, Dagron S, Eccleston-Turner M, Forman L, Gostin LO, Meier BM, Negri S, Ooms G, Sekalala S, Taylor A, Yamin AE, Hoffman SJ (2020) Do not violate the international health regulations during the COVID-19 outbreak. Lancet 395:664–666. https://doi.org/10.1016/S0140-6736(20)30373-1

Ho A, Dascalu I (2020) Global disparity and solidarity in a pandemic. Hast Cent Rep 50:65–67. https://doi.org/10.1002/hast.1138

Hübner D (2018) Einführung in die philosophische Ethik. Vandenhoeck & Ruprecht, Göttingen

Jonsen AR (2003) The birth of bioethics. Oxford University Press, New York

Karp DJ (2020) What is the responsibility to respect human rights? Reconsidering the ‚respect, protect, and fulfill‘ framework. Int Theory 12:83–108. https://doi.org/10.1017/S1752971919000198

Lau H, Khosrawipour V, Kocbach P, Mikolajczyk A, Schubert J, Bania J, Khosrawipour T (2020) The positive impact of lockdown in Wuhan on containing the COVID-19 outbreak in China. J Travel Med 27:taaa037. https://doi.org/10.1093/jtm/taaa037

Lebret A (2020) COVID-19 pandemic and derogation to human rights. J Law Biosci 7. https://doi.org/10.1093/jlb/lsaa015

Maehle A-H (1996) Organisierte Tierversuchsgegner. Gründe und Grenzen ihrer gesellschaftlichen Wirkung (1879–1933). In: Dinges M (ed) Medizinkritische Bewegungen im Deutschen Reich (ca. 1870 – ca. 1933). Steiner, Stuttgart, pp 109–127

Mutua M (2009) Human rights. A political and cultural critique. Penn Press, Philadelphia

NN (2020a) Konjunkturpaket beschlossen: Familienbonus und weniger Mehrwertsteuer. 29.06.2020. https://www.aerzteblatt.de/nachrichten/114198/Konjunkturpaket-beschlossen-Familienbonus-und-weniger-Mehrwertsteuer. Accessed 04 Nov 2020

NN (2020b) Amnesty sieht Beschäftigte im Gesundheitswesen in Gefahr. 13.07.2020. https://www.aerzteblatt.de/nachrichten/114637/Amnesty-sieht-Beschaeftigte-im-Gesundheitswesen-in-Gefahr. Accessed 29 Oct 2020

Nooke G, Lohmann G, Wahlers G (eds) (2008) Gelten Menschenrechte universal? Begründungen und Infragestellungen. Herder, Freiburg iB

O'Neill O (2005) Bounds of justice. Cambridge University Press, Cambridge

Regin C (1995) Selbsthilfe und Gesundheitspolitik: Die Naturheilbewegung im Kaiserreich (1889 bis 1914). Steiner, Stuttgart

Roy J, Jain R, Golamari R, Vunnam R, Sahu N (2020) COVID-19 in the geriatric population. Int J Geriatr Psychiatry. https://doi.org/10.1002/gps.5389

Sanders CJ (1994) European-American ethos and principlism: an African-American challenge. In: DuBose ER, Hamel RP, O'Connell LJ (eds) A matter of principles? Ferment in U.S. bioethics. Trinity Press International, Valley Forge, pp 148–163

Sekalala S, Forman L, Habibi R, Meier BM (2020) Health and human rights are inextricably linked in the COVID-19 response. BMJ Glob Health 5. https://doi.org/10.1136/bmjgh-2020-003359

Sikkink K (2020) The hidden face of rights. Toward a politics of responsibilities. Yale University Press, New Haven

Tasioulas J (2007) The moral reality of human rights. In: Pogge T (ed) Freedom from poverty as a human right. Who owes what to the very poor? Oxford University Press, Oxford, pp 75–101

Taylor AL, Habibi R, Burci GL, Dagron S, Eccleston-Turner M, Gostin LO, Meier BM, Phelan A, Villarreal PA, Yamin AE, Chirwa D, Forman L, Ooms G, Sekalala S, Hoffman SJ (2020) Solidarity in the wake of COVID-19: reimagining the international health regulations. Lancet 396:82–83. https://doi.org/10.1016/S0140-6736(20)31417-3

UN Economic and Social Council (1984) The Siracusa Principles on the limitations and derogation provisions in the International Convenant on Civil and Political Rights, E/CN.4/1985/4. https://undocs.org/pdf?symbol=en/E/CN.4/1985/4. Accessed 07 Jan 2021

UN General Assembly (1948) Universal Declaration of Human Rights (UDHR), A/RES/217. https://www.un.org/en/about-us/universal-declaration-of-human-rights. Accessed 03 Feb 2023

UN General Assembly (2006) The United Nations Convention on the Rights of Persons with Disabilities. https://www.un.org/development/desa/disabilities/convention-on-the-rights-of-persons-with-disabilities/article-19-living-independently-and-being-included-in-the-community.html. Accessed 03 Feb 2023

UN General Assembly (2015) Transforming our world: the 2030 agenda for sustainable development, A/RES/70/1. http://www.un.org/ga/search/view_doc.asp?symbol=A/RES/70/1&Lang=E. Accessed 07 Jan 2021

UN Human Rights Council (2020) Disease pandemics and freedom of opinion and expression. Report of the Special Rapporteur on the promotion and protection of the right to freedom of opinion and expression. A/HRC/44/49. https://www.undocs.org/A/HRC/44/49. Accessed 07 Jan 2021

UN Human Rights Office of the High Commissioner (2011) Guiding principles on business and Human Rights. Implementing the United Nations ‚Protect, Respect and Remedy' Framework, HR/PUB/11/04, New York and Geneva. https://www.ohchr.org/Documents/Publications/GuidingPrinciplesBusinessHR_EN.pdf. Accessed 07 Jan 2021

UNESCO (2005) Records of the general conference: resolutions Volume 1, 33/C/Res15 Art. 13. https://www.unesco.de/sites/default/files/2018-09/UN-Resolution_Tag_audivisuelles_Erbe.pdf. Accessed 07 Jan 2021

WHO (1946/1948) Constitution of the World Health Organization. https://www.who.int/governance/eb/who_constitution_en.pdf. Accessed 09 Nov 2020

WHO (2005) International Health Regulations (IHR), 2nd edn. WHO, Geneva. https://www.who.int/publications/i/item/9789241580410. Accessed 07 Jan 2021.

WHO (2007) Ethical considerations in developing a public health response to pandemic influenza. WHO/CDS/EPR/GIP/2007.2. https://apps.who.int/iris/bitstream/handle/10665/70006/WHO_CDS_EPR_GIP_2007.2_eng.pdf. Accessed 28 Oct 2020

WHO (2011) Implementation of the international health regulations (2005). Report of the Review Committee on the Functioning of the International Health Regulations (2005) in relation to Pandemic (H1N1) 2009. WHA/A64/10. https://apps.who.int/gb/ebwha/pdf_files/WHA64/A64_10-en.pdf?ua=1. Accessed 11 Nov 2020

WHO (2015) Ethics in epidemics, emergencies and disasters: research, surveillance and patient care: training manual. http://apps.who.int/iris/bitstream/10665/196326/1/9789241549349_eng.pdf?ua=1. Accessed 11 Nov 2020

WHO (2016) Guidance for managing ethical issues in infectious disease outbreaks. https://apps.who.int/iris/handle/10665/250580. Accessed 09 Nov 2020

WHO (2020) Ethics and COVID-19: resource allocation and priority-setting. WHO/RFH/20.2. https://www.who.int/ethics/publications/ethics-and-covid-19-resource-allocation-and-priority-setting/en/. Accessed 15 Dec 2020

Wolff J (2012) The human right to health. W.W. Norton & Co, New York

Wolff J (2018) An introduction to moral philosophy. W.W. Norton & Company, New York/London

Duties and Rights of Health Professionals During a Pandemic

Reflections on Professional Ethics

Annabel Seebohm and Otmar Kloiber

Contents

1 Introduction 54
2 The Hippocratic Oath and its Interpretations.... 54
  2.1 Altruism in Medicine and Nursing 55
3 Human Rights Since the Enlightenment 55
4 The Understanding of Statehood and Civic Duties 57
  4.1 The State as a Community of Solidarity.... 57
  4.2 Obligation to Render Assistance.... 57
  4.3 Interventions by the States 58
  4.4 Compulsory Obligation or 'civil conscription'?.... 59
  4.5 Professional Obligations.... 60
  4.6 The Development of Medical Deontology 61
  4.7 The Geneva Declaration of 1948 (Geneva Pledge).... 62
  4.8 The Geneva Declaration and the Protection of One's Own Health.... 62
  4.9 The Geneva Declaration and the Duty to Provide Assistance.... 62
  4.10 The International Code of Medical Ethics of 1949 and the Medical Code of Conduct.... 63
  4.11 The International Code of Medical Ethics, the National Code of and the Duty to Provide Assistance 63
5 Rights of Health Professionals as Employees and Self-Employed 64
  5.1 Securing the Workplace and Workflows 64
  5.2 Assessment of the Risk Situation 64
  5.3 Securing Occupational Diseases.... 65

A. Seebohm (✉)
Lawyer, Wachtberg, Germany
e-mail: annabel_seebohm@hotmail.com

O. Kloiber
World Medical Association (WMA), Ferney-Voltaire, France
e-mail: otmar.kloiber@wma.net

© The Author(s), under exclusive license to Springer-Verlag GmbH, DE, part of Springer Nature 2023

A. Reis et al. (eds.), *Pandemics and Ethics*,
https://doi.org/10.1007/978-3-662-66872-6_5

5.4 Rights of Refusal in the Context of Contractual Commitment.................. 65
6 Conclusions 66
References 67

1 Introduction

The chapter on the rights and duties of health professionals during a pandemic focuses on doctors and nurses. While similar ethical and legal requirements exist for the dental and pharmacy professions, requirements for health professions are, at least in Europe, largely limited to licensing requirements for the profession.

The Covid-19 pandemic of 2020 found many parts of the world completely unprepared. This applies both to the provision of material resources such as protective clothing, respirators or other materials, medicines, ventilators as well as to human resources, in particular in anesthesia and intensive medicine. With the pandemic's arrival in Central Europe, the scarcity of resources in efficiency- optimised health systems became quickly visible. By the end of January 2020, a shortage of personal protective equipment was already apparent. Soon afterwards, the shortage of health care personel, particularly in the nursing and medical professions, became apparent.

As with SARS and Ebola, many members of the health professions became ill and died from Covid-19 (see CPME 2021). In view of the dangerous situation to which many health professions are exposed to Covid-19, questions arise as to the duties and rights of professional groups and their ethical foundations, which face the expectations of help from the sick and the population. This chapter will pursue these questions by first distinguishing ethics and professional law in the context of current regulations from historical considerations. Then, the obligations that can be discerned from this will be weighed up against the rights and protection of health professionals.

2 The Hippocratic Oath and its Interpretations

The deployment of health care professionals in dealing with a potentially deadly pandemic has been surprisingly little questioned. The duty to help was repeatedly linked in the press and in particular in specialist publications to the Hippocratic Oath. A relationship that is highly questionable in several respects.

The Hippocratic Oath not only obliged the ancient physician to the Greek gods, but also prohibited him from exercising activities that are today carried out by physicians, such as surgical interventions or abortions. The required avoidance of all dangerous, potentially deadly interventions is also due to the fact that the ancient physician lacked the legitimacy of a university education or a formal examination. His standing relied on his reputation. The Hippocratic Oath probably had much less the function of an ethical obligation in mind than the maintenance of the income source, which should not be compromised by either risky interventions or caring for the dying and therefore incurable patients. But the most fundamental misperception of the Hippocratic Oath lies in the fact that hardly any physician trained and active in Central Europe would ever have sworn it (cf. Deichgräber 1983; Schubert 2005; van der Eijk 2010).

2.1 *Altruism in Medicine and Nursing*

The Hippocratic Oath does not really contribute to the understanding of a medicine based on humanity or empathy. For the European culture, Christianity with its values of caritas and misericordia is of relevance. The medicine that developed in the late Middle Ages, which was strongly influenced by Arabic writings and scholars, also introduced the ethos of dedication and vocation up to self-sacrifice through its "Christianization" at the early European universities. Hospitals were mostly founded by Christians and often carried by religious communities. The physician was only active as a guest in early hospitals. The owners were crusaders, religious sisters or, after the Reformation, also lay organizations with a religious orientation. Relatively late secular organizations such as the Red Cross movement stepped in. All of them have in common the altruistic and Judeo-Christian tradition of caritas (charity, love, care, in English: care) and misericordia (compassion, mercy). The caring for the sick and their nursing became one of the core virtues of Christianity.

3 Human Rights Since the Enlightenment

The freedom of the individual or all individuals is a historically new achievement. The understanding of personal autonomy in legislation and jurisprudence has only slowly become established since the end of the Second World War. Civil and human rights have been increasingly incorporated into national and international legal documents. This also established the right to health in the canon of human rights, although its concretization took decades (cf., inter alia, Frewer and Bielefeldt 2016).

While social legislation in Europe codified the essential health rights, these remained more ambitious than concrete in international law for a long time. With the founding of the World Health Organization (WHO) in 1946, its constitution states:

> "The enjoyment of the highest attainable standard of health is one of the fundamental rights of every human being without distinction of race, religion, political belief or economic or social condition." (World Health Organization 1946)

This very vague statement becomes much more concrete by the Universal Declaration of Human Rights of the then young United Nations on 10 November 1948 in Article 25, paragraph 1:

> "Everyone has the right to a standard of living adequate for the health and well-being of himself and of his family, including food, clothing, housing and medical care and necessary social services, and the right to security in the event of unemployment, sickness, disability, widowhood, old age or other lack of livelihood in circumstances beyond his control." (United Nations 1948)

In Article 12 of the International Covenant on Economic, Social and Cultural Rights of 16 December 1966, the United Nations become even more specific:

> "(1) The States Parties recognize the right of everyone to the enjoyment of the highest attainable standard of physical and mental health.
>
> (2) The steps to be taken by the States Parties to achieve the full realization of this right shall include those necessary for:
>
> (a) The reduction of the stillbirth rate and of infant mortality and for the healthy development of the child;
>
> (b) The improvement of all aspects of environmental and industrial hygiene;
>
> (c) The prevention, treatment and control of epidemic, endemic, occupational and other diseases;
>
> (d) The creation of conditions which would assure to all medical service and medical attention in the event of sickness." (United Nations 1966)

This also sets out the state's obligations to prevent, treat and combat epidemics in international law. Which must be assumed to include pandemics.

In a very detailed commentary No. 14 on Article 12 of the International Covenant, the United Nations Committee on Economic, Social and Cultural Rights strengthened the rights of each individual, regardless of their individual economic situation:

> "States have a special obligation to provide those who do not have sufficient means with the necessary health insurance and health-care facilities, and to prevent any discrimination on internationally prohibited grounds in the provision of health care and health services, especially with respect to the core obligations of the right to health." (United Nations 2000)

This clearly sets out the international obligation of states to create efficient health care systems as the realization of a human right. With the inclusion of the prevention and control of epidemics, this obligation goes far beyond the provision of health insurance systems and regular curative, rehabilitative and palliative care.

Since the outbreak of SARS in 2002/2003, the WHO has not tired of emphasizing the likelihood of a pandemic, also and above all with an unknown pathogen. Medical associations such as the World Medical Association (see World Medical Association 2011, 2017a, b, 2018), in which medical associations and medical organizations from 115 countries and territories work together, and the Standing Committee of European Doctors (see CPME 2014), have repeated the warning with concrete proposals for pandemic preparedness. However, with the exception of the regions of Asia directly affected by SARS, this remained limited to desktop simulations. Preparations were either not made or, for cost reasons, even further reduced (see Kirkpatrick et al. 2020). Whether most states have complied with their self-imposed obligations to protect the health of their population in the event of a pandemic is therefore doubtful.

4 The Understanding of Statehood and Civic Duties

4.1 The State as a Community of Solidarity

Seen from an international perspective the states of the European Union, the European Economic Area, Switzerland and Great Britain have, generally efficient health systems that are all based in one way or another on the idea of solidarity. The degree of direct state organisation or involvement is highly variable. It ranges from purely state-run systems in the Nordic countries to mixed forms with a significant proportion of private insurance (e.g. Great Britain), to social insurance systems (e.g. Germany or Austria) or systems in which private insurers are included in a solidary system (e.g. Switzerland). But all have in common that the states fulfil their task of providing healthcare for all through legally regulated processes.

Continuous efforts to economise healthcare have led to reductions in reserve and stock-piling capacity in the healthcare systems since the 1980s at the latest. With the end of the Eastern Bloc, in addition, reserve stocks of drugs and medical products as well as reserve hospitals that were intended for use in the event of war were also dismantled, at least in Germany. After the financial crisis of 2008, the austerity measures of the European Union hit the healthcare systems of the Southern European member states particularly hard, with the effect that any reserve capacities of these systems were completely lost.

In addition, globalisation of the markets created massive dependence on international supply chains and thus made the functioning of healthcare systems much more vulnerable to external factors, factors which can neither be fully controlled by the states themselves nor by the European Union. The crisis situation during spring 2020 reflexively led to a rejection of international cooperation. Border closures between EU member states and export bans on medical products left the EU institutions paralysed. The model of an international community of solidarity has failed in its first serious test against national egoisms.

4.2 Obligation to Render Assistance

The obligation to render assistance to a fellow human being in need, applies not only on a state level, but of course, also in interpersonal relations. The laws of most states obligate persons to render assistance if the life or limb of another person is endangered.

According to § 323c paragraph 1 of the German Penal Code (StGB), the failure to render assistance is punishable:

> Whoever, in the event of accidents or common danger or distress, does not render assistance, even though this is required and can be expected of him under the circumstances, in particular without considerable personal danger and without violating other important duties, shall be punished with imprisonment of up to one year or with a fine.

The obligation to render assistance may be judged to be different for different individuals. It will be assessed differently for a healthy person than for a frail person; it will be valued differently for medical personnel or firefighters than for laymen who have no specific knowledge or skills to engage in dangerous situations. While the exception from the duty to render assistance "without violating other important duties" leaves room for interpretation, it is clear that no one is expected to put themselves in danger.

4.3 *Interventions by the States*

In constitutional states the freedoms of the individual are limited when the interests of others are affected. This is especially true for the endangering of life and limb or the environment. Examples of this are speed limits on roads or smoking bans as protection for non-smokers.

These restrictions on the freedom of the individual as a measure to protect others can and must also be used in dangerous epidemics in order to limit the spread and thus the endangerment of further persons. This includes quarantine, but also the mandatory notification of diseases, the mask mandates, hygiene regulations or contact restrictions, including the closure of businesses and the restriction of communal activities.

States make use of various instruments, which range from Covid-19-specific laws (e.g. Austria), via infection protection laws (e.g. Germany) to the declaration of a state of emergency (e.g. France). These measures also allow for an expanded recruitment of health personnel, for example by recruiting already retired specialists, simplifying and accelerating the licensing of nurses and doctors and the special deployment of junior professionals and medical students (cf. CPME 2020a, pp. 7 ff.). The latter needs to be emphazised because of the dangerous situation they are put in. Being exposed to a particularly dangerous pathogen requires targeted training as well as supervision and must be justified accordingly. The occasional reports by medical students of the compulsory recruitment for nursing activities on Covid-19 wards as a replacement for nursing staff or their permanent use for taking Covid-19 swabs cannot be justified as being part of the medical education. This is to be distinguished from the voluntary and paid engagement, which in turn is only acceptable after training and with sufficient protection measures.

The deployments on Covid wards (as part of the training) described in isolated reports by students, without sufficient personal protective equipment, cannot be justified, nor can the refusal to vaccinate trainees in exposed areas be accepted (cf. Seebohm and Kloiber 2020).

4.4 *Compulsory Obligation or 'civil conscription'?*

In Germany, neither the amendments introduced by the so-called emergency laws of 1968 into the Basic Law (GG) nor the Infection Protection Act (IfSG) allow for a compulsory obligation towards individuals to provide healthcare. In principle, according to Article 12 Paragraph 2 GG, nobody "(…) may be forced to do a certain job, except within the framework of a traditional general public service obligation that is the same for everyone". Article 12a GG describes the State's recruitment options in the event of defence. They concern the recruitment of conscripts for defence and civilian services, including medical services or civilian nursing services or medical activities.

However, the Infection Protection Act IfSG does not allow for a compulsory obligation to combat infectious diseases. However, it provides for the possibility in § 5a IfSG to entrust certain health professions with medical tasks that they are not normally allowed to perform.

Most disaster protection acts of the German States (Länder) also allow for the obligation of third parties to provide assistance in the event of a declared disaster. These regulations are also likely to allow access to health professions. It is unclear how these disaster protection regulations could be implemented in the event of a pandemic, just as the efficiency of such measures is unclear.

On 25.03.2020, Bavaria included the possibility of compulsory recruitment of medical staff in Article 6 Paragraph 1 of its Infection Protection Act (BayIfSG):

> If this is necessary to cope with the health emergency, Article 9 Paragraph 1 Sentence 1 BayKSG shall apply subject to the proviso that the competent authority may also order the assignment to medical or nursing care facilities for the provision of training-typical services, goods and services. Such an entitlement is not permissible if the person concerned is thereby disproportionately endangered in their health or physical integrity. The competent authority shall take the place of the disaster protection authority. (BayIfSG 2020, S. 174)

Whether this Bavarian regulation is permissible under general law is disputed (Scientific Service of the German Parliament 2020).

On 28.03.2020, the state government of North Rhine-Westphalia presented a draft law "for the consistent and solidary coping with the Covid-19 pandemic in North Rhine-Westphalia and for the adaptation of state law with regard to the effects of a pandemic". Article 1, § 15 paragraph 1 "Conscription of medical and nursing staff" provided for:

> The competent authorities according to § 3 may require persons who are authorized to practise medicine or who have completed training in nursing, rescue services or another health profession to provide services, goods and services if this is urgently required and appropriate in order to cope with the epidemic situation according to § 11. The authorities may also assign and oblige any person referred to in sentence 1 to provide services, goods and services to medical or nursing care facilities under the same conditions. (Landtag Nordrhein-Westfalen 2020)

The initiative from North Rhine-Westphalia was abandoned after massive protests and significant legal concerns (cf. Biermann and Gutensohn 2020).

In several US states (cf. Coleman and Reis 2008) and in Canada (cf. Cara et al. 2010) there are legal possibilities of obligations to medical activity in pandemics, which are often subject to penalty ("civil conscription"). However, their practical relevance has never been proven. Apparently effective is the exit ban, some states, e.g. the Netherlands and Israel, have imposed on clinically active physicians and other health professionals during the pandemic.

4.5 Professional Obligations

Professional self-understanding

While the medical profession has had a continuous academic tradition since the late Middle Ages, nursing has been in the domain of religiously influenced organizations or church orders until well into modern times. Even the formerly used German professional name of the "Krankenschwester" (Sister) still reminds us of the religious sisters who for a long time were the only ones to operate institutionalized nursing care. Their professional self-understanding was determined by Christian morality, the religious obligation to assist the sick, disabled and the dying. With the professionalization and secularization of nursing, the need for an independent professional ethos has developed. However, developing an own professional ethos is kind of contradicted by the overwhelming perception of the Christian-influenced professional image, which is associated with an extremely high reputation.

The increasing professionalization and secularization of nursing since Florence Nightingale has also led to the codification of professional ethics. In Great Britain, for example, 'Nurses' are required to make a promise before entering the profession. In Germany, professionalization of nursing has not progressed as far formally, as is also reflected in the fact that only three federal states have chambers of nurses. The state chamber of nurses of Rhineland-Palatinate requires prospective nursing staff to make a 'solemn promise' when it came into force in early 2020, which is modeled on the procedure at the medical chambers. However, neither the solemn promise of the nursing board nor the ethical code of the International Council of Nurses (International Council of Nurses) contain any obligation to act. Rather, they regulate the therapist-patient relationship. A general self-commitment to provide assistance cannot be derived from this.

The American Nurses Association defines criteria that allow nursing staff to refuse to work in a pandemic situation. These include belonging to a vulnerable group oneself, insufficient protective equipment, inadequate working conditions, unclear legal situations and ethically questionable circumstances (cf. American Nurses Association 2020).

Shortly after the founding of the World Medical Association (1947), a new version of a medical oath and an International Code of Medical Ethics was commissioned. The Declaration of Geneva, first published in 1948, the Pledge, later became and is still part of the (model) Code of Medical Ethics for German physicians. Like the Hippocratic Oath on which it is based, the Declaration of Geneva Pledge does not contain a strict obligation to act. However, a powerful self-commitment can be found right at the beginning:

> "As a member of the medical profession, I solemnly pledge to dedicate my life to the service of humanity. The health and well-being of my patients will be my first consideration". (WMA 2017b)

These first two rules correspond more to the Christian tradition than to the medical ethics of the Greek antiquity.

4.6 *The Development of Medical Deontology*

Medical deontology has always played a leading role in the development of professional ethics in healthcare. Since the middle of the 20th century, the acceptance of individual autonomy in the sense of a patient autonomy has increasingly gained importance. While the Hippocratic Oath—and with it professional morality—has served more to protect oneself and one's profession, modern professional ethics focuses on the protection of patients and the patient-doctor relationship. Elements such as confidentiality, general decency, respect for colleagues and the protection of life and health are largely interwoven.

4.7 *The Geneva Declaration of 1948 (Geneva Pledge)*

The Geneva Declaration added conscientiousness, respect for human rights and the prohibition of (non-medically justified) discrimination to the canon in 1948 (WMA 2017b). However, patient autonomy, care and justice were not included. As a basic document of the medical profession and as a modernized form of the Hippocratic Oath, the Declaration of Geneva remained largely unalterd until 2017. In parallel, however, professional rules had developed and addressed sub-areas such as abortion or respect for the patient's self-determination. With the revision in 2017, respect for patient autonomy was given a dominant position. In addition, a duty to pass on knowledge in the sense of research and teaching, a scientific, evidence-based approach and the protection of practitioner's own health were included.

4.8 The Geneva Declaration and the Protection of One's Own Health

The following self-commitment is worth a closer look in the context of the pandemic: "I will attend to my own health, well-being and abilities in order to provide care of the highest level."

Several objectives are behind this: On the one hand, the doctor should be as a role model for healthy lifestyle. On the other hand, the pledge serves as a delination against a demanded self-sacrificing work performance. This is often came as a malign interpretation of the Hippocratic Oath. Yet the most important objective is the protection of the doctor as a resource. IF the doctors are sick (or even deceased) themselves, they can no longer help their patients.

4.9 The Geneva Declaration and the Duty to Provide Assistance

The Geneva Declaration does not contain a general and explicit obligation to provide assistance that goes beyond general civic duties. The only really overpowering obligation is to human rights: "I will not use my medical knowledge to violate human rights and civil liberties, even under threat."

Neither the Hippocratic Oath nor the Declaration of Geneva provides an obligation to enter into a patient-doctor relationship. However, once a patient-doctor relationship has been entered into, the Declaration of Geneva speaks of "duties" towards the patient and emphasizes: "The health and well-being of my patient will be my first consideration" (WMA 2017b).

4.10 The International Code of Medical Ethics of 1949 and the Medical Code of Conduct

On a global level, the 'International Code of Medical Ethics' plays the role of a worldwide medical code of conduct (WMA 2006a). This code is not a legal text, but rather summarizes the community's basic understanding of medical duties. Over the years, the document has been further developed in a few points since its first adoption in 1949. The actual developments in medicine and the resulting deontological principles are mostly contained in individual guidelines. As an example, the Declaration of Helsinki on research on humans (see Schmidt et al. 2020) or the prohibition of participation of physicians in torture contained in the Declaration of Tokyo (see WMA 2006b) may be mentioned here.

The rapid development in medicine and in our societies requires a constant review of the duties contained in the Code and often an interpretation of the underlying principles, which (at least initially) can only be recorded in guidelines. Only at larger intervals can these developments be incorporated into the international code.

4.11 The International Code of Medical Ethics, the National Code of and the Duty to Provide Assistance

The International Code of Medical Ethics also does not contain a general obligation to provide treatment except in an emergency: "A physician shall give emergency care a humanitarian duty unless he/she is assured that others are willing and able to give such care" (WMA 2006a).

However, this is hardly more than the legal obligation to provide assistance, which is likely to exist in most countries. The (model) Code of the German Medical Association (the obligation to establish a legally binding Code of Medical Ethics lies with the state chambers of physicians in Germany) regulates the medical profession in a much more detailed way than the International Code of Medical Ethics (see Bundesärztekammer 2018). However, large parts of the Code have more of an administrative than an ethical character. In Austria, the Code of Medical Ethics is part of the national Medical Act.

Even though the German (model) Code of Medical Ethics stipulates that "physicians (…) serve the health of the individual and the population", neither this one nor the Austrian Code of Conduct contain a duty to enter into a new patient-physician relationship.

The obligation to provide treatment (apart from the emergency already mentioned above) usually results from contractual obligations—whether through participation in a contract with the social insurance or as an employee in a hospital. But even in such relationships, the obligation to work is usually fulfilled collectively, so that an individual patient cannot necessarily force treatment by a specific doctor.

5 Rights of Health Professionals as Employees and Self-Employed

5.1 Securing the Workplace and Workflows

In the European Union, workers have a right to high occupational safety and health (see EU 1989). This includes, in addition to the prevention of accidents at work, the avoidance of exposure to dangerous substances and pathogens. In addition, most countries have compensation systems that cover the treatment and rehabilitation of occupational accidents and diseases, as well as compensation in the event of incapacity for work or death. This applies to all employees, including those in the health sector.

5.2 Assessment of the Risk Situation

In healthcare, there is constant contact with potentially infectious patients or materials. In accordance with the risk, the protective and preventive measures are very high. Nevertheless, the safety measures differ qualitatively and quantitatively from normal operation to operations during a pandemic or epidemic. Epidemics are characterized by a high degree of contagiousness and therefore require specific containment measures that go beyond normal hygiene procedures. These include the increased use of protective clothing and respirators, intensified disinfection measures, and, in the case of airborne transmission, also specially ventilated rooms.

When an epidemic occurs, the consumption of protective materials can increase exponentially from one day to the next. What is normally equivalent to one year's consumption of protective clothing, masks and disinfectant can suddenly become a week's consumption. The "just-in-time" supply chains trimmed for cost efficiency in our healthcare systems do not take this increased demand into account, especially if producers and logistics providers are themselves affected by the epidemic. The Covid-19 pandemic has demonstrated this impressively.

However, the safety instructions for dealing with (potentially) infectious patients do not change just because the supply situation deteriorates or even protective materials are no longer available. Unlike in industrial operations, where a dangerous work situation must be shut down before work can safely continue, an emergency situation usually arises in healthcare. Suspending operations, i.e. treatment of seriously ill patients, would have serious consequences for many of them (and for the population in terms of public health) and often death.

5.3 Securing Occupational Diseases

It is therefore not permissible to continue working without protective equipment. For example, in Germany, until recently, a deliberate failure to use protective measures and procedures resulted in the loss of occupational accident protection and the coverage of an occupational disease. Although the emergency situation should be obvious in the case of the pandemic, it remains to be seen whether all cases will be sufficiently compensated. It should not be forgotten that the occupational protection in Germany, for example through the statutory occupational accident insurance, provides an extremely high-quality coverage that cannot be found in most countries of this world. In addition, in most countries self-employed physicians are depending on their own private coverage in the event of incapacity for work or death.

5.4 Rights of Refusal in the Context of Contractual Commitment

The refusal of work is then permitted if the physicians as employees or, in some countries, also as contract physicians, are in a labor dispute. The professional code of conduct also provides for the conscientious exercise of their activity, which in turn can lead to the refusal (conscientious objection) of activities (e.g. abortions or physician-assisted suicide) for moral reasons. Both the strike and the refusal on grounds of conscience are subject to strict limits by deontology, as neither the endangerment of the lives of patients nor the refusal of medically necessary treatment (e.g. in the case of severe pain) are tolerable.

A refusal of work is even required from the physician if it is a matter of participation in torture, or of degrading or inhuman treatment or punishment. Examples of this are participation or preparation for executions, amputation of limbs or blinding as punishment, force-feeding of hunger strikers or the forced administration of emetics to drug couriers who have been apprehended (cf. WMA 2006b). In all of these procedures, the physician is prohibited from participating or assisting.

In most European health care systems, the rejection of a new patient is usually only permitted due to overload or the lack of treatment options. Even then, emergencies must still be seen, treated, admitted to hospital or transferred immediately—depending on where the initial treatment takes place.

While emergency assistance is not only ethically but also legally required, no one, not even a contractually bound physician or a physician employed in a hospital, can be forced to put themselves in danger. Such a danger is also present if the patients with potentially life-threatening pathogens are to be treated without the availability of adequate protective measures. Apart from self-protection, treatment under this extremely high risk is not meaningful because only a healthy physician can help other patients. Just as one would not send firefighters into a collapsing house, one would not want to send health personnel into an unpredictable risk.

The considerations of what is reasonable must therefore be made in view of the danger posed by the situation, the available protective measures and procedures, and the treatment options available. However, the high number of deceased physicians, nurses and other health professionals in pandemics such as SARS, Ebola or Covid-19 shows that the situation is often underestimated.

6 Conclusions

Most health care systems in Europe have mechanisms in place to ensure that all individuals have access to medical care (and often also to general health care). In addition, there is a duty of continuity for an existing patient-physician relationship from medical professional ethics. A patient-physician relationship that has been entered into once with mutual consent creates obligations that arise, for example, from the Declaration of Geneva. A refusal to treat must not lead to a health impairment of the patient. On the other hand, medical ethics does not provide for a treatment obligation that goes beyond the general duty of care of every citizen, taking into account the medical knowledge and skills.

From an ethical point of view, there is no special obligation to provide services for physicians or other health professionals, although such an obligation may exist as a general moral obligation. This means, conversely, that such an obligation would have to be understood and accepted by the general public. It cannot be demanded unilaterally by the health professions. This means that a compulsory obligation of individual professions is ethically not acceptable and questionable under the principle of equality before the law. A compulsory obligation that is in addition associated with considerable risks to life and limb must be called into question even more. Increased risks to the population would therefore first have to be averted by the use of all available means before the restriction of civil rights or even the compulsory obligation of individual professions is considered.

In most cases, however, these questions are probably only academic, as physicians, nurses and other health professionals have themselves chosen a profession that is potentially hazardous in principle. The handling of dangerous or potentially deadly infectious diseases has always been part of the work and will continue to be in the future. The epidemics and pandemics of recent decades have shown that health professionals are willing to work overtime to an extreme extent, without any material compensation that would even come close to being adequate. This is also indicated by the fact that actual refusals to work in the health sector have been rather rare so far.

During an epidemic or pandemic, students and trainees in health professions must continue to be trained theoretically and practically. Particular care must be taken to protect them as inexperienced persons. Unaccompanied exposure to danger is strictly to be rejected from an ethical point of view. Compulsory recruitment of students and trainees in health professions such as the use of medical students as cheap labor in intensive care units or the performance of mass tests, for example under the threat of expulsion, are neither ethically nor legally justifiable.

In 2007, in a detailed discussion of the ethical considerations for developing a strategy against pandemic influenza, the World Health Organization (WHO) not only pointed to the moral, legal, contractual and professional obligations of health personnel, but also to reciprocal obligations of the state and employers (see World Health Organization 2007). These include, for example, the stockpiling of drugs, protective equipment and other medical products that ensure safe and meaningful work in a pandemic. At least in Europe, such pandemic preparedness on the part of states, the European Union and employers has unfortunately been insufficient. A fundamental reorientation of health systems away from a "just-in-time" approach towards a "just-in-case" approach for any disaster situation is desirable (see CPME 2020b; WMA 2011, 2017a, 2018). The Covid-19 pandemic shows that the precautionary principle is not an empty formula.

References

American Nurses Association (2020) Nurses ethics and the response to the Covid-19 pandemic. https://www.nursingworld.org/~4981cc/globalassets/covid19/nurses-ethics-and-the-response-to-the-covid-19-pandemic_pdf-1.pdf. Accessed 25 Jan 2021

BayIfSG – Bayerisches Infektionsschutzgesetz vom 25. März 2020 (2020) Bayerisches Gesetz- und Verordnungsblatt Nr. 7/2020. https://www.verkuendung-bayern.de/files/gvbl/2020/07/gvbl-2020-07.pdf#page=2. Accessed 7 Feb 2021

Biermann K, Gutensohn D (2020) Corona-Krise. Ärzte und Pfleger warnen vor Zwangsarbeit. https://www.zeit.de/arbeit/2020-04/corona-krise-aerzte-pflegekraefte-arbeit-verpflichtung-armin-laschet? Accessed 25 Jan 2021

Bundesärztekammer (2018) (Muster-)Berufsordnung für die in Deutschland tätigen Ärztinnen und Ärzte – MBO-Ä 1997. https://www.bundesaerztekammer.de/recht/berufsrecht/muster-berufsordnung-aerzte/muster-berufsordnung/. Accessed 15 Feb 2021

Cara E, Davies CE, Zlotnik Shaul R (2010) Physicians' legal duty of care and legal right to refuse to work during a pandemic. Can Med Assoc J 182(2):167–170

Coleman CH, Reis A (2008) Potential penalties for health care professionals who refuse to work during a pandemic. JAMA 299(12):1471–1473

CPME (Ständiger Ausschuss der Europäischen Ärzte) (2014) CPME statement on Ebola virus disease and pandemic preparedness. https://www.cpme.eu/cpme-statement-on-ebola-virus-disease-and-pandemic-preparedness/. Accessed 25 Jan 2021

CPME (Ständiger Ausschuss der Europäischen Ärzte) (2020a) CPME report on COVID-19 in Europe. https://www.cpme.eu/european-doctors-publish-cpme-report-on-covid-19-in-europe/. Accessed 25 Jan 2021

CPME (Ständiger Ausschuss der Europäischen Ärzte) (2020b) Pandemic preparedness European doctors' recommendations to the EU. https://www.cpme.eu/index.php?downloadunprotected=/uploads/adopted/2020/11/CPME_AD_Brd_21112020_111.FINAL_.CPME_.COVID19.pandemic.preparedness.lessons.learned.pdf. Accessed 7 Feb 2021

CPME (Ständiger Ausschuss der Europäischen Ärzte) (2021) COVID-19 in Europe: Status report from the National Medical Associations. https://www.cpme.eu/covid-19-section/national-updates/. Accessed 7 Feb 2021

Deichgräber K (1983) Der hippokratische Eid, 4. edn. Hippokrates, Stuttgart

Eijk van der PJ (2010) Medicine and philosophy in classical antiquity. Doctors and philosophers on nature, soul, health and disease. University Press, Cambridge

Europäische Union (1989) Rahmenrichtlinie über Sicherheit und Gesundheitsschutz bei der Arbeit (Richtlinie 89/391/EWG). https://osha.europa.eu/de/safety-and-health-legislation/european-directives. Accessed 25 Jan 2021

Frewer A, Bielefeldt H (eds) (2016) Das Menschenrecht auf Gesundheit. Normative Grundlagen und aktuelle Diskurse. Transcript, Bielefeld

Kirkpatrick DD, Apuzzo M, Gebrekidan S (2020) Europe said it was pandemic-ready. Pride was its downfall. The New York Times. https://nyti.ms/2WDjiiN. Accessed 25 Jan 2021

Landtag Nordrhein-Westfalen (2020) Gesetzentwurf der Landesregierung. Gesetz zur konsequenten und solidarischen Bewältigung der COVID-19-Pandemie in Nordrhein-Westfalen und zur Anpassung des Landesrechts im Hinblick auf die Auswirkungen einer Pandemie (Drs. 17/8920). https://www.landtag.nrw.de/portal/WWW/dokumentenarchiv/Dokument/MMD17-8986.pdf. Accessed 16 Feb 2021

Schmidt U, Frewer A, Sprumont D (eds) (2020) Ethical research. The declaration of Helsinki, and the past, present and future of human experimentation. Oxford University Press, Oxford/New York

Schubert C (2005) Der hippokratische Eid. Medizin und Ethik von der Antike bis heute. Wissenschaftliche Buchgesellschaft, Darmstadt

Seebohm A, Kloiber O (2020) persönliche Berichte von Studentenvertretern

United Nations (1948) Universal declaration of human rights A/811. Deutsche Übersetzung A/RES/217 A (III). https://www.un.org/Depts/german/menschenrechte/aemr.pdf. Accessed 25 Jan 2021

United Nations (1966) International covenant on social economic and cultural rights. Deutsche Übersetzung. https://www.humanrights.ch/de/ipf/grundlagen/rechtsquellen-instrumente/uno/pakt-i/. Accessed 25 Jan 2021

United Nations (2000) CESCR general comment no. 14: The right to the highest attainable standard of health (article 12 of the International covenant on economic, social and cultural rights) E/C.12/2000/4. https://www.refworld.org/pdfid/4538838d0.pdf. Accessed 16 Feb 2021

Wissenschaftliche Dienste des Bundetages (2020) Gesetzgebungskompetenz für den Infektionsschutz. Ausarbeitung WD 3 3000 081/20. https://www.bundestag.de/resource/blob/691276/d7b39e76d5cd2649a5ffe3e6596df907/WD-3-081-20-pdf-data.pdf. Accessed 7 Feb 2021

World Health Organization (1946) Constitution of the World Health Organization. https://apps.who.int/gb/bd/PDF/bd47/EN/constitution-en.pdf?ua=1. Accessed 25 Jan 2021

World Health Organization (2007) WHO ethical considerations in developing a public health response to pandemic influenza. https://www.who.int/csr/resources/publications/WHO_CDS_EPR_GIP_2007_2c.pdf. Accessed 25 Jan 2021

World Medical Association (2006a) WMA international code of medical ethics. https://www.wma.net/policies-post/wma-international-code-of-medical-ethics/. Accessed 25 Jan 2021

World Medical Association, (2006b) WMA declaration of Tokyo – guidelines for physicians concerning torture and other cruel, inhuman or degrading treatment or punishment in relation to detention and imprisonment. https://www.wma.net/policies-post/wma-declaration-of-tokyo-guidelines-for-physicians-concerning-torture-and-other-cruel-inhuman-or-degrading-treatment-or-punishment-in-relation-to-detention-and-imprisonment/. Accessed 25 Jan 2021

World Medical Association (2011) WMA declaration of Montevideo on disaster preparedness and medical response. https://www.wma.net/policies-post/wma-declaration-of-montevideo-on-disaster-preparedness-and-medical-response/. Accessed 25 Jan 2021

World Medical Association (2017a) WMA statement on epidemics and pandemics. https://www.wma.net/policies-post/wma-statement-on-epidemics-and-pandemics/. Accessed 25 Jan 2021

World Medical Association (2017b) Deklaration von Genf. https://www.bundesaerztekammer.de/fileadmin/user_upload/downloads/pdf-Ordner/International/Deklaration_von_Genf_DE_2017.pdf. Accessed 25 Jan 2021

World Medical Association (2018) WMA statement on avian and pandemic influenza. https://www.wma.net/policies-post/wma-statement-on-avian-and-pandemic-influenza/. Accessed 25 Jan 2021

Restrictions on Fundamental Rights in the Name of Public Health. Fundamental Rights as an Regulative Elements of Proportionate Pandemic Management

Stephan Rixen

Contents

1 Introduction: Fundamental Rights-Related Problems of Measures to Cope with the Pandemic 69
2 Restrictions on Fundamental Rights as a means of Collective Health Protection (Public Health) 71
2.1 Scope of Protection, Intervention, Justification 71
2.2 Principle of Proportinality 72
2.3 Democracy-Theoretically Motivated, Limited Relativization of the Binding Nature of Fundamental Rights 73
2.4 Precision and Proceduralization of the Principle of Proportionality 74
3 Conclusion and Outlook 79
References 80

1 Introduction: Fundamental Rights-Related Problems of Measures to Cope with the Pandemic

The way in which the consequences of the Corona crisis have been dealt with has given rise to strategies and instruments for coping which, in the pre-pandemic period, that is to say before March 2020, would have been considered completely abnormal. Although there had been initial approaches to thinking about pandemic coping from a public health law perspective in the last ten years (see Rixen 2011; Klafki 2017; Trute 2018), they had hardly been taken into account in the legal debate. Pandemics seemed to be relevant only for other regions of the planet, not for (Western) Europe or Germany—an misconception, as we now know. Terms such as *containment*, *shutdown* or *lockdown* were, at best, only used by specialists

S. Rixen (✉)
Faculty of Law, University of Cologne, Cologne, Germany
e-mail: stephan.rixen@uni-koeln.de

© The Author(s), under exclusive license to Springer-Verlag GmbH, DE, part of Springer Nature 2023

A. Reis et al. (eds.), *Pandemics and Ethics*,
https://doi.org/10.1007/978-3-662-66872-6_6

in disease control who were just as unknown to the general public as virologists. Who would have thought that compulsory mask wearing, curfews, bans on visits, restrictions on domestic travel (in the 30th year of German reunification), the ban on demonstrations, religious services, cultural and leisure events, emergency provision in the education and training sector, the shutdown of commercial businesses and their compensatory support through gigantic state debt financing would be possible? Who would have thought that an entire society, right down to the micro level of the closest social relationships, would be exposed to the grip of ubiquitous pandemic regulation for such a long time? Who would not have considered such a degree of biosafety governance to be an irreparable dystopia? We are witnessing a live experiment in social regulation of an epidemiological nature in which virally threatened freedom is restricted in order to enable its unlimited use *à la longue* (see Nullmeier 2020 for this context).

The freedom-restricting measures taken in the course of the Corona crisis, as many believe, have led society and government into a state of emergency (cf. Rixen 2020a, c). What is meant by this is not always clear. Descriptive terms that aim to describe the loss of the previously known normality stand next to normatively tinted interpretations that often refer very associatively to Carl Schmitt as the alleged great theorist of the state of emergency. Schmitt is a kind of *walking dead* of constitutional theory. He always has his say when the usual ideas of normality come into question. If you read on (Schmitt 1928/1996, pp. 18 f.), you will quickly realize that his concept of the state of emergency refers to a privilege-based, unlimited power. This does not fit the coping with the Corona crisis, because it is structured by numerous protective forms of power limitation. Nevertheless, those who whisper about the state of emergency as a normative exceptional situation assume that the constitutional state is not able to cope with the exceptional situation with its means (cf. Rixen 2020c; in general on the state of emergency Barczak 2020; Kaiser 2020).

As tempting as the fixation on the figure of the state of emergency beyond the law is, it leads astray rapidly. Modern societies are constitutively crisis-prone (cf. Kersten and Rixen 2020, p. 13). Crises, meaning situations that go beyond what is customary according to all experience, are part of the normality of modern societies. The mere existence of an area of law such as disaster protection law shows that events that massively interfere with the usual course of coexistence belong to the normality assumptions on which the entire legal system is based (cf. Rixen 2011, pp. 69 f.). But this means that the law, including and especially constitutional law, must reflect the crisis not as a para-legal exceptionality, but as a legally regulable normality. This means above all to let oneself be guided by the logic of weighing, which sets the fulfilment of state tasks, to which the anti-pandemic health protection belongs, in relation to proportionate restrictions of fundamental rights. This weighing logic is embedded in a state organizational law institutional setting that has to prove itself as a flanker of fundamental rights protection precisely in the crisis.

2 Restrictions on Fundamental Rights as a means of Collective Health Protection (Public Health)

Dealing with the Covid-19 pandemic ('Corona crisis') in 2020 and 2021 has led to extensive restrictions on basic rights. The interference with basic rights serves the protection against infection, that is, a collective good (public health), because the aim is to prevent the Coronavirus SARS-CoV-2 from spreading and, as a result, people from becoming infected with Covid-19 or dying. Based on the Infection Protection Act (IfSG), which has been amended several times during the course of the pandemic, numerous measures have been taken in Germany, which, from a legal point of view, are based on ordinances (§ 32 IfSG), general and individual orders, typical instruments of administrative law. They shorten the fundamental freedom (interference with basic rights), without the basic rights being violated by such interference. In legal language, the German legal community only speaks of a violation of basic rights if the interference with basic rights cannot be justified.

The principle of proportionality is probably the most important justification criterion for dealing with the pandemic. It is supposed to dose the use of state force as differentially as possible, that is, to contribute to distinguishing legitimate state force, which serves the fulfilment of tasks, from illegitimate state violence. Behind this is the idea of the rule of law, that is, a political rule which is hedged in by the protective forms of law, but not as an end in itself, but as a regulative element which structures and directs the fulfilment of state tasks, but does not want to make it impossible. The task of infection control is therefore to be realised, but not in a disproportionate, but in a proportionate way. If, in the words of the well-known *Max Weber*, rule in everyday life is primarily administration (cf. Weber 2013, p. 459), it becomes clear that the struggle for the proportionate limitation of the measures for dealing with the pandemic must primarily limit the activity of the administration, but at the same time also the legislator, who essentially defines the scope of action of the administration. However, the principle of proportionality must be observed in general and is not specific to the pandemic, even though the various measures for combating epidemics make the problem of how state force can be appropriately dosed particularly clear.

2.1 Scope of Protection, Intervention, Justification

In German legal theory, the handling of liberty rights as a subcategory of fundamental rights is structured by three distinctions (see, for example, Kingreen and Poscher 2020, pp. 84–102): scope of protection, intervention and justification. The scope of protection refers to the area of human freedom that is protected by the fundamental right (freedom of opinion, freedom of assembly, freedom of religion, etc.). With 'interference', any measure attributable to the state is referred to that makes it impossible or more difficult for a behaviour protected by the scope of protection. This can be laws, but also individual measures of the administration that prohibit or forbid a certain behaviour. Justification means that the interference must meet certain requirements that identify it as a legitimate form of state power. This includes, for example, that a measure of the administration can ultimately be traced back to a parliamentary law; but the most important thing is the principle of proportionality. This structure according to scope of protection, intervention and justification has developed since the beginning of the 1980s in constitutional law theory, has then been received and further developed by the German Federal Constitutional Court and can now be generally accepted with terminological and content-related deviations.

2.2 Principle of Proportinality

The principle of proportionality consists of several criteria (see Kaiser 2020, p. 234; Kingreen and Poscher 2020, pp. 99–102): First, the measure chosen by the state must be eligible at all, which is unproblematic, for example, with a parliamentary act, a legal regulation issued by the administration or an administrative act issued by the administration in individual cases. In addition, the state must pursue a constitutionally legitimate goal with the measure chosen by it. This is the case if the regulatory goal either takes up a constitutionally regulated task or if the regulatory goal at least does not contradict any constitutional requirements. The measure in question must also be suitable, necessary and appropriate (= reasonable or proportionate in the narrower sense). "Suitable" means that the chosen regulatory instrument can promote the achievement of the regulatory goal. The word "can" is important because it gives the state a certain margin to determine how a regulatory goal pursued by it can be achieved. In particular, the norm-setting state therefore has a scope for assessment and design that allows it to choose the regulatory instrument for which it can at least reasonably be said that it can achieve the regulatory goal. "Necessary" means that there is no equally effective, but milder, means by which the regulatory goal can be achieved. Also in this respect, the state, in particular the parliamentary legislator or an administrative norm-setter who issues a legal regulation, has a scope for assessment and design that allows it to act on the basis of at least plausible assumptions and -connections.

The further relevant criterion of proportionality—"appropriate" or "reasonable"—is intended to prevent the state measure in question from excessively restricting the fundamental right. This requires a balancing of goods which takes into account the weight of the pursued regulatory goal on the one hand and the importance of the fundamental right in question in the concrete application context on the other hand and tries to bring both dimensions into a "practical concordance" (the well-known term of the constitutional law scholar and former judge of the Federal Constitutional Court Konrad Hesse), which gives both the greatest possible effective protection. This criterion, the application of which—unlike suitability and necessity—does not allow for any legislative assessment and design discretion, acts as a "final safety net" to filter out regulatory excesses that have not been complained at the previous stages.

2.3 Democracy-Theoretically Motivated, Limited Relativization of the Binding Nature of Fundamental Rights

The following should be noted with regard to non-specific human rights discourse: With the exception of human dignity (Article 1, Paragraph 1 of the German Constitution, the Basic Law [Grundgesetz = GG]), basic rights are not absolute values; rather, their effective protective intensity can be minimized, which of course must be justified. This is based on the idea that basic rights should primarily moderate and discipline state activity, but not stop it. The principle of proportionality contributes to this, with the criteria of suitability and necessity reflecting the embedding of basic rights in state activity in particular. By recognizing assessment and design options, in particular those of the legislator, the legislator is given a presumption of trust that he will find solutions that are compatible with basic rights. At the same time, it is recognized that regulation—the specific balancing of opposing interests, which leads to the selection of certain control instruments—is not a mathematically unambiguous task, but requires certain tolerances in the sense of design (play) options. From a constitutional law perspective, there can be several equally "right" solutions that may appear to be politically unwise, but are nevertheless constitutionally defensible. The fact that things can be seen differently for good or less good reasons is a hallmark of democracy. This relativizes the basic rights binding, in particular of the legislature (Article 1 Paragraph 3 of the German Constitution), because this binding acts, so to speak, with a democratic theoretical reservation. Democracy is therefore not generally suspected of being potentially incompatible with basic rights, but is on the contrary a way of giving effective force to basic rights without there always being only one right way to do so. This democratic theoretical relativization—better: relationing—of the basic rights binding, which is part of the principle of proportionality, is hardly noticed in non-legal discourse on basic rights. The element of appropriateness or acceptability, which complements the criteria of suitability and necessity, limits this democratic theoretical presumption of trust and explicitly asks from the perspective of the holders of basic rights what loss of freedom is still tolerable. Where the limit of what is still or no longer tolerable lies cannot be said abstractly. It depends on the regulatory problem in question, the regulatory goal, the regulatory instruments discussed and the basic rights affected.

In contrast to some non-legal human rights discourse, where the inviolability and inalienability of human rights are emphasized with great emphasis, it is necessary to stress: Of course, fundamental rights as legal constructs are based on the tradition of "inviolable and inalienable human rights" (Art. 1 para. 2 GG). But they want to make human rights operable as part of a constitution of political rule, which establishes a certain form of democratic rule as a parliamentary government system. Fundamental rights, legally understood, are not a value compass that floats purely appellative over things. Rather, they want to steer the course of democratic institutions very finely, which means that their effectiveness must come to fruition in the formal language of a democratic constitutional state. Fundamental rights must therefore shape the regulatory instruments of the democratic constitutional state in concrete detail, so that their effectiveness can come into operation in an operable manner. This shows a specific legal approach to fundamental rights, a specific legal style of operationalization, which reformulates vaguely formulated fundamental rights texts in everyday-usable action directives for the state in a principled-open, indeed confessionally-vague manner. This legal style, which is based on operable distinctions, also explains, for example, why the proportionality principle is structured by practically well-manageable criteria. That fundamental rights are to be respected thus becomes more tangible and simplifies the argumentation with the fundamental rights.

2.4 Precision and Proceduralization of the Principle of Proportionality

2.4.1 Overview

In the course of the pandemic, the Infection Protection Act (IfSG) was amended by the "Third Act to Protect the Population in the Event of an Epidemic of National Importance" of 18.11.2020 (Federal Law Gazette 2020) in order to pandemic-specific concrete the principle of proportionality, which is to protect the effective fundamental rights. The new, seven-part, partly long § 28a IfSG, which supplements the general provision on protective measures of § 28 IfSG, is to specify in detail which measures of pandemic management are proportionate; this is flanked by some procedural requirements.

For the duration of the declaration of an epidemic situation of national scope by the German Bundestag, the federal parliament, comprehensive protective measures are permissible in the areas specifically mentioned of private and public life (§ 28a para. 1 nos. 1 to 17 IfSG), which can be combined (§ 28a para. 6 sentence 1 IfSG). In sum, this allows intervention in every field of social coexistence through restrictions, bans and obligations, but differentiation is possible. This means that a complete, all-encompassing *lockdown* is conceivable, just as measures that only apply to certain fields and only set certain measures in motion (also § 28a para. 7 IfSG). Measures in certain areas (in particular religious gatherings, restrictions on leaving the house that affect the private home; restrictions on visits to nursing homes) are subject to even higher requirements (§ 28a para. 2 sentence 1 IfSG). This is also illustrated by the provision that states that in nursing homes and similar stationary facilities of the health and social welfare system, protective measures "must not lead to the complete isolation of individual persons or groups"; "a minimum of social contacts must be maintained" (§ 28a para. 2 sentence 2 IfSG, see also German Ethics Council 2020b).

According to § 28a para. 5 IfSG: "Ordinances which are issued according to § 32 in connection with § 28 para. 1 and § 28a para. 1 shall be accompanied by a general statement of reasons and shall be limited in time. The period of validity shall generally be four weeks; it may be extended." On the one hand, this is intended to highlight the time dimension of proportionality, on the other hand, the expiration date makes it possible to re-evaluate the situation, possibly with the result that the previous measures are modified. The justification provides an account of the 'general', i.e. overarching, reasons that were decisive for the selection of measures.

2.4.2 Public Health: Target Hierarchies, Target Conflicts, Weighing Parameters

"Decisions on measures to prevent the spread of the coronavirus disease 2019 (COVID-19) [...] are to be primarily based on the protection of life and health and the functioning of the health care system" (§ 28a para. 3 sentence 1 IfSG). 'In particular' means primarily, while the functioning of the health care system, which is to be protected from being overloaded by Covid-19 patients requiring ventilation for weeks, concretizes the protection of life and health only with regard to medical infrastructure including personnel. This is supplemented by general requirements for the intensity of the measures, which depend on the incidence of new infections (§ 28a para. 3 sentences 2 to 12 IfSG). This goal, which has the entire health care system in mind, can be reformulated as a public health goal, even though the term public health did not play a role in the parliamentary debates on the law.

The law further states: "In decisions on measures to prevent the spread of the coronavirus disease 2019 (COVID-19), social, societal and economic effects on individuals and the general public are to be taken into account and considered to the extent that this is compatible with the goal of effective prevention of the spread of the coronavirus disease 2019 (COVID-19)" (§ 28a para. 6 sentence 2 IfSG). The main goal is to be achieved with as little loss of effectiveness as possible by scaling the extent of the restrictions on fundamental rights taking into account the foreseeable social, societal and economic effects on individuals and the general public, which are to be "taken into account", i.e. considered. The law speaks of "social" and "societal" effects, without it being clear how to delimit the terms. While it is relatively clear what is meant by economic effects, this is less clear in the case of societal and social effects. Societal effects could, for example, be the consequences for family life if the closure of nurseries and schools were to bring parents who may be working from home into a permanent state of overload and possibly even lead to a re-conventionalization or re-traditionalization of roles in the field of care work. Social effects are likely to refer more to aspects that have to do with protection, support and neediness in a broader sense and thus have more to do with individual effects. These include loneliness, lack of social participation and the risk of domestic violence, which can be exacerbated by the restricted low-threshold availability of assistance services, for example in a *lockdown*.

The dominance of the public health goal (protecting life and health, including the functioning of the health care system) remains, the fine-tuning of the effective measures of infection control should take into account the effects. This can also lead to the fact that, because of these effects, measures are less intensive in some places: "Individual social, societal or economic areas that are of particular importance to the general public may be exempt from the protective measures to the extent that their inclusion is not absolutely necessary to prevent the spread of the coronavirus disease 2019 (COVID-19)" (§ 28a para. 6 sentence 3 IfSG).

We see: The law frames the decision-making process of the administration. The administration fills this frame. For this purpose, the law provides primary and supplementary goals. Fundamental rights act as important weighing parameters, as they shape the areas of life in question. The administration must and may make use of a sort of regulatory toolbox, which can lead to very different measures depending on the infection situation. The effective rule of law therefore depends on the administrative design of a possibly very confusing situation, which can only be framed and structured by law. Once again it becomes clear: Fundamental rights, understood legally, should create space for the freedom of the human being in very complex decision-making processes, without making it impossible to fulfill the state task of "Public Health through Infection Control", which in the long term contributes to the fact that freedom is ideally possible again to the extent that it is familiar from the prepandemic period.

2.4.3 No Freedom Restrictions for Vaccinated People?

Another topic of proportionality are the so-called immunity or vaccination certificates, which are supposed to enable the regain of freedom after the Covid-19 vaccination has been carried out (German Ethics Council 2020a). The talk of 'special rights' or 'privileges' is wrong from a fundamental rights perspective, because it is about the restoration of the normative normal state, which is a state of as little restricted freedom as possible. As with all fundamental rights violations, the question arises as to whether and, above all, how long they can be justified if the persons involved no longer endanger others. Where there is no longer any danger, the continuation of restrictions on freedom would be disproportionate. However, the empirical situation is not clear in every respect. The efficacy of the vaccination administered in two doses in terms of protection against contracting Covid-19 is very high according to the current scientific findings, but how long does the protection last? And does the vaccination also protect against infecting others? This is indeed likely, but not yet certain. Ultimately, it always depends on whether, from the perspective of effective infection protection, which must also take into account practical problems of compliance with protection or hygiene concepts, the sector-specific withdrawal of restrictions on freedom can be justified. In a highly dynamic situation in which there are new scientific findings on a daily basis, the legislator must have a greater scope for assessment and design than usual, combined, however, with a strict duty to observe and also to improve. According to the current state of natural science, vaccination is not a 'fundamental rights joker' that makes all restrictions on freedom unconstitutional from one day to the next.

In any case, the whole debate only makes sense if each person has a real chance of being vaccinated within a reasonable period of time. The state must ensure the quickest possible availability of the vaccine. In this respect, it is subject to a duty of care (cf. Art. 2 para. 2 sentence 1 GG, protection of life and limb, in connection with the principle of the welfare state, Art. 20 para. 1 GG, and the principle of equality, Art. 3 para. 1 GG). This is designed to organise the quickest possible access to vaccination, whereby the prioritised access of particularly vulnerable persons can justify the later vaccination of other persons. The (denied) re-establishment of freedom also leads to equality problems (Art. 3 para. 1 GG) in so far as every restoration of freedom leads to the question of whether it must also apply to areas of life which resemble the areas of life for which freedom has been restored. The Federal Constitutional Court also takes the principle of proportionality into account in the assessment of possible infringements of the principle of equality and, in the end, asks whether there are any reasons for withholding a benefit which necessarily distinguish one constellation from the other. The more similar the areas of life which are treated differently, the higher the requirements for a sustainable unequal treatment. Here too, the assessment and design discretion of the legislator must be taken into account (usually, in the case of infection protection, it is a question of ordinances which are issued by a state government or a state ministry).

2.4.4 Constitutional Protection of Divergent Constructions of Reality?

The problem of how the state and society should react to the fact that in the Covid-19 pandemic not a few people have said goodbye to a shared world which is connected by an undivided construction of reality leads to the limits of the world access framed by constitutional rights. This is not just about traditional differences of opinion, but about very fundamental controversies about what is actually the case. This is particularly evident in the absurd theses about vaccination as "a technique controlled by secret powers to subdue free people", which epistemically secures the will to political and moral self-determination. This competition of constructions of reality is due to a vulgarised, because completely misunderstood, social constructivism, which confuses the perspectivity of human knowledge with the absolutely given subjectivity of the person who takes a perspective. Driven by a kind of right to epistemic self-determination, the everyday-theoretical motto of which is "everyone has to know that for themselves", the question of what is relevant knowledge and why, central to sociological knowledge, is transformed into a problem of appreciation, because the rejection of theses which are incompatible with common ideas of rationality and reality is quickly seen as devaluation of the subject which represents them. The rejection of not being taken seriously with one's own version of world access is intensified because the whole person is at stake in the debate.

Anyone who denies the existence of virological conditions or the efficacy of vaccination in principle questions the nature-friendly construction of reality that underlies the Basic Law. The catalogue of legislation of the Basic Law lists numerous areas of life that cannot be reasonably regulated without natural science and technical assumptions: Art. 73 para. 1 no. 6 GG (air traffic), Art. 73 para. 1 no. 6a (railway traffic), Art. 73 para. 1 no. 12 GG (firearms and explosives law), Art. 73 para. 1 no. 14 GG (generation and use of nuclear energy for peaceful purposes, disposal of radioactive substances), Art. 74 para. 1 no. 19 GG (measures against dangerous or contagious diseases), Art. 74 para. 1 no. 20 GG (protection of plants against diseases and pests), Art. 74 para. 1 no. 24 GG (air pollution, noise abatement), Art. 74 para. 1 no. 26 GG (medically assisted generation of human life, investigation and artificial alteration of hereditary information, regulations on the transplantation of organs, tissues and cells). Anyone who regulates air traffic should not doubt gravity. A law that orders 'gravity is forbidden' would be about as sensible as a law that forbids the sun to give light. These natural science-explainable givennesses of a legal system are rarely discussed because they appear so self-evident. But the conspiratorial distorted debates about viruses or vaccines make it necessary to make the implicit knowledge about the natural science-based construction of reality of the applicable legal system explicit.

There is no doubt that criticism of the natural scientific quality of certain virological studies or even of vaccination studies is constitutionally protected, whether as specific scientific criticism that must be measured against the criteria of academic freedom (Art. 5 para. 3 sentence 1 GG), or as an expression of opinion (Art. 5 para. 1 sentence 1 GG) taking into account that having an opinion does not require having an idea. For example, no one can be forbidden to believe that the earth is flat. However, there is no fundamental right to the effect that the state and society declare their own, nature-skeptical view of the world to be the only relevant view. Anyone who disregards the official order to wear a mask at a demonstration questions the construction of reality based on natural science premises that the legislator was allowed to follow with a view to the Basic Law's understanding of reality when he enacted norms of the right of assembly and the right of infection protection. The requirement to wear a mask at a demonstration proves to be a reasonable non-recognition of divergent constructions of reality that endanger others when they become socially consequential behaviour from the mere idea.

2.4.5 Completion of the Proportionality Thinking by Judicial Control

The effect of the principle of proportionality is completed by the role of the courts. Of course, the rule of law character of a community does not exhaust itself in the fact that measures of the administration can also be reviewed by independent courts in the Corona crisis. But it is still an important indication that rule of law prevails, which *rule of law* is effective. Hundreds of court decisions that have been issued in Germany since March 2020—mainly by administrative courts and higher administrative courts, the Federal Constitutional Court, but also by constitutional courts of the federal states—show that the legally framed measures of the administration are put to the test. As the Constitutional Court of the Saarland aptly put it, it is a "accompanying justification control" (Constitutional Court 2020, p. 11). This means that the measures issued by the administration in the execution of the parliamentary law-making powers, which in particular must take into account the principle of proportionality, are closely examined by the courts. This can lead to the fact that—again in the light of the principle of proportionality—prohibitions are interpreted restrictively in the light of fundamental rights or exceptions to prohibitions are applied in a fundamental rights-friendly manner or a violation of statutory provisions or the principle of proportionality—and thus a violation of fundamental rights—is established (cf. Rixen 2020b, p. 1101). At the same time, the courts respect that the norm-setting and norm-applying administration needs a margin of assessment in the proportionality test—specifically: on the level of suitability and necessity—in order to be able to react adequately to the often empirically diffuse risk situation, which is characterized by particularly great uncertainty in the pandemic (Trute 2020). This is reflected in a regularly not too strictly applied judicial control density, which does not call the effectiveness of infection control into question (Rixen 2020a, b).

3 Conclusion and Outlook

In coping with the Covid-19 pandemic, there have been massive restrictions on fundamental rights. Whether and to what extent these are permissible, and in particular for how long, is primarily a question of proportionality. The principle of proportionality is constitutionally guaranteed and implemented in the Infection Protection Act, specifically by § § 28, 28a. Fundamental rights may be restricted for the purposes of public health or public health. Here, in particular, the legislators at federal and especially at state level, where most ordinances are issued, have a discretion and design space. Fundamental rights, legally understood, are supposed to moderate and discipline the fulfilment of state tasks, without contravening the legitimate state task—infection protection. For this reason, fundamental rights can be restricted, but these restrictions (interferences) must be justified, which is to be measured by the principle of proportionality. Fundamental rights, legally understood, are—with the exception of the guarantee of human dignity—less absolute, static variables than scalable regulative elements that grant more or less protection.

The term public health does not play a prominent role in the political debate on the reform of the Infection Protection Act. It is missing in the justifications of the laws that have amended the Infection Protection Act during the Covid-19 pandemic. In this respect, the term public health rather serves as a placeholder for the goal of protecting the lives and health of people in the pandemic. There is thus no meaningful connection to the debates on public health that are taking place in medicine, health economics, health care research or medical ethics. The Corona crisis should be seen as an opportunity to take notice of the international debates on public health that are taking place outside the legal sciences and to make them fruitful for the further development of the proportionality test in particular. In particular, the unclear relationship in the Infection Protection Act between the health interests of individuals and the interests of the general public in health-promoting conditions and health-promoting, for example infection-avoiding, behaviour could be clarified in this way. With the help of the impulses from the public health debate, it would be possible to determine more precisely what is proportionate in pandemic regulation and what is not.

References

Barczak T (2020) Der nervöse Staat – Ausnahmezustand und Resilienz des Rechts in der Sicherheitsgesellschaft. Mohr Siebeck, Tübingen

Bundesgesetzblatt (2020) Teil I, pp 2397–2413

Deutscher Ethikrat (2020a) Immunitätsbescheinigungen in der Covid-19-Pandemie – Stellungnahme. www.ethikrat.org. Accessed 6 Jan 2021

Deutscher Ethikrat (2020b) Mindestmaß an sozialen Kontakten in der Langzeitpflege während der Covid-19-Pandemie – Ad-hoc-Empfehlung. www.ethikrat.org. Accessed 6 Jan 2021

Kaiser A-B (2020) Ausnahmeverfassungsrecht. Mohr Siebeck, Tübingen

Kersten J, Rixen S (2020) Der Verfassungsstaat in der Corona-Krise. C.H. Beck, München

Kingreen T, Poscher R (2020) Grundrechte – Staatsrecht II, 20th edn. C.F. Müller, Heidelberg

Klafki A (2017) Risiko und Recht. Risiken und Katastrophen im Spannungsfeld von Effektivität, demokratischer Legitimation und rechtsstaatlichen Grundsätzen am Beispiel von Pandemien. Mohr Siebeck, Tübingen

Nullmeier F (2020) Covid-19-Pandemie und soziale Freiheit. Online-Vorabpublikation aus der Zeitschrift für politische Theorie (ZPTh). www.theorieblog.de/wp-content/uploads/2020/11/Nullmeier_Corona_und_soziale_Freiheit_ZfPT_2020.pdf. Accessed 6 Jan 2021

Rixen S (2011) Befugnisse und Grenzen des staatlichen Infektionsschutzrechts. In: Kloepfer M (ed) Pandemien als Herausforderung für die Rechtsordnung. Nomos Verlagsgesellschaft, Baden-Baden, pp 67–84

Rixen S (2020a) Grenzenloser Infektionsschutz in der Corona-Krise? Konturen eines grundrechtssensiblen Pandemie-Krisenrechts. R Polit 56(2):109–117

Rixen S (2020b) Gesundheitsschutz in der Coronavirus-Krise – Die (Neu-)Regelungen des Infektionsschutzgesetzes. Neu Jurist Wochenschr 73(16):1097–1103

Rixen S (2020c) Die epidemische Lage von nationaler Tragweite – einfachrechtliche Regelungen und verfassungsrechtliche Problematik. In: Kluckert S (Hrsg) Das neue Infektionsschutzrecht. Nomos Verlagsgesellschaft, Baden-Baden, pp 133–146

Schmitt C (1996) Politische Theologie, 7th edn Duncker & Humblot, Berlin

Trute H-H (2018) Pandemien als potentiell globale Katastrophe. GSZ – Z Gesamte Sicherheitsrecht 1(4):125–133

Trute H-H (2020) Ungewissheit in der Pandemie als Herausforderung. GSZ – Z Gesamte Sicherheitsrecht 3(3):93–101

Verfassungsgerichtshof des Saarlandes (2020) Beschluss vom 28.4.2020, Lv 7/20. www.verfassungsgerichtshof-saarland.de. Accessed 6 Jan 2021

Weber M (2013) Wirtschaft und Gesellschaft. Max Weber Gesamtausgabe Bd. I/23. Mohr Siebeck, Tübingen

Ethical Challenges of Resource Allocation in Pandemics

Foundations and Concretization for the Prioritization of Therapies and Vaccines

Georg Marckmann

Contents

1 Introduction 83
2 General Requirements for a Fair Allocation of Scarce Resources 85
3 Prioritization of (Intensive) Medical Treatment During the Covid-19 Pandemic 87
4 Prioritization of SARS-CoV-2 Vaccines 90
5 Outlook 93
References 93

1 Introduction

A pandemic is characterized by the worldwide spread of an infectious disease, which is associated with severe courses of disease. Pandemics usually pose a significant threat to the health of the population; often the global spread of the infectious disease is associated with many severe cases of disease and high mortality rates. Again and again, pandemics have shaken the lives of people. While in the Middle Ages, bacterial infections such as the plague repeatedly claimed many lives, in modern times the greatest danger comes from virus pandemics. The so-called Spanish flu claimed the lives of many millions of people in the years 1918 to 1920, triggered by a particularly virulent influenza virus. In 2009, there was a threat of a pandemic by the H1N1 variant of the influenza virus, colloquially known as "swine flu". Most recently, the enormous challenges associated with a pandemic have been shown impressively by the worldwide spread of the SARS-CoV-2 virus (severe acute respiratory syndrome coronavirus 2), which was declared a "Public Health Emergency of International Concern" by the World

G. Marckmann (✉)
Ludwig Maximilian University of Munich, Munich, Germany
e-mail: marckmann@lmu.de

© The Author(s), under exclusive license to Springer-Verlag GmbH, DE, part of Springer Nature 2023

A. Reis et al. (eds.), *Pandemics and Ethics*,
https://doi.org/10.1007/978-3-662-66872-6_7

Health Organization (WHO) on 30 January 2020 and a pandemic on 11 March 2020.

Pandemics pose significant challenges to the international community and national health systems. The WHO has developed various recommendations for pandemic management, the Pandemic Influenza Preparedness (PIP) Framework recommends a global strategy for preparing for and responding to an influenza pandemic.[1] In addition, many countries have drawn up pandemic plans to better prepare for the sudden spread of an infectious disease. When a pandemic occurs with a new pathogen for which there is neither sufficient population immunity nor an effective vaccine, health systems can quickly reach the limits of their capacity, as the SARS-CoV-2 pandemic illustrates. If many patients become seriously ill in a short period of time, the material and personnel resources are no longer sufficient to treat all patients adequately (see Emanuel et al. 2020). The situation in northern Italy during the first wave of the SARS-CoV-2 pandemic has impressively shown how dramatically the shortage of resources can escalate—with the most difficult allocation decisions for the health personnel involved, which are often referred to as a triage, a term primarily used in disaster and military medicine (see Truog et al. 2020). But even on this side of the allocation of limited intensive care capacities, questions of resource allocation arise (see Garrett et al. 2020): For example, in order to keep intensive care beds free for seriously ill Covid-19 patients, hospitals have reduced the number of operations, so that the question arises as to which patients should have priority in access to the limited number of operating room capacities (see Brindle et al. 2020). Questions of resource allocation arise not only in the field of medical treatment, but also in preventive measures to combat infections. In particular, at the beginning of the SARS-CoV2 pandemic, there was still a significant shortage of personal protective equipment; later on, the prioritization of the still insufficiently available vaccines were at the centre of the debate (see Persad et al. 2020).

In view of the diverse questions of resource allocation in a pandemic, this article addresses the question of how the inevitable allocation decisions can be made in a fair manner. To this end, procedural and material requirements for a fair allocation of scarce resources are first presented in general. The two following sections then discuss questions of resource allocation or prioritization in the context of a pandemic in the allocation of intensive care beds—as an example of allocation decisions for therapeutic measures—and in the distribution of vaccines—as an example of allocation decisions for preventive measures. Both sections will also focus on how the questions of resource allocation for intensive care capacities and vaccines have been discussed or are being discussed in Germany.

[1] See https://www.who.int/influenza/pip/en/ (Accessed 31 Jan 2021).

2 General Requirements for a Fair Allocation of Scarce Resources

Health has a special moral significance: No matter what individual life plans people pursue, they always need at least sufficient health to be able to realize their goals. Health is thus a particularly fundamental, transcendental good. Norman Daniels has convincingly demonstrated how and why health is an essential prerequisite for equal opportunity in society (see Daniels 2008). For reasons of justice, not only must equal access to health care be guaranteed, but also the socio-economic conditions for a healthy life are of central importance (see Lampert et al. 2016). The distribution of preventive and therapeutic measures thus raises questions of justice when resources are limited.

In general, two requirements must be met for a fair distribution of scarce goods: On the one hand, the distribution decisions must be based on a fair decision-making process, on the other hand, they must be ethically well founded. Table 1 provides an overview of the formal ethical requirements for fair distribution decisions (see the "accountability of reasonableness" by Daniels and Sabin 2002). With population-based measures, these formal requirements of treatment decisions are particularly important for the legitimacy and acceptance of the measures, since they involve a very large number of healthy people.

However, allocation decisions should not only be made in a fair process, but also justified by convincing ethical arguments. In questions of distributive justice, it is usually about priorities, i.e. the question of which persons should have priority in access to scarce goods. In the international and national discussions on priority

Table 1 Formal criteria for fair allocation decisions (according to Marckmann 2008)

Criterion	Explanation
Transparency	Allocation decisions and the underlying criteria should be communicated openly
Consistency	In comparable situations, similar allocation rules and criteria should be applied
Legitimacy	Distribution decisions should be made by democratically legitimate institutions and procedures
Justification	Distribution decisions should be based on a comprehensible, relevant justification
Evidence-based decision-making	Distribution decisions should take into account the available evidence on the benefits and risks as well as the costs
Minimization of conflicts of interest	Distribution decisions should be regulated in a way that minimizes conflicts of interest
Participation opportunities	Those affected by a distribution decision should have opportunities to participate in the decision-making process
Regulation	Voluntary or state regulation should ensure compliance with these formal requirements

setting in health care, three criteria have emerged that are ethically best justified (Central Commission for the Observation of Ethical Principles in Medicine and its Border Areas (Central Ethics Commission) at the German Medical Association 2007; Marckmann 2009b):

Health need: According to this criterion, those patients who need medical help the most should have priority in health care, measured by the (temporal) urgency of treatment and the severity of the illness. With public health measures such as health promotion and prevention, the need would be greatest among those population groups who have a poor health status, a high risk of illness or a high risk of a serious or fatal course of illness (high vulnerability).

Expected (individual) health benefit: With this criterion, those people who would benefit most from a measure have priority. Those with a small expected benefit are treated secondarily.

Cost-benefit ratio (efficiency): This criterion tries to optimize the efficiency of resource use: those measures that can achieve the greatest health benefit overall in relation to the resources used should have priority, for example, measured by the gain in quality of life and life expectancy. In particular, with population-based measures, it may be a legitimate goal to use the limited resources available in such a way that the greatest possible health benefit results for the target population. However, from an ethical point of view, the distribution of the health benefit must also be taken into account, in particular with regard to the priority health need. The aim would be to achieve a "benefit maximization with fairness constraints" (Marckmann 2009a).

In addition, there are allocation criteria or procedures that are ethically more controversial but have also been discussed repeatedly in the context of the Covid-19 pandemic (see Emanuel et al. 2020). On the one hand, procedures based on formal equality are discussed, such as 'first come first served' or random allocation (lottery). On the other hand, distribution could take into account the instrumental value of people, either retrospectively with regard to relevant services for others in the past or prospectively with a view to future importance for other people. With this justification, for example, health personnel could be given priority in access to life-saving treatment or preventive measures. Last but not least, the age of those affected is also discussed as a prioritization criterion: on the one hand in terms of remaining life years, on the other hand as a life cycle argument, according to which younger people should be given priority because they have had fewer chances to go through the various stages of life (see Williams 1997). There are good reasons to combine various ethical criteria in distribution decisions (see, for a current example, the allocation of intensive care ventilators in the Covid-19 pandemic by White and Lo 2020), with a key challenge to determine the relative weight of the different ethical criteria in the resulting distribution scheme.

As explained at the beginning, the dynamics of the Covid-19 pandemic has led to a shortage of resources in various areas, thus raising questions of ethically appropriate allocation. Within the scope of this contribution, it is not possible to discuss all allocation problems in the context of the Covid-19 pandemic in detail.

Therefore, the following two allocation scenarios will be discussed exemplarily in the order of their occurrence during the Covid-19 pandemic: the allocation of intensive care beds and the prioritization of SARS-CoV-2 vaccines.

3 Prioritization of (Intensive) Medical Treatment During the Covid-19 Pandemic

The first wave of the Covid-19 pandemic in spring 2020 was accompanied by a high number of patients with a acute respiratory distress syndrome (ARDS), so that the available intensive care capacities in many regions became scarce or even no longer sufficient for the care of all Covid-19 patients requiring ventilation. For the involved actors, this posed the difficult question of who of the seriously ill patients should receive one of the scarce intensive care beds and who should only be given palliative care. While there are guidelines for such triage situations in mass casualty medicine, there are no comparable guidelines for intensive care. However, as early as 2012, a risk analysis "Pandemie durch Virus Modi-SARS" by the Robert Koch Institute had already pointed to a possible pandemic-related overload of the health care system:

> So far, there are no guidelines on how to deal with a mass outbreak of infected people in a pandemic. This problem requires complex medical, but also ethical considerations and should not be considered only in a special crisis situation. (German Bundestag 2013, p. 65)

For this reason, medical associations in many countries took up these questions and developed recommendations for dealing with a possible shortage of intensive care resources. From a perspective of procedural justice, however, the question arises as to whether medical associations are legitimate in making provisions for situations in which decisions have to be made about the allocation of insufficiently available life-saving treatments. While medical ethics provides clear guidelines for the treatment of patients in individual cases, there is no comparable orientation for the allocation of scarce resources. After all, this is not a medical, but rather a societal, i.e. state task. The legislature has made corresponding provisions, for example, in the Transplantation Act for the allocation of organs. Accordingly, the assessment of the German Ethics Council is somewhat surprising that the state has only very limited opportunities to "make abstract binding provisions for the allocation of scarce resources", as it may not assess human life (German Ethics Council 2020). Rather, it is quite understandable that people with disabilities have filed a constitutional complaint following the recommendations of the medical associations (see AbilityWatch 2020): The legislature, so the criticism, should have immediately enacted legal regulations for a possible triage situation, which would ensure that people with disabilities are neither directly nor indirectly disadvantaged. In its final ruling, The Federal Constitutional Court agreed that legislative action is constitutionally required to protect people with disabilities (1 BvR 1541/20, 16 December 2021).

In view of the lack of corresponding state regulations, it was preferable from the perspective of procedural justice that there were at least recommendations from medical associations: These can help that unavoidable prioritization decisions are made according to uniform, transparent, clearly defined and medically and ethically well-founded criteria in a process that ensures equal treatment of patients and does not leave the responsible health care personnel alone with the decision.

In decision-making, it must first be ensured that all available options have been used to mobilise further intensive care capacity or transfer patients to another hospital. It must also be ensured that intensive care in the individual case has a realistic prospect of success and is still wanted by the patient. In particular, older people, who have the highest risk of serious disease and death from Covid-19, often do not want everything medically possible to be done to save their lives. However, this requires that patients have previously specified, in the context of advance care planning, which life-sustaining therapies they still wanted in a severe health crisis (cf. Curtis et al. 2020; Feddersen et al. 2020).

If intensive treatment is promising and desired by the patient, decisions must be made about which material criteria should guide the then inevitable prioritizations if there are insufficient intensive care capacities. To do this, one could go behind a Rawlsian "veil of ignorance" (Rawls 1975) and ask which distribution scheme people would choose if they knew nothing about themselves and their position within society. There are many good reasons to believe that people in this 'original position' would choose to distribute the limited intensive care capacities in such a way that most lives could be saved. This would also maximize the a priori survival probability of the individual. This can be achieved by prioritizing according to the criterion of treatment success—here understood as the probability of surviving the current intensive course—as proposed by eight German medical societies (see Marckmann et al. 2020a,b):[2] This gives priority to those patients who are very ill but can be successfully treated over those patients who would also die with intensive medical treatment with a high probability. This prioritization cannot eliminate the tragedy of the decisions, but it may reduce it somewhat, as life-sustaining therapy would only be foregone in those patients who would have a very low chance of survival with intensive care. However, the proposed prioritization process is not a consistent implementation of the maxim of saving the lives of most people, as the (expected) resource intensity, i.e. in particular the expected length of stay of intensive care patients, is not taken into account (see Lübbe 2020). On the one hand, there are currently no reliable models for predicting the expected length of stay of intensive care patients, on the other hand, the question arises as to whether there are also good ethical reasons not to take resource consumption at the level of the individual patient into account as an independent factor: A patient should not have worse chances of being saved because the treatment requires more resources.

The underlying criterion for the clinical prospects of success therefore relates to the probability of surviving the current intensive treatment. The assessment is made in each individual case taking into account 1) the severity of the acute illness, 2) prognostically relevant comorbidities and 3) the general state of health, insofar as it has effects on the current survival. These three factors could

[2] The corresponding S1 guideline is available online from the AWMF https://www.awmf.org/leitlinien/detail/ll/040-013.html (Accessed 3 Feb 2021).

be summarised in a points score, which would allow prioritization across a larger number of patients (cf. Riessen et al. 2020). The general exclusion of certain patient groups regardless of individual assessment, as proposed by the Swiss recommendations (cf. Schweizerische Akademie der Medizinischen Wissenschaften und Schweizerische Gesellschaft für Intensivmedizin 2020), appears ethically problematic, as clinical prospects do not result from the presence of a certain illness, but rather from the interplay of various prognostically relevant factors.

The prioritisation proposed by the German medical professional societies according to the criterion of clinical prospects of success and the underlying ethical justification of saving as many lives as possible in the acute crisis with the limited resources available has been criticised primarily from a constitutional law perspective (cf. Fateh-Moghadam and Gutmann 2020) and by representatives of people with disabilities (cf. AbilityWatch 2020). The criticism is directed primarily at the aggregation in the ethical justification and the possible discrimination against older people and people with disabilities when applying the criterion of clinical prospects of success. However, neither age nor the presence of a disability are per se associated with worse outcomes. Only if, for example, frailty is high in old age or if a disability significantly (!) reduces the probability of survival, would those affected—not apriori, but depending on the clinical ourse in the individual case—possibly have a worse chance of getting an intensive care bed in the event of a prioritisation decision. But this also applies to people with serious comorbidities who lead to a significant (!) deterioration in prognosis (very high probability of death despite intensive care) in the event of a serious illness with Covid-19.

If one wants to avoid this effect, one has to think about alternative triage criteria (see Emanuel et al. 2020 for an overview). A procedure oriented towards formal equality of opportunity such as first-come-first-served or a lottery would be a reasonable approach. However, it is doubtful whether the latter really guarantees equality of opportunity, as people have different chances of being quickly admitted to hospital with a severe Covid-19 illness due to different geographical, socio-economic or physical conditions. From an ethical point of view, it is more problematic that both allocation procedures have a significant moral price: There will be more avoidable deaths, fewer lives can be saved because even patients with a very poor prognosis will be given an intensive care bed and will occupy it for a long time. In the same time, several patients with a better prognosis could have been saved. In addition, the unavoidable tragedy of triage decisions would be increased because even patients with a good chance of survival would have to die if they came too late or were not allocated an intensive care bed by lottery. It is doubtful whether this would be a regulation that most people would agree to behind a Rawlsian veil of ignorance, i.e. without knowing their individual situation, as this would worsen the individual's a priori survival probability during the pandemic.

Other possible allocation criteria, such as the instrumental value of the patient (e.g. priority for health personnel), could not be used as a fundamental alternative, but only as an additional criterion. However, this would require a corresponding social consensus. The same applies to the ethically debatable question of whether younger people should be given preference over older people, as the latter have less chance of a fulfilled life (see the "life-cycle principle" for example by White and Lo 2020). It has therefore been suggested that age should be used as a secondary criterion ("tiebreaker") if two patients have the same chance of surviving the acute intensive course (see Emanuel et al. 2020; White and Lo 2020). The recommendations of the Italian Society of Anaesthesia, Analgesia, Reanimation and Intensive Therapy (SIAARTI) contain life expectancy as a secondary prioritisation criterion (see Società Italiana di Anestesia Analgesia Rianimazione e Terapia Intensiva 2020)—which tends to favour younger patients, but does not represent a consistent implementation of the "life-cycle principle", as it is not the fulfilled life cycle, but the remaining years of life that are taken into account in the decision. However, a corresponding social deliberation process would also be required here before implementation. This is why they are not included in the recommendations of the German professional societies. However, these considerations once again underscore the urgent need for parliament to deal with the question of an appropriate way of dealing with such a dramatic shortage of life-saving therapies—also with a view to comparable shortages in future pandemics. Finally, in December 2022, the German parliament passed a legal regulation for allocation decisions in a national spread of communicable diseases. Accordingly, intensive care resources should be allocated only according to the criterion of the acute and immediate probability of survival of the patient. However, patients who are already on intensive care treatment are excluded from the allocation decisions. This has been criticized especially from the medical societies because it will involve more avoidable deaths and disadvantage especially vulnerable population subgroups with a high probability of a severe or deadly course of the Covid-19-disease.

4 Prioritization of SARS-CoV-2 Vaccines

Since the beginning of the Covid-19 pandemic, intensive work has been underway worldwide to develop a vaccine against the SARS-CoV-2 virus. In view of the high infection rates with a large number of seriously ill Covid-19 patients and the occurrence of mutations of the SARS-CoV2 virus with a possibly higher infectivity, great hopes had been placed in effective vaccines against the SARS-CoV2 virus. The developments since the beginning of 2021 showed, however, that not only the production of the already approved vaccines were limited, but also that distribution problems further delayed access to vaccination for many people. Not everyone who wanted to be vaccinated and would have had a benefit from the vaccination could be vaccinated. This raised the ethical question of which criteria should be used to distribute the scarce vaccine: Which population groups should be vaccinated first if the vaccine capacity is not enough for everyone? (for an overview see Williams and Dawson 2020).

An effective vaccine against the SARS-CoV-2 virus has the potential to prevent severe courses of disease and death as long as Covid-19 can only be treated to a limited extent. In addition, it can reduce the transmission and thus the spread of the infection. From an ethical point of view, it is therefore imperative to regulate early who should have priority in the allocation of scarce vaccines. However, questions of prioritization are delicate and are often avoided by politics, as they make transparent what is inevitable: Some people will get the potentially life-saving goods (earlier), others will have to wait. A prioritization according to clearly defined procedures and criteria can help to ensure that the limited resources are used in such a way that they cover urgent needs and achieve the greatest possible benefit overall. In addition, a transparent discussion and a clearly defined prioritization scheme can prevent uncertainties in the population and strengthen confidence in the health system in times of crisis. The question of vaccination prioritization once again highlights the importance of procedural justice.

What should the prioritization of vaccines against the SARS-CoV-2 virus be based on? The overarching goal should be to reduce the harm caused by the Covid-19 pandemic as much as possible. This includes not only health related harm caused by severe course of the disease and death, but also negative social effects such as poverty, isolation and insecurity, which in turn have a negative impact on health. At the same time, it must be ensured that all people have equal access to the prioritized vaccines, regardless of factors like age, place of residence or socio-economic status. This prioritization, based on the ethical criterion of benefit maximization, should take into account that it must also be ensured that the groups of people who need the protection of the SARS-CoV-2 vaccine the most are vaccinated first, as they have a high risk of a severe or even fatal course of Covid-19. The prioritization would thus correspond to a benefit maximization with fairness constraints (see Sect. 2). Interestingly, the position paper of the joint working group of members of the Standing Vaccination Commission, the German Ethics Council and the National Academy of Sciences Leopoldina does not mention the principle of benefit maximization among the ethical principles (see Standing Vaccination Commission et al. 2020). The well-being of patients cannot be promoted in the event of severe shortages of suitable resources—although the well-being of vaccinated persons can be protected by an effective vaccination. The working group primarily recommends that the prioritization should be based on the criterion of "urgency", where apparently not—as is usual—the temporal urgency, but rather the need is meant, which results from the vulnerability of the groups of people.

From the overarching goal—to avoid as much harm as possible through the pandemic while securing the priority need for infection protection—specific criteria can then be derived to determine which groups of people should have priority in access to vaccination (see National Academies of Sciences Engeneering and Medicine 2020). These include 1) a high risk of severe illness and death from Covid-19, 2) a high probability of infection with the SARS-CoV-2 virus due to professional activity, 3) a high risk of negative social impacts in the event of illness and 4) a great importance for the transmission and spread of infection. Based on these criteria, it can then be determined which groups of people should be supplied with the scarce vaccine in which order. For this purpose, current knowledge about the course of the Covid-19 pandemic and the efficacy of the available vaccines in different population groups, including possible harm potentials, is required. The following considerations can therefore only give a preliminary impression of how a strategy for the prioritization of SARS-CoV-2 vaccinations could look like.

The highest priority should be given to those people who, due to their age or certain diseases, have a high risk of developing Covid-19 severely or dying from it. In particular, those people should be taken into account who, due to their living conditions, cannot protect themselves well against an infection (for example, very old residents in nursing homes) or who, due to their socio-economic living conditions, have an increased risk of severe course of the disease (Schmidt et al. 2021). In addition, the health personnel with the highest priority for access to the SARS-CoV-2 vaccination would be those who, through the care of Covid-19 patients, have a high risk of infection and/or care for particularly vulnerable people (e.g. staff in nursing homes for the elderly). Subsequently, such occupational groups could be given access, which have a high risk of infection and a great importance for the maintenance of public life, that is, who work in areas such as infrastructure, food supply, communication, school and child care. Then, such groups of people could be considered who could a significant role in the spread of the pandemic, even if they themselves do not have a high risk of a severe course of the disease. In a final phase, all other persons could then be given access to vaccination. This general prioritization scheme must be further specified. In Germany, the Standing Committee on Vaccination (STIKO) at the Robert Koch Institute is responsible for this, which regularly updates its recommendations for Covid-19 vaccination, also depending on the approved vaccines (cf. Standing Committee on Vaccination 2021). The Committee rightly emphasizes that the proposed prioritization scheme cannot explicitly map all clinical pictures and indications for vaccination, so that there must be room for individual decision-making on the state level.

Even if the questions of prioritizing SARS-CoV-2 vaccines are controversial and sometimes very emotional, one should consider that, in comparison to a shortage of intensive care capacities, these are decisions of significantly lower impact. After all, it is not a question here of allocating life-saving acute treatments, but of the chronological order of access to a preventive measure. Those who cannot be vaccinated in the first phases as part of a prioritization have a comparatively low risk of infection and a severe course of the disease (otherwise they would have been vaccinated early) and can further reduce the probability of infection through appropriate measures. In addition, it is in the interest of everyone that the negative effects of the Covid-19 pandemic on health and our lives be minimized as much as possible. We can achieve this goal most effectively with a prioritization of the SARS-CoV2 vaccination.

5 Outlook

The global spread of infectious diseases with a high burden of disease can also bring highly developed health systems to the limits of their capacity. As the Covid-19 pandemic has shown, this results in questions of appropriate allocation of scarce resources in various sectors and at different levels. From an ethical perspective of justice, the inevitable allocation and prioritization decisions should be made in fair procedures and on the basis of well-justified criteria. The present contribution has discussed the challenges involved using the examples of allocating scarce intensive care beds and prioritizing SARS-CoV-2 vaccines. Since these are (potentially) life-saving goods, the legislature—as in the case of organ transplantation—should at least specify the essential allocation criteria in order to create legitimate and legally secure framework conditions for local actors. This in turn requires that the possible questions of resource allocation be addressed and discussed at an early stage in society, as there is no time for a careful discussion and balancing of the relevant aspects in the acute crisis. It is to be hoped that the SARS-CoV-2 pandemic will be used to develop socially accepted guidelines for the inevitable allocation and prioritization decisions—also with a view to future pandemics.

References

AbilityWatch (2020) Verfassungsbeschwerde gegen Triage-Verfahren. https://abilitywatch.de/2020/07/21/verfassungsbeschwerde-gegen-triage-verfahren/. Accessed 23 Feb 2021

Brindle ME, Doherty G, Lillemoe K, Gawande A (2020) Approaching surgical triage during the COVID-19 pandemic. Ann Surg 272(2):e40–e42. https://doi.org/10.1097/SLA.0000000000003992

Curtis JR, Kross EK, Stapleton RD (2020) The importance of addressing advance care planning and decisions about do-not-resuscitate orders during novel Coronavirus 2019 (COVID-19). J Am Med Assoc 323(18):1771–1772. https://doi.org/10.1001/jama.2020.4894

Daniels N (2008) Just health: meeting health needs fairly. University Press, Cambridge

Daniels N, Sabin JE (2002) Setting limits fairly. University Press, Oxford

Deutscher Bundestag (2013) Unterrichtung durch die Bundesregierung. Bericht zur Risikoanalyse im Bevölkerungsschutz 2012. https://dipbt.bundestag.de/dip21/btd/17/120/1712051.pdf. Accessed 23 Feb 2021

Deutscher Ethikrat (2020) Solidarität und Verantwortung in der Corona-Krise. Ad-hoc-Empfehlung. Deutscher Ethikrat, Berlin

Emanuel EJ, Persad G, Upshur R, Thome B, Parker M, Glickman A, Zhang C, Boyle C, Smith M, Phillips JP (2020) Fair allocation of scarce medical resources in the time of Covid-19. N Engl J Med 382(21):2049–2055. https://doi.org/10.1056/NEJMsb2005114

Fateh-Moghadam B, Gutmann T (2020) Gleichheit vor der Triage: Rechtliche Rahmenbedingungen der Priorisierung von COVID-19-Patienten in der Intensivmedizin. In: Verfassungsblog. https://verfassungsblog.de/gleichheit-vor-der-triage/. Accessed 23 Feb 2021

Feddersen B, Petri S, Marckmann G, der Schmitten J (2020) Implementing patient-centered advance care planning in the outpatient setting during the COVID-19 pandemic. MMW Fortschr Med 162(9):45–48. https://doi.org/10.1007/s15006-020-0476-x

Garrett JR, McNolty LA, Wolfe ID, Lantos JD (2020) Our next pandemic ethics challenge? Allocating „normal" health care services. Hastings Cent Rep 50(3):79–80. https://doi.org/10.1002/hast.1145

Lampert T, Richter M, Schneider S, Spallek J, Dragano N (2016) Soziale Ungleichheit und Gesundheit: Stand und Perspektiven der sozialepidemiologischen Forschung in Deutschland. Bundesgesundheitsbl Gesundheitsforsch Gesundheitsschutz 59(2):153–165. https://doi.org/10.1007/s00103-015-2275-6

Lübbe W (2020) Orientierung in der Corona-Krise? Nicht mit Doppelbotschaften. Medizinrecht 38:434–439

Marckmann G (2008) Gesundheit und Gerechtigkeit. Bundesgesundheitsbl Gesundheitsforsch Gesundheitsschutz 51(8):887–894

Marckmann G (2009a) Nutzenmaximierung mit gerechtigkeitsethischen Einschränkungen: Perspektiven einer ethisch vertretbaren Kosten-Nutzen-Bewertung. Das Gesundheitswesen 71(Suppl. 1):28

Marckmann G (2009b) Priorisierung im Gesundheitswesen: Was können wir aus den internationalen Erfahrungen lernen? Z Evid Fortbild Qual Gesundheitswes 103(2):85–91

Marckmann G, Neitzke G, Schildmann J (2020a) Triage in der COVID-19-Pandemie – was ist gerecht? DIVI 11(4):172–178

Marckmann G, Neitzke G, Schildmann J, Michalsen A, Dutzmann J, Hartog C, Jobges S, Knochel K, Michels G, Pin M, Riessen R, Rogge A, Taupitz J, Janssens U (2020b) Entscheidungen über die Zuteilung intensivmedizinischer Ressourcen im Kontext der COVID-19-Pandemie: Klinisch-ethische Empfehlungen der DIVI, der DGINA, der DGAI, der DGIIN, der DGNI, der DGP, der DGP und der AEM. Med Klin, Intensivmed Notfallmed 115:477–485. https://doi.org/10.1007/s00063-020-00708-w

National Academies of Sciences Engeneering and Medicine (2020) Framework for equitable allocation of COVID-19 vaccine. The National Academies Press, Washington, DC. https://doi.org/10.17226/25917

Persad G, Peek ME, Emanuel EJ (2020) Fairly prioritizing groups for access to COVID-19 vaccines. J Am Med Assoc. https://doi.org/10.1001/jama.2020.18513

Rawls J (1975) Eine Theorie der Gerechtigkeit. Suhrkamp, Frankfurt am Main

Riessen R, Haap M, Marckmann G, Mahling M (2020) Rationale Therapieentscheidungen bei Intensivpatienten [Rational therapeutic decisions in intensive care patients]. Dtsch Med Wochenschr 145(20):1470–1475. https://doi.org/10.1055/a-1216-7614

Schmidt H, Weintraub R, Williams MA, Miller K, Buttenheim A, Sadecki E et al (2021) Equitable allocation of COVID-19 vaccines in the United States. Nat Med. https://doi.org/10.1038/s41591-021-01379-6

Schweizerische Akademie der Medizinischen Wissenschaften, Schweizerische Gesellschaft für Intensivmedizin (2020) COVID-19-Pandemie: Triage von intensivmedizinischen Behandlungen bei Ressourcenknappheit. Hinweise zur Umsetzung Kapitel 9.3. der SAMW-Richtlinien intensivmedizinische Massnahmen (2013). Schweizerische Akademie der Medizinischen Wissenschaften (SAMW), Bern

Società Italiana di Anestesia Analgesia Rianimazione e Terapia Intensiva (2020) Raccomandazioni di etica clinica per l'ammissione a trattamenti intensivi e per la loro sospensione, in condizioni eccezionali di squilibrio tra necessità e risorse disponibili. Società Italiana di Anestesia Analgesia Rianimazione e Terapia Intensiva. https://doi.org/10.1701/3347.33183

Ständige Impfkommission (2021) Beschluss der STIKO zur 2. Aktualisierung der COVID-19-Impfempfehlung und die dazugehörige wissenschaftliche Begründung. STIKO-Empfehlung zur COVID-19-Impfung. Aktualisierung vom 29. Januar 2021 In: Epidemiologisches Bulletin 5/2021. https://www.rki.de/DE/Content/Infekt/EpidBull/Archiv/2021/Ausgaben/05_21.pdf?__blob=publicationFile. Accessed 23 Feb 2021

Ständige Impfkommission, Deutscher Ethikrat, Nationale Akademie der Wissenschaften Leopoldina (2020) Wie soll der Zugang zu einem COVID-19 Impfstoff geregelt werden? https://www.leopoldina.org/publikationen/detailansicht/publication/wie-soll-der-zugang-zu-einem-covid-19-impfstoff-geregelt-werden-2020/. Accessed 23 Feb 2021

Truog RD, Mitchell C, Daley GQ (2020) The toughest triage allocating ventilators in a pandemic. N Engl J Med 382(21):1973–1975. https://doi.org/10.1056/NEJMp2005689

White DB, Lo B (2020) A framework for rationing ventilators and critical care beds during the COVID-19 pandemic. J Am Med Assoc 323(18):1773–1774. https://doi.org/10.1001/jama.2020.5046

Williams A (1997) Intergenerational equity: an exploration of the ‚fair innings' argument. Health Econ 6(2):117–132. https://doi.org/10.1002/(sici)1099-1050(199703)6:2<117::aid-hec256>3.0.co;2-b

Williams JH, Dawson A (2020) Prioritising access to pandemic influenza vaccine: a review of the ethics literature. BMC Med Ethics 21(1):40. https://doi.org/10.1186/s12910-020-00477-3

Zentrale Kommission zur Wahrung ethischer Grundsätze in der Medizin und ihren Grenzgebieten (Zentrale Ethikkommission) bei der Bundesärztekammer (2007) Priorisierung medizinischer Leistungen im System der Gesetzlichen Krankenversicherung (GKV). Dtsch Ärztebl Int 104(40):A2750–A2754

Ventilator Triage and Vaccine Rationing in Covid-19: A New Paradigm for Promoting Social Justice in Allocation with Disadvantage Indices

Harald Schmidt

Contents

1 Introduction . . . 97
2 Resource Scarcity During Covid-19 . . . 99
3 Triage in the Allocation of Ventilators . . . 99
3.1 Cross-cutting Principles of Triage Frameworks . . . 99
3.2 Allocation Frameworks in Societal Context . . . 100
3.3 The Limitations of Allegedly Objective Data within the SOFA Points System . . . 103
3.4 Specific Improvement Proposals and Important Changes in Triage Framework Programs . . . 105
3.5 Interim Conclusion: The Shortfalls of Maximizing Benefits Alone Have Become Unignorable . . . 107
4 Allocation of Vaccines . . . 108
4.1 Overarching Principles in Allocation Framework Programs: A New Development . . . 109
4.2 The Conceptual Role of Disadvantage Indices in Social Justice . . . 110
4.3 The Practical Implementation of Disadvantage Indices to Promote Social Justice . . . 112
4.4 Four Main Uses of Disadvantage Indices to promote Social Justice . . . 113
5 Conclusion . . . 115
References . . . 116

1 Introduction

The concept of triage originated on battlefields. War metaphors have been used frequently since early 2020 (Chapman and Miller DeMond 2020; Sabuced et al. 2020), as those involved in politics and science sought to understand the actual

H. Schmidt (✉)
University of Pennsylvania, Philadelphia, USA
e-mail: schmidth@upenn.edu

© The Author(s), under exclusive license to Springer-Verlag GmbH, DE, part of Springer Nature 2023

A. Reis et al. (eds.), *Pandemics and Ethics*,
https://doi.org/10.1007/978-3-662-66872-6_8

extent of the threat posed by SARS-CoV-2 and, simultaneously, to find appropriate political and policy responses. Such comparisons are typically used when it is necessary to mobilize a comprehensive response from the entire society. At the same time, however, it must be noted that SARS-CoV-2 did not actually represent a war situation. Furthermore, the costs that may be acceptable in a war situation are not directly transferable to the various issues raised by SARS-CoV-2, in particular with regard to rationing and triage. This urgency is all the more acute as the pandemic has exposed social inequalities in brutal clarity in many countries. Certain disadvantaged groups were much harder than others, for example in terms of unemployment, infection risks, hospitalization and death, raising the question of how to respond to this in policy (APM Research Lab 2020; McClung et al. 2020; National Academies of Sciences, Engineering and Medicine 2020; Schmidt 2020a). There are essentially three possible responses: these inequalities can be maintained, exacerbated or alleviated. The focus on war metaphors can quickly push the consideration of inequality to the periphery as a detail—but this would be short-sighted for several reasons (Chapman and Miller DeMond 2020; Sabuced et al. 2020). Rationing has taken place in various areas where demand outstripped supply, for example in access to tests, antibody medications, protective masks or clothing (Emanuel et al. 2020). This chapter focusses on two of the most controversial rationing questions: the allocation of ventilators and of vaccines. The social inequalities surfaced by SARS-CoV-2 were particularly pronounced in the USA, which led to an unprecedented innovation in policy. While, to some extent, the discussion is therefore specific to the USA, many of the general lessons also apply to other countries, policy option.

Soldiers must be healthy enough to be able to fight successfully. When Napoleon undertook campaigns in Egypt and Syria from 1797 to 1801, he encountered bad weather, poor sanitation and the plague: His army was reduced by one fifth and his war goals were in major jeopardy. In view of this situation, formal triage is said to have been used for the first time, which meant that those soldiers who were most likely to continue fighting should be medically treated—while all others were abandoned (Nakao and UkaiI 2017). In the logic of war and in view of Napoleon's goals, this approach can be compelling. But the concept of triage as well as the circumstances under which it was deployed and justified have changed over time (Antommaria et al. 2020; Maves et al. 2020; Trotter 2010). Triage is generally activated when demand for medical care exceeds the available resources. Paradigmatic cases are situations such as natural disasters, for example, earthquakes, because there is not enough time to prepare for them. Likewise, health systems can be overwhelmed by pandemics–even if adequate preparations have been mad (Emanuel et al. 2018).

2 Resource Scarcity During Covid-19

In the case of the Covid-19 pandemic, individual states or regions in the USA differed in the extent to which they anticipated, or were willing to anticipate, the need to ration resources. Effective political leadership proved to be a critical factor. Federal governments, states, municipalities and government agencies can mobilize financial or other resources so that more medical supplies, protective clothing for staff or access to intensive care units are made available. Macro-level decisions directly affect the need and urgency of rationing measures at the meso- and micro-levels, such as at the hospital or individual patient-level (Emanuel et al. 2018). Whether a patient or a patient receives access to a scarce resource therefore depends not only on the behavior of the health personnel and the policy of the health facilities; rather, the type of interventions available, and the magnitude of scarcity are typically determined to a large extent by political measures at higher levels. These regulate both the general access to resources that are to be distributed and the principles that are to be applied.

3 Triage in the Allocation of Ventilators

The great majority of patients infected with SARS-CoV-2 recovered without requiring hospitalization, but around 15% became seriously ill and needed oxygen, around 5% become critically ill and need to be treated in intensive care units, most often with mechanical ventilation (World Health Organization 2020a). As the virus spread rapidly and no country had sufficient capacity for intensive care units and ventilators, the first major wave of infection in spring 2020 sparked an international race for these resources. The United States responded slowly and uncoordinatedly to this challenge (Himmelstein et al. 2018; Woolhandler et al. 2021). At a time when 200,000 people were already infected and 6,000 had died, the President invoked the Defense Production Act to require private companies to produce ventilators and protective masks. New York City was one of the epicenters, and Governor Cuomo warned that the supply of ventilators would last only another six days (Klebnikov 2020). In New York and elsewhere, it increasingly seemed necessary to ration at the micro level.

3.1 Cross-cutting Principles of Triage Frameworks

An earlier and more effective response would have alleviated the pressure on hospitals to some extent; but even adequate policy measures at the macro level would have entailed the need to deal with the shortage at the meso and micro levels

(Emanuel et al. 2018). In response, hospitals, academic researchers, and policy makers developed guidelines for the allocation of ventilators. There is a clear public interest in disclosing the criteria for who gets a ventilator when not all can. Unfortunately, however, a systematic review found that as of May 10, 2020, when the need had already peaked during the first wave, only 26 states had published guidelines (Piscitello et al. 2020).

Typically, these documents proposed that allocation should aim to maximize overall benefits (Emanuel et al. 2020; Feinstein et al. 2020; Antommaria et al. 2020; Piscitello et al. 2020). Such an orientation could be viewed as being motivated by utilitarianism alone, but it is important to see that there are other options, also, such as multi-criteria approaches, in which a range of different values and principles are combined (Emanuel et al. 2020; White and Lo 2020). For example, New Jersey (NJ), like other states, issued a framework for triaging ventilators with the classic utilitarian credo of "the greatest good for the greatest number" as one of its goals (Grewal 2020). The overarching premise of benefit-maximizing frameworks is that, in a situation of absolute scarcity of ventilators, it would be wrong to offer a ventilator to someone who would die during ventilation or soon after discharge from the hospital. Instead, maximizing benefits should strive to give ventilators to save the most lives, and the most live years, by allocating ventilators to those who are most likely to respond to treatment or live long enough afterwards—whoever that may be.

The focus on survival is also not limited to Anglo-Saxon countries, which can be viewed as aligning more closely with consequentialist approaches. It can also be found in Germany. Together with six other professional societies, the German Interdisciplinary Association for Intensive and Emergency Medicine published Clinical-ethical recommendations in March 2020 and explained: "The prioritization of patients should therefore be based on the criterion of prognosis, which does not mean a decision in the sense of the 'best choice', but rather the renunciation of treatment of those for whom there is no or only a very small prospect of success" (German Interdisciplinary Association for Intensive and Emergency Medicine 2020).

3.2 Allocation Frameworks in Societal Context

The allocation guidelines created in spring 2020 generally abstracted from the specific historical and social context. This means that no consideration was given to the extent to which a person belongs to a historically or currently socially privileged or disadvantaged group, with a strong focus on clinical data alone. This can be understandable if the aim is to develop procedures that aim to be as objective as possible. But especially in countries like the USA, such an approach also raises profound questions about whether the allocation guidelines maintain, intensify or reduce social inequalities. In spring 2020, New York was the largest hotspot of the Covid-19 pandemic in the USA. The city can be used as a instructive case study for surfacing major challenges with focussing on a narrow set of seemingly objective criteria. When the Covid-19 pandemic spread, many wealthy people withdrew to their vacation homes. But many other New Yorkers had to stay in the city because their work (whether in formal or informal employment) was such that it could not be done from a distance, or because they could not afford not to travel. The analysis of inner-city transit data data from the end of March 2020 showed that the use of the subway had decreased sharply, but varied greatly in different parts of the city. Of the five boroughs, Manhattan has the highest average income at $80,000 per year, and morning subway usage there decreased by 75%. In the Bronx, however, where the average income is only $38,000 per year, this decrease was only 55% (Goldbaum and Cook 2020). These differences are plausibly explained by the fact that the residents in these boroughs differed in the extent to which they were able to prioritize their health over their income. People with low incomes were therefore more exposed to the environmental risks associated with the use of mass transit. In addition, they often had less secure housing and were more exposed to health risks in their formal or informal employment. Due to historic and ongoing forms of structural racism, US society is structured in such a way that most communities of color have significantly reduced economic opportunities (Himmelstein et al. 2018; O'Brien et al. 2020). This means that a larger share of people among the disadvantaged were (and are) people of color, facing a disproportionate impact from the pandemic (Yearby and Mohapatra 2020).

Similar disparities were also observed in the more health-related measures. At the end of April, deaths due to Covid-19 were almost two times as high in the Bronx as in Manhattan; 224 to 122 per 100,000 inhabitants (Wadhera et al. 2020). Just over a year later, in February 2021, this basic pattern had not changed—Bronx: 314, Manhattan: 178 (NYC Health 2021). The deaths also differed by ethnic groups. In April 2020, twice as many African Americans died as white New Yorkers, and the Latino population fared similarly: 127 to 114 to 63 per 100,000 residents (Wadhera et al. 2020). The trend continued in February 2021, per 100,000 residents: white New Yorkers 163, Latinos 311, African Americans 283. These trends were unfortunately confirmed at the national level (see Table 1).

For the rationing of ventilators, the question arises as to whether and how such disparities should be taken into account. Consider the following scenario (Schmidt 2020b; Schmidt et al. 2021): Three patients are waiting to be admitted to an intensive care unit where only one bed is still available. All three have severe Covid-19 symptoms to the same extent. John is a healthy white man aged 40. Rosa is a 45-year-old African American woman with pre-existing conditions. Linda is a 56-year-old white woman with Down syndrome. Who should be admitted?

It is helpful to discuss these three patients and the underlying general equity question against the background of the dominant allocation guideline at the time, the Model guidance for the Allocation of Scarce Critical Care Resources During a Public Health Emergency (henceforth: Model Guidance), which, according to the authors, was adopted in different ways in hundreds of hospitals across the US,

Table 1 Covid-19 cases, hospitalizations, deaths by ethnic group

Ratio relative to white non-Latinos				
	American Indian, Alaska Native, non-Latino	Asian, non-Latino	Black, African American, non-Latino	Latino
Cases	2,5 times higher	1,1 times higher	2,6 times higher	2,8 times higher
Hospitalizations	5,3 times higher	1,3 times higher	4,7 times higher	4,6 times higher
Deaths	1,4 times higher	No increase	2,1 times higher	1,1 times higher

Source US Centers for Disease Control and Prevention, Risk for COVID-19 Infection, Hospitalization, and Death By Race/Ethnicity, available at: https://www.cdc.gov/coronavirus/2019-ncov/covid-data/investigations-discovery/hospitalization-death-by-race-ethnicity.html

some US states and in all hospitals in Mexico (University of Pittsburgh 2020a, b). The guidelines were revised in December 2020 in important points that are directly relevant for the discussion presented here (White and Lo 2021). I will first describe the conclusions from the widely adopted version of April 3 and then the changes that were proposed in December 2020 (at the time of writing this chapter, these changes were not yet reflected in a new version of the guidelines published on a dedicated website at the Department of Critical Care Medicine at the University of Pittsburgh).

Linda suffers from high blood pressure and complications from a previous heart operation. Her treatment would take longer than John's. Under clinical aspects, her age would also play a role. The life expectancy of people with Down syndrome is 60 years. Linda has fewer years ahead of her than John and Rosa. Implicitly or explicitly, clinical aspects would probably be interpreted as speaking against treatment (Chapman et al. 2013). Rosa grew up in a part of the city that was "redlined" (i.e. geographic areas that banks and insurance precluded from major lending, such as mortgage loans—in general neighborhoods with African American populations, see Jan 2018). Access to health services can be as difficult as access to credit or healthy food. Due to historic and ongoing experiences, her community is often mistrustful of the health system. For example, the Tuskegee Syphilis Study (CDC 2020a, b), still cast a long shadow, and discriminatory experiences of Black patients when it comes to prescribing pain medication or accessing hospitals do little to change this (Cuevas et al. 2016; Nelson 2002, 2003). Rosa had health insurance for some years, but lacked it in other years (Yearby and Mohapatra 2020). She also has kidney problems (Cobb et al. 2019), and all in all, her statistical chances of survival look similar to Linda's. John has the best chances; if the overarching goal of maximizing benefits is paramount, he should be admitted according to the points system of the Model Guidance. While the thought process is relatively clear, the outcome also raises considerable social justice tensions.

3.3 *The Limitations of Allegedly Objective Data within the SOFA Points System*

A central aim of the Model Guidance is to avoid unfair results that can typically result from alternative approaches such as "first come, first served". The guideline also expressly states that "race, ethnicity, gender, insurance status, perceptions of social worth, immigration status, among others" should be irrelevant (University of Pittsburgh 2020a). Yet, a fair allocation is considerably hampered by the fact that the guidelines proposes each patient be assessed based on an "objective and validated measure of acute physiology (e.g., the SOFA point system) [taking into account] a critically shortened life expectancy, even if the person would survive the acute illness crisis" (ibid.).

The SOFA point system (Sequential Organ Failure Assessment) is widespread in the USA (Antommaria et al. 2020; Maves et al. 2020; Piscitello et al. 2020; Vincent et al. 1996) and integrates eight individual clinical measurements to derive an overall assessment that allows statements to be made about the probability of death in the intensive care unit. The higher the score, the more likely the death of the patient. When integrated into the Model Guidance, the prioritization of patients results from a combination of SOFA points with points for the remaining estimated life expectancy, from which a total value is derived that leads to a classification into three groups (see Fig. 2). In addition to the total points, in the April 2020 version of the guideline, it was proposed to consider two additional secondary criteria: the age of the patients and whether they were employed in the health care sector; in this way, a multi-criteria framework was set up in which other aspects should also be taken into account, although not with the same weight as the central criteria.

A first problem with the focus on objective data is that that across different racial, ethnic, income or insurance status populations, shares of people with major health conditions are not equal. Uncontroversial, comprehensive and detailed data makes it clear that baseline health is significantly worse among lower income, uninsured, disabled and particular racial and ethnic groups, who are all far more likely to be assigned "low priority" status on the Point system. (all data cited in this paragraph from: Centers for Disease Control and Prevention (CDC) 2013; National Center for Health Statistics 2019). For example, while 8% of whites lack insurance, 14% of non-Hispanic blacks have no insurance, and 27% of Hispanics. Smoking is significantly more common among adults without high school (35%) compared to those with a college degree (13%). Blacks have a 25% increased cancer death rate, compared to whites. Diabetes prevalence is highest among non-Hispanic blacks (11% vs 7% whites), persons with less than high school education (12% vs. 6% college or higher), those who are poor (11% vs 6% high income) and those with a disability (12% vs. no disability: 5%). Non-Hispanic blacks have a higher rate of hypertension (41%) than non-Hispanic whites (29%) and Hispanics (28%). Rates of blood pressure control are lowest among those without health insurance (28%), Mexican-Americans (30%), and those born outside the United States (39%). Asthma is significantly more common among adults with incomes 450%FPL (49%). And health is highly connected to place (For example, Black people are 75 percent more likely to live near oil, gas and petrochemical facilities than the average American because these industries are so concentrated in black communities).(Fleischman 2017).

The reasons for these disparities are mainly structural and historical (Dwyer-Lindgren et al. 2017; Forde et al. 2020; Khazanchi et al. 2020; O'Brien et al. 2020; Yearby and Mohapatra 2020). Without affordable universal health coverage, poorer and uninsured people have a harder time managing health problems. And the collective experiences of communities like Rosa's mean that even with access to health care, a lack of trust can have the same consequence as a lack of means.

From a broader social justice perspective, these background conditions should matter in allocating ventilators. But they don't. In requiring at least 5 years of longer-term survival, the Model Guidance ignores that life expectancy across geographic, income and racial groups can vary by up to 30 years (City Health Dashboard 2020). For example, inner-city residents of Chicago, who are more likely to be black, can expect to live to 60 years. Those in suburban areas, who are typically white, live to 90, and variations of this magnitude are also found in New York City and Philadelphia. (Robert Wood Johnson Foundation online database 2020).

Under the Model Guidance, the Downs patient and the inner-city Black patient could receive a penalty point, whereas a 60-year-old white suburban patient would receive none. And chances are far higher that Black patients receive an additional penalty point due to their SOFA score. To determine how well kidneys work, SOFA incorporates a creatinine score, a waste product of muscles, found in blood. The main problem with creatinine is that it is myopic to view it as an objective measure of kidney function alone: it simultaneously measures social disadvantages driven by structural or historical patterns of unequal opportunities. Some literature has suggested uniform differences in creatinine levels by race, and historically higher average creatinine levels in Black people have been attributed to higher muscle mass (Grubbs 2020). However, there is weak scientific evidence for this hypothesis, and increasing awareness that measuring differences across races is severely complicated by the fact that race is a social construc. (Omi and Winant 2014). Further, a biological trait cannot be mapped categorically onto a group of people that is both socially defined and composed of widely differing physiological profiles that reflect different circumstances of living far more than genetics (Morris and Mohan 2020; Yudell et al. 2016). For example, limited evidence suggests that genetic factors substantially increase the risk of end-stage kidney disease in 13% of African-Americans (Dummer et al. 2015), but even then, by implication, the vast majority of the higher prevalence of the disease is non-genetic, and due to different living circumstances that are more common for the respective group (Forde et al. 2020). Related, creatinine is higher in Black communities because of higher rates of chronic kidney disease, due to higher rates of diabetes and high blood pressure(Cobb et al. 2019; Grubbs 2020)that are best understood as the consequences of health inequities and structural racism. (Dwyer-Lindgren et al. 2017; Forde et al. 2020; Khazanchi et al. 2020; O'Brien et al. 2020; Yearby and Mohapatra 2020).

Creatinine becomes relevant for social justice due to the way SOFA functions and is integrated into the Model Guidance's Point System. SOFA measures creatinine in 5 tiers. The first assigns 0 points to patients with levels (see Fig. 1). However, 1 point is assigned for levels 1.2–1.9, and up to 4 for levels ≥ 5. A single added point can therefore make the difference between getting, and not getting, a ventilator, and as noted, chances for this are even higher when there are additional point assessments for reduced life expectancy.

3.4 *Specific Improvement Proposals and Important Changes in Triage Framework Programs*

In focusing on baseline health alone, the Point system is objective in one sense, but does not establish a level playing field that would give structurally and historically disadvantaged populations a fair chance at receiving life-saving treatment. In attempts to reduce adverse outcomes, several concrete proposals were made, including adjusting the overall point score by using weights constructed with a statistical measure of disadvantage (which will be described in more detail below) so that the further disadvantage that already disadvantaged patients face from the scoring system can be neutralized or adding points for past disadvantage more broadly (Chomilo et al. 2020; Manchanda et al. 2020; Schmidt et al. 2021; Sederstrom 2020). Regarding reducing unfairness from the use of SOFA, concrete policy proposals were made to reduce unjust outcomes through: improving diversity in decision processes; numerically adjusting creatinine scores (so that they are benchmarked to the average values by race, rather than an overall value), dropping creatinine (i.e. use SOFA without the creatinine score); finding alternative measures (such as cystatin); avoiding disadvantage by adding equity weights using a disadvantage index; and rejecting the SOFA model altogether(Schmidt et al. 2021).

Of note, the authors of the model guidance published a revised version of the point system in December 2020, that, among other changes, reduces the life expectancy requirement to 1 year, no longer mentions SOFA, and applies equity weights to consider social disadvantage, see Fig. 2 (White and Lo 2021).

Recent empirical studies of triage procedures at Covid-19 have shown that black patients have been disproportionately disadvantaged, depending on which scoring system was used (Ashana et al. et al. 2021; Parker et al. 2021). For this reason as well, it is welcome that the guidelines have been revised, although it remains unclear how the weightings were determined: for example, if they were

1. Multi-criteria strategy for the allocation of intensive care resources in Public Health Emergencies					
Ethical Principle	Specification	Point system			
		1	2	3	4
Save Lives	Prognosis for short-term survival	SOFA-Score <6	SOFA-Score 6-8	SOFA-Score 9-11	SOFA-Score 12
Save Life Years		...	Life expecancy < 5 years despite succesful treatment of acute condition	...	Death likely within 1 year despite successful treatment of acute condition
*Sequential Organ Failure Assessment. Instead of this scoring system, another method can be used to assess survival in the ICU (such as LAPS2) and should then also be divided into four sections.					

2. *Conversion of baseline scores from the multi-criteria strategy to prioritize patients.*	
Red - Highest	Priority score 1-3
Orange - Medium (reassess as needed).	Priority score 4-5
Yellow - Lowest (re-evaluation at discretion).	Priority score 6-8
*Source: Directive Regarding Non-Prosecution of Healthcare Facilities and Professionals Adhering to Triage Protocols During COVID-19 Pandemic - Attorney General Law Enforcement Directive No. 2020-03. Office of the Attorney General, Department of Law and Public Safety. [Reformatting of original layout to conform to publisher's design template; full original illustrations should be used for further citation].	

Fig. 1 Guidelines for prioritization in ventilator access (April 3 version. 2020, part of New Jersey's framework), reproducing schematic overviews of two central elements in the overall decision-making process*

derived empirically on the basis of a review of admitted patients, it would be helpful to know the extent to which the adjustments meant that disadvantages relative to other groups were reduced. Provided the changes are capable to reduce disadvantage, a further non-trivial challenge is to ensure that policy makers and administrators across several states and hundreds of hospitals who adopted the April versions of the Guidance are alerted to the fact that they should implement the proposed changes, to address what its authors highlighted as "important equity problems" (White and Lo 2021).

1. Multi-criteria strategy for allocation of intensive care resources in public health emergencies.

Principle	Criterion	Points system*			
		1	2	3	4
Promote population health outcomes	Prognosis for hospital survival (assessed using a validated severity of illness score)	Quartile 1: lowest risk of death (i.e., risk of death, 25%)	Quartile 2 (i.e., risk of death 25–49%)	Quartile 3 (i.e., risk of death 50–75%)	Quartile 4: highest risk of death (i.e., risk of death .75%)
	Presence of end-stage medical condition (medical assessment of near-term prognosis)				Death expected within 1 yr from end-stage condition
Promote justice	1. Correction for structural inequities using ADI	Subtract one point from the Triage Priority Score if the patient's ADI score is 8, 9, or 10 (on a 1–10 scale)			
	2. Priority to frontline essential workers	Subtract one point from the Triage Priority Score if the patient is an essential worker in a high-risk occupation			
	3. Priority to those who've had the least chance to live through life's stages	Tiebreaker: In the event that two patients have identical Triage Priority Scores, give priority to the younger patient when a significant age difference exists			
	4. Equal chances	Second tiebreaker: In the event that two patients have identical Triage Priority Scores and are of similar ages, use random selection to determine who receives the resource			

Fig. 2 Triage framework to promote population health outcomes and justice. (Revised version of Model Guidance (published only in the academic literature at the time of writing, see White and Lo 2021, reformatting of original layout to conform to publisher's design template; full original illustrations should be used for further citations.

3.5 *Interim Conclusion: The Shortfalls of Maximizing Benefits Alone Have Become Unignorable*

Encouragingly, the Biden-Harris administration announced in its National Covid-19 strategy, published in January 2021, that it the newly established Health Equity Task Force would strengthen enforcement of anti-discrimination requirements in several ways, including issuing federal guidance for crisis standards of care, which may be one way of resolving both equity and logistical challenges(Office of the President 2021).

For now, the review of ventilator triage during the Covid-19 pandemic has shown that while, initially, a focus on maximizing benefit in traditional ways seemed appropriate in the frenzied efforts to manage the consequences of the pandemic spring 2020, a year on, in which the country wrestled with countless other forms of structural racism, there is a broader recognition that continuing as before entails major risk of either maintaining, or exacerbating inequities. A directly parallel development can be observed regarding vaccine allocation.

4 Allocation of Vaccines

Aside from the health impact on disadvantaged minority groups, the covid-19 pandemic is striking in its substantial economic impact. A central question is hence to what extent policymakers should prioritize worse-off groups in allocating vaccines, and, by extension minority populations. (Schmidt 2020a). The US government started the vaccine development process in January 2020. But work on frameworks that govern how to allocate vaccines only began in the summer. (National Academies of Sciences, Engineering, and Medicine 2020; Schmidt 2020a). In part, this is understandable. Many questions that affect the sequence in which vaccines should be offered to different population groups depend on how vaccines work: particularly in terms of how effective they are at reducing the risk of death, and limiting the spread of infection. Research data are particularly important for deciding in which sequence to offer vaccines to groups at increased, but also differing, risk of acquiring and spreading Covid infection, such as older populations, essential workers, or people with multiple comorbidities. But in addition to data on the characteristics of vaccines, Covid-19's impact in the US also requires us to consider other data: for, from as the discussion of ventilator rationing showed, from early spring 2020, it became clear that disadvantaged populations, and particularly racial and ethnic groups, were far harder hit in terms of unemployment, infections, and deaths. (APM Research Lab 2020; NYC Health 2021; Wadhera et al. 2020). Conscious of this impact, the National Institutes of Health (NIH) and the Centers for Disease Control and Prevention (CDC) requested the National Academies of Science, Engineering, and Medicine (NASEM) to offer advice on equitable allocation to the CDC's Advisory Committee on Immunization Practices (ACIP). Starting work in July 2020, the NASEM committee published an important landmark report in early October. (National Academies of Sciences, Engineering, and Medicine 2020).

4.1 *Overarching Principles in Allocation Framework Programs: A New Development*

The NASEM report includes a review of both general resource allocation frameworks as well as ones focused on covid-19, and on the context of vaccines more specifically. Under dominant utilitarian, consequentialist, and multicritieria approaches, most models center on maximising benefits or achieving the greatest good for the greatest number of people in a way that, as in the case of ventilator guidance, sets aside the concrete historic, cultural and social circumstances in which people, and particularly disadvantaged groups, find themselves. The focus is hence, again, on maximizing abstract disembodied metrics such as life years gained by an intervention, or the total number of lives saved (with an influential multi-value framework suggesting in broad overview guidance that both aims should simultaneously receive the highest priority, and that worst off groups should only be prioritised insofar as this aligns with maximising benefits) (Emanuel et al. 2020). But life years and lives belong to people in social settings. And these settings occur in societies that frequently commit to treating everyone equally, but often fail to do so (Economic Policy Institute 2020; Schmidt 2020a; World Health Organization 2020b). In a major shift in the overall debate, NASEM, along with guidance from the WHO's SAGE group, urges that "unjust disparities" be reduced in allocating vaccines (National Academies of Sciences, Engineering, and Medicine 2020; World Health Organization 2020b). NASEM require not just assessing the grand total of benefits that might be secured by different strategies, but also which population groups stand to secure what share of benefits, urging, in particular, to consider consequences for those experiencing past and ongoing societal injustice.

The primary goal of the NASEM framework is to "Maximize societal benefit by reducing morbidity and mortality caused by transmission of the novel coronavirus." As such, it is in close continuity with dominant models. Yet, the committee also expressly recognises a further important sub-theme in established and emerging frameworks, some of which urge more direct consideration of the situation of the worst-off. (Nuffield Coucil on Bioethics 2020; World Health Organization 2020c). Importantly, the report notes that "the vaccine allocation criteria should mitigate the negative effects of existing health inequities". (National Academies of Sciences, Engineering, and Medicine 2020).

—see Fig. 3.

Phase 1	Phase 2	Phase 3	Phase 4
Phase 1a, "Jumpstart phase" • High risk health workers • First responders Phase 1b • People of all ages with comorbid and underlying conditions that put them at significantly higher risk • Older adults living in congregate or overcroweded settings	• K-12 teachers and school staff and child care workers • Critical workers in high-risk settings-workers who are essential to the functioning of society and at substantially higher risk of exposure • People of all ages with comorbid and underlying conditions that put them at moderately higher risk • People in homeless shelters or group homes for individuals with disabilities, including serious mental illness, developmental and intellectual disabilities, and physical disabilities or in recovery, and staff working in such settings • People in prisons, jails, detention centers, and similar facilities, and staff who work in such settings • All other older adults not included in phase 1	• Young adults • Children • Workers in industries and occupations important to the functioning of society and and at increased risk of exposure not included in phases 1 or 2	• Everyone residing in the United States who did not have access to the vaccine in the previous phases
Equity is a cross-cutting consideration: In each poulation group, vaccine access should be prioritized for geographic areas identified through CDC's Social Vulnerability Index or another more specific index			

Fig. 3 National Academies of Science, Engineering, and Medicine—Prioritized vaccine groups, with special emphasis that within each group should be prioritized according to the degree of disadvantage (National Academies of Sciences, Engineering, and Medicine 2020)

4.2 *The Conceptual Role of Disadvantage Indices in Social Justice*

In recommending the Social Vulnerability Index (SVI) the NASEM adapted an earlier proposal from the academic literature to use a disadvantage index as a means of addressing social justice considerations (Schmidt 2020a). Such indices integrate a number of separate variables to capture how vulnerable or deprived, on average, are the people living in a particular geographic area. They combine data on relevant variables to compute an overall score that can capture not just single layers of disadvantage, but potentially also the cumulative effects of ethically important "clusters of disadvantage" (Wolff and De-Shalit 2007).

The SVI was initially constructed to guide prioritisation in disasters such as hurricanes or earthquakes. Based on U.S. Census data, it assigns county or tract-level geographic regions a numeric score that integrates 15 factors that are grouped under four related themes: socioeconomic status; household composition; race, ethnicity, and language; and housing and transportation. As such, the SVI recognises the close and concerning linkage between health and place, and health and social status.(Dasgupta et al. 2020; Karaye and Horney 2020; Karmakar et al. 2021; Robert Wood Johnson Foundation 2020; Webb Hooper et al. 2020).

While the NASEM committee proposed using the SVI, a number of further indices exist that could be used in principle, which raises both practical and ethical issues around what clusters of disadvantage are captured, and in which geospatial areas (Schmidt et al. 2020a), For example the Multidimensional Deprivation Index integrates standard of living, education, health, economic security, housing quality, and neighborhood quality(Bureau 2017). There are also indices that combine SVI metrics with ones deemed particularly relevant for the pandemic context, such as the NIH's covid-19 Pandemic Vulnerability Index (National Institute of Environmental Health Sciences 2020). The Area Deprivation Index integrates 17 variables from the American Community Survey, that are grouped under the domains of income, education, employment, and housing quality, and has been developed specifically to inform health delivery and policy (Kind and Buckingham 2018). Unlike the SVI, that has the census tract as its geographical reference point, the ADI is focused on neighborhoods (termed block-group level by the Census Bureau) comprising between 600–3000 people (Similar to measures that have been used in Europe since the 1980s, the ADI captures more directly the impact of the social determinants on health see Schmidt et al. 2020a). The relevance of these indices is readily illustrated. For example, due to their age, two 70 year-old women are both at increased risk of dying from covid-19. But a well-off white suburban woman living only with her husband in a spacious house still faces a lower risk than a more disadvantaged inner-city Hispanic woman living in a crowed setting with multiple generations. Likewise, while both neurosurgeons and nurses are health workers, at work and at home, the former are at far less risk than the latter. Reflecting such differences therefore considerably improves fairness.

4.3 The Practical Implementation of Disadvantage Indices to Promote Social Justice

Helpfully, and innovatively, the NASEM report recognizes this in stipulating that—within each phase and priority group, worse-off populations should be offered vaccines before better off ones. In addition, the framework also recommended that indices such as the SVI be used to increasing the amount vaccines allocated to more disadvantaged groups. Specifically, it recommended that 10% of the total nationally available amount be reserved as additional allocations for populations in the worst-off quartiles (i.e., in addition to the allocations that these groups would have received based on population alone. NASEM also instructs stats to undertake additional "special efforts" to reach worse-off populations. (National Academies of Sciences, Engineering, and Medicine 2020).

Historically, in the case of pandemics, the US does not require that the same allocation framework be implemented in all states. Instead, the CDC's ACIP offers central, non-binding guidance to its administrative units that then develop specific binding guidance: 64 immunization grantees, referred to here collectively as jurisdictions (50 states, the District of Columbia, 5 large cities, and 8 territories). The CDC issued basic guidance on operational procedures in its Covid Playbook and requested its jurisdictions to provide initial allocation plans by the end of October, with the vast majority complying (Centers for Disease Control and Prevention (CDC) 2020a, b).

The first two vaccines received emergency use authorization in mid-December 2020; depending on how their evidence was evaluated, the ACIP released guidelines for the first allocation phase in the relevant jurisdictions at the end of December 2020, which also integrated previously published ethical guidelines (Dooling et al. 2020, McClung et al. 2020).

ACIP's framework differs from NASEM in the sequence of priority groups, and in how it seeks to promote equity otherwise, declining, in particular, the proposal of integrating disadvantage index in a similarly salient way (published guidance does not refer to the concept (Dooling et al. 2020; McClung et al. 2020). In terms of establishing priority groups, ACIP orders 7 population groups: first, healthcare personnel and long-term care facility residents (1a); second people older than 75 years along with frontline essential workers (1b); third people 65–74 years old, together with 16–64 year olds with high-risk medical conditions, and essential workers not deemed frontline workers (1c), see Dooling et al. 2020.

Yet, in January 2021, 28 states (Lucy Tompkins et al. 2020) began offering vaccines to people 65 and older alongside healthcare workers, and the national covid-19 strategy by the Biden Administration also endorsed this change and announced it would "work with states to open up vaccinations to more priority groups." (Office of the President 2021).

The reasons for this variation are not uniform. Two central ones are that demographic compositions differ across states (for example, one quarter of the US' population over 65 lives in California, Florida, and Texas(cf. Census Office 2021) and the share of disadvantaged people is not the same across states, but differs, with, for example 16 states having more than a quarter of their population in the nationwide most disadvantaged group, which can factor into decisions around the sequence of priority groups. Further, even when states are relatively similar, the tradeoffs associated with different scenarios often simply present dilemmas, and can therefore express different ways of balancing these tradeoffs. However, as the NASEM report illustrates, equitable allocation is not determined by the sequence of priority groups alone. In a review of jurisdictions' initial allocation plans, colleagues and I found several distinct uses of a disadvantage index to promote equity Schmidt et al. 2020b).

4.4 Four Main Uses of Disadvantage Indices to promote Social Justice

First, the most obvious use is for planning where to place dispensing sites so locations are easy to reach, especially for populations who may have less flexible working hours, informal caring obligations that make it difficult to spend several hours on a vaccine appointment, or transportation challenges. New Jersey already indicates it is doing this. This approach will also help plan locations for nontraditional sites for vaccinating Americans such as school gyms, sports stadiums, community centers, and mobile clinics that were announced under the Biden administration's national strategy. This use can also help more fully engage pharmacies, which are intended to be tapped to help with the vaccination effort: an index such as the ADI can enable mapping to the level of neighborhoods, and hence help ensure that people in more disadvantaged areas are not skipped over, in offering vaccines.(Schmidt et al. 2020b). Second, disadvantage indices can be used to plan outreach and communication strategies, something that Arizona, Vermont, and Washington are doing. Such efforts matter immensely: Vaccine dispensing sites are worth nothing if people don't use them, or don't trust them, perhaps because of patterns of unfair treatment in interactions with health care providers and government services. Working proactively with community groups in disadvantaged areas to determine easily reachable and trusted sites can help match supply with uptake among communities in greatest need. (Schmidt et al. 2020b). Third, an important way of promoting equity is to ensure that more vulnerable groups are offered larger shares of vaccines each time a state or city-level jurisdiction receives a new batch. Doing so reduces scarcity for these groups and means they can receive vaccines more quickly. In adapting the National Academies proposal for equitable allocation, planners in Massachusetts, New Hampshire, and Tennessee already adjust the number of vaccines shipped to allocation sites so more-vulnerable populations are offered more than they would have received based on numbers alone. This approach can also counteract the tendency of better-off and well-connected groups to work the system to their advantage. (Schmidt et al. 2020b). Fourth, each new vaccine shipment offers an important opportunity to monitor equitable allocation and course-correct, where needed, and in this sense, disadvantage indices can serve as a guiding compass for equitable distribution of Covid-19 vaccines. (Schmidt et al. 2020b).

Importantly, the national strategy recognizes this and instructs the CDC to "work with states and localities to update their pandemic plans to describe how they have or will provide equitable access to Covid-19 resources within highly vulnerable communities, including Tribal communities, using CDC's Social Vulnerability Index [SVI] or other indices as appropriate." (Office of the President 2021).

The Biden-Harris administration's commitments to allocate vaccines equitably and in ways that reduce disparities could not be more clear or timely. And it is encouraging that states as different as Ohio, Michigan and California have already committed to using indices for monitoring purposes, which can, and should be, adopted far more widely, and will help to dovetail the federal commitment towards equity with the range of innovative uses of the SVI and other indices in state-level allocations. Such an approach would become even more effective if the allocation formula to states would be revised from one that allocates vaccine proportionate to population, favored under the Tump administration's Health secretary as "fair, simple, and consistent" (Huang 2020) to one that adjusts for the share of a jurisdiction's disadvantage, which, as noted, is not equal across states. For example, in New Mexico. more than 3 in 10 people are in the nationwide worse-off group. But in New Hampshire, just over 1 in 10 is in this group. Allocating by population alone means that worse off groups, and particularly worse-off minorities, face more scarcity in states in which they account for a larger share of the population—but this is not their fault, and should be addressed through a distribution formula that reflects the unequal shares of disadvantaged populations. At the time of writing there is active consideration of this aspect. (Schmidt et al. 2020c).

On a final point, it is also important to appreciate the unique potential of disadvantage indices as a practical vehicle for navigating the intersection of racial and social justice. Justice does not require us to ensure that Barak Obama receives a Covid-19 vaccine before Bill Clinton, or Condoleezza Rice before Nancy Pelosi. Race is irrelevant here, as all four people can live equally safely until it is their turn to be vaccinated. Instead, justice requires us to respond to the fact that communities of color have been hit harder by Covid-19 because they account for larger shares of the nations' disadvantaged people which is due, in turn, to society being structured in ways that reduce their economic mobility and odds of leading long and healthy lives. Addressing equity through an index that measures a generalized concept of disadvantage therefore helps directly address the situation of worse-off populations but is not limited to race-based justice, and as such, it can avoid legal challenges and recognizes that disadvantage can take many different forms that matter independently. (Dasgupta et al. 2020; Karaye and Horney 2020; Karmakar et al. 2021; Robert Wood Johnson Foundation 2020; Webb Hooper et al. 2020).

5 Conclusion

Covid-19 has torn at the fabric of society in countless different ways. As this review sought to demonstrate, this included what might be described as a seismic shift in the rationing debate. While, in the frenzied efforts of coming to grips with the magnitude of the threat in Spring 2020, approaches that were centered on maximizing overall benefit relatively easily embedded themselves in the emerging policy framework, over the course of the year it became clear that more attention needed to be paid to the distribution of benefits, too. 'Colorblind', and disadvantage-blind allocation models that ignore the vastly disparate impact that the pandemic had on, especially, worse off minorities, risk becoming complicit in structures that, once again, systematically disadvantage worse-off populations. It is therefore encouraging that there is now an awakening to more fully integrate disadvantage metrics with primarily risk-based frameworks. (Dasgupta et al. 2020; Karaye and Horney 2020; Karmakar et al. 2021; Robert Wood Johnson Foundation 2020; Webb Hooper et al. 2020).

As difficult as it can be with the myriad of decisions that we are still facing right now, it is worth bearing in mind that covid-19 is a generation defining event, and, more likely, will have an impact lasting beyond just a single generation. So, when we look back at how, ultimately, we responded—whether in a decade, two, or later—there seem to be two basic options. The first is, that we find that even though there were efforts towards reducing, rather than maintaining, or increasing further equity, in the end, we failed. The other, that we really started to do what was long overdue, and that is to make real and measurable progress in reducing inequities in health, and economic mobility. For better or worse, Rudolf Virchow already observed some 170 years ago that "Medicine is a social science, and politics is nothing more than medicine on a grand scale" (Mackenbach 2009). History since then has show, that, collectively, we have been slow to act accordingly. As in many areas, progress is seldom linear, but proceeds in fits and starts, sometimes requiring major events for real and lasting reorientation. Hopefully a sliver lining in our current covid response will be that there will be fuller appreciation of the decades of work of colleagues in the field of social determinants of health, and a broader exploration of practical, yet meaningful measures such as disadvantage indices to improve more equitable access to scarce resources such as ventilators or vaccines, as well as healthcare more broadly.

Acknowledgements I am grateful to various co-authors for essential insights published in joint articles and also this chapter, as noted in the bibliography, in particular: Amaka Eneanya, Lawrence Gostin, Whitney Kerr, Parag Pathak, Dorothy Roberts, Tayfun Sönmez, Utku Ünver, Michelle Williams.

Postscript Parallel to the finalisation of the proofs, the final version of the review on the use of indices of disadvantage in the USA was published, cited in the text as Schmidt et al. 2020b. Among other things, the adoption of disadvantage indices has continued to expand (to 34 states as of the end of March 2021). For research, citation and related purposes, the following reference should therefore be used: Schmidt H, Weintraub R, Williams MA, Buttenheim A, Sadecki E, Wu H, Doiphode A, Gostin LO, Shen A. Equitable allocation of COVID-19 vaccines in the United States. Nature Medicine (2021). https://doi-org.proxy.library.upenn.edu/10.1038/s41591-021-01379-6 Online first May 18, 2021.

References

Antommaria A, Gibb T, McGuire A, Wolpe P, Wynia M, Applewhite M, Eberl J (2020) Ventilator triage policies during the COVID-19 pandemic at U.S. hospitals associated with members of the association of bioethics program directors. Ann Intern Med. https://doi-org.proxy.library.upenn.edu/10.7326/M20-1738

APM Research Lab (2020) The color of coronavirus: covid-19 deaths by race and ethnicity in the U.S. https://www.apmresearchlab.org/covid/deaths-by-race. Accessed 5 Mar 2021

Ashana DC, Anesi GL, Liu VX, et al (2021) Equitably Allocating Resources During Crises: Racial Differences in Mortality Prediction Models. American journal of respiratory and critical care medicine.

Bureau UC (2017) Multidimensional deprivation in the United States: 2017. https://www.census.gov/library/publications/2019/acs/acs-40.html. Accessed 5 Mar 2021

Census Bureau (2021) Population and housing unit estimates. https://www.census.gov/programs-surveys/popest.html. Accessed 5 Mar 2021

Centers for Disease Control and Prevention (CDC) (2013) CDC health disparities and inequalities report – United States, 2013. MMWR Morb Mortal Wkly Rep, 62

Centers for Disease Control and Prevention (CDC) (2020a) COVID-19 vaccination program interim playbook for COVID-19 vaccination program jurisdiction operations interim operational guidace, version 2.0

Centers for Disease Control and Prevention (CDC) (2020b) U.S. public health service syphilis study at Tuskegee. https://www.cdc.gov/tuskegee/index.html. Accessed 5 Mar 2021

Chapman C, Miller DeMond S (2020) From metaphor to militarized response: the social implications of "we are at war with COVID-19" – crisis, disasters, and pandemics yet to come. Int J Sociol Soc Policy 40(9/10):1107–1124. https://doi-org.proxy.library.upenn.edu/10.1108/IJSSP-05-2020-0163

Chapman E, Kaatz A, Carnes M (2013) Physicians and implicit bias: how doctors may unwittingly perpetuate health care disparities. J Gen Intern Med 28(11):1504–1510. https://doi-org.proxy.library.upenn.edu/10.1007/s11606-013-2441-1

Chomilo N, Heard-Garris N, DeSilva M, Blackstock U (2020) The harm of a colorblind allocation of scarce resources. https://www-healthaffairs-org.proxy.library.upenn.edu/do/10.1377/hblog20200428.904804/full/. Accessed 5 Mar 2021

City Health Dashboard (2020) New York city – metrics overview for New York, NY. https://www.cityhealthdashboard.com/ny/new%20york/city-overview?metric=837. Accessed 5 Mar 2021

Cobb R, Thorpe R, Norris K (2019) Everyday discrimination and kidney function among older adults: evidence from the health and retirement study. J Gerontol A 75(3):517–521. https://doi-org.proxy.library.upenn.edu/10.1093/gerona/glz294

Cuevas A, O'Brien K, Saha S (2016) African American experiences in healthcare: "I always feel like I'm getting skipped over". Health Psychol 35(9):987–995. https://doi-org.proxy.library.upenn.edu/10.1037/hea0000368

Dasgupta S, Bowen V, Leidner A, Fletcher K, Musial T, Rose C, Oster A (2020) Association between social vulnerability and a county's risk for becoming a COVID-19 hotspot – United States, June 1–July 25, 2020. MMWR Morb Mortal Wkly Rep 69(42):1535–1541. https://doi-org.proxy.library.upenn.edu/10.15585/mmwr.mm6942a3

Deutsche Interdisziplinäre Vereinigung für Intensiv- und Notfallmedizin (2020) Entscheidungen über die Zuteilung von Ressourcen in der Notfall und der Intensivmedizin im Kontext der COVID-19-Pandemie (Von den Fachgesellschaften verabschiedete Fassung vom 25.03.2020). https://www.divi.de/empfehlungen/leitlinien-intensivmedizin. Accessed 5 Mar 2021

Dooling K, McClung N, Chamberland M, Marin M, Wallac M, Bell BP, Oliver SE (2020) The advisory committee on immunization practices' interim recommendation for allocating initial supplies of COVID-19 vaccine – United States, 2020. MMWR Morb Mortal Wkly Rep 69(49):1857–1859. https://doi-org.proxy.library.upenn.edu/10.15585/mmwr.mm6949e1

Dummer P, Limou S, Rosenberg A, Heymann J, Nelson G, Winkler C, Kopp J (2015) APOL1 kidney disease risk variants: an evolving landscape. Semin Nephrol 35(3):222–236. https://doi-org.proxy.library.upenn.edu/10.1016/j.semnephrol.2015.04.008

Dwyer-Lindgren L, Bertozzi-Villa A, Stubbs R, Morozoff C, Mackenbach J, van Lenthe F, Murray C (2017) Inequalities in life expectancy among US counties, 1980 to 2014: temporal trends and key drivers. JAMA Intern Med 177(7):1003–1011. https://doi-org.proxy.library.upenn.edu/10.1001/jamainternmed.2017.0918

Economic Policy Institute (2020) Black workers face two of the most lethal preexisting conditions for coronavirus – racism and economic inequality. Washington, DC. https://www.epi.org/publication/black-workers-covid/. Accessed 5 Mar 2021

Emanuel E, Steinmetz A, Schmidt H (2018) Rationing and resource allocation in healthcare. Oxford University Press, Oxford

Emanuel E, Persad G, Upshur R, Thome B, Parker M, Glickman A, Phillips J (2020) Fair allocation of scarce medical resources in the time of Covid-19. N Engl J Med 382(21):2049–2055. https://doi-org.proxy.library.upenn.edu/10.1056/NEJMsb2005114

Feinstein M, Niforatos J, Hyun I, Cunningham T, Reynolds A, Brodie D, Levine A (2020) Considerations for ventilator triage during the COVID-19 pandemic. Lancet Respir Med 8(6):e53. https://doi-org.proxy.library.upenn.edu/10.1016/S2213-2600(20)30192-2

Fleischman L (2017) Fumes across the fence-line: the health impacts of air pollution from oil & gas facilities on African American communities. Boston Branch, Boston

Forde A, Sims M, Muntner P, Lewis T, Onwuka A, Moore K, Diez Roux A (2020) Discrimination and hypertension risk among African Americans in the Jackson Heart Study. Hypertension (online first, July 1, 2020). https://doi-org.proxy.library.upenn.edu/10.1161/HYPERTENSIONAHA.119.14492

Goldbaum C, Cook L (30 March 2020) They can't afford to quarantine. So they brave the subway. New York Times

Grewal GS (2020) Directive regarding non-prosecution of healthcare facilities and professionals Adhering to triage protocols during COVID-19 pandemic – Attorney general law enforcement directive no. 2020-03. State of New Jersey, Office of the Attorney General. Department of Law and Public Safety, Trenton

Grubbs V (2020) Precision in GFR reporting: let's stop playing the race card. Clin J Am Soc Nephrol. https://doi-org.proxy.library.upenn.edu/10.2215/CJN.00690120

Himmelstein D, Woolhandler S, Cooney R, McKee M, Horton R (2018) The Lancet commission on public policy and health in the Trump era. Lancet 392(10152):993–995. https://doi-org.proxy.library.upenn.edu/10.1016/S0140-6736(18)32171-8

Huang P (2020) Initial batch of COVID-19 vaccines will go to states based on population, not risk. NPR. https://www.npr.org/sections/health-shots/2020/11/24/938617836/initial-batch-of-covid-19-vaccines-will-go-to-states-based-on-population-not-risk. Accessed 5 Mar 2021

Jan T (28 March 2018) Redlining was banned 50 years ago. It's still hurting minorities today. The Washington Post

Karaye I, Horney J (2020) The impact of social vulnerability on COVID-19 in the U.S.: an analysis of spatially varying relationships. Am J Prev Med 59(3):317–325. https://doi-org.proxy.library.upenn.edu/10.1016/j.amepre.2020.06.006

Karmakar M, Lantz P, Tipirneni R (2021) Association of social and demographic factors with COVID-19 incidence and death rates in the US. JAMA Netw Open 4(1):e2036462. https://doi-org.proxy.library.upenn.edu/10.1001/jamanetworkopen.2020.36462

Khazanchi R, Evans C, Marcelin J (2020) Racism, not race, drives inequity across the COVID-19 continuum. JAMA Netw Open 3(9):e2019933. https://doi-org.proxy.library.upenn.edu/10.1001/jamanetworkopen.2020.19933

Kind A, Buckingham W (2018) Making neighborhood-disadvantage metrics accessible – the neighborhood atlas. N Engl J Med 378(26):2456–2458. https://doi-org.proxy.library.upenn.edu/10.1056/NEJMp1802313

Klebnikov S (2020) Cuomo: New York has only six days of ventilators left in stockpile (2. April 2020). Forbes

Lucy Tompkins A, Lee J, Ivory D, Smith M (2020) More than half of states widen access to vaccine, raising hopes as well as chaos (Published Jan. 15, 2021, Updated Jan. 28, 2021). New York Times. https://www.nytimes.com/2021/01/15/us/coronavirus-vaccine-states.html. Accessed 5 Mar 2021

Mackenbach J (2009) Politics is nothing but medicine at a larger scale: reflections on public health's biggest idea. J Epidemiol Community Health 63(3):181–184. https://doi-org.proxy.library.upenn.edu/10.1136/jech.2008.077032

Manchanda E, Couillard C, Sivashanker K (2020) Inequity in crisis standards of care. N Engl J Med. https://doi-org.proxy.library.upenn.edu/10.1056/NEJMp2011359

Maves R, Downar J, Dichter J, Hic J, Devereaux A, Geiling J, Christian M (2020) Triage of scarce critical care resources in COVID-19 an implementation guide for regional allocation: an expert panel report of the task force for mass critical care and the American College of Chest Physicians. Chest 158(1):212–225. https://doi-org.proxy.library.upenn.edu/10.1016/j.chest.2020.03.063

McClung N, Kinlaw K, Bowen Matthew D, Wallace M, Bell B, Lee G, Talbot H, Romero J, Oliver S, Dooling K (2020) The advisory committee on immunization practices' ethical principles for allocating initial supplies of COVID-19 vaccine – United States, 2020. MMWR Morb Mortal Wkly Rep 69:1782–1786. https://doi-org.proxy.library.upenn.edu/10.15585/mmwr.mm6947e3external

Miller WD, Han X, Peek ME, Charan Ashana D, Parker WF. Accuracy of the sequential organ failure assessment score for in-hospital mortality by race and relevance to crisis standards of care. JAMA Network Open. 2021;4(6):e2113891–e2113891.

Morris H, Mohan S (2020) Using race in the estimation of glomerular filtration rates: time for a reversal? Curr Opin Nephrol Hypertens 29(2):227–231. https://doi-org.proxy.library.upenn.edu/10.1097/MNH.0000000000000587

Nakao H, Ukail KJ (2017) A review of the history of the origin of triage from a disaster medicine perspective. Acute Med Surg 4(4):379–384. https://doi-org.proxy.library.upenn.edu/10.1002/ams2.293

National Academies of Sciences, Engineering, and Medicine (2020) A framework for equitable allocation of vaccine for the novel coronavirus. Washington, DC. https://www.nationalacademies.org/our-work/a-framework-for-equitable-allocation-of-vaccine-for-the-novel-coronavirus. Accessed 5 Mar 2021

National Center for Health Statistics (2019) Health, United States, 2018. Hyattsville, Maryland

National Institute of Environmental Health Sciences (2020) COVID-19 Pandemic Vulnerability Index (PVI). https://covid19pvi-niehs-nih-gov.proxy.library.upenn.edu. Accessed 5 Mar 2021

Nelson A (2002) Unequal treatment: confronting racial and ethnic disparities in health care. J Natl Med Assoc 94(8):666–668

Nelson A (2003) Unequal treatment: report of the Institute of Medicine on racial and ethnic disparities in healthcare. Ann Thorac Surg 76(4):S1377–S1381. https://doi-org.proxy.library.upenn.edu/10.1016/s0003-4975(03)01205-0

Nuffield Council on Bioethics (2020) Rapid policy brief: fair and equitable access to COVID-19 treatments and vaccines. https://www.nuffieldbioethics.org/assets/pdfs/Ethical-considerations-inresponding-to-the-COVID-19-pandemic. Accessed 5 Mar 2021

NYC Health (2021) COVID-19: data – by Borough. https://www1.nyc.gov/site/doh/covid/covid-19-data-totals.page#rates. Accessed 5 Mar 2021

O'Brien R, Neman T, Seltzer N, Evans L, Venkataramani A (2020) Structural racism, economic opportunity and racial health disparities: evidence from U.S. counties. SSM Popul Health 11:100564. https://doi-org.proxy.library.upenn.edu/10.1016/j.ssmph.2020.100564

Office of the President (2021) National strategy for the COVID-19 response and pandemic preparedness. https://www.whitehouse.gov/wp-content/uploads/2021/01/National-Strategy-for-the-COVID-19-Response-and-Pandemic-Preparedness.pdf. Accessed 21 Jan 2021

Omi M, Winant H (2014) Racial formation in the United States. Routledge, London

Piscitello G, Kapania E, Miller W, Rojas J, Siegler M, Parker W (2020) Variation in ventilator allocation guidelines by US state during the coronavirus disease 2019 pandemic: a systematic review. JAMA Netw Open 3(6):e2012606. https://doi-org.proxy.library.upenn.edu/10.1001/jamanetworkopen.2020.12606

Robert Wood Johnson Foundation (2020) [Online database] Life expectancy: could where you live influence how long you live? Last updated January 2020. https://www.rwjf.org/en/library/interactives/whereyouliveaffectshowlongyoulive.html?rid=0034400001rlscZAAQ&et_cid=1675803. Accessed 5 Mar 2021

Sabuced J, Alzate M, Hur D (2020) COVID-19 and the metaphor of war (COVID-19 y la metáfora de la guerra). Int J Soc Psychol 35(3):618–624. https://doi-org.proxy.library.upenn.edu/10.1080/02134748.2020.1783840

Schmidt H (2020a) Vaccine rationing and the urgency of social justice in the Covid-19 response. Hast Cent Rep 50(3):46–49. https://doi-org.proxy.library.upenn.edu/10.1002/hast.1113

Schmidt H (2020b) The way we ration ventilators is biased – not every patient has a fair chance. April 15, 2020, New York Times

Schmidt H, Pathak P, Sönmez T, Ünver M (2020a) Covid-19: how to prioritize worse-off populations in allocating safe and effective vaccines. BMJ 371:m3795. https://doi-org.proxy.library.upenn.edu/10.1136/bmj.m3795

Schmidt H, Weintraub R, Williams M, Buttenheim A, Sadecki E, Wu H, Doiphode A, Gostin L, Shen A(2020b) Equitable allocation of COVID-19 vaccines: an analysis of the initial allocation plans of CDC's jurisdictions with implications for disparate impact monitoring (December 1, 2020). SSRN: https://ssrn-com.proxy.library.upenn.edu/abstract=3740041. Accessed 21 Jan 2021

Schmidt H, Ünver U, Williams M, Pathak P, Sönmez T, Gostin L (2020c) Rationing safe and effective COVID-19 vaccines: allocating to states proportionate to population may undermine commitments to mitigating health disparities. SSRN Working Paper. https://papers-ssrn-com.proxy.library.upenn.edu/sol3/papers.cfm?abstract_id=3729069. Accessed 5 Mar 2021

Schmidt H, Roberts D, Eneanya N (2021) Rationing, racism and justice: advancing the debate around ‚colourblind' COVID-19 ventilator allocation. J Med Ethics. https://doi-org.proxy.library.upenn.edu/10.1136/medethics-2020-106856

Sederstrom N (2020) The „give back": is there room for it? http://www.bioethics.net/2020/07/the-give-backis-there-room-for-it/. Accessed 5 Mar 2021

Trotter G (2010) Sufficiency of care in disasters: ventilation, ventilator triage, and the misconception of guideline-driven treatment. J Clin Ethics 21(4):294–307. https://www.ncbi.nlm.nih.gov/pubmed/21313863. Accessed 21 Jan 2021

University of Pittsburgh, Department of Critical Care Medicine (2020a) A model hospital policy for allocating scarce critical care resources (version dated April 15). Available at: https://www.nytimes.com/2020/04/15/opinion/covid-ventilator-rationing-blacks.html_. Accessed 5 Mar 2021

University of Pittsburgh, Department of Critical Care Medicine (2020b) A model hospital policy for allocating scarce critical care resources. Available onlline now. https://ccm.pitt.edu/?q=↖content/model-hospital-policy-allocating-scarce-critical-care-resources-available-online-now. Accessed 5 Mar 2021

Vincent J, Moreno R, Takala J, Willatts S, De Mendonca A, Bruining H, Thijs L (1996) The SOFA (Sepsis-related Organ Failure Assessment) score to describe organ dysfunction/failure. On behalf of the Working Group on Sepsis-Related Problems of the European Society of Intensive Care Medicine. Intensive Care Med 22(7):707–710. https://doi-org.proxy.library.upenn.edu/10.1007/BF01709751

Wadhera R, Wadhera P, Gaba P, Figueroa J, Joynt Maddox K, Yeh R, Shen C (2020) Variation in COVID-19 hospitalizations and deaths across New York City Boroughs. JAMA. https://doi-org.proxy.library.upenn.edu/10.1001/jama.2020.7197

Webb Hooper M, Napoles A, Perez-Stable E (2020) COVID-19 and racial/ethnic disparities. JAMA 323(24):2466–2467. https://doi-org.proxy.library.upenn.edu/10.1001/jama.2020.8598

White D, Lo B (2020) A framework for rationing ventilators and critical care beds during the COVID-19 pandemic. JAMA 323(18):1773–1774. https://doi-org.proxy.library.upenn.edu/10.1001/jama.2020.5046

White D, Lo B (2021) Mitigating inequities and saving lives with ICU triage during the COVID-19 pandemic. Am J Respir Crit Care Med 203(3):287–295. https://doi-org.proxy.library.upenn.edu/10.1164/rccm.202010-3809CP

Wolff J, De-Shalit A (2007) Disadvantage. Oxford University Press, Oxford

Woolhandler S, Himmelstein D, Ahmed S, Bailey Z, Bassett M, Bird M, Venkataramani A (2021) Public policy and health in the Trump era. Lancet. https://doi-org.proxy.library.upenn.edu/10.1016/S0140-6736(20)32545-9

World Health Organization (2020a) Coronavirus disease (COVID-19). WHO, Genf. https://www-who-int.proxy.library.upenn.edu/news-room/q-a-detail/coronavirus-disease-covid-19. Accessed 5 Mar 2021

World Health Organization (2020b) WHO SAGE values framework for the allocation and prioritization of COVID-19 vaccination. WHO, Genf. https://apps-who-int.proxy.library.upenn.edu/iris/handle/10665/334299. Accessed 5 Mar 2021

World Health Organization (2020c) Resource allocation and priority-setting. WHO/RFH/20.2. WHO, Genf. https://www-who-int.proxy.library.upenn.edu/ethics/publications/ethics-covid-19-resource-allocation.pdf?ua=1. Accessed 5 Mar 2021

Yearby R, Mohapatra S (2020) Law, structural racism, and the COVID-19 pandemic. Journal of Law and the Biosciences (2020, Forthcoming), Saint Louis U. Legal Studies research paper no. 2020–08, Indiana University Robert H. McKinney School of Law research paper no. 2020-. SSRN working paper. https://papers-ssrn-com.proxy.library.upenn.edu/sol3/papers.cfm?abstract_id=3612824. Accessed 21 Jan 2021

Yudell M, Roberts D, DeSalle R, Tishkoff S (2016) Taking race out of human genetics. Science 351(6273):564–565. https://doi-org.proxy.library.upenn.edu/10.1126/science.aac4951

Vaccination Against Infectious Diseases—A Bioethical Debate in the Pandemic

Personal Responsibility and Social Responsibility

Christiane Druml

Contents

1 Introduction 121
1.1 Historical Aspects and Discourse on Voluntariness 122
2 The Right to Health—Vaccination and Ethics 123
2.1 Basics Using the Example of the Discussion in the Austrian Bioethics Commission on Measles Vaccination (2014/2015) 124
3 The Covid-19 Pandemic 126
3.1 Vaccine Debates in Times of a Pandemic 127
3.2 Placebo Control 128
3.3 "Human Challenge Trials" 128
4 Vaccination Requirement 130
4.1 Terminology 130
4.2 Healthcare Professionals 130
5 Information Responsibility, Conspiracy Theories and "Fake News" 131
6 Shortage of Vaccines—Prioritization 132
7 Immunity and the Exercise of Fundamental Rights in the Pandemic 133
8 Concluding Remarks 134
References 134

1 Introduction

Hardly any topic has triggered so many emotions in the months of the Corona pandemic as vaccination. Vaccinations, in addition to improvements in hygiene and general improvements in the health care system, are one of the greatest achievements of medicine, which have led to an increase in life expectancy, prosperity and social justice. Through vaccinations, the threat from many human-to-human

C. Druml (✉)
Medical University of Vienna, Vienna, Austria
e-mail: christiane.druml@meduniwien.ac.at

© The Author(s), under exclusive license to Springer-Verlag GmbH, DE, part of Springer Nature 2023

A. Reis et al. (eds.), *Pandemics and Ethics*,
https://doi.org/10.1007/978-3-662-66872-6_9

transmissible infectious diseases has been weakened or extinguished. Vaccinations are therefore among the measures that have saved the most lives of all medical interventions. They not only protect the individual, but also the community through collective defense ('herd immunity'). A correspondingly high vaccination rate can also contribute to the worldwide eradication of individual diseases, as the example of smallpox in 1979 shows.

It was already very early in the Corona pandemic that it became apparent that there would be no effective drugs, no antiviral 'magic bullet', for the treatment of Corona Virus Disease-19 (Covid-19) in the short term. This made it clear that containment of the pandemic would be most likely possible through an effective vaccination. Therefore, an unprecedented amount of money was spent worldwide to focus science on the development of effective vaccines—in the recent history probably unique. Previous vaccine development had usually taken more than five years; the reduced development time compared to previous vaccines was expected to be 18 months (see Gavi 2020).

Two essential factors then contributed to an unforeseen acceleration of the development, on the one hand a massive financial commitment, both from public funds and from the pharmaceutical industry, to support research internationally coordinated and bundled, on the other hand the large number of infected people, which made it possible to carry out the large clinical studies necessary for the development of vaccines in a short time. Just think back to SARS1, where drug development was made impossible by the extinction of the epidemic, because even promising drugs could not (any longer) be tested in clinical studies. However, research was stopped by the similarity of the then SARS-CoV virus with SARS-CoV-2, which unfortunately could have provided effective drugs and vaccines for the current pandemic (see Zhang et al. 2020).

Surprisingly, it has been possible to develop several vaccines in less than twelve months and to register them for general use, while complying with all quality and safety criteria, through this bundled effort. This is accompanied by a discussion, also fuelled by statements from politicians, scientists and ethicists, about vaccination in general and about a potential legal obligation of people to be vaccinated, an ***obligation to vaccinate.*** Vaccination has been an extremely emotionally charged topic for decades, if not since its introduction at the end of the eighteenth century; the current pandemic has flared up this discussion to an unprecedented intensity, with the term ***voluntary,*** also mantra-like repeated by politicians, at the centre of the controversy.

1.1 Historical Aspects and Discourse on Voluntariness

Discussions about a vaccination obligation have been very emotional for a long time and are as old as vaccination itself. If you look back in history, you can see that as early as the 18th century, a form of vaccination against smallpox—variolation—was common, which we owe to the English aristocrat Lady Mary Wortley

Montague in Europe. She had learned about this immunization against smallpox at the court in Constantinople in the Ottoman Empire, where her husband was ambassador of England, and brought it back to England. This form of vaccination, in which the secretion of people slightly infected with smallpox was incised into the skin of healthy people, which was supposed to lead to a mild form of the disease, also came to Vienna via the Dutchman Jan Ingen-Housz. At the request of Maria Theresa, he carried out his vaccination method in the Austrian hereditary lands from 1769. Maria Theresa apparently did not know that variolation had been practiced for decades in one of her provinces, Transylvania. From 1780, an annual "vaccination course" was held in a so-called "inoculation house". Only from 1801 were people vaccinated with the cowpox vaccine according to the method of Edward Jenner, thus the beginning of "vaccination".

Until Ingen-Housz began to vaccinate at the behest of the prince of the country, vaccination was not an issue in the hereditary lands, because a very powerful opponent of vaccination, Anton de Haen, held a chair at the University of Vienna and is considered one of the founders of clinical medicine. Even the French opponents of vaccination had based their arguments on his—just to illustrate an ambivalent situation between proponents and opponents, which is not a phenomenon of our time alone.

The great philosopher Immanuel Kant also belonged to the well-known opponents of vaccination (cf. Kordelas and Grond-Ginsbach 2000). Already at that time there were opponents of vaccination in most European countries, who had also organized themselves. Above all, there was great opposition in England, which led to a state enquiry into the scientificity of vaccination itself. Joseph II had already demanded the keeping of accurate death registers in the spirit of the Enlightenment in order to bring scientificity into the debate about vaccination and to increase the explanatory power of the numbers of people who died of smallpox in comparison to those who were saved by variolation.

At the beginning of the 19th century, an indirect compulsion to vaccinate children, especially by "reminding of their duties" of subjects, was applied, which was also proclaimed from the pulpits of the churches and could lead to consequences if it was not observed (cf. Lesky 1959). The smallpox vaccination was also introduced in Bavaria in 1807 and, shortly afterwards, in Baden, Württemberg and Kurhessen by means of compulsory vaccination of infants, which was supposed to bring about a health turnaround, since at that time around 80% of the population in Europe was infected with smallpox (cf. Meyer and Reiter 2004). In addition, the German Vaccination Act was introduced in 1874, which provided for the compulsory vaccination of all children.

2 The Right to Health—Vaccination and Ethics

The discussion about **vaccination** has—triggered by a postulated but refuted association of measles vaccination with the occurrence of autism (cf. Wakefield et al. 1998 retracted; Dyer 2010)—in the United States in recent decades assumed the character of highly emotional "wars of faith". This has also overflowed to Europe in recent years and initially affected measles vaccination here. In this context, the question of the welfare of the child became significant due to the lack of willingness of many parents to have their children vaccinated. Measles are not a harmless childhood disease, but are associated with complications and serious long-term consequences, such as severe cerebral damage leading to death.

2.1 Basics Using the Example of the Discussion in the Austrian Bioethics Commission on Measles Vaccination (2014/2015)

Inadequate measles vaccination is a phenomenon that has been visible in many countries and also in Austria in the last ten years and led to the Austrian Minister of Health's commission in April 2014 to the national bioethics commission to discuss the ethical aspects of vaccination (cf. Paules et al. 2019). The Austrian Bioethics Commission was founded by the Chancellor of the Republic of Austria in 2001; it consists of 25 independent scientists and advises the Chancellor on all ethical issues arising from the rapid development in the life sciences. Their statements are publicly available on the website of the Federal Chancellery.[1] For the declining willingness in an increasing part of the population, especially in industrial countries, to have themselves or their children vaccinated, various causes are responsible (cf. Larson 2018): On the one hand, the very low risk of side effects or complications is overestimated, on the other hand, world-view movements, such as the "back to nature" wave in some parts of the population, contribute to the fact that vaccinations against infectious diseases such as measles or influenza are not accepted to the extent they should be. Vaccination not only prevents the vaccinated person from acquiring a disease, but also protects others, such as those who cannot be vaccinated for health reasons (e.g. age, immunosuppression). For these, diseases that are considered harmless can develop much more dangerously, they can only be protected by building up collective immunity, ***herd immunity.***

Ultimately, vaccination leads to a *vaccination paradox,* so that vaccination becomes its own enemy through its successes: Through its effect, the diseases prevented by it are no longer visible and existent, for many also no longer known, so that the awareness of the dangers of these diseases is lacking and a vaccination is considered unnecessary. Many parents, whose healthy upbringing as children and adolescents was well protected by the earlier vaccinations, no longer have their own children vaccinated, the number of children who no longer receive basic vaccination is increasing sharply in industrial countries. In 2018, for example, about

[1] https://www.bundeskanzleramt.gv.at/themen/bioethikkommission.html. Accessed on 23.02.2021.

21,000 children between the ages of five and nine were completely unvaccinated (cf. Der Standard 2018). This discussion essentially concerns the conflict of interest between the welfare of the child, the right of parents to raise their children according to their ideas, and the question of vaccination as a social responsibility. Children have a right to the highest possible level of health, which the state must grant them by recognizing the UN Convention on the Rights of the Child. The United Nations, together with UNICEF, has stated that every child has a right to vaccinations against preventable diseases, which also includes the acceptance of any possible minor side effects of vaccination.

Ultimately, the Bioethics Commission came to uniform recommendations in its statement, which were placed under the motto ***Information—Motivation—Transparency*** and published in 2015. They concern the following aspects and can be seen as the basis for the discussions in all further dealings of the Commission with the topic of vaccination against human-to-human transmissible infectious diseases in comparison to a vaccination against Covid-19.

Central recommendations from 2015 are as follows (abridged):

- Demand for the creation of publicly accessible documentation on the benefits and side effects of vaccinations as well as on the cases of unvaccinated persons
- Publication of data from surveillance programs
- transparent information to parents about (free) child vaccination programs
- Strengthening of the relevant teaching content of the medical curricula of all health professions
- (obligatory) information to parents before their children enter daycare and school
- legal basis for school vaccination programs and their extension to kindergartens
- Vaccination as a professional requirement for personnel in health facilities in the sense of an ethical obligation in accordance with the non-harm principle on the basis of the recommendations of the National Vaccination Board; demand for a legal vaccination obligation due to the considerable risk potential (cf. Bioethics Commission 2015).

Although the discussion in 2014/2015 placed particular emphasis on the vulnerability of children and, above all, on the right of children to be protected from avoidable infectious diseases, the Bioethics Commission made the clearest demands with regard to the ethical obligations of health personnel in this statement. People in health professions are often not sufficiently protected and affected by infectious diseases that they can transmit to the people entrusted to them. They have contact with vulnerable people who are particularly at risk of contracting infections because they are already confronted with an existing underlying disease or cannot be vaccinated themselves. In the statement of the Bioethics Commission, which deals mainly with measles, the interference with autonomy, which a vaccination obligation represents, is justified by the protection of the public. With measles, a collective immunity must be achieved, which is to be seen as a ***public good.*** As many or all people should contribute to this herd immunity so that as many people as possible are then protected.

The World Health Organization's (WHO) efforts to eradicate measles—like smallpox in 1979—have been setback over the years, as reflected in Austria by increased infection rates, prompting the Bioethics Commission in May 2019 to unanimously call for not only health personnel, but also, from an ethical perspective, all people to be vaccinated. The following argument was put forward for this obligation (press release of the Bioethics Commission of 8 May 2019):

The proportionality of the measures is decisive for the obligation to vaccinate:

> The less harmful the intervention is for the individual, the 'more dangerous' the disease is for the health of the population and the greater the benefit of a vaccination obligation in general, the more justified the intervention appears to be in the physical integrity of the individual. For the current situation, the Bioethics Commission sees the proportionality in measles to be maintained and therefore calls for a general obligation to vaccinate. The Bioethics Commission calls for any possible extension of the vaccination obligation to be evidence-based and regularly reviewed. (Bioethics Commission 2019)
>
> Unlike in Austria, where the Bioethics Commission's recommendation for a vaccination obligation has not been implemented in national legislation, Germany has regulated a vaccination obligation for children from the age of one and for health personnel and teachers with the Measles Protection Act 2020. In nine other European countries—Bulgaria, Croatia, Czech Republic, France, Hungary, Italy, Poland, Slovakia and Slovenia—a measles vaccination is also required (see Attwell et al. 2018).

In Austria, with the exception of the smallpox vaccination, which was abolished in 1980 (BGBl. 1980/583), there has never been a compulsory vaccination. It is currently possible, on the basis of § 17 para. 3 Epidemics Act, to order vaccinations for doctors, nurses and midwives in the event of a pandemic; more on this later.

3 The Covid-19 Pandemic

Since the World Health Organization (WHO) became aware of cases of a new lung inflammation of unknown origin in the Chinese city of Wuhan on 31 December 2019, caused by a new coronavirus (SARS-CoV-2), events and statements have been piling up. As early as 30 January 2020, WHO Director-General Tedros Adhanom Ghebreyesus declared the outbreak of the new coronavirus to be "a public health emergency of international concern" (WHO 2020a), the highest warning level of the WHO. Due to the rapid increase in infections outside China, the WHO Director-General declared the outbreak an official pandemic on 11 March 2020 (see WHO 2020b).

Corona hit the world in a situation of unpreparedness. Although the WHO, but also experts like Anthony Fauci, director of the National Institute of Allergy and Infectious Diseases, NIAID, and even Bill Gates have been warning of a pandemic for years (see Gates 2015), the threat was not taken seriously. Epidemics—so the general opinion—take place far away in the rainforest (like Ebola) or South America (Zika). Guidelines for the management of infectious disease outbreaks had a greater focus on these diseases than on those that can affect the south as well as the north (see WHO 2016).

This, although dangerous new infectious diseases ("Emerging Infectious Diseases") have already occurred mainly in densely populated regions such as Western Europe, on the coasts of the United States or China, and less in the rainforest.

In addition, the world has proven to be very vulnerable to globalization, characterized by worldwide travel and the worldwide **division of labor** in the production of consumer goods to drugs. This vulnerability affected both the containment of the disease and the dependencies in the provision of essential consumer goods and necessary drugs, as can be seen in the example of antibiotics or even heparin, the latter of which was produced in China to 80% for reasons of insufficient profit margin and lack of production in Europe (see Vilanova et al. 2019).

Since the beginning of the pandemic, we have been confronted with new challenges as well as classical ethical problems on a weekly basis (cf. Druml 2020). These included the following questions:

- How can effective medications and therapies be found?
- How can a global shortage of protective clothing be remedied?
- How do I generate evidence for protective measures (e.g. masks)?
- How and when can an intervention in basic rights be justified (e.g. personal freedoms and mobility, right to education, employment, right to data protection)?
- How can the risk of misinformation be prevented as part of conspiracy theories and 'fake news'?
- How do I solve medical dilemmas in times of scarcity when there is a shortage of medical resources (e.g. medical protective clothing, **triage** in intensive care)?

And above all: How can the topic of 'vaccination under the difficult conditions of a pandemic' be discussed objectively?

3.1 *Vaccine Debates in Times of a Pandemic*

At the beginning of the pandemic, in addition to the search for effective antiviral drugs, the hope was nourished for a soon-to-be natural group immunity, which quickly turned out to be a dead end, as this would have been associated with extremely high rates of hospitalization and also deaths, and the health system of every country would have been overwhelmed. Even nations that initially followed this plan, i.e. keeping structures open while simultaneously accepting higher death rates, such as England or Sweden, have abandoned this strategy in the further course of the pandemic (see Lindström 2020). After some setbacks in terms of initially promising drugs, such as Remdesivir, ultimately the expectations of an efficient pandemic control rested on the development of an effective and safe vaccine that could bring people's lives back to more normal conditions.

By now, almost 200 different Corona vaccines are under development, at least 89 preclinical vaccines are in the stage of animal testing and, as of January 28, 2021, 67 of these vaccines are in clinical trials on humans; 20 vaccines have already reached the final stages of testing (phase 3 of drug development). Ten vaccines are currently approved or in various stages of registration.[2] The vaccines are developed on different bases, such as on the basis of mRNA, on the basis of viral vectors or DNA and others.

3.2 *Placebo Control*

For the development of vaccines—as for other drugs—randomized controlled clinical trials are indispensable. The efficacy of a vaccine candidate, since there is no standard vaccination against Covid-19 and thus no withholding of an effective vaccine, is tested against a sham vaccination, a placebo. As a rule, when several drugs are being studied for the same indication and one of them already receives approval, all other drugs are then tested against the already approved drug—as the "current standard drug"—and no longer against the placebo, since this would no longer be scientifically or ethically justified.

In a critical situation like the Corona pandemic, however, there are good reasons to deviate from this rule, above all in order to be able to produce the enormous demand of many hundreds of millions of doses of the vaccine for the whole world. A large part of humanity needs a vaccine against Covid-19, so that a wide range of different vaccines is desirable, with vaccines that are easier to handle, transport, cheaper or more effective for individual different groups of the population.

Another reason to continue to allow placebo controls as a comparison (which neither affects the efficacy nor the safety of a vaccine), is the time factor, since vaccines have to be developed as quickly as possible without any time loss. A possible solution to this problem of the control group is to inform all participants of a placebo-controlled study about this and to promise them that, if they were randomized to the placebo group, they will receive an effective vaccination after the study has been completed (cf. Wendler et al. 2020).

3.3 *"Human Challenge Trials"*

Another ethical question that was particularly discussed in spring 2020 is in relation to 'Human Challenge Trials'; these are studies on healthy volunteers who are

[2] https://www.nytimes.com/interactive/2020/science/coronavirus-vaccine-tracker.html. Accessed on 23.02.2021.

deliberately infected with the virus under strictly controlled conditions in order to accelerate the development of an effective vaccine. This special type of clinical trial has, for example, been used in the development of a vaccine against malaria (see Metzger et al. 2019). For Covid-19 there was the initiative "1 Day Sooner" from Harvard,[3] and in October 2020 plans for such studies were published in the United Kingdom. The scientific background here is to divide the participants into two groups; one group could be immunized with the experimental vaccine, the other would receive a placebo and, during a subsequent targeted infection, it could quickly become apparent whether the vaccine had worked or not (see Plotkin and Caplan 2020).

Such studies are obviously problematic from an ethical point of view and only very rarely to be recommended. The central argument for such studies is the possibility of acquiring knowledge about the disease itself and the effectiveness of a possible vaccine very quickly. The disadvantages are clear: with SARS-CoV-2 it is an infection often associated with severe course of the disease and potentially also with fatal complications, for which it is not foreseeable who—even in the absence of individual risk factors—will become more seriously ill or not. For such studies, a secure implementation with intensive monitoring and the preceding information and clarification of the subjects about their potential danger is essential. For these reasons, such study concepts were not used for Covid-19 (see Kirby 2020). However, in February 2021 such a study was approved by an ethics committee in the United Kingdom for 90 healthy volunteers aged 18 to 30 years.[4]

In general, all vaccine development has in common that, during a pandemic, special requirements are placed on the breadth (age, ethnicity) of the population groups included in the studies. In the end, data must be available for all age groups and ethnic groups that can be vaccinated. The tested populations must be representative—otherwise the principle of fairness that everyone should share in the progress of science would not be fulfilled. Just as different ethnic populations must be studied, all age groups, as well as men and women of childbearing age and people with pre-existing conditions must be included in studies. These are demands that must be met not only from a scientific, but also from an ethical point of view. The ethics committees that approve the conduct of the studies and the responsible authorities must continuously control these basics.

The inclusion of women in clinical studies is a much-discussed topic. Women are still underrepresented because of their childbearing ability and the risks associated with it for the fetus. Practically no data have been collected for pregnant women, as they have not been included in studies due to their vulnerability (see Beigi 2021).

---

[3] www.1daysooner.org. Accessed on 23.02.2021.

[4] See https://ukcovidchallenge.com/;https://www.gov.uk/government/news/worlds-first-coronavirus-human-challenge-study-receives-ethics-approval-in-the-uk. Accessed on 23.02.2021.

4 Vaccination Requirement

4.1 Terminology

The term **'vaccination requirement'** needs to be clarified linguistically: everyone understands something different under this term, and some think that the term vaccination requirement signifies 'compulsory vaccination' by state compulsion. But 'vaccination requirement' can include many things, such as a professional requirement, a requirement for entry into a country or participation in a school event. As the legislature stipulates in the Epidemics Act, it may be a vaccination protection that is imposed as a prerequisite for a certain activity and is intended to prevent a risk—to the affected persons themselves but above all to third parties. The effort to eradicate smallpox was implemented by a vaccination requirement and finally achieved in 1979.

In its statement of November 2020 on the 'Ethical Questions of a Vaccination against Covid-19', the Austrian Bioethics Commission devoted itself to this term on the occasion in question and suggested that the terminology be fundamentally reconsidered in order to avoid misunderstandings here through clarity of language (see Bioethics Commission 2020b). Language influences our thinking and thus our actions and often leads to inexplicable decisions in the emotionally heated area of vaccination.

4.2 Healthcare Professionals

There is considerable skepticism and rejection of vaccinations among employees in the health care sector. From an ethical perspective, the responsibility of those employed in the health care sector is manifold:

People employed in the health care sector, that is, doctors and nurses, care staff, physiotherapists, but also midwives, medical and technical professions and all those who have to do with vulnerable patients, have a guarantor position to these people entrusted to them. Their right to self-determination can be restricted for the benefit of the community. They must do everything in their power to avoid damage caused by the spread of a disease. This duty not only affects those who work in the profession, but also the legal entity of the institution in which they work, for example the hospital.

The autonomy of the individual and the right to privacy (Article 8 of the European Convention on Human Rights) do not stand in opposition to this, as the vulnerability of patients must also be protected and the interference with the basic rights of the staff must therefore be justified, necessary and, above all, proportionate: the interference with private life is negligible—only a short sting—the benefit is—with a low risk of serious side effects—great, both for the individual and for public health.

Carrier institutions also have organizational and protective duties and must ensure that patients do not suffer any health risks from the staff of the institution. In addition, it can be assumed that the members of the health professions were already aware of these requirements when they chose their profession. Here it is about the autonomy of the individual, but the non-damage principle stands in direct tension with it, as it is to be seen as an essential part of medical and nursing ethics.

In addition, the credibility of the health care staff is no longer given when they reject vaccinations, as they are "role models" for preventive medicine. The potential for harm posed by unvaccinated staff is great. Patients have a legitimate trust that they will not be exposed to any additional health risks in a medical facility; therefore, a legal vaccination obligation for such groups of people would be justified.

The new vaccines developed specifically for the Corona pandemic now have the disadvantage, in comparison to an established and long-term tested vaccine, such as the measles vaccine, that they were only developed and approved recently, so that we cannot look back on long-term experience and do not yet fully know some aspects of their properties. For example, there is currently a discussion about how much the vaccinations, in addition to protecting the vaccinated person from illness, also prevent infection of others, whether they have a "sterilizing" effect, for example. However, the question is whether the reduced virus load in vaccinated people also leads to a reduction in infections.

The vaccines that have been approved so far are trustworthy because the European Medicines Agency (EMA) guarantees a high-quality approval process and, as part of pharmacovigilance, sufficient data is collected and evaluated after approval, even with an initially "conditional" approval, in order to be able to detect any negative effects of the new vaccines as quickly as possible. It should be emphasized that even with this accelerated approval process, no compromises or compromises have been made with regard to the efficacy, quality and safety of the vaccines.

5 Information Responsibility, Conspiracy Theories and "Fake News"

Today, the Internet and social media are driving a general skepticism towards scientific facts and, as a result, vaccination. This is about conspiracy theories, myths, "fake news" and other misinformation. This is also an ethical issue because these false and selective statements can cause damage by preventing people from being protected and because they undermine efforts to get a pandemic under control as quickly as possible. Conspiracy theories are not a special characteristic of a pandemic, but are fueled by it. The legislature has the moral obligation to counter this with transparent and scientifically sound information. It is not just about the false information itself, but rather about the underlying intention of the authors of these messages to influence people in certain directions. Disinformation is one of the most pressing issues of our time.

It is essential to strengthen knowledge about vaccinations, to inform the population in a clear and understandable way and from reliable sources that are recognizable as such about the benefits and possible side effects of vaccinations, as well as to make the scientific basis for the development of vaccination programs and the conditions for access to immunization ("prioritization") available (cf. Johnson et al. 2020).

6 Shortage of Vaccines—Prioritization

The newly developed vaccines will be available at different times depending on when they are approved, as the industry has already started production in parallel with the approval process. At the end of 2020, the beginning of 2021, the vaccines from BioNTech/Pfizer and Moderna became available in the European Union under a conditional approval. The vaccination started on Sunday, December 27, 2020, in a coordinated action within the European Union. However, the demand for the vaccine exceeded the supply, so that the individual countries were confronted with a shortage, which led to medical, ethical and legal questions of prioritization.

Corona mainly affects people over the age of 65; the mortality rate increases sharply from 65 onwards, while in contrast to influenza, children and adolescents do get sick, but are hardly characterized by severe cases. Therefore, in clinical studies, people over the age of 16 or 18 were only included in the first step, unlike with the swine flu A/H1N1, for which the vaccine Pandemrix was developed as part of the swine flu pandemic, which mainly threatened children and young adults, for whom there were cases of suspected narcolepsy (see Nohynek et al. 2012); an argument that was repeatedly put forward in relation to potential risks of a quickly developed Covid-19 vaccine (see Karlsson et al. 2021).

In Germany, the issue of priorities was dealt with in a joint statement by the Standing Vaccination Commission at the Robert Koch Institute with the German Ethics Council and the National Academy of Sciences Leopoldina. Nevertheless, the Ordinance on Vaccination Priorities of the Federal Ministry of Health has made further differentiation. In Austria, too, the Bioethics Commission, parallel to the National Vaccination Commission, has published a recommendation on the priority guidelines, as well as on any effects of the individual's vaccination status on the exercise of fundamental rights (see Bioethics Commission 2020a). On 4 February 2021, the German Ethics Council issued a statement on the latter (see German Ethics Council 2021).

The priorities were generally guided by the idea of avoiding hospitalizations and deaths. The principle of 'helping the helpers', which means vaccinating health care workers first, is generally implemented and relies on avoiding damage: in many countries, doctors and nurses, as well as members of the nursing profession, have suffered an almost unimaginable number of illnesses and deaths as a result of the Corona pandemic (see Bandyopadhyay et al. 2020). In Austria, too, members of the health professions can be vaccinated compulsorily in accordance with the Austrian Epidemics Act, which provides an indication of the relevance of such a ranking.

In Austria, too, the most vulnerable of the older and very old people, especially those who are accommodated in institutions, were ranked together with the health care staff in the first vaccination priority.

The following principles are particularly relevant for prioritization: the autonomy of the individual with his or her desire to be protected; the beneficence principle with regard to the individual willing to be vaccinated and the principle of care with regard to the other people in relation to the vaccinated person, as well as finally the principle of care for society as a whole.

7 Immunity and the Exercise of Fundamental Rights in the Pandemic

Since the successful development of vaccines against Covid-19 was foreseeable, an increasingly emotionally charged discussion about the possible effects of immunity or the individual's vaccination status on the restriction of fundamental rights, in particular freedom of movement and respect for private life, has taken place. The question at stake here is whether, with the vaccination the conditions for interfering with their fundamental rights have been eliminated for the vaccinated. A question that cannot be finally answered at the moment, as the vaccination situation in EU countries is rather characterized by a shortage. Nevertheless, it should be mentioned here that, with the increasing number of vaccinated people, the restrictions on fundamental rights, such as quarantine, and isolation, are to be increasingly withdrawn. It is not a question of whether the population has "understanding" for the individual withdrawal of the measures or whether they find them "unjust" (cf. Deutscher Ethikrat 2021). The vaccination is not a "reward" or a "privilege", but a return to a normal time, in which it is even necessary to reduce and end state interventions in private life. If mild restrictions such as wearing masks, social distancing and hygiene measures have to take place for the next few months—if only because it cannot be recognized until the actual end of the pandemic whether the person sitting in the city bus without a mask is vaccinated or is opposed to the state measures. In order to avoid this demoralization of society, clear rules for self-protection and protection of fellow human beings are necessary. Monopolists, such as state transport companies or others, are subject to a duty to contract and may not discriminate between users, which private companies, which do not have a monopoly position, can and will probably do in the interests of safety and thus greater attractiveness for consumers. However, the greater freedom of the vaccinated is limited by the practicability of the control until the end of the pandemic. A control seems to be possible only with such measures, which are more complex, like the purchase of tickets for cultural events or, for example, the issuance of ship's passports or air tickets (2020).

Especially for those people who had to suffer greatly from the fundamental rights restrictions, such as people in nursing homes who were isolated for a long time and were only allowed very little social contact in order to avoid exposing them to the risk of infection, the withdrawal of the fundamental rights restrictions is required after successful immunization, all the more so as the constantly increasing possibilities of testing also the external visit of family members and friends can be controlled.

8 Concluding Remarks

Vaccination is a prime example of how humans should orient their lives in society according to the principles of solidarity, justice, and the common good. Our possibilities for individual self-determination, which we have achieved through social and medical progress, must not be used arbitrarily and entirely at random; responsible action remains bound to social responsibility. This also includes the possible individual responsibility for the elimination of avoidable suffering in society, as caused by a pandemic.

The pandemic has not only led to the most severe and diverse health problems of individual people as "collateral damage", but has also severely impaired the health care of non-Covid patients. It has not only posed great organizational and logistical problems for the health care system, but has also had massive consequences for economy, culture, and our coexistence in society as a whole. The **Generational Contract** and inclusion were called into question.

Vaccination is a key measure to not only secure the health of the individual, but to avert these dramatic consequences for our community and to enable us to lead a "normal" life again. The possible side effects and complications of a vaccination are in no way proportionate to the enormous benefit for the vaccinated person themselves, but also for our society. From an ethical point of view, it must be demanded that as many people as possible be vaccinated and that action be taken globally by ensuring a fair distribution of vaccines for all people around the world. A demand that can only be implemented in solidary cooperation of all countries.

References

Attwell K, Navin MC, Lopalco PL, Jestin C, Reiter S, Omer SB (2018) Recent vaccine mandates in the United States, Europe and Australia: a comparative study. Vaccine 36(48):73777384

Bandyopadhyay S, Baticulon RE, Kadhum M et al (2020) Infection and mortality of healthcare workers worldwide from COVID-19: a systematic review. BMJ Glob Health 5:e003097. https://doi.org/10.1136/bmjgh-2020-003097

Beigi RH et al (2021) The need for inclusion of pregnant women in COVID-19 vaccine trials. Vaccine 39(6):868

Bioethikkommission (2015) Impfen ethische Aspekte. https://www.bundeskanzleramt.gv.at/themen/bioethikkommission/publikationen-bioethik.html. Accessed 23 Feb 2021

Bioethikkommission (2019) Stellungnahme der Bioethikkommission zum Impfen. https://www.bundeskanzleramt.gv.at/themen/bioethikkommission/pressemitteilungen-bioethik/stellungnahme-der-bioethikkommission-zum-impfen.html. Accessed 23 Feb 2021

Bioethikkommission (2020a) Versorgung der Bevölkerung mit dem Influenza-Impfstoff in der Saison 2020/21. https://www.bundeskanzleramt.gv.at/themen/bioethikkommission/publikationen-bioethik.html. Accessed 23 Feb 2021

Bioethikkommission (2020b) Ethische Fragen einer Impfung gegen COVID-19. https://www.bundeskanzleramt.gv.at/themen/bioethikkommission/publikationen-bioethik.html. Accessed 23 Feb 2021

Der Standard (2018) In Österreich wird „zu spät und zu wenig geimpft". https://www.derstandard.at/story/2000089390748/in-oesterreich-wird-zu-spaet-und-zu-wenig-geimpft. Accessed 23 Feb 2021

Deutscher Ethikrat (2021) besondere Regeln für Geimpfte? Ad-hoc Empfehlung. https://www.ethikrat.org/publikationen/kategorie/ad-hoc-empfehlungen/. Accessed 23 Feb 2021

Druml C (2020) COVID-19 and ethical preparedness?. Wien Klin Wochenschr 132(13):400402

Dyer C (2010) Lancet retracts Wakefield's MMR paper. BMJ 340:c696

Gates B (2015) The next epidemic – lessons from Ebola. N Engl J Med 372(S):13811384

Gavi (2020) A COVID-19 vaccine might be ready within 18 months. But what happens then?. https://www.gavi.org/vaccineswork/covid-19-vaccine-might-be-ready-within-18-months-what-happens-then. Accessed 23 Feb 2021

Johnson NF, Velásquez N, Restrepo NJ, Leahy R, Gabriel N, El Oud S, Lupu Y et al (2020) The online competition between pro-and anti-vaccination views. Nature 582(7811):230233

Karlsson LC, Soveri A, Lewandowsky S, Karlsson L, Karlsson H, Nolvi S, Antfolk J et al (2021) Fearing the disease or the vaccine: the case of COVID-19. Pers Individ Differ 172:110590

Kirby T (2020) COVID-19 human challenge studies in the UK. Lancet Respir Med 8(12):e96

Kordelas L, Grond-Ginsbach C (2000) Kant über die „moralische Waghälsigkeit" der Pockenimpfung. NTM 8:2233

Larson HJ (2018) The state of vaccine confidence. Lancet 392(10161):22442246

Lesky E (1959) Österreichisches Gesundheitswesen im Zeitalter des aufgeklärten Absolutismus. In: Archiv für österreichische Geschichte. R M Rohrer, Wien

Lindström M (2020) The COVID-19 pandemic and the Swedish strategy: epidemiology and postmodernism. SSM Popul Health 11:100643

Metzger WG, Ehni HJ, Kremsner PG, Mordmüller BG (2019) Experimental infections in humans – historical and ethical reflections. Tropical Med Int Health 24(12):13841390

Meyer C, Reiter S (2004) Impfgegner und Impfskeptiker. Bundesgesundheitsbl-Gesundheitsforsch-Gesundheitsschutz 47(12):11821188

Nohynek H, Jokinen J, Partinen M, Vaarala O, Kirjavainen T, Sundman J, Kilpi T et al (2012) AS03 adjuvanted AH1N1 vaccine associated with an abrupt increase in the incidence of childhood narcolepsy in Finland. PLoS One 7(3):e33536

Paules CI, Marston HD, Fauci AS (2019) Measles in 2019 going backward. N Engl J Med 380(23):21852187

Plotkin SA, Caplan A (2020) Extraordinary diseases require extraordinary solutions. Vaccine 38(24):39873988

Ständige Impfkommission beim Robert Koch-Institut, Deutscher Ethikrat, Nationale Akademie der Wissenschaften Leopoldina (2020) Wie soll der Zugang zu einem COVID-19-Impfstoff geregelt werden? https://www.leopoldina.org/publikationen/detailansicht/publication/wie-soll-der-zugang-zu-einem-covid-19-impfstoff-geregelt-werden-2020/. Accessed 23 Feb 2021

Vilanova E, Tovar AMF, Mourao PAS (2019) Imminent risk of a global shortage of heparin caused by the African Swine Fever afflicting the Chinese pig herd. J Thromb Haemost 17(2):254–256

Wakefield AJ, Murch SH, Anthony A, Linnell J, Casson DM, Malik M, Berelowitz M, Dhillon AP, Thomson MA, Harvey P, Valentine A, Davies SE, Walker-Smith JA (1998) Ileal-lymphoid-nodular hyperplasia, non-specific colitis, and pervasive developmental disorder in children. Lancet 351(9103):637641 RETRACTED

Wendler D, Ochoa J, Millum J, Grady C, Taylor HA (2020) COVID-19 vaccine trial ethics once we have efficacious vaccines. Science 370(6522):12771279

WHO (2016) Guidance for managing ethical issues in infectious disease outbreaks. https://apps.who.int/iris/bitstream/handle/10665/250580/9789241549837-eng.pdf;jsessionid=06F65C795DA936FDBF476BEE979030F2?sequence=1. Accessed 23 Feb 2021

WHO (2020a) 2019-nCoV-Ausbruch zur gesundheitlichen Notlage von internationaler Tragweite erklärt. https://www.euro.who.int/de/health-topics/health-emergencies/pages/news/news/2020/01/2019-ncov-outbreak-is-an-emergency-of-international-concern. Accessed 23 Feb 2021

WHO (2020b) Pandemie der Coronavirus-Krankheit (COVID-19). https://www.euro.who.int/de/health-topics/health-emergencies/coronavirus-covid-19/novel-coronavirus-2019-ncov. Accessed 23 Feb 2021

Zhang H, Penninger JM, Li Y, Zhong N, Slutsky AS (2020) Angiotensin-converting enzyme 2 (ACE2) as a SARS-CoV-2 receptor: molecular mechanisms and potential therapeutic target. Intensive Care Med 46(4):586590

Immunity and Vaccination Certificates in the Covid-19 Crisis

Ethical and Legal Problems of a Possible Need for Differentiation

Steffen Augsberg

Contents

1 Problem Overview: Why Individual Freedom of Choice is Important 137
2 Epistemic and Risk-Ethical Foundations 139
2.1 Epistemological Assessment 139
2.2 Normative Framework 140
3 Weighing Opportunities and Risks 142
3.1 Opportunities 142
3.2 Risks 143
3.3 Criteria and Methods for Weighing Up 143
4 Regulatory Requirements 144
4.1 Flexible, Self-Reflective Regulation 144
4.2 In Particular: Complementary (test) Procedures 145
4.3 Special Situations: Differential Treatment Carried Out by Private Individuals and State Travel Conditions 145
5 Final Considerations: Accountability as a Permanent Challenge 146
References 146

1 Problem Overview: Why Individual Freedom of Choice is Important

After about a year of "corona crisis", it became clear that even very strict and comprehensive hygiene protection measures alone were not enough to return to at least a tolerable (proto-)normality. From this insight, the hopes associated with the different Covid-19 vaccines gain their special importance. We know now (and could and probably should have known much earlier) that the vaccinations do not significantly reduce infectivity. At the time, though, and under the given circumstances

S. Augsberg (✉)
University of Giessen, Giessen, Germany
e-mail: Steffen.Augsberg@recht.uni-giessen.de

© The Author(s), under exclusive license to Springer-Verlag GmbH, DE, part of Springer Nature 2023

A. Reis et al. (eds.), *Pandemics and Ethics*,
https://doi.org/10.1007/978-3-662-66872-6_10

it was not unreasonable to assume that this was the case. Furthermore, because with the vaccinations it is highly probable that at least severe or even fatal courses of the disease can be avoided, they act against an overload of the health system and the resulting, society-wide problematic "domino effect". As far as this is the central, if not the decisive justification for the far-reaching and serious infection protection-based restrictions on freedom (cf. German Ethics Council 2020a, 2021), it must be considered whether and to what extent these—especially in view of already existing and future "collateral damage" (cf. Nicola et al. 2020)—may still be maintained. The general argument of epidemic control is not enough for this. In order to avoid a "operation successful, patient dead!" scenario, a balanced approach is required that reflects and monitors the legitimately pursued goals as well as the intended and unintended consequences on a continuous basis. Complete eradication of Sars-CoV-2 is not a realistic and situation-appropriate purpose in this sense: Whoever demands this underestimates the expected practical difficulties, both with regard to the unavoidable and desired international contacts in open societies and with regard to the possible pathogen reservoir in the animal kingdom. At the same time and above all, such an absolutization of infection control would only be possible at the price of numerous additional, massive impairments of freedom and health. In the end, this would lead to an authoritarian biopolitical scheme that could only achieve its goal of saving lives (or more precisely: life years) at the price of endangering and sacrificing essential moral and legal rights up to and including life. This is neither ethically nor legally acceptable. Therefore, the restrictions applicable to the general population are to be lifted step by step to the extent that the (primary) goal of preventing severe and fatal Covid-19 courses has been achieved (cf. German Ethics Council 2021).

At the same time, the goals pursued by infection control can already run empty for individual persons before such a general withdrawal of freedom restrictions is possible or advisable. In principle, it simply corresponds to the principle of proportionality to allow widespread freedom restrictions only where no more specific and precise instruments are available. The existing infection control measures are based on the basic idea of risk prevention; they thus presuppose no actual, but at least a potential danger to oneself and others, and they also allow for a very low individual probability (cf. Kießling 2020). If this general (un-) probability is further reduced in the individual case and therefore the risk potential is lacking or at least significantly reduced, the measures must be lifted or at least their justifications exchanged. Here it is, as has been repeatedly pointed out and yet to be emphasized again, not about "special rights", "special rules" or even "privileges", but about the return to the rule of law. Against this background, specific attention is to be paid not only to vaccinations, but also to a possible natural immunity after recovery from Covid-19. In both cases[1] it has to be clarified what consequences

[1] For the sake of simple distinguishability, they are referred to here as immunity and vaccination certificates, without thereby pre-determining a specific model. The terminological jungle (e.g. immunity / vaccination certificate, -nachweis, -pass, -zertifikat etc.) recognizable in the corresponding debate cannot be pursued any further here.

arise if the basic assumption of an existing danger is no longer maintained or at least the probability that the danger will materialize has decreased significantly. This is to be pursued below by examining similarities, but also differences between these two basic constellations in more detail. In particular, the epistemic and risk-ethical assumptions underlying them are to be set out (see Sect. 2). Furthermore, the risks and chances existing in each case are to be viewed and weighted in more detail, whereby arguments of appearance are to be distinguished from actual problems and special attention is to be paid to freedom-theoretical or constitutional basic assumptions (see Sect. 3). Furthermore, the possibilities of consistent regulation are to be taken into account (see Sect. 4). A (interim) conclusion concludes the contribution, but certainly not the discussion (see Sect. 5).

2 Epistemic and Risk-Ethical Foundations

It is obvious at first that there are still considerable uncertainties from an epistemic point of view (cf. only Greely 2020): How an overcome Covid-19 disease or vaccination affects, whether there are differences with different disease course and different vaccines used, how long a possible immunity or reduced infectivity lasts—all this is being researched, but there are only tentative, evidence-based statements at best (cf. for example Voysey et al. 2021). That is precisely why a risk-ethical assessment of the available information is needed.

2.1 Epistemological Assessment

To begin with, the sometimes encountered idea is to be rejected that the decisive questions in medical-scientific research are merely *not yet* clarified. To assume this would point to an exaggerated need for security as well as to a certain epistemological naivety: In view of the dynamics of the infection process and the relevant research, it is not possible to establish a stable "state of the art"; at most, there are short-lived snapshots that become outdated very quickly due to the constantly changing knowledge. As the increase in knowledge typically goes hand in hand with an increase in ignorance, it is not to be expected that there will be a significantly better epistemic basis in the future. Rather, as in numerous other areas (cf. I. Augsberg 2009), a certain degree of uncertainty must be expected on a permanent basis. This makes a specific fixation on security and certainty not only unhelpful, but even paralysing, counterproductive and dangerous (cf. generally Sunstein 2009)—not only for individual freedoms, but also for collective infection control. A level of knowledge certainty may not be demanded that would hardly be offered or acceptable in any other social context. Otherwise, in view of the uncertainties present there as well, all relaxation measures would have to be omitted as a matter of principle. Because it is not possible to predict precisely whether or how strongly these will lead to a resurgence of infections. So crisis management can actually only be understood as escalation or at least long-term maintenance of protective measures; this goes back behind the awareness of the risks and consequences threatening in this way. The "feeling" procedure of the state, which is based on more or less well-founded assumptions, model calculations and risk assessments, is thus in a clear tension with a strongly pronounced need for security. Even the German Corona Warning App would appear irresponsible to the latter. Because it suggests a security ("low risk") that it cannot guarantee due to its limited distribution and the problematic reporting behaviour of the users tested positive. This is even more true for vaccinations against Covid-19: despite the expected, pleasingly high efficacy, it is nevertheless obvious that relatively large margins of uncertainty are accepted—and must be accepted. It is apparent that in the case of probabilities, without further justification, rounding up or down once is inconsistent.

In addition, it is epistemologically problematic to assume that the empirical (natural-scientific-medical) level can be discussed separately from the normative level for the risk assessment required. Cognitive and normative aspects are practically and theoretically closely interwoven (cf. comprehensively I. Augsberg 2014). Empirical studies are therefore not to be considered in isolation, but are influenced to at least a considerable extent by non-empirical factors such as research objectives, pre-understanding and choice of methods as well as different evaluations. This does not call the relevance of empirical knowledge into question. However, it should be remembered in view of a simplifying dichotomy of factuality and validity that normative orders, in particular the law, are characterized by a selection and filtering function. Even allegedly purely empirically based statements are not simply found, but (co-)constructed. Anyone who ignores this and instead treats empiricism and normativity as strictly separate phenomena pursues an outdated ideal of knowledge. Whether there is a "sufficient" degree of epistemic certainty can only be determined contextually and taking into account the specific risks and opportunities. It is not a question of knowledge, but of assessing reality (cf. Augsberg 2019).

2.2 *Normative Framework*

In view of the highly dynamic situation of (non-)knowledge about Sars-CoV2 and Covid-19, a normative orientation is therefore required. This refers to a risk-ethical analysis taking into account the constitutional framework. Here, the inevitable epistemic uncertainty—with regard to the medical as well as the social effects—is not understood as an obstacle, but rather motivates and justifies this methodological approach (cf. Gethmann 2018; cf. Nida-Rümelin et al. 2012). How we should act despite lacking or changing knowledge is not determined by the current state of (non-)knowledge, but follows from the assessment of which reasons make risky behavior appear justifiable. Instead of assuming medium- to long-term clarity, the central task is therefore to formulate conditions under which, for example, the use of immunity or vaccination certificates may be permissible under conditions of uncertainty.

Thus, what is required is a reflexive and communicative process of judgment that should not be limited to scientific discourse, let alone a single disciplinary perspective. Rather, in addition to research, also social, political and legal actors should be involved. (Risk-)ethical reflection must therefore distinguish between mere fears and plausible concerns based on experience, between argumentatively justified skepticism and exaggerated security concerns. In an largely unprecedented situation like the current epidemic situation, neither the description of the risk nor the expectations of risk management can simply be taken over from other areas. Nevertheless, there are analogies that support the approach proposed here. In particular, the comparative view of evidence-based medicine is particularly helpful: It almost serves as a prime example of the described intertwining of normative and cognitive elements, because it transfers the proof *(evidence)* of a legal epistemological model to medicine, the basic idea and point of which is precisely that it does not require certainty, but only a procedural, situationally adaptive approach to this (degrees of certainty). and offers (cf. Ladeur 2011; cf. Augsberg 2012). In this sense, it makes sense to accentuate categorical as well as gradual differences. Therefore, a distinction should be made between empirically observable risk perception (with varying evidence) and rational risk assessment, as well as between expressed intuitions of justice and their ethically reflected classification.

The risk-ethical assessment can in any case only be convincing if it integrates fundamental constitutional normative requirements into the weighing program. This refers to the ethically and legally central function of immunity or vaccination certificates: in view of a reduced danger to be able to reduce individual restrictions on freedom to the extent possible. Because in the rule of law, in principle, it is not the freedom of the individual, but the limitation of this freedom by the state that requires legitimation, the burden of justification and explanation changes: the (in principle prohibited) state restriction of fundamental freedom is to be more strictly judged than the (in principle required) restoration of this freedom. Sharp, but not incorrect: "Freedom that has to prove its unimportance is abolished" (Wißmann 2021). Accordingly, the risk assessment must proceed from the assumption that, in doubt, the individual's freedom of choice is to be preferred. Of course, this does not mean an absolute priority. However, in the required weighing process, the individual's freedom of choice must not be too quickly and simply subordinated to allegedly higher (collective) goods. In particular, serious, possibly existential impairments should be given special attention. As correct as it is to take into account the social and economic consequences of the fight against epidemics at the societal level, it is just as important to ask whether certain measures or relaxations contribute (can) to avoiding or ending individual unbearable burdens and borderline situations (cf. already German Ethics Council 2020b, p. 32).

3 Weighing Opportunities and Risks

The concept of immunity and vaccination certificates arouses great, sometimes unrealistic hopes, but also not inconsiderable concerns in the public (cf. also Schmidhuber and Stöger 2020). Some see them as an easy way back to a normal life free from infection control-based restrictions. Others fear a two-class society, and internationally there is criticism of a possible *immunocapitalism* (cf. Mills 2020). In fact, as has been shown, the instrument proves to be legally and ethically versatile and difficult. A central part of a normative analysis corresponding to the above considerations is the examination of specific opportunities and risks. These are not only to be listed and contrasted with each other, but also to be questioned and, in structured processes, to be weighted on the basis of explicitly named criteria and contrasted with possible consequences of action and decision-making. This has to be done in a schematic and keyword-like manner here for reasons of space, but even in this rudimentary form the basic intention and task can be seen.

3.1 Opportunities

The first and foremost argument that can be put forward for the introduction of immunity or vaccination certificates is the already mentioned argument that they serve to at least partially, namely individually, rescind existing infection control measures that infringe on basic rights. This corresponds to the ethically and legally central goal of minimizing individual freedoms as much as possible (see German Ethics Council 2020b; Voo et al. 2020a, b for this and the following). In addition, other individual and collective advantages of the certificates can be identified: They can not only enable a faster opening of at least parts of the economy and thus contribute to limiting negative economic effects. They also allow long-time isolated, isolated people to have more interpersonal contacts again in social terms. This is associated with a possible advantage for general infection control, because on the one hand the individually reduced risk allows organizational improvements, in particular in nursing and care for the elderly, and saves resources, for example with regard to tests. On the other hand, it also opens up additional areas of application, for example through the stronger involvement of voluntary social engagement. In close connection with this is the possibility of relieving those (mentally) who are exposed to a great extent or intensively in contact with at-risk groups as a result of their profession.

3.2 *Risks*

The risks to be considered (cf. Brown et al. 2020 et seq.) include in particular the danger that, in view of the uncertainties regarding the hoped-for sterile immunity, an early opening could mean additional infections. Where there are few contacts with unvaccinated persons, however, this argument obviously loses much of its significance. It is therefore not so much the special stress situation that makes an earlier withdrawal of (internal) contact restrictions appear particularly advisable in long-term care facilities (cf. German Ethics Council 2021), but rather their relative isolation. This also makes it clear that the reference to a possibly still existing infectivity is at least partially empty also in other "closed systems". However, concerns regarding the use of tests of questionable quality (antibodies) must be taken seriously and implemented regulatively. The same applies to concerns about the tamper-proofness, data protection compliance or specific abuse potentials.

With regard to the relevant risks, a correlation can also be seen with the extent to which the restoration of freedom took place. This affects in particular the incentive problem, which, however, has different effects on immunity and vaccination certificates: While in the former case the incentives would work counterproductive due to the uncertain consequences of voluntary infection, there is a considerable interest in the highest possible vaccination rate, and at least so far no relevant side effects occur. However, the risks for general compliance with norms are more uniform if freedom restrictions were only withdrawn in favour of recovered/vaccinated persons: In fact, individual releases from general infection control measures could cause unrest and have negative effects on the willingness to comply with the rules. However, it would be too general to equate possible control problems with an impossibility of differentiated control. It should also be noted that the feared unrest would mainly be an expression of insufficient information. There would therefore be possibilities to counteract these risks. It would not be convincing, however, to use irrational fears and mere envy as a reason not to implement measures that would otherwise be advisable. This also applies to the wide range of fears that the introduction of immunity/vaccination certificates would lead to discrimination or stigmatisation.

3.3 *Criteria and Methods for Weighing Up*

The aforementioned aspects must be integrated into a transparent, comprehensible weighing-up process in each individual case. It is to be assumed from the legally unassailable premise described that restrictions on freedom are in need of justification. This means, firstly, that the burden of proof does not lie with those who demand (re-)establishment of freedom, but with those who withhold it (further). This contradicts blanket references to uncertain knowledge and, at the same time, makes it necessary to distinguish precisely between (legal) ethically relevant arguments for freedom, solidarity and justice and, if applicable, sociologically relevant debates about envy. With regard to freedom, the aspect of weight here is primarily that the individual restoration of freedom for those who have recovered/been vaccinated does not mean any loss of freedom for the rest of the population. However, there is no (moral or even legal) entitlement to "shared suffering". It therefore also appears unconvincing to regard the first phase of vaccinations, in which vaccinations are carried out on the basis of a normatively prescribed priority, as a special case. Apart from the fact that corresponding rankings will also be required for the next phase, this fails to take account of the importance of priority: if its criteria are convincing, it is not clear why their importance should end with the genuinely life-/health-relevant consequences. Furthermore, the parameters used to justify restrictions on freedom must be explained; they may not simply be adapted or exchanged at will. Moreover, either altruistic action is not always to take precedence over other interests in freedom, or there is no unlawful discrimination if different treatment is based on the factual ground of (presumably) non-existent or at least significantly reduced infectivity. Corresponding fears in the public media do not change this. On the contrary, it is precisely the task of enlightened ethical reflection to counter such misconceptions and exaggerations; they must not be accepted uncritically. The same applies to the criticism voiced in entirely different systemic contexts as part of the international ethical debate. The weighing-up process is context-sensitive, i.e. it must be carried out in relation to the concrete situation on the ground, as is shown here in an exemplary manner.

4 Regulatory Requirements

An important role is played here by the question of to what extent feared developments can be countered by effective regulation. First and foremost, it should be emphasized that immunity and vaccination certificates are not panaceas, but only one of many means of partially reversing the restrictions on freedom introduced in the context of combating epidemics. They are therefore part of a comprehensive, flexibly designed range of instruments and, in particular, need to be supplemented by a more sophisticated testing strategy.

4.1 Flexible, Self-Reflective Regulation

The above-mentioned reservations can be contained to the extent that they do not concern rather remote concerns, by means of appropriate regulatory measures (cf. German Ethics Council 2020b, p. 33 ff.). In this respect, it is necessary to proceed in accordance with the awareness of epistemic uncertainties: what is required is a reflexive approach that anticipates and processes negative and positive developments as well as the special regulatory effects as far as possible. A state procedure that is "exploratory" in this sense, based on more or less well-founded assumptions, model calculations and preliminary risk assessments, is in clear tension with rigid and exaggerated security concepts. Instead, the risk-ethical assessment, which responds flexibly and adaptively to the dynamics of the pandemic, implies a self-critical and learning-capable regulation. Uncertainty thus does not imply a—cost-producing—prohibition of action, but above all the obligation to continuously check whether the original assumptions still hold, and to make adjustments if necessary. For this purpose, communication-, procedure- and organisation-related requirements are to be combined (cf. Augsberg 2021, p. 44 ff.): In order to make the social dimension of risk acceptance accessible in particular and to ensure the necessary learning capability, complex structures of knowledge generation and dissemination are required, but also special cooperation mechanisms and procedural rules that ensure adaptability (e.g. through time limits, monitoring or reevaluation requirements).

4.2 In Particular: Complementary (test) Procedures

Complementary testing can be used as a complementary instrument, in particular for persons who have not yet received vaccinations—due to initial shortages or due to special incompatibilities. Corresponding, sufficiently reliable and user-friendly tests are now available that do not require special medical training. What is lacking is a coordinated strategy for who and for what purpose they can or may be used. Here, there is an urgent need for political improvement.

4.3 Special Situations: Differential Treatment Carried Out by Private Individuals and State Travel Conditions

Barely worth mentioning are finally differential treatments based on immunity/vaccination, carried out by private individuals. In principle, there is no doubt that the principle of private autonomy also includes the right to choose one's own contracting partners at will (cf. German Ethics Council 2021). Only in very limited constellations, in particular in the context of so-called social welfare and in parts of the transport and health system, there is a so-called obligation to contract. In general, private individuals can choose their contracting partners at will: For example, the owner of a nightclub can in principle reject guests because he does not like their appearance or outfit. This is, and this is regardless of whether the potential contracting partner could meet the condition, a legal choice of selection, which has to be accepted. In addition, under the described conditions of reduced infectivity, there would also be a factual reason for differentiation. For example, restaurants, theatres, sports and singing clubs, etc. could resume their operations in "normal" form, i.e. without social distancing, etc. This would represent a significant relief for those affected and thus contradicts the comparison with clearly inadmissible, for example racist, discrimination. It is also to be countered that anti-discrimination regulations be correspondingly extended. The same applies in principle to the decision of individual states to make immunity/vaccination documentation a condition for entry or exit. However, additional considerations concerning the international dimension have to be taken into account here (cf. WHO 2021).

5 Final Considerations: Accountability as a Permanent Challenge

It would be paradoxical if, at the end of this short overview dedicated to the fluidity of knowledge, a final finding were to stand. On the contrary, if the past years have taught us one thing, then it should be this: to always remain vigilant and skeptical, especially towards those who claim to have all the answers. Therefore, only a plea for a continued discussion. However, it should be clear that certain argumentative dead ends should have been avoided. Risk ethics cannot replace political decisions, and political decisions require public debate. A careful, sensibly conditioned use of immunity or vaccination certificates therefore appeared to be responsible at one point and the fact that we now are aware of the Covid vaccines' limitations doesn't change the general point. It is, however, of great concern that many of the restrictions placed on the unvaccinated were introduced not in reaction to reduced threat but rather as a incentive to overcome vaccination hesitancy. Keeping this in mind, vaccination passports, immunity certificates et al., understood as a possible additional regulatory option, should by no means be ruled out categorically (cf. Greely 2020). Instead, such certificates—secured, for example, by time limits and monitoring obligations—should be taken seriously as an additional instrument that at least partially alleviates the hardship of general restrictions on freedom. It should be noted that the decision-relevant knowledge is constantly changing. Therefore, temporary solutions are sensible, and it is necessary to ensure that the procedures used are open to innovation. Given our experience with the Covid crisis, it must be to recognized that epistemic uncertainties are not just an obstacle that might hinder us short-term but will be surmountable over time. Rather, they form an ongoing and unavoidable background for the necessary risk management.

References

Augsberg I (ed) (2009) Ungewissheit als Chance. Perspektiven eines produktiven Umgangs mit Unsicherheit im Rechtssystem. Mohr Siebeck, Tübingen

Augsberg S (2012) Kooperative Wissensgenerierung im Gesundheitsrecht. Zum Umgang der Sozialgerichte mit Evidenzbasierter Medizin, Gesundheitsrecht, pp 595–601. Otto Schmidt, Köln

Augsberg I (2014) Informationsverwaltungsrecht. Zur kognitiven Dimension der rechtlichen Steuerung von Verwaltungsentscheidungen. Mohr Siebeck, Tübingen

Augsberg S (2019) Gleichheit angesichts von Vielfalt. Der philosophische und der juristische Diskurs. In: Veröffentlichungen der Vereinigung der Deutschen Staatsrechtslehrer 78. de Gruyter, Berlin, pp 7–51

Augsberg S (2021) § 8: Maßstäbe des Verwaltungshandelns. In: Voßkuhle et al., vol 1. i.E. Beck, München

Brown R et al (2020) The scientific and ethical feasibility of immunity passports. Lancet Infect Dis:1–6. https://doi.org/10.1016/S1473-3099(20)30766-0

Deutscher Ethikrat (2020a) Solidarität und Verantwortung in der Corona-Krise. Deutscher Ethikrat, Berlin

Deutscher Ethikrat (2020b) Immunitätsbescheinigungen in der Covid-19-Pandemie. Deutscher Ethikrat, Berlin

Deutscher Ethikrat (2021) Besondere Regeln für Geimpfte?. Deutscher Ethikrat, Berlin

Gethmann CF (2018) In: Mittelstraß J (ed) Risikotheorie. Enzyklopädie Philosophie und Wissenschaftstheorie, vol 7. Metzler, Stuttgart, pp 153–160

Greely HT (2020) COVID-19 immunity certificates: science, ethics, policy, and law. J Law Biosci 7:1–29

Kießling A (2020) In: dies. (ed) Infektionsschutzgesetz, Kommentar, § 28. Beck, München

Ladeur K-H (2011) Wissenserzeugung im und durch Recht – und das Problem der „evidenzbasierten Medizin". Gesundheitsrecht 2012:455–459

Mills P (2020) (Nuffield Council) Background discussion paper COVID-19 antibody testing and „immunity certification": a discussion paper. London

Nicola M et al (2020) The socioeconomic implications of the coronavirus pandemic (COVID-19): a review. Int J Surg 78:185–193

Nida-Rümelin J, Rath J, Schulenburg B (2012) Risikoethik. de Gruyter, Berlin

Rubin R (2020) The challenges of expanding rapid tests to curb COVID-19. JAMA 324:1813–1815

Schmidhuber M, Stöger K (2020) Personenbezogene Gesundheitsdaten in einer Pandemie—ethische und rechtliche Aspekte. Wien Med Wochenschr. https://doi.org/10.1007/s10354-020-00785-8

Sunstein CR (2009) Laws of fear. Beyond the precautionary principle. Cambridge University Press, Cambridge

Voo TC et al (2020a) Immunity certification for COVID-19: ethical considerations. Bulletin of the World Health Organization, Geneva

Voo TC et al (2020b) Ethical implementation of immunity passports during the COVID-19 pandemic. J Infect Dis 2020:715–718

Voßkuhle A, Eifert M, Möllers C (eds) (2021a) Grundlagen des Verwaltungsrechts, vol 1. i.E. Beck, München

Voysey M et al. (2021) Single-dose administration and the influence of the timing of the booster dose on immunogenicity and efficacy of ChAdOx1 nCoV-19 (AZD1222) vaccine: a pooled analysis of four randomised trials. The Lancet 397(2021):881–891

WHO (2021) Interim position paper: considerations regarding proof of COVID-19 vaccination for international travelers

Wißmann H (2021) Verfassungsbruch? Schlimmer: Ein Fehler. Die Aufkündigung der Moderne durch die Pandemiepolitik 2.0, Verfassungsblog v. 06.02.2021. https://verfassungsblog.de/verfassungsbruch-schlimmer-ein-fehler/. Accessed 24 Feb 2021

Pandemics and Research Ethics. An Overview of Central Challenges

Alice Faust, Lana Saksone, Stefanie Weigold, Lena Woydack and Daniel Strech

Contents

1 Introduction . . . 150
2 Challenges and Possible Solutions for Research Ethics in Pandemics . . . 151
2.1 Social Value . . . 151
2.2 Scientific Validity . . . 152
2.3 Favorable Risk-Benefit Ratio . . . 153
2.4 Fair Selection of Study Participants . . . 154
2.5 Informed Consent . . . 155
2.6 Collaborative Partnership . . . 156
2.7 Respect for Study Participants . . . 157
2.8 Independent Review . . . 157
3 Overarching Fundamental Questions . . . 158
3.1 Challenge Studies . . . 158
3.2 Impact on Other Research . . . 159
4 Summary and Final Considerations . . . 159
References . . . 160

A. Faust (✉) · L. Saksone · S. Weigold · L. Woydack · D. Strech
Berlin Institute of Health at Charité – Universitätsmedizin Berlin, QUEST Center for Transforming Biomedical Research, Berlin, Germany
e-mail: alice.faust@charite.de

L. Saksone
e-mail: lana.saksone@charite.de

S. Weigold
e-mail: stefanie.weigold@charite.de

L. Woydack
e-mail: lena.woydack@charite.de

D. Strech
e-mail: daniel.strech@bih-charite.de

© The Author(s), under exclusive license to Springer-Verlag GmbH, DE, part of Springer Nature 2023
A. Reis et al. (eds.), *Pandemics and Ethics*,
https://doi.org/10.1007/978-3-662-66872-6_11

1 Introduction

Since pandemics are usually caused by such infectious diseases for which there are hardly any evidence-based, effective approaches to prevention, diagnosis and therapy, a worldwide need for arises in a very short time. The urgency can vary depending on the characteristics of the pandemic. The Covid-19 pandemic caused worldwide dramatic effects on health and economy, resulting in a worldwide prioritization of Covid-19 research in the biomedical sciences. Within a few months, thousands of clinical studies were planned, reviewed, funded, conducted and published on the same disease. This extremely high number of clinical studies in combination with the strong time pressure, the very uncertain evidence base and the pronounced infection control measures also leads to an intensification of many research ethics challenges and in some cases even to very pandemic- or Covid-19-specific challenges.

For the structure of our chapter we use the internationally recognized framework for research ethics by Ezekiel Emmanuel et al. (Emanuel et al. 2008). With this, ethical challenges in clinical research can be subordinated to eight normative principles, i.e. social value, scientific validity, beneficial risk-benefit assessment, fair selection of study participants, informed consent, collaborative partnership, respect for study participants and independent review. In the context of the Covid-19 pandemic, the WHO published a document on research ethics, which also refers to this framework, whereby the principles of informed consent and fair selection of study participants are combined (World Health Organization 2020b).

For this chapter we considered both literature that deals generally with research during pandemics (Saxena et al. 2019; Alirol et al. 2017) and further specialized literature that deals specifically with research ethics in pandemics (Calain et al. 2009; Calain 2018; Gailits et al. 2019; Montgomery 2016). We would like to point out two comprehensive international documents at this point. The 2015 report "Ethics in epidemics, emergencies and disasters: research, surveillance and patient care" published by the WHO, which addresses general ethical challenges in epidemics, emergencies and disasters (World Health Organization 2015) and the (pre-corona) report "Research in Global Health Emergencies" published by the Nuffield Council on Bioethics in 2020 (Nuffield Council on Bioethics 2020).

In addition, there is a steadily growing number of contributions on the topic of Covid-19 and research ethics. For both areas, the authors are not aware of any systematic review, which is why we each carried out a scoping review on research ethics in pandemics in general and on research ethics in Covid-19 and used the results as the basis for this chapter. The chapter is also informed by a survey carried out by one of the authors in April 2020 with all German research ethics committees on the topic of challenges and possible solutions for research proposals for Covid-19 (Faust et al. 2020).

2 Challenges and Possible Solutions for Research Ethics in Pandemics

2.1 Social Value

In order to justify the risks for study participants and the public funding for clinical trials, these studies must generate social value or socially relevant knowledge (Raspe et al. 2012, p. 2). A pandemic event triggers pressure on relevant actors involved in research to contribute significantly to contain the pandemic through the rapid research of treatment and vaccination options. Under such conditions, it is necessary for researchers to critically question whether the planned research is at least on a minimum scale clinically relevant and whether the goals and objectives are appropriately aligned with social benefit (Townsend et al. 2020). For further explanations of how research in pandemics should define its goals and objectives in order to achieve social value, see the article by London and Kimmelman (2020).

In particular, in the context of the Covid-19 pandemic, the need arose to prioritize research projects. In addition, hundreds of non-Covid-19 specific clinical studies were stopped for logistical, legally restrictive, and other reasons (Singh et al. 2020). (Sect. 3.2 and the website: https://covid19.bgcarlisle.com/). What criteria should be used to decide, for example, whether resources should be allocated more to drug and vaccine development or to prevention and primary health research (see Tangwa and Munung 2020)? Unlike in prioritization processes in the context of clinical decision-making, such as the allocation of intensive care beds (see other chapters in this book), there are no established guidelines for prioritization processes for research projects in pandemic settings to date. A special prioritization question as in the Covid-19 context not only arises in the decision of which studies should be publicly funded, but also which clinical studies are allowed to recruit Covid-19 patients if there are not enough patients available (Spector-Bagdady et al. 2020; Wieten et al. 2020).

Closely linked to the question of resource allocation is the challenge of how to achieve efficient and effective study coordination at national and international level. The timely implementation of new, relevant findings from research into patient care is also relevant for the social value of research. In Germany, the "Network University Medicine" was founded during the Covid-19 pandemic for this purpose, in which all university hospitals in Germany will cooperate in perspective (Netzwerk Universitätsmedizin 2020).

A concrete challenge during the Covid-19 pandemic were several simultaneous studies on different therapeutics that were partially poorly differentiated from each other (London and Kimmelman 2020). An extreme example is the drug hydroxychloroquine, for which more than 150 clinical studies were registered, many of which were stopped or could not provide usable results due to insufficient patient recruitment (Pai 2020).

The results of the already mentioned survey with the ethics committees also pointed to problems with the coordination of studies and the submission of study applications with unclear objectives (Faust et al. 2020). Examples of national and international efforts to coordinate clinical research on Covid-19 are the British RECOVERY study (Nuffield Department of Population Health 2021) and the WHO-organized SOLIDARITY study (World Health Organization 2021b).

International collaboration and communication can help effectively fight a pandemic as a global event (Saxena et al. 2019). Therefore, it is particularly important to deal transparently with research data, sources and methods (Barton et al. 2020; Mietchen and Li 2020), in order to, for example, prevent redundant repetitions of experiments that have already proven to be ineffective and thus expose study participants to unnecessary risks. Increased transparency thus creates the opportunity to quickly integrate new knowledge into research. A central element for timely transparency on study progress are international clinical trial registers such as the US-based clinicaltrials.gov or the "International Clinical Trials Registry Platform (ICTRP)" of the WHO (World Health Organization 2021a).

2.2 *Scientific Validity*

In order for research to generate social value, it must produce valid, credible data that can be interpreted and used meaningfully (Raspe et al. 2012, p. 3).

As mentioned at the beginning, the characteristic of a pandemic is the spread of an infectious disease for which hardly any evidence-based knowledge is available. As the pandemic with SARS-CoV-2 shows, this has consequences for the focus of basic research, but also for exploratory studies with regard to pandemic containment measures. This aspect illustrates the importance of high scientific validity of study results at different levels, since newly published results can have an immediate consequence for clinical practice or health policy debates in the pandemic (Bramstedt 2020).

The high time pressure can negatively affect the scientific validity. The strong desire to develop a therapy or vaccine as quickly as possible carries the risk of circumventing ethical and scientific standards to some extent. However, in the context of a pandemic, it is precisely these core elements of high-quality research, such as randomization, blinding or the calculation of appropriate case numbers, that should not be dispensed with (London and Kimmelman 2020). Studies with small case numbers often generate false indications of possible effects, which then divert other scarce resources into ineffective treatment approaches. At the same time, studies with small case numbers discover smaller, but still clinically significant, benefits less well.

The rapid spread of infections with new pathogens creates situations of great uncertainty with regard to effective treatments and simultaneously great therapeutic need. This has led to a controversial discussion of the use of investigational drugs, with insufficiently secured preclinical or clinical evidence (Spector-Bagdady et al. 2020). For example, the government of Upper Bavaria temporarily allowed hospitals in Upper Bavaria, Lower Bavaria and Swabia to use Remdesivir for individual treatment attempts ("Individuelle Heilversuche") (Government of Upper Bavaria 2020).

The wide use of individual treatment attempts carries the risk that a meaningful assessment of the effectiveness and safety of certain medications and interventions in controlled clinical studies is no longer possible because they are already being used therapeutically.

An example of this was the use of plasma from patients who had previously been infected with the Corona virus as a therapy for patients acutely infected with the virus. According to the hypothesis, the antibodies present in the plasma against the virus should support the immune response in the fight against the disease. The Trump administration provided financial support to the Mayo Clinic to ensure that up to 53,000 patients received plasma as a therapy for Covid-19. As a result of the use of plasma outside of clinical studies, there were significantly fewer participants for research, out of fear of receiving a placebo instead of the plasma which they deemed to be effective (Thomas and Weiland 2020). The question of how ethically justifiable it is to give a placebo to study participants is also part of medical or research ethics debates and goes beyond the scope of this chapter (Schüklenk 2014).

2.3 *Favorable Risk-Benefit Ratio*

Research on humans always entails potential benefits and harms. The risks to the participants should be in an appropriate ratio to the social benefits of the desired knowledge gain. Such a risk-benefit assessment always remains associated with uncertainty (Raspe et al. 2012, p. 4).

Since pandemics are usually caused by an unknown pathogen, researchers and ethics committees often face particularly difficult risk-benefit-assessments (Faust et al. 2020). However, the risk-benefit assessment in times of pandemics is not only a special challenge in the run-up to a clinical study. Since many studies testing different drugs against the same pathogen are carried out simultaneously during a pandemic, risk-benefit assessments must be partly adapted during the course of clinical studies. The equipoise principle (see didactic element) must be continuously evaluated. As a rule, there is no established standard at the beginning of a pandemic, which means that a placebo can be given in the control arm of a study. However, if there are increasingly indications of the efficacy of a (new) medication, which then quickly establishes itself as a therapeutic standard, it may not be possible to give a placebo to participants in the control arm of other studies anymore. It must be ensured that all participants in the control arm of the study are supplied with the current standard or that harmful and ineffective therapies are stopped (Alirol et al. 2017). In the course of the Covid-19 pandemic, some vaccines have been approved for use in the population before the end of their test phase. For studies with other vaccines against Covid-19, this raises questions, for example, about the ethical legitimacy of administering a placebo in the control arm or blinding the study. The WHO Access to Covid-19 Tools (ACT) Accelerator Ethics and Governance Working Group has developed a policy for this purpose (World Health Organization 2020a).

Another problem in connection with the equipoise principle can arise from the administration of experimental drugs outside of studies. Due to the small number of cases and the lack of a control group, the impression of the safety and efficacy of a medication can be falsely created, even when it is not save and effective. In such a situation there would be no equipoise anymore, which in turn would prevent practice-relevant, randomized controlled trials (RCTs) with a placebo in the control arm from being carried out (Ramnath et al. 2020).

In general, the question is raised to what extent higher risks for study participants in exceptional situations such as pandemics can be justified by a particularly high social value. The justification of higher risks has been discussed mainly in the context of provocation studies (Shah et al. 2020) (see Section 3).

In particular, in pandemics with highly infectious pathogens, such as the Covid-19 pandemic, there are not only general risks for study participants, but also for the study team. The peculiarity lies in the potential endangerment of the staff by an infection with the virus. Therefore, it is important to ensure adequate protection for the study team, e.g. by means of medical protective clothing. A risk-benefit assessment must therefore also be made for the study team (Spector-Bagdady et al. 2020).

Didactic Element

Equipoise principle: There is a real uncertainty among experts with regard to the evidence as to which of the drugs/interventions to be tested in the study has a better risk-benefit ratio. Participants in the control arm must receive the medical standard, i.e. if there is an established therapy, it is given. Only if there is no established standard a placebo is given (Raspe et al. 2012, p. 86).

2.4 Fair Selection of Study Participants

A fair selection of study participants requires that the selection is made on the basis of scientific criteria so that valid and relevant results can be produced with the study (Raspe et al. 2012, p. 3 ff.). Furthermore, the principle includes the demand for a selection that can ensure a minimization of the risks for study participants. In addition, it makes sense to select participants in such a way that they can also benefit from the possible benefits of research. Finally, it is important to take the vulnerability of the selected groups into account and critically question whether the selection is justified. This should prevent privileged groups from having priority access to promising research, as was the case with the HIV pandemic in the 1980s (Macklin and Friedland 1986). At the same time, it should prevent high-risk research from being carried out primarily on economically disadvantaged groups or certain groups from being excluded from research, even though clinical research is urgently needed for their effective and safe health care, such as children, pregnant women or older people (Childress 2008).

A concrete challenge that was also relevant during the Covid-19 pandemic is the inclusion of subgroups that are in relationships of dependence with the study conductors, such as hospital staff (Faust et al. 2020). Particular care must be taken here, just as the ensuring of voluntariness is binding.

For certain population groups, such as pregnant women and children, the challenges associated with conducting research are particularly complex, as the risks they entail can have particularly serious consequences. At the same time, these groups also have a right to evidence-based healthcare. However, if, for example, pregnant women are categorically excluded from participating in studies, as was the case with the majority of Ebola and Covid-19 research, there is hardly any opportunity to create an evidence base for safe medication use in this subgroup. Results generated in a non-pregnant population are usually not directly generalizable to pregnant women (Costantine et al. 2020).

During the Covid-19 pandemic, social inequalities and structural disadvantages are particularly evident. For example, People of Colour communities in the USA are primarily affected by infection and, moreover, by a severe course of the disease, due to the unequal access to healthcare (Fortuna et al. 2020). Therefore, it is a special challenge to enable people from these communities to participate in research. Community engagement can be an important strategy in this regard.

At the beginning of a pandemic, there are usually no or only a few effective new drugs against the rampant pathogen, which is why a large number of clinical studies are conducted. However, despite a rapid spread of infection, it may still happen that more patients want to participate in the studies than there are places available. During the Covid-19 pandemic, the conduct of a lottery for the fair distribution of study places has been proposed. However, a lottery must be weighed against other possible distribution strategies. Which strategy is the right one depends, among other things, on the risk-benefit profile of the medication to be tested (Iyer et al. 2020).

2.5 *Informed Consent*

The principle of informed consent is intended to safeguard respect for the autonomy of the potential participants (Raspe et al. 2012, p. 5 ff.). Only those who receive all the important information about the study, understand it and remain free in the decision to participate or not, can give their informed consent to participate in research.

In a pandemic situation, challenges arise for the processes of informed consent due to the infection protection measures required in research contexts, such as distance rules and isolation measures for patients or entire hospital departments. In order to protect hospital staff and relatives, a strict isolation rule applies to patients suffering from Covid-19. On the one hand, this leads to logistical problems in carrying out informed consent with patients who are still able to give consent if, for example, documents are not allowed to leave the isolated rooms. On the other hand, difficulties arise in implementing alternative consent forms, such as consent by relatives or guardians, if they are not allowed to enter the hospital to talk to patients (Spector-Bagdady et al. 2020; Faust et al. 2020).

A special challenge in connection with informed consent is the so-called therapeutic misconception. This exists if relatives and patients attribute a primarily therapeutic goal to participation in research instead of perceiving it as primarily oriented towards gaining knowledge (Silverman and Lemaire 2006). The problem of the therapeutic misconception is not pandemic-specific. However, as described in Sect. 2.4, there is a special risk of the therapeutic misconception in pandemic situations.

Intensive care patients are a particularly vulnerable group who urgently need medical help. In order to provide this help evidence-based data must be generated through research that can only be carried out to a certain extent by this vulnerable subgroup itself. Intensive care patients are often no longer able to give consent or only severely restricted in their ability to consent (Furyk et al. 2017; Berg et al. 2013). Alternative types of consent that are discussed in this context are deferred consent, consent by proxy and waiver of consent (Foex 2001). When exactly which type of consent is to be applied possibly also in combination and how these are to be carried out in a high-quality manner was described as a central challenge in the Covid-19 context (Faust et al. 2020; van der Graaf et al. 2020).

Epidemiological studies or public health surveillance measures are just as essential as clinical research for a better understanding of a pandemic. To what extent informed consent should be necessary for such research is controversial (Ma et al. 2020) and also depends on the legal regulations of the respective country (World Health Organization 2017).

2.6 Collaborative Partnership

The goal of collaborative partnership is to enable people and their communities to actively participate in research. Participants should be able to participate in decision-making about the goals of research and benefit from its results (Raspe et al. 2012, p. 7). The example of the British 'MQ COVID-19 and mental health initiative' has advocated for the inclusion of those affected in the design and prioritization of research. The initiative consists of members of the 'Academy of Medical Sciences' (AMS), the charity 'MQ Transforming Mental Health' and those affected (Townsend et al. 2020; Balmer 2020). Another aspect in the debate about collaborative partnership is the involvement of local actors at all decision-making levels in research to increase the acceptability of research (Alirol et al. 2017; Sigfrid et al. 2020).

Since a pandemic is a global event, research processes are also taking place worldwide (see, for example, the WHO-coordinated SOLIDARITY study mentioned above). The unequal distribution of wealth and access to medical care in the world creates special ethical challenges in relation to research in the global South. One challenge, for example, is ensuring access to the results of research, such as a vaccine, especially if studies are conducted in countries of the global South (cf. Tangwa and Munung 2020).

Research in a pandemic can be in a partly competitive relationship to healthcare, for example if healthcare personnel are also required for research work in addition to clinical care (Iyer et al. 2020). Although medical care should be given priority (Moodley et al. 2020), research can ideally provide new insights that improve care for everyone. Therefore, considering different processes in the context of a broader understanding of collaborative partnership are inevitable.

2.7 *Respect for Study Participants*

Respect for study participants includes the obligation of researchers to monitor the physical and mental health of participants in general and not only in view of the disease under investigation (Townsend et al. 2020). Furthermore, the decisions of the participants regarding the termination of a study need to be respected. Under certain circumstances, follow-up care for former participants can also be part of this principle (Raspe et al. 2012, p. 6).

The economic effects of pandemics can put people in financial distress. For example, the rapid spread of the Corona virus led to drastic economic lockdown measures in various countries. In such a crisis, people may be more inclined to participate in studies if there are financial incentives for doing so (Largent and Lynch 2020). The conditions that must be met in order to combine voluntary study participation and financial incentives, especially in the context of a pandemic, are still being controversially discussed (Largent and Lynch 2020; Gelinas et al. 2018).

2.8 *Independent Review*

In Germany, independent ethical and legal review and approval of medical research is conducted by research ethics committees and, in certain areas, additionally by federal authorities. The members of these committees and authorities are not involved in the planning, implementation, etc. of the study to be examined and are independent in this sense. Nevertheless, conflicts of interest can also arise in ethics committees, for example if members of a local ethics committee know the local applicants professionally or personally. The review by ethics committees serves to protect the welfare of the study participants and to advise and support researchers and their institutions ethically and scientifically (Raspe et al. 2012, p. 5).

In the context of a pandemic, there may be a sharp increase in biomedical research. This also results in an increase in the workload of ethics committees. An accelerated review is expected due to the pandemic circumstances, without a loss of consultation quality. How this goal is to be achieved with little time available is a challenge and raises questions about criteria for prioritizing applications and organizing special sessions (Spector-Bagdady et al. 2020). The WHO has issued general recommendations for the rapid review of research applications by ethics committees during public health emergencies. It recommends the development of national SOPs to be created in advance of a pandemic (World Health Organization 2020c). Some countries, such as New Zealand (Health and Disability Ethics Committees 2020) and India (Indian Council of Medical Research 2020) have implemented this promptly for the Covid-19 pandemic.

3 Overarching Fundamental Questions

3.1 Challenge Studies

Provocation studies are defined as the deliberate infection of subjects/patients with a pathogen in order to gain knowledge about the disease caused by it and to research potential drugs or a vaccine. Although not new (Roestenberg et al. 2018), the topic was intensively discussed in the context of the Covid-19 pandemic (Shah et al. 2020; Chappell and Singer 2020; Holm 2020). The conduct of provocation studies raises various questions from the areas of "social value", "fair selection of study participants", "informed consent" and "favourable risk-benefit assessment" dealt with above.

An intentional infection with pathogens is initially clearly in contradiction to the general medical ethics principle of non-maleficence. This challenge is further exacerbated in the case of the SARS-CoV2 pandemic, as there are no treatment approaches available for Covid-19. On the other hand, there is also a particularly high potential for benefit, so that proponents of provocation studies assess the risks to study participants under certain conditions (such as risk reduction, fair selection, robust informed consent) as potentially appropriate with a particularly high social value (Shah et al. 2020). In particular, as the general knowledge of low-risk groups and treatment approaches increases, the ratio of benefits and risks can become increasingly favourable. Furthermore, the WHO has developed criteria for the ethical conduct of provocation studies on Covid-19 (World Health Organization 2020d).

3.2 *Impact on Other Research*

The conduct of research that contributes to a better understanding and combating of a pandemic has an impact on research in other areas. The question of a fair and meaningful allocation of resources therefore affects not only pandemic-related research projects, but also research in other areas (Meagher et al. 2020). The infection risk can also have an impact on other research. In the course of the Covid-19 pandemic, for example, there was a particularly high risk for cancer patients who were treated as part of studies. On the one hand, they were dependent on the continuation of the studies and on the other hand particularly vulnerable to infection with the Corona virus (Shuman and Pentz 2020).

4 Summary and Final Considerations

In this chapter, we have given a primarily descriptive overview of research ethics challenges in the pandemic context. The focus was on challenges that are being discussed internationally in the context of the SARS-CoV-2 pandemic. Many of the challenges presented have already been normatively analyzed in national and international literature and general recommendations have been published as to which principles are to be weighed against each other taking different circumstances into account. See, for example, the WHO recommendations for a rapid ethics review outlined above (World Health Organization 2020c), articles on post-hoc informed consent (van der Graaf et al. 2020), on the prioritization of Covid-19 studies (Spector-Bagdady et al. 2020) or on provocation studies (Shah et al. 2020). However, there are hardly any reports on the implementability or the concrete implementation of these normative recommendations. This is an area of particular research need. Results on the facilitating and hindering factors in the practical implementation of the normative recommendations are needed in order to continuously optimize the current research ethics practice of pandemic control and to prepare research ethics for future pandemics with other pathogens in the best possible way.

Note/Acknowledgement The present contribution of the research group arose within the framework of the project "PRECOPE" (Preparedness and Response for Ethical Challenges in Human Subject Research during Covid-19 and similar Pandemics) funded by the German Federal Ministry of Education and Research (BMBF) (01KI20123), see https://www.bihealth.org/de/forschung/quest-center/projekte/translationale-bioethik/precope.

We would like to thank the chairman and the employees of the secretariat of the Working Group of Medical Ethics Committees in Germany for their cooperation in a survey of all German research ethics committees, the results of which are taken into account in several places in this article. We would also like to thank the editors of this volume for their helpful feedback on our contribution, which has been taken into account in revisions.

References

Alirol E, Kuesel AC, Guraiib MM, de la Fuente-Núñez V, Saxena A, Gomes MF (2017) Ethics review of studies during public health emergencies—the experience of the WHO ethics review committee during the Ebola virus disease epidemic. BMC Med Ethics 18(1):43. https://doi.org/10.1186/s12910-017-0201-1

Balmer N (2020) MQ and AMS convene expert group to rapidly develop a mental health research response to COVID-19. https://www.mqmentalhealth.org/posts/mq-and-ams-convene-expert-group-to-rapidly-develop-a-mental-health-research-response-to-covid-19. Accessed 12 Oct 2020

Barton CM, Alberti M, Ames D, Atkinson J-A, Bales J, Burke E, Chen M, Diallo SY, Earn DJ, Fath B (2020) Call for transparency of COVID-19 models. Science 368(6490):482–483

Berg RM, Møller K, Rossel PJ (2013) An ethical analysis of proxy and waiver of consent in critical care research. Acta Anaesthesiol Scand 57(4):408–416. https://doi.org/10.1111/aas.12083

Bramstedt KA (2020) Luxembourg's approach to research integrity during the COVID-19 pandemic. Account Res 27(6):396–400. https://doi.org/10.1080/08989621.2020.1778473

Calain P (2018) The ebola clinical trials: a precedent for research ethics in disasters. J Med Ethics 44(1):38. https://doi.org/10.1136/medethics-2016-103474

Calain P, Fiore N, Poncin M, Hurst SA (2009) Research ethics and international epidemic response: the case of ebola and Marburg hemorrhagic fevers. Pub Health Ethics 2(1):729

Chappell RY, Singer P (2020) Pandemic ethics: the case for risky research. Res Ethics. https://doi.org/10.1177/1747016120931920

Childress LAMJF (2008) What is fair participant selection? In: The Oxford textbook of clinical research ethics. Oxford University Press, Oxford, p 377

Costantine MM, Landon MB, Saade GR (2020) Protection by exclusion: another missed opportunity to include pregnant women in research during the coronavirus disease 2019 (COVID-19) pandemic. Obstet Gynecol 136(1):26–28. https://doi.org/10.1097/aog.0000000000003924

Emanuel EJ, Wendler D, Grady C (2008) An ethical framework for biomedical research. In: Emanuel EJ (ed) The Oxford textbook of clinical research ethics. Oxford University Press, Oxford, pp 123–135

Faust A, Sierawska A, Krueger K, Wisgalla A, Hasford J, Strech D (2020) Challenges and proposed solutions in making clinical research on COVID-19 ethical. A status quo analysis across German research ethics committees. medRxiv. https://doi.org/10.1101/2020.08.11.20168773

Foex B (2001) The problem of informed consent in emergency medicine research. Emerg Med J 18(3):198–204

Fortuna LR, Tolou-Shams M, Robles-Ramamurthy B, Porche MV (2020) Inequity and the disproportionate impact of COVID-19 on communities of color in the United States: the need for a trauma-informed social justice response. Psychol Trauma Theory Res Pract Policy 12(5):443–445. https://doi.org/10.1037/tra0000889

Furyk JS, Lawton LD, Ting JY, McD Taylor D, Group ACfEMCT (2017) Informed consent in emergency care research: an oxymoron? Emerg Med Australas 29(1):110–112

Gailits N, Nouvet E, Pringle J, Hunt M, Lu D, Bernard C, Elit L, Schwartz L (2019) Blurring lines: complexities of ethical challenges in the conduct of West African Ebola Research. A Review of the Literature. https://www.elrha.org/wp-content/uploads/2019/10/Gailits-et-al.-Blurring-Lines-Ethical-Challenges-in-West-African-Ebola-Research.pdf. Accessed 26 Nov 2020

Gelinas L, Largent EA, Cohen IG, Kornetsky S, Bierer BE, Fernandez Lynch H (2018) A framework for ethical payment to research participants. N Engl J Med 378(8):766–771. https://doi.org/10.1056/NEJMsb1710591

van der Graaf R, Hoogerwerf M-A, de Vries MC (2020) The ethics of deferred consent in times of pandemics. Nat Med 26(9):1328–1330. https://doi.org/10.1038/s41591-020-0999-9

Health and Disability Ethics Committees (2020) COVID-19 emergency response: Ethical Review Operating Procedures (eSOP). https://ethics.health.govt.nz/operating-procedures. Accesssed 13 Jan 2021

Holm S (2020) Controlled human infection with SARS-CoV-2 to study COVID-19 vaccines and treatments: bioethics in Utopia. J Med Ethics 46(9):569–573

Indian Council of Medical Research (2020) National guidelines for ethics committees reviewing biomedical and health research during COVID-19 pandemic. https://main.icmr.nic.in/sites/default/files/guidelines/EC_Guidance_COVID19_06_05_2020.pdf. Accessed 13 Jan 2021

Iyer AA, Hendriks S, Rid A (2020) Advantages of using lotteries to select participants for high-demand Covid-19 treatment trials. Ethics Human Res. https://doi.org/10.1002/eahr.500061

Langhof H, Strech D (2017) Off-label use, compassionate use und individuelle Heilversuche: ethische Implikationen zulassungsüberschreitender Arzneimittelanwendungen, Angewandte Ethik in der Neuromedizin. Springer, Berlin, pp 95–105

Largent EA, Fernandez Lynch H (2020) Paying participants in COVID-19 trials. J Infect Dis. https://doi.org/10.1093/infdis/jiaa284

London AJ, Kimmelman J (2020) Against pandemic research exceptionalism. Science 368(6490):476–477. https://doi.org/10.1126/science.abc1731

Ma X, Wang Y, Gao T, He Q, He Y, Yue R, You F, Tang J (2020) Challenges and strategies to research ethics in conducting COVID-19 research. J Evid Based Med 13(2):173–177. https://doi.org/10.1111/jebm.12388

Macklin R, Friedland G (1986) AIDS research: the ethics of clinical trials. J Law Med Ethics 14(5-6):273–280

Meagher KM, Cummins NW, Bharucha AE, Badley AD, Chlan LL, Wright RS (2020) COVID-19 ethics and research. Mayo Clin Proc 95(6):1119–1123. https://doi.org/10.1016/j.mayocp.2020.04.019

Mietchen D, Li J (2020) Quantifying the impact of data sharing on outbreak dynamics (QIDSOD). Research Ideas Outcomes 6:e54770

Montgomery J (2016) Conducting research and innovation in the context of global health emergencies: what are the ethical challenges? Nuffield Council on Bioethics, London

Moodley K, Allwood BW, Rossouw T (2020) Consent for critical care research after death from COVID-19: arguments for a waiver. S Afr Med J 110(7):16

Netzwerk Universitätsmedizin (2020) FAQ zum Nationalen Forschungsnetzwerk der Universitätsmedizin. https://www.bmbf.de/de/faq-zum-nationalen-forschungsnetzwerk-der-universitaetsmedizin-11570.html. Accessed 02 July 2020

Netzwerk Universitätsmedizin Netzwerkpartner. (o. J.) https://www.netzwerk-universitaetsmedizin.de/netzwerkpartner. Accessed 05 Oct 2020

Nuffield Council on Bioethics (2020) Research in global health emergencies. https://www.nuffieldbioethics.org/publications/research-in-global-health-emergencies. Accessed 05 Feb 2021

Nuffield Department of Population Health NDoM, University of Oxford (2021) Recovery randomised evaluation of COVID-19 therapy. https://www.recoverytrial.net/. Accessed 22 Jan 2021
Pai M (2020) Covidization of research: what are the risks? Nat Med 26(8):1159. https://doi.org/10.1038/s41591-020-1015-0
Ramnath VR, McSharry DG, Malhotra A (2020) Do no harm: reaffirming the value of evidence and equipoise while minimizing cognitive bias in the COVID-19 era. Chest 158(3):873–876
Raspe H, Hüppe A, Strech D, Taupitz J (2012) Empfehlungen zur Begutachtung klinischer Studien durch Ethik-Kommissionen. Deutscher Ärzteverlag, Köln.
Regierung von Oberbayern (2020) Vollzug des Arzneimittelgesetzes (AMG). Einzeleinfuhr von Remdesivir im Rahmen von individuellen Heilversuchen von an COVID-19 erkrankten Menschen. https://www.regierung.oberbayern.bayern.de/mam/dokumente/bereich5/coronavirus/2020-03-20_allgemeinverfügung-vollzug-des-arzneimittelgesetzes-einzeleinfuhr-von-remdesivir.pdf. Accessed 05 Feb 2021
Roestenberg M, Hoogerwerf M-A, Ferreira DM, Mordmüller B, Yazdanbakhsh M (2018) Experimental infection of human volunteers. Lancet Infect Dis 18(10):e312–e322
Saxena A, Horby P, Amuasi J, Aagaard N, Köhler J, Gooshki ES, Denis E, Reis AA, Gangbo F, Compaore GM, Ngaba ON, Komas NP, Munday F, Aglanu LM, Wellington K, Maiga-Ascofaré O, Bah-Sow OY, Diallo AA, Souaré O, Penali L, Mason GT, Mfutso-Bengo J, Doumbia A, Iliyasu Z, Folayan MO, Mbaye EH, Ndiaye BP, Touré A, Touré P, Nyan O, Bouacha H, Seryazi IS, Jahan M, Al-Atiyyat NMH, Shah A, Aasim A, De Castro L, Marodin G, Ascurra M, Rethymiotaki E, Peicius E, Farnon EC, Taieb FN, Taverne B, Moore CE, de Almeida JR, Whittall H, Saenz C, Sathiyamoorthy V, Ravinetto R, the A-WHOW (2019) Ethics preparedness: facilitating ethics review during outbreaks – recommendations from an expert panel. BMC Med Ethics 20(1):29. https://doi.org/10.1186/s12910-019-0366-x
Schüklenk U (2014) Access to unapproved medical interventions in cases of catastrophic illness. Am J Bioethics 14(11):20–22. https://doi.org/10.1080/15265161.2014.957626
Shah SK, Miller FG, Darton TC, Duenas D, Emerson C, Lynch HF, Jamrozik E, Jecker NS, Kamuya D, Kapulu M (2020) Ethics of controlled human infection to study COVID-19. Science. https://doi.org/10.1126/science.abc1076
Shuman AG, Pentz RD (2020) Cancer research ethics and COVID-19. Oncologist 25(6):458–459. https://doi.org/10.1634/theoncologist.2020-0221
Sigfrid L, Maskell K, Bannister PG, Ismail SA, Collinson S, Regmi S, Blackmore C, Harriss E, Longuere K-S, Gobat N, Horby P, Clarke M, Carson G (2020) Addressing challenges for clinical research responses to emerging epidemics and pandemics: a scoping review. BMC Med 18(1). https://doi.org/10.1186/s12916-020-01624-8
Silverman HJ, Lemaire F (2006) Ethics and research in critical care. Intensive Care Med 32(11):1697–1705
Singh JA, Bandewar SV, Bukusi EA (2020) The impact of the COVID-19 pandemic response on other health research. Bull World Health Organ 98(9):625
Spector-Bagdady K, Higgins PD, Lok AS et al (2020) COVID-19 clinical trial oversight at a major academic medical center: approach of the Michigan medicine. COVID-19 clinical trial committees. Clin Infect Dis 71(16):2187–2190. https://doi.org/10.1093/cid/ciaa560
Tangwa GB, Munung NS (2020) COVID-19: Africa's relation with epidemics and some imperative ethics considerations of the moment. Res Ethics. https://doi.org/10.1177/1747016120937391
Thomas K, Weiland N (2020) As trump praises plasma, researchers struggle to finish critical studies. The New York Times, 04.08.2020. https://www.nytimes.com/2020/08/04/health/trump-plasma.html. Accessed 05 Feb 2021
Townsend E, Nielsen E, Allister R, Cassidy SA (2020) Key ethical questions for research during the COVID-19 pandemic. Lancet Psychiatry 7(5):381–383
Wieten S, Burgart A, Cho M (2020) Resource allocation in COVID-19 research: which trials? Which patients? Am J Bioethic 20(7):86–88. https://doi.org/10.1080/15265161.2020.1779392

Wild V (2010) Arzneimittelforschung an schwangeren Frauen: Dilemma, Kontroversen und ethische Diskussion. Campus, Frankfurt

World Health Organization (2015) Ethics in epidemics, emergencies and disasters: research, surveillance and patient care: WHO training manual. https://www.who.int/ethics/publications/epidemics-emergencies-research/en/. Accessed 05 Feb 2021

World Health Organization (2017) WHO guidelines on ethical issues in public health surveillance. https://apps.who.int/iris/bitstream/handle/10665/255721/9789241512657-eng.pdf;jsessionid=3A12BA9698CD8A5E7632969552A49D73?sequence=1. Accessed 02 Feb 2021

World Health Organization (2020a) Emergency use designation of COVID-19 candidate vaccines: ethical considerations for current and future COVID-19 placebo-controlled vaccine trials and trial unblinding. https://www.who.int/publications/i/item/WHO-2019-nCoV-Policy_Brief-EUD_placebo-controlled_vaccine_trials-2020.1. Accessed 29 Jan 2021

World Health Organization (2020b) Ethical standards for research during public health emergencies: distilling existing guidance to support COVID-19 R&D. https://www.who.int/publications/i/item/ethical-standards-for-research-during-public-health-emergencies. Accessed 01 July 2020

World Health Organization (2020c) Guidance for research ethics committees for rapid review of research during public health emergencies. https://www.who.int/ethics/publications/guidance-for-research-ethics-committees/en/. Accessed 13 Jan 2021

World Health Organization (2020d) Key criteria for the ethical acceptability of COVID-19 human challenge studies. https://apps.who.int/iris/bitstream/handle/10665/331976/WHO-2019-nCoV-Ethics_criteria-2020.1-eng.pdf. Accessed 29 Jan 2021

World Health Organization (2021a) International clinical trials registry platform (ICTRP). https://www.who.int/clinical-trials-registry-platform. Accessed 28 Jan 2021

World Health Organization (2021b) "Solidarity" clinical trial for COVID-19 treatments. https://www.who.int/emergencies/diseases/novel-coronavirus-2019/global-research-on-novel-coronavirus-2019-ncov/solidarity-clinical-trial-for-covid-19-treatments. Accessed 22 Jan 2021

Ethical and Legal Challenges of Digital Medicine in Pandemics

Opportunities—Risks—Compromises

Timo Minssen and Sara Gerke

In general, this chapter could only incorporate developments that have occured before July 2021.

Contents

1 Introduction 166
2 New Developments in Digital Medicine and Applications in Pandemics 167
3 Ethics and Law 170
4 Selected Issues at the Intersection of Ethics and Law 171
4.1 Data, Privacy, and Consent 171
4.2 Data Access, (Intellectual) Property Rights, and Competition Law 175
4.3 Robustness, Cybersecurity, Liability, Accountability, and Licensing 178
4.4 Transparency, Traceability, and Explainability 182
4.5 Bias, Discrimination, and Social Justice 186
5 Discussion 189
6 Conclusions and Outlook 193
References 193

The research for this article was supported by a grant from the Collaborative Research Program for Biomedical Innovation Law, a scientifically independent collaborative research program supported by a Novo Nordisk Foundation grant (NNF17SA0027784). Special thanks go to the student assistant Verda Sigura for her support in organizing the literature list. The research of Timo Minssen was also supported by the initiative of the Wallenberg Foundation for Humanities and Social Sciences Research in AI and Autonomous Systems (WASP-HS).

T. Minssen (✉)
Center for Advanced Studies in Biomedical Innovation Law (CeBIL), Faculty of Law, University of Copenhagen, Copenhagen, Denmark
e-mail: timo.minssen@jur.ku.dk

T. Minssen
Research Affiliate, Centre for Law, Medicine and Life Sciences (LML), University of Cambridge, Cambridge, UK

S. Gerke
Assistant Professor of Law, Penn State Dickinson Law, Carlisle, PA, USA
e-mail: sgerke@psu.edu

© The Author(s), under exclusive license to Springer-Verlag GmbH, DE, part of Springer Nature 2023
A. Reis et al. (eds.), *Pandemics and Ethics*,
https://doi.org/10.1007/978-3-662-66872-6_12

1 Introduction

The Covid-19 pandemic and the resulting restrictions on mobility, contact bans, mobile phone surveillance apps, and other strategies for containment of infection chains have led to an increase in the use of digital applications in public and private health care in recent years (Whitelaw et al. 2020, p. e435). The possibility of avoiding contact through remote monitoring of patients in hospitals and in home care also contributes to this trend. Moreover, improved data analysis in research, development, and testing of new therapies, as well as the growing potential of artificial intelligence (AI) for rapidly developed diagnostic methods and vaccine candidates, result in increased demand and use of digital aids by doctors, patients, hospitals, researchers and companies.

Although many of these new digital possibilities have received enthusiastic support and encouragement from the population, it soon became clear that not all applications are fully developed and that new responses to a wide range of risks and security deficiencies need to be found (O'Shea 2020, p. 1). The use of these technical innovations was therefore accompanied not only by socio-economic and political discussions but also by ethical and legal debates. Issues such as data protection, cyber security, consent, liability, transparency, discrimination, ownership, and a fair distribution and access to digital possibilities play an important role here. Many of these AI-related topics have been widely discussed in public and professional circles for some time, but the Covid-19 pandemic has clearly intensified and concretized these debates. The pandemic has had not only a direct impact on various emergency laws and the ethical debates on risk prevention and the organization of health care (DAV 2020, p. 1) but also an indirect effect on legislation of the "pre-Covid era". In Germany, for example, the interplay of the Covid-19 crisis with the entry into force of a number of groundbreaking new laws in the field of digital medicine, which had been planned for some time, has only recently become apparent. Examples of this are the Digital Healthcare Act (DVG 2019) and the Hospital Future Act (KHZG 2020). It quickly became clear that the Covid-19 pandemic intensified the sometimes heated debates about these new laws and thus highlighted the burning questions at the intersection of ethics and law even further (Gerke et al. 2020d, p. 5).

Against this background, we will first give a brief overview of the possibilities and areas of application of digital medicine in pandemics in Sect. 2. Our selection focuses primarily on case studies that have emerged in the current Covid-19 pandemic and that we consider to be particularly relevant for the discussion of ethical and legal issues. Then, in Sect. 3, we will briefly discuss the interaction of ethics and law, which also includes the question of distinguishing and interacting between ethics and law. This provides the basis for a detailed discussion of selected ethical and legal topics in Sect. 4. Here, not only a short overview of legal framework conditions and legal developments will be provided but also the specific legal-ethical problem areas, risks, and future options will be shown. The focus will be on the legal analysis and discussion in the German and European context, while ethical aspects and points of contact will be taken into account as far as possible. In addition, in Sect. 4 we will focus on *digital* solutions and problems relevant to Covid-19 and pandemics. A large number of other ethical and legal problems relevant to Covid-19 such as legality and proportionality issues with regard to restrictions on freedom (Gunnarsdóttir et al. 2020, p. 1), drug prices, or global distribution issues with regard to vaccines (Price et al. 2020, p. 914; Druedahl et al. 2020, p. 582) will therefore not be the focus of this study. It should also be emphasized that this chapter serves the purpose of providing an overview of the ethical aspects and legal challenges of digital medicine in pandemics. A comprehensive analysis of the various areas of law, such as European anti-discrimination law or human and fundamental rights, is not possible due to the limit on space. Sect. 5 analyses, links, and discusses the insights gained from the previous sections from a broader perspective. Finally, Sect. 6 summarizes the results of our study and provides an outlook on future challenges and opportunities.

2 New Developments in Digital Medicine and Applications in Pandemics

Digital medicine has developed rapidly in recent years. In particular, the expansion of the 5G broadband network, new telemedicine platforms and biomedical peripheral devices, the increasing networking of modern home and entertainment electronics in the "Internet of Things (IoT)", and new mobile phone and smartwatch functions have significantly contributed to the fact that telemedicine applications are moving more and more towards individuals and households (Watson et al. 2020, p. 1110). The Covid-19 pandemic and new legislation have exacerbated this trend and not only created an increased demand for digital solutions in medicine but also showed new possibilities for relieving and improving the health care system (ibid.). Digital technologies are now being used increasingly to support measures against the Covid-19 pandemic as quickly and comprehensively as possible and to protect public health worldwide. This includes both population and quarantine monitoring, infection identification, prediction of infection development, contact tracing, and intervention evaluation with mobility data, as well as targeted and effective public communication (Whitelaw et al. 2020, p. e435; Sava 2020; Budd et al. 2020, p. 1183) and, more recently, even digital vaccination certificates (WHO 2021, p. 1). Many of the immediate measures taken against the Covid-19 pandemic use billions of mobile phones, enormous online data sets and interconnected devices, enormous computer resources and advances in machine learning (a subgroup of AI technology) and in language analysis (Budd et al. 2020, p. 1183).

There is currently particularly active digital innovation and development in the field of contact tracing. Contact tracing is essential to combating the Covid-19 pandemic in order to identify people who have had close contact with a Covid-19 patient and may have been infected with the virus. Since there are not enough workers available for contact tracing in many countries of the world and to reduce the burden on staff (Lewis 2020, p. 384; Shachar et al. 2020, p. 18), many countries have now implemented so-called Corona warning apps (also “contact-tracing apps” or more accurately “exposure-notification apps”). The general idea of these warning apps is that they notify the user if they have come into close contact with a person who has been diagnosed with Covid-19. The user of the app can then take appropriate measures, such as testing themselves and/or going into voluntary or forced quarantine. Apple and Google have developed an “Exposure Notifications System” that uses Bluetooth technology. Health authorities around the world can use this system as the basis for developing their contact-tracing apps or Corona warning apps (Google 2021, p. 1). For example, Germany made use of the system developed by Apple and Google (Rahman 2021, p. 1). The so-called “Corona warning app” has been available in Germany since June 2020. According to the Robert Koch Institute, the Corona warning app has been downloaded almost 25 million times (as of January 2021; Robert Koch Institut 2021, p. 1), which corresponds to approximately 30% of the population. It is assumed that the Corona warning app shows already positive effects if approximately 15% of the German population participates (Hurtz 2020, p. 1). Furthermore, it is assumed that the spread of the virus could be stopped with the participation of approximately 60% of the population (ibid.).

In order to reduce the exposure of employees in the healthcare sector and outside the healthcare sector, the Covid-19 pandemic has also led to increased integration of AI technologies into home healthcare. Technology-supported, remotely controlled, and remotely monitored assessment of voice analysis and vital functions such as pulse rate, body temperature, blood pressure, or also the respiratory rate can be used to assess people who are isolated at home or quarantined to provide care for others and to determine times when home care is provided (Gerke et al. 2020a, p. 1176). Remote monitoring can also be used in conjunction with so-called “intelligent pills” (“smart pills” or “ingestible electronic sensors”) to promote compliance with medication intake (Gerke et al. 2019, p. 329) or to decide when admission to a hospital due to Covid-19 complications is necessary. For cases where private care at home is not an option, such digital technologies and remote monitoring systems are also being used, developed, or considered by hospitals to an increasing extent (Wittbold et al. 2020, p. 1). For example, systems with AI have been developed that can predict the course of disease in patients with Covid-19 and thus make the planning of therapy, care, and resource allocation in hospitals more effective (Li et al. 2020, p. 1; see also Rajkomar et al. 2019, p. 1347). In addition, ambient intelligence systems (“ambient intelligence”) based on continuous video recordings (Gerke et al. 2020b, p. 601) and robot-supported systems for contact avoidance are being developed for hospital use, test centers, and outpatient care (Guizzo and Klett 2020, p. 1).

Another important area of application of new digital technologies relates to the research and development of pandemic-relevant drugs, therapeutic methods, and vaccines, or also to finding new applications for already approved medications

(Loucera et al. 2020, p. 1). Rapid progress in bioinformatics, often referred to as "computational biology", contributes to this (Vamathevan et al. 2019, p. 463). Although there are still some problems to be overcome in connection with the in vivo complexity of biological processes, and the performance of these technologies often depends on the quality of the data (Bender and Cortés-Ciriano 2020, p. 511), high-performance computers, neural networks, advancing developments in AI, and quantum computing with increasing precision and speed allow billions of biological molecules and (bio-)chemical compounds to be examined to find suitable active ingredients and drug candidates against the Covid-19 virus and to decipher cellular mechanisms (Preeti 2020, p. 1; Arshadi et al. 2020, pp. 7–9). Deep learning technologies—a subgroup of machine learning—are also used here, which in combination with modern image analysis, accelerate the prediction of molecular structure and function as well as the automated generation of innovative chemical units with tailor-made therapeutic properties (Jiménez-Luna et al. 2020, p. 573). However, the growing number of successful and potential applications is also accompanied by the problem that the mathematical models underlying the interpretations and conclusions are often difficult to understand for the human mind (ibid.). This highlights the need for sufficiently transparent and interpretable digital methods in molecular biology and health technology (Minssen et al. 2020a, p. 114). In addition, AI is currently still facing limitations in the conduct and control of crucial clinical trials. But even in this area, the Covid-19 pandemic has increasingly led to the use of digital technologies, such as the use of machine learning to process data from clinical trials (Zame et al. 2020, p. 506) or the exploration of possibilities by medical authorities to conduct clinical trials at home and in private apartments (Danish Medicines Agency 2020, p. 1; cf. European Medicines Agency 2019, p. 1). Finally, it should be mentioned that digital programs in the rapidly developing field of three-dimensional (3D) printing technology also offer new possibilities that are not only used in the field of production of personal protective equipment but also in the development and construction of medical devices and isolation rooms (Choong et al. 2020, p. 637). In summary, it can therefore be said that digital technologies show an enormous range of solutions and approaches to coping with the pandemic. Some applications are already very concrete; others are not yet fully developed or dependent on high-tech infrastructure. It also becomes clear that the increased demand for digital solutions, the expanded data access, and the necessary incentives for the quick and immediate application of digital solutions caused by the Covid-19 pandemic will further drive these developments (Monroe 2020, p. 10). It is interesting that digital technologies, such as 3D printers and telemedicine, can actually contribute to eliminating regional differences and imbalances between supply and demand caused by socio-economic trends and disruptions in supply chains (Choong et al. 2020, p. 637). However, many helpful digital technologies also lead to a variety of concrete or potential problems, such as privacy intrusions and discrimination, as well as future issues in terms of distribution issues and global access to high-tech infrastructure (Atik and Jeutner 2019, p. 1).

3 Ethics and Law

It is obvious that the technical developments, applications, and possibilities explained above raise a number of important ethical and legal questions. However, the terms "ethics" and "law" are often confused. This can be explained by the fact that ethics and law often overlap, and the transitions between delimitation and interaction sometimes appear fluid. However, there are also clear differences. In particular, in the medical field, a large number of very detailed analyses and interesting discussions can be found in academic literature (see, for example, Scott 2000, p. 245 and Oduncu 2012, p. 359). However, this short chapter only allows for a very brief discussion of the relationship between ethics and law.

There are many more or less detailed definitions of ethics and law in the literature. Simply put, ethics can be understood as the "theory or doctrine of acting according to the distinction between good and evil", with the subject of ethics being morality (Suchanek and Lin-Hi 2018, p. 1). While original theories of ethics, such as Greek ethics, could be both empirical and normative, today, a strict distinction is made between empirical, descriptive, and normative ethics (ibid.). Normative ethics formulates a "should", which claims general binding force (ibid.). The terms "law" ("Recht") and "legal system" ("Rechtsordnung") in the objective sense are all state-institutionalized rules that influence or guide human behavior and stand in a hierarchical order to each other (BPB 2020, p. 1; see also Klunzinger 1993, p. 1). Claims that arise for an entitled person from the objective law are, however, understood as law in the subjective sense (BPB 2020, p. 1; see also Alexy et al. 2019, p. 1; see also Klunzinger 1993, p. 2). The law differs from ethics and other normative systems, such as custom, morality, and tradition, by its state institutionalization and enforcement with the help of certain decision, recognition, and change rules (BPB 2020, p. 1; see also Klunzinger 1993, pp. 1–2). Roughly speaking, one can say that ethics is mainly concerned with the question of what someone should do, while the law prescribes what rights the individual has and how to act in accordance with the legal system. Ethics mainly refers to human behavior, which is understood as morally right, while the law rather functions as the "ethical minimum" (Jellinek 1878, p. 42). The law, as such, is subject to the obligation of legitimacy, which it has to meet on the one hand through its democratic origin and confirmation, on the other hand through a problem-solving that is fair to the facts and interests (BPB 2020, p. 1). Ethical and legal considerations are often considered and discussed in an overall view, usually with the aim of achieving the greatest possible agreement in order to avoid or resolve any conflicts. Ethical and legal principles are often considered together in view of fundamental values such as equality, freedom, and human dignity in order to formulate, interpret, and correctly implement new laws. This can lead to the expansion or restriction of certain rights and obligations of the individual—or of companies, states, and other interest groups. In this sense, the ethical and normative evaluation of existing law, that is, the law as it is ("de lege lata"), also contributes to the reform and development of future law, that is, the law as it should be ("de lege ferenda"). The four principles of biomedical ethics, namely (1) patient's right of self-determination, (2) avoidance of harm, (3) patient welfare, and (4) justice (Beauchamp and Childress 2012; see also Gillon 2003, p. 307) also play an important role. Ethical principles can either support or provide a significant counterweight to other factors, such as economic or political considerations.

4 Selected Issues at the Intersection of Ethics and Law

The application of new digital technologies to combat the pandemic has led to a large number of ethical and legal debates in the areas of data protection, data transfers, and ownership, as well as issues of cybersecurity, consent, and transparency. In addition, important questions about fair distribution, discrimination, and access to digital opportunities have been and are being discussed intensively. In the following, we will deal with selected legal issues in these areas and, where possible, also take into account ethical aspects.

4.1 Data, Privacy, and Consent

The increased use of digital technologies during the Covid-19 pandemic has raised a variety of data protection issues. When is the processing of health data legally possible? How can the privacy of patients be adequately protected? How should a Corona warning app be designed? In contrast to other continents and countries in the world, such as the USA or China, Europe is a pioneer in legally anchored data protection. The General Data Protection Regulation (2016/679—GDPR) has been applicable throughout the EU since 25 May 2018 (Article 99(2) of the GDPR). The GDPR, in particular, protects the right of natural persons to the protection of personal data (Article 1(2) of the GDPR). The regulation has a wide material scope and territorial scope. According to Article 2(1) of the GDPR, the Regulation generally "applies to the processing of personal data wholly or partly by automated means and to the processing other than by automated means of personal data which form part of a filing system or are intended to form part of a filing system". "Personal data" is "any information relating to an identified or identifiable natural person ('data subject')" (Article 4(1) of the GDPR). The term "processing" is defined in Article 4(2) of the GDPR as "any operation or set of operations which is performed on personal data or on sets of personal data, whether or not by automated means". This includes, for example, the recording, collection, storage, disclosure by transmission, erasure, or destruction (Article 4(2) of the GDPR). The GDPR is not only relevant to companies in the EU but can even apply to companies established outside the EU—for example, in the USA. According to Article 3(1) of the GDPR, the "Regulation applies to the processing of personal data in the context of the activities of an establishment of a controller or a processor in the

Union, regardless of whether the processing takes place in the Union or not". The term "controller" is defined as "the natural or legal person, public authority, agency or other body which, alone or jointly with others, determines the purposes and means of the processing of personal data" (Article 4(7) of the GDPR). A processor is "a natural or legal person, public authority, agency or other body which processes personal data on behalf of the controller" (Article 4(8) of the GDPR). Article 3(2) of the GDPR makes it clear that the Regulation also applies in two cases "to the processing of personal data of data subjects who are in the Union by a controller or processor not established in the Union". The first case is when the processing of personal data is related to "the offering of goods or services" to data subjects in the EU. This applies regardless of whether the offer is free or subject to a fee (Article 3(2)(a) of the GDPR). The second case is when the processing of personal data is related to the monitoring of the behavior of data subjects insofar as their behavior takes place in the EU (Article 3(2)(b) of the GDPR). If the GDPR applies, the principles in Article 5 must be followed, in particular during the Covid-19 pandemic. Article 5 of the GDPR includes, for example, the principle of data minimization. Personal data must therefore be "adequate, relevant and limited to what is necessary in relation to the purposes for which they are processed" (Article 5(1)(c) of the GDPR). In addition, for example, the principle of integrity and confidentiality must also be observed. Personal data must therefore be processed in such a way that its appropriate security is ensured. This also includes the protection against unlawful or unauthorized processing and against accidental destruction, damage, or accidental loss by means of appropriate organizational and technical measures (Article 5(1)(f) of the GDPR). The GDPR also regulates special categories of personal data, such as genetic data and data concerning health. Genetic data are personal data on the acquired or inherited genetic characteristics of a natural person that provide clear information about the health or physiology of this person and are particularly obtained from the analysis of a biological sample (Article 4(13) of the GDPR). Data concerning health includes all "personal data related to the physical or mental health of a natural person, including the provision of health care services, which reveal information about his or her health status" (Article 4(15) of the GDPR). Genetic data and data concerning health as special categories of personal data may not be processed according to Article 9(1) of the GDPR. However, the ban does not apply if an exception under Article 9(2) of the GDPR applies (see also Price et al. 2019b, p. 449). This means that, for example, genetic data and data concerning health can usually only be processed if the person concerned "has given explicit consent to the processing of those personal data for one or more specified purposes" (Article 9(2)(a) of the GDPR). In times of Covid-19, other exceptions can also be considered, which allow the processing of genetic data and data concerning health without the consent of the person concerned under certain conditions. For example, according to Article 9(2)(h) of the GDPR, the processing of special categories of personal data is possible if the "processing is necessary for the purposes of preventive or occupational medicine, (...) medical diagnosis, the provision of health (...) care or treatment or the management of health (...) systems and services on the basis of Union or Member State law or pursuant to contract with a health professional and subject to the conditions and safeguards referred to in paragraph 3". Article 9(3) of the GDPR stipulates that personal data may only be processed for these purposes if the processing is carried out by a professional (or under their responsibility) who is subject to professional secrecy under the law of a Member State or Union law or the provisions of national competent bodies. The processing may also be carried out by another person who is subject to secrecy under the law of a Member State or Union law or the provisions of national competent bodies. Another exception to the processing of genetic data and data concerning health, which is of particular relevance in the fight against the Covid-19 pandemic, is Article 9(2)(i) of the GDPR. According to this Article, the processing must be "necessary for reasons of public interest in the area of public health, such as protecting against serious cross-border threats to health or ensuring high standards of quality and safety of health care and of medicinal products or medical devices, on the basis of Union or Member State law which provides for suitable and specific measures to safeguard the rights and freedoms of the data subject, in particular professional secrecy". In addition, the processing of genetic data and data concerning health is also possible without the consent of the data subject for scientific research purposes in exceptional cases and under certain conditions. This is the case in accordance with Article 9(2)(j) of the GDPR if the "processing is necessary for archiving purposes in the public interest, scientific or historical research purposes or statistical purposes in accordance with Article 89(1) based on Union or Member State law which shall be proportionate to the aim pursued, respect the essence of the right to data protection and provide for suitable and specific measures to safeguard the fundamental rights and the interests of the data subject". Article 89(1) of the GDPR, in particular, provides that the data must be pseudonymised if the purpose can be achieved in this way. The GDPR also gives data subjects rights (Articles 12—23 of the GDPR). For example, the data subject has a general "right to obtain from the controller the erasure of personal data concerning him or her without undue delay" (also known as a "right to be forgotten") in accordance with Article 17 of the GDPR. However, an exception may apply in times of the Covid-19 pandemic. The right to be forgotten does not apply if the processing is carried out "for reasons of public interest in the area of public health" (Article 17(3)(c) in conjunction with Article 9(2)(h) and (i) and Article 9(3) of the GDPR). The GDPR also gives the data subject, for example, a general right to data portability against the controller (Article 20 of the GDPR). However, the right does "not apply to processing necessary for the performance of a task carried out in the public interest or in the exercise of official authority vested in the controller" (Article 20(3) sentence 2 of the GDPR). During the pandemic, the exchange of data has also been essential. For example, the GDPR does not apply if the data is anonymised. However, if personal data is to be exchanged, for example, between the EU and the USA, it becomes more complicated, as the same level of data protection does not apply in the USA (Minssen et al. 2020c, p. 34). The Court of Justice of the European Union therefore declared the so-called "EU-US Privacy Shield" invalid in its *Data Protection Commissioner v. Facebook Ireland Limited and Maximillian Schrems*

(C-311/18—Schrems II) judgment of 16 July 2020, which hitherto ensured the international flow of data between the USA and Europe. However, the Court also held that data transfers carried out in accordance with the standard data protection clauses recognised by the EU can still be valid. However, this requires that "appropriate safeguards" (see Article 46 GDPR) are in place to compensate for the lack of data protection in a third country. Despite this possibility of legal data transfer, this judgment is criticised by many companies, scholars, and authorities (e.g., Commission Nationale Informatique & Libertés 2020), as it could complicate or practically make impossible the exchange of personal data between EU and non-EU countries like the USA (Bradford et al. 2021, lsab007; Corrales et al. 2020, p. 160).

The already described Corona warning apps in Section 2, but also the recently introduced digital vaccination certificates, have raised questions about data protection and privacy. In April 2020, for example, the EU member states, with the support of the European Commission, developed a so-called EU "toolbox" for the use of contact tracing apps or Corona warning apps (European Commission 2020d, p. 1). The EU toolbox sets out the essential requirements for such an app. In particular, the apps should be in line with the EU data protection rules as set out in the *Guidelines of the European Data Protection Board (EDPB) on the use of location data and contact tracing tools in the context of the Covid-19 outbreak* (EDPB 2020a, p. 1–22). In its guidelines, the EDPB, for example, recalls that both the GDPR and the Directive 2002/58/EC (ePrivacy Directive) are relevant in the context of contact tracing (ibid., p. 5). The ePrivacy Directive, which has been implemented into national law by the EU member states, must be taken into account in the processing of electronic communication data like mobile location data (EDPB 2020b, p. 1). In a statement in March 2020, the EDPB Chair had already emphasised that authorities should initially aim to process anonymised location data (ibid.; see also Shachar et al. 2020, p. 19). In addition to compliance with the EDPB guidelines, the EU toolbox provides further essential requirements for the implementation of contact tracing apps or Corona warning apps. For example, the apps should be implemented in close consultation with the health authorities and with their approval (European Commission 2020d, p. 1). In addition, the use of the apps should be voluntary (ibid.). The toolbox also recommends that the apps should use Bluetooth technology (ibid.). This recommendation is particularly welcome as the use of Bluetooth is less invasive in terms of the privacy of an individual than contact tracing using, for example, location data (Gerke et al. 2020a, p. 1181). The toolbox also emphasises that the apps should be based on anonymised data, that is, without revealing the identity of Covid-19 patients to users (European Commission 2020d, p. 1). In addition, the apps should be secure, effective, and interoperable across the EU (ibid.). It is obvious that the required balancing must also take into account ethical questions and values. In particular, the four principles of biomedical ethics (Beauchamp and Childress 2012) are to be considered—for example, with regard to access to modern phones, on which the apps have to work. Furthermore, it is already becoming increasingly clear that, for example, so-called "trade-offs" between the adequate protection of privacy and various fundamental rights on the one hand, and the precision, impartiality, transparency, and international competitiveness of pandemic-relevant digital technologies on the other hand, must be taken into account. Since effective data exchange is crucial for combating the Covid-19 pandemic and future pandemics, laudable initiatives such as the WHO's "Technology Access Pool" (C-TAP) (WHO 2020, p. 1; see also WHO 2021, p. 1) or data portals within the European Open Science Cloud will have to make increasingly decisions on such "trade-offs" (EOSC-Data 2020, p. 1; EOSC-Covid 2020, p. 1). In addition, property rights and competition law may play a role here (Graber-Soudry et al. 2020).

4.2 *Data Access, (Intellectual) Property Rights, and Competition Law*

One the one hand, different forms of property rights can—similar to data protection rights—make the use of digital technologies in the Covid-19 pandemic and access to important data more difficult. On the other hand, however, such rights can also create the necessary incentives for the development of new pandemic-relevant technologies. However, this requires that the prerequisites for the creation or granting of such rights and the scope of protection for such rights be designed and enforced in a proportionate, meaningful, and correct manner. In particular, intellectual property rights and their importance in terms of ownership and access to data sets pose particularly great challenges for legislators, authorities, health systems, companies, and international organizations during the Covid-19 pandemic (Gunnarsdóttir et al. 2021; Minssen and Pierce 2018, p. 311). Data mining methods or data analyses often require the copying of or references to information or databases (Gunnarsdóttir et al. 2021). However, all of these can be protected by different and often overlapping intellectual property rights (Gunnarsdóttir et al. 2021; Minssen and Pierce 2018, p. 311), which in turn can lead to problems for the legal interoperability of digital technologies (Graber-Soudry et al. 2020, pp. 19–21). The most important intellectual property rights for the protection of medical data typically include the protection of trade secrets and confidential information, as well as exclusive rights with respect to data and marketing rights granted by medical authorities (Gunnarsdóttir et al. 2021). In addition, copyright and—at least in Europe—special sui generis database rights may also be of great importance (ibid.). It is also important to note that data "as such" are not patentable under the principles enshrined in the European Patent Convention and national patent laws (Graber-Soudry et al. 2020, pp. 44–45). However, specific uses of algorithms, AI, and functional data that contribute to technical effects and applications can be claimed in patents and patent applications under certain conditions (Minssen and Pierce 2018, p. 311). In addition, the publication or exchange of Covid-19-relevant data can have decisive effects on IPR strategies, such as compliance with important conditions for the protection of trade secrets or the patent law criteria of novelty and inventive step (Graber-Soudry et al. 2020, p. 44; see also Carroll 2015, p. 8). In order not to jeopardize the availability of patent protection and the protection of a trade secret for Covid-19-relevant inventions, inventors may therefore tend to forego the publication of data (Graber-Soudry et al. 2020, p. 45; Gunnarsdóttir et al. 2021).

Contract law is another important and flexible but also complex tool to clarify, restrict, and control ownership issues for data use and data transfer in a pandemic. For example, approvals for access to and reuse of pandemic-relevant data and digital technologies or underlying rights can be granted or required by licensing agreements or other contractual conditions (Carroll 2015, p. 8; Minssen and Pierce 2018, pp. 311 et seq.; Gunnarsdóttir et al. 2021). In special cases, the data user has to rely on exceptions to limitations of the scope of protection, infringements, or—in some cases even—compulsory licenses: This may be necessary, for example, if data protected by intellectual property rights are not disclosed or licensed or if in a medical emergency, such as a pandemic, completely unaffordable or grossly disproportionate license fees are demanded, and no agreement could be reached. However, such compulsory licenses are subject to strict requirements and are only appropriate in exceptional cases. This has led to a range of urgent and highly relevant issues at the interface between intellectual property rights, other property relationships, competition law, and data (Minssen and Pierce 2018, p. 311). These discussions are further intensified by the Covid-19 pandemic, as evidenced by the global efforts to pool data resources and improve the (legal) interoperability of these data (Graber-Soudry et al. 2020), as well as international IPR debates and recent reports of data theft (Gunnarsdóttir et al. 2021). These discussions between data researchers/owners, government agencies, non-profit/international organizations, patient associations, civil society organizations, and state/private companies that provide large research infrastructure, technologies, and standardization platforms are both legally and ethically very complex (Gunnarsdóttir et al. 2021). They raise extremely difficult global questions about innovation economics, fair wealth distribution, fair competition, solidarity and global sustainability, responsibility, and fairness (ibid.). There is also a highly relevant interplay between (intellectual) property rights, data protection law, and competition law in accordance with Articles 101 and 102 of the Treaty on the Functioning of the European Union and the EC Merger Regulation. Competition law may prohibit or slow down certain forms of cooperation in order to protect free competition (Szentesi 2021, p. 1). These competition law interventions can, for example, relate to the sharing of data sets among certain companies, the joint development and production of medicines or aids, or cooperation in supply chains (ibid.). However, in times of crisis, it may be in the public interest that suppliers of certain and essential goods can communicate and cooperate without the risk of breaching competition law (ibid.). Therefore, competition authorities have granted special exceptions in individual decisions subject to certain conditions during the Covid-19 pandemic (e.g., so-called "Comfort Letters"). However, this does not mean that Covid-19 grants a "carte blanche" to ignore competition law in digital cooperation (ibid.; see also Kakkar et al. 2020, p. 1).

Competition law can also be used as a concrete means to combat excessive and unjustified price increases (Kianzad 2021, p. 251) or to compel market-dominant companies to disclose essential data sets in the fight against the pandemic in specific cases. The recently reformed German competition law plays a pioneering role here and has gained particular relevance in the Covid-19 pandemic (Van Dorpe 2021, p. 1). With the entry into force of the 10th Amendment of the German Competition Act (GWB-Digitalisierungsgesetz 2021, p. 1) on 19 January 2021, the German Bundestag has introduced a new cartel law framework for access to data. This is done, inter alia, in the form of two data access claims anchored in the provisions on abuse control of the GWB (Schweda and von Schreiter 2021, p. 1). In other European countries, such as Belgium, several competition authorities have announced in recent months that they would try to apply competition law in order to grant access to data collected by companies to third parties (Federle and Benoit 2020, p. 1). However, if the data concerned are personal data, the enforcement of such access obligations is difficult (ibid.). It is also quite conceivable that companies could abuse the rules of the GDPR and thus a dominant position in order to avoid data access and achieve a competitive advantage (Këllezi 2019, p. 343). In this sense, there are still many open legal questions with ethical implications. However relevant the interplay of intellectual property rights, data protection, and competition law may be, it is also important to take into account important differences between intellectual property rights and "general" individual property rights. Intellectual property rights typically require a certain level of performance, such as an innovative technical invention or function in patent law. This requirement makes it possible to distinguish intellectual property from the "public domain", such as simple data or discoveries, and to define the scope of protection. Intellectual property rights therefore only cover a limited, time-limited facet of—often "created"—property. Even rights to personal data, for example, under the GDPR, constitute a *sui generis* right. In this context, it is argued that data protection rights could be seen as property rights or personal rights at first glance (Hummel et al. 2020, p. 1 ff.; Hughes 2006, p. 993–1084; Lemley and Weiser 2007, pp. 783–842; Pearce 2018, p. 190). However, other authors reject such a broad interpretation (Nadezhda Purtova 2015, p. 83–111).

In view of these limitations and independently of the open questions with regard to intellectual property rights, data protection rights, and exceptions to such rights, the following questions therefore arise: Would it also be possible to see an ethical and moral responsibility to provide individual medical data? How would data that could be of great importance in addressing the Covid-19 pandemic influence such a discussion and deliberation? Would financial incentives play a role? I. Glenn Cohen already discussed three years ago the important normative question of whether there be a duty to share personal medical data for the benefit of the public or to achieve other non-pecuniary benefits such as better health or quality of life (Cohen 2018, p. 209; see also Gunnarsdóttir et al. 2021). A recently published US study on genetic data provides general indications of the willingness of citizens to share their data (Briscoe et al. 2020, p. 1; Gunnarsdóttir et al. 2021). The study shows that only about 12% of those surveyed would allow the free use of their data for altruistic purposes, while more than half of those surveyed would allow the use of their data if they were compensated financially, and about 38% of those surveyed would not share their data (Gunnarsdóttir et al. 2021). In addition, the study confirmed that almost two-thirds of those surveyed would be inclined to submit genetic data if the data were not rented, sold, or passed on to third parties, and any future use would depend on their permission (Briscoe et al. 2020, p. 1; Gunnarsdóttir et al. 2021). Even if it can be assumed that individual attitudes toward genetic and other types of medical data differ, this study indicates that the exploitation of the full potential for the collection and use of medical data can depend very much on individual attitudes toward property and financial incentives (Gunnarsdottir et al. 2021). However, it is also important that the value of sharing their medical data is conveyed to the public. So instead of financial incentives, there is also the possibility that companies that use the data create added value for the health of the "data donors" (Gerke et al. 2020c, p. 305; Gunnarsdottir et al. 2021).

4.3 Robustness, Cybersecurity, Liability, Accountability, and Licensing

With the far-reaching and invasive deployments of digital technologies during the Covid-19 pandemic and due to the growing number of AI-based medical applications, security issues are becoming increasingly important. This also raises the extremely important question of who is responsible and ultimately liable if digital solutions and the application of AI in combating pandemics do not work properly or make mistakes that lead to individual or collective damage. This could be software errors or technologies that are not sufficiently protected against cyber attacks, smartphones, digital vaccine certificate apps, or programs that damage patients or lead to false Covid-19 diagnoses or recommendations. It is also possible to forge test results or three-dimensional image analyses controlled by AI using "deep learning" technology (Mirsky et al. 2019, p. 1). How can such application errors, fraudulent abuse, errors in programming and data selection, system-internal errors in "self-learning" AI technology, and cyber attacks be prevented by security measures, rules, and technical requirements? Who has claims for damages and on what basis against whom, and under what conditions? Answering these questions is very complex and case-specific, but it is crucial for legal certainty and thus for the confidence of the economy and society in the technology.

4.3.1 Robustness and Cybersecurity

The security and robustness of such an important and invasive technology depends, on the one hand, on technical standards, regulations, precautionary measures, and training programs for proper use. On the other hand, the question of cybersecurity has gained enormous importance worldwide (Gerke et al. 2020c, pp. 323–325). This can be explained by the aforementioned growing use of digital technologies that increasingly penetrate into particularly sensitive private settings and health areas. Moreover, the increasing number of cyberattacks worldwide, which reached another peak during the Covid-19 pandemic (Dubsky 2020, p. 1), also plays a role. It is therefore not surprising that several national laws and regulatory structures have already been tightened up in the field of cybersecurity (Bischoff 2020, p. 1; Gerke et al. 2020c, pp. 323–325; Minssen et al. 2020a, p. 122). In December 2020, the European Commission also published a series of proposals on cybersecurity, which include a new cybersecurity strategy (European Commission 2020a, p. 1) and a proposal for a directive on ensuring a high common level of cybersecurity in the EU (European Commission 2020b, p. 1). The European Commission thus appears to have recognised the enormous importance of cybersecurity for the confidence of users in online activities, as well as for economic activities and growth (Wieler 2021, p. 1). This also seems to include the insight that far-reaching measures and initiatives are necessary in order for Europe to benefit safely and effectively from innovation, automation, and connectivity (ibid.). It should also be noted that cybersecurity should not only include technical upgrading and legally regulated technical security standards. Since a chain is only as strong as its weakest link, it will be just as important to train both specialists and the population in cybersecurity and to issue practically easy-to-implement and understandable behaviour guidelines.

4.3.2 Liability, Accountability, and Approval

But who is to be blamed if there are accidents? With regard to the question of responsibility and liability, it can be difficult to apply existing principles and concepts for civil and criminal liability, or traditional product liability rules to health software and algorithms used in advanced AI (cf. Minssen 2019, p. 1; Price 2017, pp. 11–12, Price et al. 2019a, p. 1765; Price et al. 2021, p. 15). One problem is that, to date, legislation and case law dealt primarily with software that has been used in healthcare as an integrated part of technical aids, but rarely in situations where the responsibility is inked to the software as such (Kaplan and Johnson 2020, p. 1). So far, legislations and discussions focused mainly on programs and devices that are supposed to support doctors, nursing staff, and other health care professionals in making decisions ("clinical decision support"), with the final decision to be made by a human hand (Price 2017, pp. 11–12; Gerke et al. 2020c, pp. 313–316). However, digitally based technologies and medical devices based on

AI can call this starting position into question: How can and should human users such as doctors and nursing staff be held accountable for implementing some decisions or assessing some conclusions that they do not understand? (Minssen 2019, p. 1, quoting Price 2017, pp. 11–12). How should doctors, nursing staff, and other health care professionals take responsibility for decisions proposed by opaque and highly complex algorithms that have been trained with a great variety of data? (Minssen 2019, p. 1, quoting Price 2017, pp. 11–12). In this context, the question arises as to what an appropriate balance of liability risks might look like. Perhaps it would be appropriate to consider national or international monetary funds for digital technologies and AI that would help to provide the necessary capital and to provide compensation in the event of damage (ibid. as well as Price et al. 2019a, p. 1765; Gerke et al. 2020c, p. 314). These questions are not easy to answer, especially when one considers that additional problems may arise with regard to any review obligations and guarantees to patients: Under what circumstances, for example, might doctors, nurses, health technicians, etc., be required to question AI decisions (Price 2017, p. 12)? Doctors who want to help patients to the best of their ability will certainly feel strongly obliged to intervene if an AI proposal or result appears questionable to them. This is particularly the case if an algorithm suggests a treatment that, in their opinion, is not helpful, too expensive, useless, or even dangerous for the patient (Minssen 2019, p. 1, quoting Price 2017, pp. 11–12). However, in order for doctors to be able to detect deficiencies in the AI technology being used, they must first be trained in what AI is and what advantages and disadvantages the AI technology itself, and the specific system in which it is used, entail (Katznelson and Gerke 2021). In the future, the situation could become even more complicated if patients in automated health systems are treated by technologies based on self-learning AI (Minssen 2019, p. 1; Babic et al. 2019, p. 1202; Gerke et al. 2020e, p. 53; Babic et al. 2021, p. 1). Such AI systems can learn from new data and improve and expand themselves, and it would therefore be conceivable that such systems one day—for example, in automated infection clinics—make and carry out treatment decisions independently. Who would then be responsible for any physical and/or mental harm caused to a patient? In this context and also in view of the pandemic, the question arises as to whether liability aspects in relation to such systems should be assessed under the principles of product liability or as medical malpractice or whether special liability privileges should apply due to the emergency situation. Depending on the individual case, for example, in the USA, manufacturers of some digital technologies may have liability immunity under the Public Readiness and Emergency Preparedness (PREP) Act (Gerke et al. 2020a, p. 1178).

The European Commission is dealing, inter alia, with general liability issues in its "Report on the safety and liability implications of Artificial Intelligence, the Internet of Things and Robotics" published on 19 February 2020 (European Commission 2020c, p. 1). Although the Commission still considers many existing liability rules to be applicable, it also sees a specific need for new legislative initiatives to close relevant legal gaps in terms of product liability and safety and to meet new challenges such as autonomy, connectivity, data dependence, complexity of systems and products, opacity, software updates, as well as a more comprehensive security management and better consideration of value chains (ibid.). As already pointed out by the German lawyer Claudia Otto, it should also be borne in mind that even if "the existing [EU] liability law (still) should be sufficient to assess the civil and criminal liability", it might nevertheless be necessary to "create more room for development and application in the field of artificial intelligence" in order to "increase the attractiveness of the location" (from German, Otto 2020, p. 1). At the same time, Otto admonishes that "in order to achieve a balance of interests, a corresponding simplification of the enforcement of claims by victims is needed in order to not throw the legal system out of balance" (from German, ibid.).

The European Parliament has also considered such questions as it can be seen in its recently published resolution "with recommendations to the Commission on a civil liability regime for artificial intelligence" (European Parliament 2020, p. 1). The Resolution contains the following formulation in Consideration B:

> "[...] whereas any future-oriented civil liability legal framework has to instil confidence in the safety, reliability and consistency of products and services, including in digital technology, in order to strike a balance between efficiently and fairly protecting potential victims of harm or damage and, at the same time, providing enough leeway to make it possible for enterprises, and particularly small and medium-sized enterprises, to develop new technologies, products or services; whereas this will help build confidence and create stability for investment; whereas ultimately, the goal of any liability framework should be to provide legal certainty for all parties, whether it be the producer, the operator, the affected person or any other third party" (European Parliament 2020, p. 3)

The draft resolution also contains detailed recommendations for the preparation of a regulation on liability for the operation of AI systems. Article 4 of the draft regulation, which would be directly applicable in the EU Member States, proposes strict liability for operators of high-risk AI systems (see also Otto 2020, p. 1, with further explanations and evaluations of the details of the proposal). Although it remains to be seen how these reports and recommendations will affect future legislative proposals, regulations and directives, it should also be noted that liability issues for AI and digital technologies in healthcare may also be based on regulatory approvals (Kaplan and Johnson 2020, p. 1). Clarifying these issues is therefore also an important concern for medical regulatory authorities such as the European Medicines Agency, the US Food and Drug Administration (FDA), the German Federal Institute for Drugs and Medical Devices, or independent testing and certification bodies for medical devices (so-called "notified bodies") (Minssen et al. 2020b, pp. 1–18). For example, the FDA considers software as a medical device if it meets the requirements of Article 201(h)(1) of the Federal Food, Drug, and Cosmetic Act and is intended, in particular, "for use in the diagnosis of disease or other conditions, or in the cure, mitigation, treatment, or prevention of disease". However, it remains to be seen whether—in particular in cases of self-learning AI—courts will deal with medical software under product liability principles or whether they will apply principles of medical malpractice (Kaplan and Johnson 2020, p. 1; Price et al. 2019a, p. 1765).

A ruling by the Court of Justice of the European Union (2017; see Minssen et al. 2020f, p. 615) of 7 December 2017 illustrates that the classification of software as a medical device has raised questions under European law. The Court had to assess a software which makes it possible to use patient data in order to, inter alia, identify contraindications, drug interactions and overdoses. However, despite this functionality, the software did not have any direct effect on or in the human body (cf. Holzer and Reinle 2018, p. 1; see also Minssen et al. 2020f, p. 615). The Court held that, as regards this function, "such software must be subject to CE marking in accordance with the provisions of the [then] European Directive on medical devices" in order for it to be placed on the market in the EU (from German, Holzer and Reinle 2018, p. 1). Member States of the EU are therefore not allowed to impose any additional certification requirements at national level (Holzer and Reinle 2018, p. 1). The principles laid down in this ruling are also in line with the rules of the new EU Regulations on medical devices (Regulation 2017/745) and in vitro diagnostic medical devices (Regulation 2017/746), which will now have to be complied with by manufacturers, national European medicines agencies, the European Medicines Agency, and notified bodies (Minssen et al. 2020b, p. 1; Minssen et al. 2020f, p. 615; Gerke et al. 2020c, pp. 310 et seq.). These authorities are therefore currently intensively searching for experts in the field of AI or machine learning who understand how the technology will develop over complex product life cycles and value chains (Minssen 2019, p. 1). One problem associated with this are the so-called "black-box" medical devices: How are medical regulatory authorities to assess digital solutions, for example, in combating pandemics, if they are opaque and it is unclear how they arrived at their result (Gerke et al. 2020c, p. 304; Minssen 2019, p. 1; Price 2015, p. 420)? How are users to trust software programs and devices whose processes they can neither influence nor understand? As already indicated above, accountability, responsibility, and liability issues therefore overlap with questions of transparency and traceability. There is a clear connection and interaction. The next section will therefore deal in more detail with these quality features.

4.4 Transparency, Traceability, and Explainability

Transparency, traceability, and explainability are often important features and regulatory requirements for digital solutions. They are not only important in order to better deal with liability issues, but can also be of particular importance for general legal certainty, confidence in the technology, and thus for product acceptance, which is particularly important for combating pandemics. In principle, human users should feel empowered by the construction and design of digital solutions to understand the effects of this technology (see Abdul et al. 2018, p. 1). During a pandemic, this could, for example, be the possibility of questioning and, if necessary, challenging the decisions made on the basis of a surveillance app or a digital health or vaccination certificate. It should also be borne in mind that algorithmic decisions can also affect people who do not interact directly with AI technology (ibid.). To address these problems, interpretable models are to be preferred if they are just as safe and effective as "black box" models. It is also important here that no disproportionate obstacles are placed in the way of data access, accuracy, and performance of digital solutions (see Mori and Uchihira 2018, pp. 1–47; Rudin and Ustun 2018, pp. 449–466). This also plays a role in the application and interpretation of the GDPR. Different rules on transparency, traceability, and explainability run through the entire text of the GDPR. These principles are reflected in different places and in different articles and must be observed exactly, otherwise this could result in high fines according to Article 83 GDPR. Due to space-limitations, only some of the most important rules should be mentioned here: For example, transparency is one of the key-principles anchored in Article 5(1)(a) of the GDPR, which stipulates that personal data should be "processed lawfully, fairly and in a transparent manner in relation to the data subject ('lawfulness, fairness and transparency')". In this way, Article 5 of the GDPR combines, as a kind of catch-all or basic provision, the requirements of lawfulness and processing in good faith with the transparency required for this (see also Felzmann et al. 2019, p. 1). Another example can be found in Article 12(1) of the GDPR, which requires, among other things, that the data controller shall take "appropriate measures to provide any information referred to in [...] [certain articles of the GDPR] and any communication under [...] [certain articles of the GDPR] relating to processing to the data subject in a concise, transparent, intelligible and easily accessible form, using clear and plain language, in particular for any information addressed specifically to a child". Article 12(2) of the GDPR makes it clear that the data controller shall facilitate the exercise of the rights of the data subject under certain articles of the GDPR, which in turn confirms the importance of transparency requirements for the effective enforcement of procedural rights. This is particularly evident in connection with Article 15(1) of the GDPR, which grants data subjects the right to "obtain from the controller confirmation as to whether or not personal data concerning him or her are being processed". If this is the case, the data subject shall have the right to obtain from the controller access to the personal data and—inter alia—the following information: "[...] the right to lodge a complaint with a supervisory authority [...]" (Article 15(1)(f) of the GDPR); or "[...] the existence of automated decision-making, including profiling, referred to in Article 22(1) and (4) [of the GDPR] and, at least in those cases, meaningful information about the logic involved, as well as the significance and the envisaged consequences of such processing for the data subject" (Article 15(1)(h) of the GDPR, see also Recital 71 of the GDPR). The aforementioned Article 22 of the GDPR generally grants data subjects the right not to be "subject to a decision based solely on automated processing, including profiling, which produces legal effects concerning him or her or similarly significantly affects him or her" (Article 22(1) of the GDPR). There are a few narrowly defined exceptions in Article 22(2) GDPR, such as contractual necessity, compatibility with EU law and national law, or the data subject's explicit consent. However, Article 22(3) GDPR provides that in these cases of exception, the controller shall implement "suitable measures to safeguard the data subject's rights and freedoms and legitimate interests, at least the right to obtain human intervention on the part of the controller, to express his or her point of view and to contest the decision". This general right to human involvement and influence, and in particular the provisions on the exceptions, could, for example, require the manufacturer and operator of a Covid-19 monitoring app or a digital diagnosis procedure to understand how a certain decision, recommendation, or reaction came about in order then to be able to make a reasoned judgement as to whether a mistake was made (cf. also Wu 2020, p. 1). If this is not possible, a high fine may be imposed for the infringement under Article 83 of the GDPR. Consequently, necessary improvements of the explainability of systems and applications can represent a particularly important challenge for providers of digital solutions (ibid.). It is therefore not surprising that today a large part of the legal and ethical debates and controversies about transparency, traceability, and explainability of digital solutions in general, and with regard to specific applications in the pandemic (idigiT 2020, p. 3), concern the area of EU data protection law. In these discussions, the explainability of decisions based on AI has taken on a central role (Hacker et al. 2020, p. 416 with reference to Wachter et al. 2017, p. 76; Selbst and Powles 2017, p. 233; Doshi-Velez and Kortz 2017, p. 1; Goodman and Flaxman 2016, p. 1; Malgieri and Comandé 2017, p. 243; Wischmeyer 2018, p. 1). It is particularly disputed whether and to what extent the GDPR contains a "right to explanation" of automated decisions (Hacker et al. 2020, p. 416 et seq.). Some academics have proposed innovative approaches and claims such as so-called "counterfactual explanations" (Wachter et al. 2018, p. 842) or a potential "right to reasonable inferences" (Wachter and Mittelstadt 2019, p. 494).

Interestingly, however, there are also voices that see other areas of law as decisive for the discussions about the explainability requirement. For example, Philipp Hacker et al. argue that the explainability requirement can be shaped not only within data protection law but also with the help of contract and tort law:

> With legal requirements under the GDPR being largely unclear at the moment, it seems fruitful to inquire into the role of explainability in other legal areas. In fact, as we argue, contract and tort law, not data protection law, may eventually impose legal requirements to use explainable machine learning models. (Hacker et al. 2020, p. 416)

An important finding of these authors is that the "trade-off between explainability and accuracy, much discussed in the technical literature", also "sits at the heart of contract and tort liability for the use of AI systems" (Hacker et al. 2020, p. 416 et seq.).

Regardless of which view within this specific legal discussion is to be followed in detail, it is at least clear that the construction and improvement of transparent technologies is of enormous importance in many cases. Some technical experts point out in this context that "much work in AI and ML communities tends to suffer from a lack of usability, practical interpretability and efficacy on real users [...]". (Abdul et al. 2018, p. 1 et seq.) and, with reference to the results of recent studies, that:

> Given HCI's [human-computer interaction] focus on technology that benefits people, we, as a community, should take the lead to ensure that new intelligent systems are transparent from the ground up. This is echoed by Shneiderman et al. [...], who discussed the need for interfaces that allow users "to better understand underlying computational processes" and give users "the potential to better control their (the algorithms') actions" as one of the grand challenges for HCI researchers. Several researchers are already contributing towards this goal, e.g. with research on interacting with machine-learning systems [...], algorithmic fairness [...] and accountability [...]. (Abdul et al. 2018, p. 1 et seq.)

More interdisciplinary research that includes technical, humanities and social sciences will therefore be necessary to integrate these requirements into the design of AI and digital systems ("ethics, privacy, intelligibility and transparency by design") and to create technical, legal, and ethical standards. The Covid-19 pandemic has further highlighted the relevance of this important undertaking.

Since—as already indicated in the previous section—the evaluation of opaque algorithms and medical software also represents an enormous challenge for medical authorities, it must be ensured that these products are safe and effective. A large number of organizations and academics demand an appropriate level of transparency in order to enable sufficient regulatory review of medical products (Meszaros et al. 2021; Minssen 2020, pp. 235–236). This does not necessarily mean that every single step must be completely traceable (Meszaros et al. 2021; Yun 2020, pp. 235–236). Complex algorithms could therefore still be used (ibid.). However, according to some commentators, it would be desirable in order to build a transparent and trustworthy AI system that "the assumptions and limitations, operating protocols, data properties and output decisions can be systematically examined and validated" (Yun 2020, p. 235–236). Other scholars also point out that the healthcare system is special and that there are already tools to provide adequate evidence of safety and effectiveness: For example, randomized clinical trials could be used to bring some "black box" algorithms to market (Gerke et al. 2020c, p. 304).

Quality, safety, and data standards as well as a technical infrastructure and a framework for improving interoperability are key factors in realizing the potential of AI and digital technologies. This will probably require international agreements. It would also be important to create the right incentives for manufacturers to develop safe, effective, and trustworthy AI systems and to use these quality features as an international competitive factor. This could be achieved, for example, by technical and legal requirements and the granting of procedural advantages and rights in compliance with or improvement of such values, or by quality certificates and (security) labels. In addition, this could ultimately also help to achieve pragmatic compromises between data access, accuracy, and performance of the products on the one hand and compliance with legal norms and essential values with regard to data protection, transparency, responsibility, and belonging on the other hand (cf. Mori and Uchihira 2018, pp. 1–47; Rudin and Ustun 2018, pp. 449–466).

In order to establish and maintain the trust among consumers and patients, which is so important for product acceptance and competitiveness, it is also important to invest in the training of specialists and in the development of AI competence ("AI-savviness") among the population. As the current pandemic makes only too clear, it is of paramount importance in this context that such efforts—in accordance with the principle of equality—aim at the entire population and also take into account vulnerable groups, minorities, and other disadvantaged groups in society. Measures which support the wide-ranging and comprehensive use of digital solutions are absolutely essential in pandemics in order to increase the (global) efficiency of digital aids.

4.5 Bias, Discrimination, and Social Justice

In medicine and telemedicine, (self-learning) AI systems, surveillance apps, and algorithms developed by humans can only be as effective and fair as the data with which they are developed and trained. This also applies to pandemic-relevant digital technologies and raises important ethical questions with regard to data quality and potential risks of systemic bias and discrimination (cf. Wahl et al. 2018, p. 1). Several examples from practice have shown that algorithmic decisions with regard to disability, age, ethnic origin (Cossins 2018, p. 1), skin color (Fefegha 2018, p. 1), socio-cultural background (Jo and Gebru 2020, p. 306), language (Bender and Friedman 2018, p. 587), or gender (Short 2020, p. 1) can act with bias or inaccuracy (Minssen et al. 2020b, p. 16). In the worst case, this can lead to false diagnoses and ineffective treatments with dangerous consequences for the patients (Minssen et al. 2020b, p. 16 et seq.). The reasons for such unequal treatment vary and are complex. They can, for example, result from personal prejudices and from the composition of expert teams developing machine learning systems or training algorithms. Inequalities can also result from the available data volume, quality, and diversity used for programming. In addition, there is also a great risk of context-related inequalities ("contextual bias") in digital medicine, in particular when using AI technology, as algorithms and AI systems developed for highly technologized elite hospitals in rich countries often require a certain level of infrastructure, expertise and/or training to use the technology safely and effectively (Price 2019, p. 66; Minssen et al. 2020b, p. 17). Also, in the private and public areas outside of hospitals, which were so important, especially during the Covid-19 pandemic, the access to and the application of digital measures to combat the pandemic can, to a high degree, depend on the education and the linguistic, cultural, and technical understanding of the population, as well as on a highly developed technical or digital infrastructure (Lebret and Minssen 2021, p. 39). This can, for example, mean that Covid-19 apps do not work correctly on older phones or that certain measures, such as digital vaccination passports, and the associated possibilities and freedom of movement, disproportionately disadvantage specific vulnerable population groups. Under certain circumstances, this can also result in AI systems recommending unsuitable, risky, confusing, and far too expensive treatments or arrangements for resource-poor environments (Price 2019, p. 66). This could make such technologies inaccessible or even dangerous for vulnerable patients. Further social science and legal studies of such AI-related access problems, prejudices, and risks of unequal treatment are therefore required so that digital technologies, which are applied in resource-poor contexts, do not create problems for those who need them most urgently (Price 2019, p. 66). It could be argued that many of these ethical and legally problematic distortions disappear and problems are alleviated when AI technology develops further and the available data, as well as their quality and diversity increase (see also Mittelstadt et al. 2016, p. 15). However, as already mentioned, many algorithms are "by nature" so-called "black boxes," that is, they are opaque and complex (Price 2015, p. 420). In addition, data protection rights as codified in the GDPR and intellectual property rights can make transparency and access to relevant data more difficult, so that so-called "trade-offs" between, for example, these rights and the performance, competitiveness, precision, and impartiality of AI technology have to be achieved (Cohen et al. 2020a, p. e376). For example, it is conceivable that software companies in the healthcare sector invoke data protection, intellectual property rights, or trade secrets to deny access to pandemic-relevant data or information about digital procedures (cf. Minssen 2019, p. 1; Banavar 2016, p. 1; Minssen and Pierce 2018, p. 311). It can therefore be left to third parties to collect data and reveal prejudices (Sharkey 2019, p. 1). For this reason, it is extremely important that these developments are anticipated and monitored within a framework that allows for appropriate control. While complete transparency is unlikely to be achievable for some highly complex medical AI applications, it is important to ensure the safety and effectiveness of the systems (Gerke et al. 2020c, p. 304). In addition, even for highly complex AI systems some academics call for a sufficient explanation of the principles on which the algorithm operates as well as precise information about the data set used (Price 2015, p. 420; Wachter et al. 2018, p. 842). Data models should be sufficiently diverse to produce unbiased results in special health applications as well. If it turns out that a result is biased or unfair, there should be procedural means available to the individual to challenge relevant decisions in healthcare. Such procedural possibilities have already been discussed in the context of transparency and responsibility for protecting privacy (Wachter and Mittelstadt 2019, p. 494). Similar considerations should also be made in healthcare and pandemic responses with regard to the discrimination and unequal treatment issue. In doing so, it is particularly important to keep in mind that AI can also lead to new types of hidden prejudices that may not be covered by current laws. Frederik Zuiderveen Borgesius explains this as follows:

> "Most nondiscrimination statutes only apply to discrimination on the basis of protected characteristics, such as racial origin. Such statutes do not apply if organisations differentiate on the basis of newly invented classes that do not correlate with protected characteristics. Such differentiation could still be unfair, however, for instance when it reinforces social inequality." (Borgesius 2018, p. 73)

It therefore appears quite appropriate that, in the event that a new interpretation of the ethical and legal non-discrimination concepts anchored in EU law, international human rights law, national constitutional law, and medical laws is not possible, careful consideration must be given to purpose-oriented rewording of directives, and, under certain circumstances, even the adoption of new laws might be necessary (Lebret and Minssen 2021, p. 39; see also Wachter et al. 2020). Central values such as human dignity, personal freedom, the right to health, fair procedure, the rule of law, and legal equality are of paramount importance here (cf. Minssen 2019, p. 1). In order to avoid bias and discrimination, it is also important that companies and authorities do not use "soft" and non-binding "ethical guidelines" as a distraction to avoid binding and enforceable AI regulations that also take human rights into account in healthcare (cf. Kaye 2018, pp. 21 ff.). The complexity and global reach of AI further show that enforceable international legal frameworks are required to properly address these problems. The findings outlined above suggest that further changes to legislation or even additional regulations may indeed be required in order to "protect fairness and human rights in the area of AI" (Borgesius 2018, p. 73). This does not necessarily mean that existing legal rules on bias and discrimination are not applicable and could not be interpreted in a fact- and expert-based manner in relation to AI (cf. also Gerards and Xenidis 2020, pp. 141 ff.). But we support Borgesius' view that "regulating AI *in general* is not the right approach" because "the use of AI systems is too varied for one set of rules" (Borgesius 2018, p. 73). It is therefore to be expected that we need "sector-specific rules"—such as in healthcare—because "different values are at stake, and different problems arise, in different sectors" (ibid.).

A good example of this would be the use of digital technologies and AI in clinical trials to avoid contact and travel during a pandemic using remote studies or studies conducted in private homes to include more population groups. The development of the very specific regulatory framework for clinical trials will have to take into account the digital and AI possibilities in terms of the inclusion of previously excluded population groups and the use of so-called "real-world data" (RWD) to achieve this goal. AI solutions should respect existing processes, but, if necessary, also design and implement new ones to ensure that algorithms include different patient groups and treat them fairly and equitably (Currie et al. 2020, p. 752). Digital solutions in clinical trials should be designed and implemented in a process that—as far as possible, feasible, and reasonable—takes into account people, human characteristics, and human values in order to protect humanitarian principles, patient interests and preferences (including social and cultural norms), and in order to extend and improve AI predictions (ibid.). When designing and implementing AI technology in clinical trials, the involvement and empowerment of all stakeholders should therefore be a high priority (ibid.). In addition, long-term approaches should ultimately also take into account global justice and solidarity aspects. Even if this may be difficult to achieve, AI manufacturers should be encouraged to develop AI applications for the specific requirements in poorer or more remote regions of the world (Minssen et al. 2020b, p. 17). This can include awareness-raising efforts in relation to the use of local population data, but also highlight the special conditions in the local context, or training initiatives that first provide expertise in AI development and applications for health care in these regions. Furthermore, the infrastructure in many countries needs to be expanded to make a digital health care system possible at all. It is also unclear whether such markets are lucrative enough to motivate developers to move to these options through traditional innovation incentives, or whether additional mechanisms ("push and pull tools") or binding international agreements, such as access to leading new technological infrastructure and high-performance computers, are needed (ibid.).

5 Discussion

There is no doubt that the Covid-19 pandemic, like many other great crises of humanity, has led to a multitude of innovations and new forms of cooperation. What distinguishes the reaction to this pandemic from other health crises is the number of new digital technologies and AI that have come into play. Although many of the digital applications used "were not always as mature as would be necessary for medical care," a "new culture of trial and error" has led to very helpful services and solutions (from German, Vorstand der Bundesärztekammer (Board of the German Medical Association) 2020, p. 1). This new "trial and error" culture often resulted in medical progress, since it focuses on the "actual needs of the population" (from German, Vorstand der Bundesärztekammer (Board of the German Medical Association) 2020, p. 1). Above all, the partially short-term implemented digital offers that have been met with a positive response should remain usable after the Covid-19 pandemic and be further developed as quickly as possible (ibid.). The Covid-19 pandemic made it clear that ethical and legal issues such as data protection, cyber security, consent, liability, transparency, explainability, accountability, discrimination, ownership, and fair distribution and access to the possibilities of digital medicine and AI pose enormous challenges for industry, science, and society at large. The pandemic has clearly intensified and concretized these debates. However, the pandemic not only represented a medical, economic, social, biological, psychological, and political catastrophe for humanity but also an opportunity to improve healthcare. It should be borne in mind that it is only a matter of time before we have to cope with the next pandemic, and any related problems, such as the spreading of antimicrobial resistance (AMR) (Minssen et al. 2020d, p. 1; see also Minssen et al. 2020e, p. 823). It would therefore be a great advance for German, European, and global healthcare if the lessons learned from the Covid-19 crisis could be quickly incorporated into the development of digital strategies, guidelines, and legislation, such as the International Health regulations (IHR). Within the already mentioned areas of focus, some overarching challenges crystallize that need to be addressed at a higher level. Three of these problems were very eloquently summarized in a recently published comment in *The Lancet* by Effy Vayena: *First,* technical and governance standards would have to be harmonized to ensure better interoperability (Vayena 2021, p. 652). Despite the increasing use of electronic patient records, there would still be gaps in the ability of software and computer systems to use and exchange information (ibid.).

Second, there would still be certain uncertainties with regard to the practically important question of what constitutes evidence of the efficiency of the many digital tools, and a demonstrable benefit for users or patients, and which bodies are authorized to assess the evidence (ibid., p. 653). *Thirdly,* various interest groups would be driven by different motives in the complex ecosystem of digital medicine (ibid.). Supervisory authorities, patients, commercial companies, researchers, health care providers, investors, and political decision-makers might pursue different goals, often using the same health data (ibid.). Competition, commercial goals and attribution would all "contribute to a splintered digital health landscape, slowing progress in data use" (ibid.). The latter is also made more difficult in particular by the need to reach compromises. For example, an effective European data protection regime without a global agreement not only has the potential to impair the performance of technologies but could also lead to discrimination and global competitive disadvantages.

As Vayena also points out, the emerging "European Health Data Space" (EHDS) (European Commission 2020e, p. 1) offers an opportunity to address these cross-cutting challenges directly. The overarching goal of this initiative is to facilitate the access and use of European health data to promote European health care systems, policy, health research, and innovation (Vayena 2021, p. 653). With this initiative, Europe has the opportunity to set an example for a human rights-based data governance approach that promotes transparency, fairness, inclusion, accountability, and, in particular, human dignity (ibid.). This also applies in a wider sense to the European AI Strategy published in February 2020 (European Commission 2020f, p. 1; see also Cohen et al. 2020a, p. e376), which is intended to lead to the development of a future legal framework for AI in Europe. Some of the emerging European legal acts should now successfully implement the principles outlined in the AI Strategy, in particular for trustworthy AI (see also HEG-AI 2019, p. 1), in terms of material rights, as well as procedural rules and applicable procedures. It is not only important to set the necessary conditions for adequate regulation but also to give impulses for ethical guidelines as "governance" tools and to achieve useful compromises as well as legally compliant and ethical application rules (see Larsson 2021, pp. 85, 111). Such considerations are, of course, not only relevant to Germany and Europe. Since pathogens—in contrast to research and treatment options—do not respect borders and passports, it is particularly important to take global perspectives into account. Unfortunately, however, the Covid-19 pandemic has mercilessly exposed the weaknesses in the world's health and care systems and the very different global responses to protecting public health (see Knawy et al. 2020, p. 1537). The evolving international Pandemic Instrument, currently being negotiated at the WHO, should therefore carefully consider new digital and AI solutions. In this way, digital technologies can help governments and health systems worldwide to effectively and sustainably respond to future pandemics and other global health challenges (ibid.). Similar to vaccination strategies, digital means against the Covid-19 pandemic can only develop their full effect if they are usable and accessible worldwide. In this context, the Riyadh Declaration on Digital Health is particularly noteworthy. It was formulated during the Global Summit on Digital Health from 11 to 12 August 2020. The declaration contains seven key priorities and nine recommendations for digital health and data that, in the opinion of the expert panel, should be adopted by the global health community in order to effectively respond to the challenges of pandemics (ibid.). The recommendations range from global communication strategies and measures against misinformation, global data standards, and other proposals to promote the worldwide interoperability of data sets and digital technology to recommendations to increase the quality and access to health data, create more incentives for digital and AI-related innovation, expand surveillance systems taking into account ethical, data protection and other legal guidelines, promote training worldwide and support global research and development of digital health technology (ibid., 1538). The declaration is primarily an international call to create the necessary global infrastructure that is required for the coordination of effective and evidence-based digital health practices and for the exchange of high-quality real-time data at global and local levels in order to provide valuable and implementable information to more countries and health systems (ibid.). As understandable, sensible, and urgent as such calls and corresponding future initiatives are, so foreseeable are international tensions, challenges, and a need for compromise solutions in view of the topics dealt with in this section. However, these problem areas are often more difficult and complex in a geopolitical context due to power and competing interests than in a national or regional context. It will therefore also be very important to support new international agreements, such as the Pandemic Instrument, or new, experience-based and goal-oriented interpretations of existing agreements and regulations, such as provisions of the TRIPS Agreement ("Agreement on Trade-Related Aspects of Intellectual Property Rights") or the IHR, through legal and ethical research, guidelines, and careful expert opinions. This includes, among other things, the precautionary principles and procedural rights not dealt with in detail here, but also a wide range of essential human rights, such as human dignity or the freedom and equality rights of the German Basic Law (see, for example, Deutsches Grundgesetz (GG) 1949, Articles 1, 2 and 3), or the rights anchored in European and international conventions, such as the right to health (see, for example, International Covenant on Economic, Social and Cultural Rights 1976, Article 12), the right to a fair and effective procedure (see, for example, European Convention on Human Rights 1950, Articles 6 and 13), the respect for private and family life (see, for example, European Convention on Human Rights 1950, Article 8; EU Charter of Fundamental Rights 2012, Article 7), and the protection of personal data (see, for example, the EU Charter of Fundamental Rights 2012, Article 8). Ethical and legal studies must also deal with the opportunities and risks for the fundamental values of many democracies from a broader perspective. This is impressively demonstrated by Harvard professor Shoshana Zuboff in her New York Times article, who concludes her contribution with the following warning:

> "We must make our choice. We may have democracy, or we may have surveillance society, but we cannot have both. We have a democratic information civilization to build, and there is no time to waste." (Zuboff 2021, p. 1)

Therefore, the urgent question arises as to what is ethically and legally possible without losing sight of the protection of democratic values. When does careful weighing even give rise to an ethical and legal responsibility to promote and implement digital solutions? And how should such applications be monitored and regulated? In our opinion, the wide range of social and humanities sciences play a decisive role in answering such questions in order to ensure a sustainable, just, and responsible application, regulation, administration, and control (governance) of technologies. Legal science, for example, is confronted with a number of challenges. A conceptual challenge is that technical and ethical aspects, developments, and implications are rarely taken into account in legal studies, while the interaction between laws, technical infrastructure, and ethical context is often overlooked. Furthermore, there is a great need to expand scientific methodology to allow more so-called "computational thinking". So far, legal scholars have often lacked the technical expertise and scientific training in terms of data and computer-related methods to carry out empirical studies in this area. On the other hand, AI experts and practitioners often lack clear design plans for AI technologies that adequately take into account ethical and legal considerations. Until recently, there have also been too few concrete examples of the development of new legal frameworks in the field of medical AI. However, this research situation is changing rapidly, and social and humanities scholars are increasingly gaining the necessary multi- and interdisciplinary networks and competencies, data, and the necessary infrastructure to effectively deal with these important issues. It remains to be hoped that such important social and humanities research will also gain increasing attention outside academic debate. The results, guidelines, recommendations, and legislative proposals stemming from such research should not only be understood as obstacles to the technical development of measures against the Covid-19 pandemic and future pandemics. They should also be regarded as necessary for anchoring new technical developments in fundamental social norms, achieving UN sustainable development goals, and ultimately also as a competitive advantage. However, in order to bridge the gap between research, theory, and practical applications, not only international standards, rules, and quality standards play an important role but also trust-building communication and training strategies. Among other things, it is necessary to also deal with human behavior and psychological factors, such as in terms of the relationship between patients and doctors (Topol 2019, p. 44). Trust in safe, compliant, fair, unbiased, useful, accessible, and effective digital medical solutions that are based on human needs is one of the key factors for the acceptance of digital technologies and AI by the public. This will be of decisive importance at both the national and European, and international levels for combating pandemics, the commercial success of digital medicine, and the global competitiveness of digital technologies and AI.

6 Conclusions and Outlook

Rapid technical developments, applications, and possibilities for combating pandemics raise many important ethical and legal questions. A careful discussion of ethical and legal rules and norms to protect fundamental values is now absolutely necessary and should significantly influence the design and competitiveness of digital products and services. It is also important to implement the insights resulting from these discussions technically, effectively, and economically sensibly, without neglecting the human factors, control options, and central values. Many of the procedures now required will require difficult compromises and a weighing of different values, such as the weighing of GDPR compliance with the accuracy and impartiality of the technology discussed in more detail here. It is therefore also of enormous importance to highlight the basic norms and values on which such specific regulations are based and to communicate them in the public debate. For Germany and Europe, this should also involve strengthening European digital sovereignty and competitiveness (Merkel et al. 2021, p. 1), and advocating for European interests and values. That said, not only during the pandemic but also afterward, this endeavour must take into account the requirements of global cooperation and an appropriate level of global solidarity as well, which highlights the future need for further global standards and basic rules.

References

Abdul A, Vermeulen J, Wang D, Lim BY, Kankanhalli M (2018) Trends and trajectories for explainable, accountable and intelligible systems: an HCI research agenda. Proc 2018 CHI Conf Hum Factors Comput Syst 582. https://doi.org/10.1145/3173574.3174156

Alexy L, Fisahn A, Hähnchen S, Mushoff T, Trepte U (2019) Das Rechtslexikon. Begriffe, Grundlagen, Zusammenhänge, 1. Aufl. Verlag J.H.W. Dietz Nachf., Bonn. Lizenzausgabe: Bundeszentrale für politische Bildung. https://www.bpb.de/nachschlagen/lexika/recht-a-z/324124/subjektives-recht. Accessed 10 Mar 2021

Arshadi AK, Webb J, Salem M et al (2020) Artificial Intelligence for COVID-19 Drug Discovery and Vaccine Development. Front Artif Intelligence 3:65

Atik J, Jeutner V (2019) Quantum computing and algorithmic law. Los Angeles Leg Stud Res Pap 38. https://doi.org/10.2139/ssrn.3490930

Babic B, Gerke S, Evgeniou T, Cohen IG (2019) Algorithms on regulatory lockdown in medicine: prioritize risk monitoring to address the "update problem". Science 366(6470):1202–1204. https://doi.org/10.1126/science.aay9547

Babic B, Cohen IG, Evgeniou T, Gerke S (2021) When machine learning goes off the rails. Harv Bus Rev. https://hbr.org/2021/01/when-machine-learning-goes-off-the-rails. Accessed 08 Feb 2021

Banavar G (2016) What it will take for us to trust AI. https://hbr.org/2016/11/what-it-will-take-for-us-to-trust-ai. Accessed 10 Feb 2021

Beauchamp TL, Childress JF (2012) Principles of biomedical ethics, 7th edn. University Press, Oxford

Bender A, Cortés-Ciriano I (2020) Artificial intelligence in drug discovery: what is realistic, what are illusions? Part 1: ways to make an impact, and why we are not there yet. Drug Discov Today 26(2):511–524. https://doi.org/10.1016/j.drudis.2020.12.009

Bender EM, Friedman B (2018) Data statements for natural language processing: toward mitigating system bias and enabling better science. Trans Assoc Comput Linguist 6:587–604. https://doi.org/10.1162/tacl_a_00041

Bischoff P (2020) Which countries have the worst (and best) cybersecurity? https://www.comparitech.com/blog/vpn-privacy/cybersecurity-by-country/ Accessed 19 Feb 2021

Borgesius FZ (2018) Discrimination, artificial intelligence and algorithmic decision-making. https://rm.coe.int/discrimination-artificial-intelligence-and-algorithmic-decision-making/1680925d73. Accessed 19 Feb 2021

Bradford L, Aboy M, Liddell K (2021) Standard contractual clauses for cross-border transfers of health data after Schrems II, J Law Biosci 8(1):lsab007. https://doi.org/10.1093/jlb/lsab007

Briscoe F et al (2020) Evolving public views on the value of one's DNA and expectations for genomic database governance: results from a national survey. PLOS ONE 15(3):e0229044. https://doi.org/10.1371/journal.pone.0229044

Budd J, Miller BS, Manning EM et al (2020) Digital technologies in the public-health response to COVID-19. Nat Med 26:1183–1192. https://doi.org/10.1038/s41591-020-1011-4

Bundeszentrale für Politische Bildung (BPB) mit Verweis auf: Duden Recht A-Z (2020) Fachlexikon für Studium, Ausbildung und Beruf, 3rd edn. Bibliographisches Institut 2015, Berlin. Lizenzausgabe Bonn: Bundeszentrale für politische Bildung. https://www.bpb.de/nachschlagen/lexika/recht-a-z/22748/recht. Accessed 10 Nov 2020

Carroll MW (2015) Sharing research data and intellectual property law: a primer. PLoS Biol 13(8):e1002235. https://doi.org/10.1371/journal.pbio.1002235

Choong YYC, Tan HW, Patel DC et al (2020) The global rise of 3D printing during the COVID-19 pandemic. Nat Rev Mater 5:637–639. https://doi.org/10.1038/s41578-020-00234-3

Cohen GI (2018) Is there a duty to share healthcare data? In: Cohen GI et al (eds) Big data, health law, and bioethics, 1 edn. University Press, Cambridge, pp 209–222. https://doi.org/10.1017/9781108147972.020

Cohen GI, Evgeniou T, Gerke S, Minssen T (2020a) The European artificial intelligence strategy: implications and challenges for digital health. Lancet Digital Health 2(7):e376–e379. https://doi.org/10.1016/S2589-7500(20)30112-6

Cohen GI, Gostin LO, Weitzner DJ (2020b) Digital smartphone tracking for COVID-19: public health and civil liberties in tension. JAMA 323(23):2371–2372. https://doi.org/10.1001/jama.2020.8570

Commission Nationale Informatique & Libertés (2020) National Council of Free Software vs. Ministry of Solidarities and Health Conseil d'Etat Section du Contentieux Ref. L. 521-2 CJA

Corrales Compagnucci M, Minssen T, Seitz C, Aboy M (2020) Lost on the high seas without a safe harbor or a shield? Navigating cross-border transfers in the pharmaceutical sector after schrems II invalidation of the EU-US privacy shield. Eur Pharm Law Rev (EPLR) 4(3):153–160. https://doi.org/10.21552/eplr/2020/3/5

Cossins D (2018) Discriminating algorithms: 5 times AI showed prejudice. In: New Scientist. https://www.newscientist.com/article/2166207-discriminating-algorithms-5-times-ai-showed-prejudice/. Accessed 10 Feb 2021

Currie G, Hawk KE, Rohren EM (2020) Ethical principles for the application of artificial intelligence (AI) in nuclear medicine. Eur J Nucl Med Mol Imaging 47:748–752. https://doi.org/10.1007/s00259-020-04678-1

Danish Medicines Agency (2020) Home-based clinical trials will be possible in the future. https://laegemiddelstyrelsen.dk/en/news/2021/home-based-clinical-trials-will-be-possible-in-the-future/#. Accessed 10 Jan 2021

Deutscher Anwaltsverein (DAV) (2020) Verbesserungsvorschläge aus zivilrechtlicher Sicht zum Gesetz zur Abmilderung der Folgen der COVID-19-Pandemie im Zivil-, Insolvenz- und Strafverfahrensrecht—BGBl Teil I 2020 Nr. 14, 27.03.2020, S. 569—Stellungnahme Nr.: 28/2020 Berlin. https://anwaltverein.de/de/newsroom/sn-28-20. Accessed 19 Feb 2021

Deutsches Grundgesetz (GG) (Grundgesetz für die Bundesrepublik Deutschland) vom 23. Mai 1949 (BGBl. p 1), zuletzt geändert durch Artikel 1 und 2 Satz 2 des Gesetzes vom 29. September 2020 (BGBl. I p 2048)

Doshi-Velez F, Kortz M (2017) Accountability of AI under the law: the role of explanation. Berkman Klein Center Working Group on Explanation and the Law, Berkman Klein Center for Internet & Society working paper. http://nrs.harvard.edu/urn-3:HUL.InstRepos:34372584. Accessed 27 Feb 2021

Druedahl LC, Lebret A, Minssen T (2020) ELSI implications of prioritizing biological therapies in times of COVID-19. J Law Med Ethics 48(3):579–582. https://doi.org/10.1177/1073110520958884

Dubsky D (2020) Angreifer setzen auf Corona und Covid-19—Interpol warnt vor alarmierender Zunahme von Cyberattacken. https://www.funkschau.de/sicherheit-datenschutz/interpol-warnt-vor-alarmierender-zunahme-von-cyberattacken.178821.html. Accessed 25 Feb 2021

EDSA, Europäischer Datenschutzausschuss (2020a) Leitlinien 04/2020 für die Verwendung von Standortdaten und Tools zur Kontaktnachverfolgung im Zusammenhang mit dem Ausbruch von COVID-19. https://edpb.europa.eu/sites/edpb/files/files/file1/edpb_guidelines_20200420_contact_tracing_covid_with_annex_de_0.pdf. Accessed 15 Mar 2021

EDSA, Europäischer Datenschutzausschuss (2020b) Statement by the EDPB Chair on the processing of personal data in the context of the COVID-19 outbreak. https://edpb.europa.eu/news/news/2020/statement-edpb-chair-processing-personal-data-context-covid-19-outbreak_de. Accessed 10 Feb 2021

EOSC-COVID (2020) COVID-19 highlights the need for EOSC. https://www.eosc-portal.eu/news/covid-19-highlights-need-eosc. Accessed 28 Feb 2021

EOSC-DATA (2020) Thousands collaborate over new COVID-19 Data Portal. https://www.eosc-portal.eu/news/thousands-collaborate-over-new-covid-19-data-portal. Accessed 10 Feb 2021

EU-Grundrechtecharta (Charter der Grundrecht der Europäischen Union (GRCh)) (2012) OJ C 326, 26.10.2012, pp 391–407. http://data.europa.eu/eli/treaty/char_2012/oj. Accessed 28Feb 2021

Europäische Kommission (2020a) The EU's cybersecurity strategy for the digital decade. https://ec.europa.eu/digital-single-market/en/news/eus-cybersecurity-strategy-digital-decade. Accessed 28 Feb 2021

Europäische Kommission (2020b) Vorschlag für eine RICHTLINIE DES EUROPÄISCHEN PARLAMENTS UND DES RATES über Maßnahmen für ein hohes gemeinsames Cybersicherheitsniveau in der Union und zur Aufhebung der Richtlinie (EU) 2016/1148. https://ec.europa.eu/transparency/regdoc/rep/1/2020/DE/COM-2020-823-F1-DE-MAIN-PART-1.PDF. Accessed 28 Feb 2021

Europäische Kommission (2020c) Bericht über die Auswirkungen künstlicher Intelligenz, des Internets der Dinge und der Robotik in Hinblick auf Sicherheit und Haftung. https://ec.europa.eu/info/sites/info/files/report-safety-liability-artificial-intelligence-feb2020_de.pdf. Accessed 06 Mar 2021

Europäische Kommission (2020d) Coronavirus: an EU approach for efficient contact tracing apps to support gradual lifting of confinement measures. https://ec.europa.eu/commission/presscorner/detail/en/ip_20_670. Accessed 10 Feb 2021

Europäische Kommission (2020e) Commission and Germany's Presidency of the Council of the EU underline importance of the European Health Data Space. https://ec.europa.eu/commission/presscorner/detail/en/IP_20_2049. Accessed 10 Nov 2020

Europäische Kommission (2020f) On artificial intelligence—a European approach to excellence and trust. https://ec.europa.eu/info/sites/info/files/commission-white-paper-artificial-intelligence-feb2020_en.pdf. Accessed 10 Feb 2021

Europäische Menschenrechtskonvention (1950) Konvention zum Schutze der Menschenrechte und Grundfreiheiten, zuletzt geändert durch Protokoll Nr. 14 vom 13.5.2004 m. w. N. 01.06.2010

Europäisches Parlament (2020) Regelung der zivilrechtlichen Haftung beim Einsatz künstlicher Intelligenz—Entschließung des Europäischen Parlaments vom 20. Oktober 2020 mit Empfehlungen an die Kommission für eine Regelung der zivilrechtlichen Haftung beim Einsatz künstlicher Intelligenz (2020/2014(INL)). https://www.europarl.europa.eu/doceo/document/TA-9-2020-0276_DE.pdf. Accessed 07 Mar 2021

European Medicines Agency (2019) Role of big data for evaluation and supervision of medicines in the EU. https://www.ema.europa.eu/en/news/role-big-data-evaluation-supervision-medicines-eu. Accessed 10 Feb 2021

Federle A, Benoit VA (2020) Data access claims under competition law and data privacy requirements. https://www.twobirds.com/en/news/articles/2020/global/data-access-claims-under-competition-law-and-data-privacy-requirements. Accessed 10 Feb 2021

Fefegha A (2018) Racial bias and gender bias examples in AI systems. Comuzi J. https://medium.com/thoughts-and-reflections/racial-bias-and-gender-bias-examples-in-ai-systems-7211e4c166a1. Accessed 15 Mar 2021

Felzmann H, Villaronga EF, Lutz C, Tamò-Larrieux A (2019) Transparency you can trust: transparency requirements for artificial intelligence between legal norms and contextual concerns. Big Data Soc. https://doi.org/10.1177/2053951719860542

Gerards J, Xenidis R (2020). Algorithmic discrimination in Europe: Challenges and opportunities for gender equality and non-discrimination law. Publications Office of the European Union. https://op.europa.eu/en/publication-detail/-/publication/082f1dbc-821d-11eb-9ac9-01aa75ed71a1/language-en#. Accessed 10 June 2021

Gerichtshof der Europäischen Union (2017) Urteil des Gerichtshofs (Vierte Kammer) vom 7. Dezember 2017, Rechtssache C-329/16, Syndicat national de l'industrie des technologies médicales (Snitem) und Philips France gegen Premier ministre und Ministre des Affaires sociales et de la Santé, Vorabentscheidungsersuchen des Conseil d'État (Frankreich), GRUR 2018, 333

Gerke S, Minssen T, Yu H, Cohen IG (2019) Ethical and legal issues of ingestible electronic sensors. Nat Electron 2:329–334. https://doi.org/10.1038/s41928-019-0290-6

Gerke S, Shachar C, Chai PR, Cohen IG (2020a) Regulatory, safety, and privacy concerns of home monitoring technologies during COVID-19. Nat Med 26:1176–1182. https://doi.org/10.1038/s41591-020-0994-1

Gerke S, Yeung S, Cohen IG (2020b) Ethical and legal aspects of ambient intelligence in hospitals. JAMA 323(7):601–602. https://doi.org/10.1001/jama.2019.2169

Gerke S, Minssen T, Cohen IG (2020c) Ethical and legal challenges of artificial intelligence-driven healthcare. In Artificial Intelligence in Healthcare 295–336 (Adam Bohr & Kaveh Memarzadeh eds., Elsevier 2020).

Gerke S, Stern AD, Minssen T (2020d) Germany's digital health reforms in the COVID-19 era: lessons and opportunities for other countries. npj Digital Medicine 3:94. https://doi.org/10.1038/s41746-020-0306-7

Gerke S, Babic B, Evgeniou T, Cohen IG (2020e) The need for a system view to regulate artificial intelligence/machine learning-based software as medical device. npj Dig Med 3:53. https://doi.org/10.1038/s41746-020-0262-2

Gesetz für ein Zukunftsprogramm Krankenhäuser (Krankenhauszukunftsgesetz—KHZG) (2020) Bundesgesetzblatt Jahrgang. Teil I No 48, ausgegeben am 28.10.2020, Seite 2208. https://www.bgbl.de/xaver/bgbl/start.xav#__bgbl__%2F%2F*%5B%40attr_id%3D%27bgbl120s2208.pdf%27%5D__1605180568792. Accessed 10 Feb 2021

Gesetz für eine bessere Versorgung durch Digitalisierung und Innovation (Digitale-Versorgung-Gesetz—DVG) (2019) Bundesgesetzblatt Jahrgang. Teil I No 49, Accessed 18 Dec 2019, p 2562. https://www.bgbl.de/xaver/bgbl/start.xav#__bgbl__%2F%2F*%5B%40attr_id%3D%27bgbl119s2562.pdf%27%5D__1605180084567. Accessed 10 Feb 2021

Gesetz zur Änderung des Gesetzes gegen Wettbewerbsbeschränkungen für ein fokussiertes, proaktives und digitales Wettbewerbsrecht 4.0 und anderer wettbewerbsrechtlicher Bestimmungen ("GWB-Digitalisierungsgesetz"). Bundesgesetzblatt Teil I No 1 vom 18.01.2021. https://www.bgbl.de/xaver/bgbl/start.xav#__bgbl__%2F%2F*%5B%40attr_id%3D%27bgbl121s0002.pdf%27%5D__1614601536463. Accessed 10 Feb 2021

Gillon R (2003) Ethics needs principles—four can encompass the rest—and respect for autonomy should be "first among equals." J Med Ethics 29(5):307–312. http://dx.doi.org/10.1136/jme.29.5.307

Goodman B, Flaxman S (2016) European Union regulations on algorithmic decision-making and a "right to explanation". https://arxiv.org/abs/1606.08813. Accessed 20 Feb 2021

Google (2021) Exposure notifications: Using technology to help public health authorities fight COVID-19. https://www.google.com/covid19/exposurenotifications/. Accessed 10 Feb 2021

Graber-Soudry O, Minssen T, Nilsson D, Corrales M, Wested J, Illien B (2020) Legal interoperability and the FAIR data principles (Version 1.0). Zenodo. https://doi.org/10.5281/zenodo.4471312

Guizzo E, Klett R (2020) How robots became essential workers in the COVID-19 response. https://spectrum.ieee.org/robotics/medical-robots/how-robots-became-essential-workers-in-the-covid19-response. Accessed 10 Feb 2021

Gunnarsdóttir H, Cohen IG, Minssen T, Gerke S (2021) The ethics and laws of medical big data. Bevorstehende Publikation. In: Marcello I et al (Hrsg) Cambridge handbook of information technology, life sciences and human rights. https://ssrn.com/abstract=3795470. Accessed 09 Mar 2021

Gunnarsdóttir HD, Sinha MS, Gerke S, Minssen T (2020) Applying the proportionality principle to COVID-19 antibody testing. J Law Biosci 7(1):lsaa058. https://doi.org/10.1093/jlb/lsaa058

Hacker P, Krestel R, Grundmann S, Naumann F (2020) Explainable AI under contract and tort law: legal incentives and technical challenges. Artif Intel Law 28:415–439. https://doi.org/10.1007/s10506-020-09260-6

High Level Expert Group on AI (HEG-AI), European Commission (2019) Ethics guidelines for trustworthy AI. https://ec.europa.eu/digital-single-market/en/news/ethics-guidelines-trustworthy-ai. Accessed 10 Feb 2021

Holzer S, Reinle M (2018) EuGH: wann gilt eine Software als Medizinprodukt? https://www.mll-news.com/eugh-wann-gilt-eine-software-als-medizinprodukt/. Accessed 08 Mar 2021

Hummel P, Braun M, Dabrock P (2020) Own data? Ethical reflections on data ownership. Philos Technol. https://doi.org/10.1007/s13347-020-00404-9

Hurtz S (2020) „Die Corona-App fängt an zu wirken, sobald 15 Prozent mitmachen". Interview mit Lucie Abeler-Dörner. https://www.sueddeutsche.de/digital/corona-app-oxford-studie-coronavirus-1.4937209. Accessed 10 Feb 2021

International Covenant on Economic, Social and Cultural Rights (ICESCR) (UN) (1976) Adopted and opened for signature, ratification and accession by General Assembly resolution 2200A (XXI) of 16 December 1966 entry into force 3 January 1976, in accordance with article 27. https://www.ohchr.org/EN/ProfessionalInterest/Pages/CESCR.aspx. Accessed 15 Mar 2021

idigiT, Institute for Digital Transformation in Healthcare (2020) Digital ethics: Corona-Warn-App. https://www.transforming-healthcare.com/wp-content/uploads/2020/09/idigiT-2020-Digital-Ethics-Quick-Check-Corona-Warn-App.pdf. Accessed 03 Mar 2021

Jellinek G (1878) Die sozialethische Bedeutung von Recht, Unrecht und Strafe. Alfred Hölder, Wien

Jiménez LJ, Grisoni F, Schneider G (2020) Drug discovery with explainable artificial intelligence. Nat Mach Intell 2:573–584. https://doi.org/10.1038/s42256-020-00236-4

Jo ES, Gebru T (2020) Lessons from archives: strategies for collecting sociocultural data in machine learning. In: FAT* '20: Proceedings of the 2020 conference on fairness, accountability, and transparency, pp 306–316. https://doi.org/10.1145/3351095.3372829

Hughes J (2006) Copyright and incomplete historiographies: of piracy, propertization, and Thomas Jefferson. South Calif Law Rev 79(5):993–1084

Kakkar A, Chauhan VPS & Verma R (2020) COVID-19 and competition law concerns. https://competition.cyrilamarchandblogs.com/2020/03/covid-19-and-competition-law-concerns/. Accessed 10 Feb 2021

Kaplan AD, Johnson H (2020) Shifting liability: AI in medical devices. https://www.crowell.com/NewsEvents/AlertsNewsletters/all/Shifting-Liability-AI-in-Medical-Devices. Accessed 16 Feb 2021

Katznelson G, Gerke S (2021) The need for health AI ethics in medical school education. Adv Health Sci Educ. https://doi.org/10.1007/s10459-021-10040-3

Kaye D (2018) UN report on the implications of artificial intelligence (AI) technologies for human rights. https://freedex.org/wp-content/blogs.dir/2015/files/2018/10/AI-and-FOE-GA.pdf. Accessed 10 Mar 2021

Këllezi P (2019) Data protection and competition law: non-compliance as abuse of dominant position. sui-generis:343. https://doi.org/10.21257/sg.114

Kianzad B (2021) Excessive pricing during the COVID-19 crisis in the EU: an empirical inquiry, February, Concurrences N° 1-2021, Art. N° 98670, pp 250–259

Klunzinger E (1993) Rechtsordnung. In: BGB: Grundlagen. Gabler-Studientexte. Gabler Verlag, Wiesbaden. https://doi.org/10.1007/978-3-663-13732-0_1

Knawy BA, Adil M, Crooks G et al. (2020) The Riyadh declaration: the role of digital health in fighting pandemics. Lancet 396(10262):P1537–1539. https://doi.org/10.1016/S0140-6736(20)31978-4

Larsson S (2021) AI in the EU: ethical guidelines as a governance tool. In: Bakardjieva Engelbrekt A, Leijon K, Michalski A, Oxelheim L (eds) The European Union and the technology shift. Palgrave Macmillan/Springer Nature Switzerland AG, Cham, pp 85–111

Lebret A, Minssen T (2021) Digital health, artificial intelligence and accessibility to health care in Denmark. Eur Hum Rights Law Rev 1:39–49

Lemley MA, Weiser PJ (2007) Should property or liability rules govern information. Texas Law Rev 85(4):783–842

Lewis D (2020) Why many countries failed at COVID contact-tracing—but some got it right. Nature 588:384–387

Li Y, Shang K, Bian W et al (2020) Prediction of disease progression in patients with COVID-19 by artificial intelligence assisted lesion quantification. Sci Rep 10:22083. https://doi.org/10.1038/s41598-020-79097-1

Loucera C, Esteban-Medina M, Rian K et al (2020) Drug repurposing for COVID-19 using machine learning and mechanistic models of signal transduction circuits related to SARS-CoV-2 infection. Signal Transduct Target Ther 5:290. https://doi.org/10.1038/s41392-020-00417-y

Malgieri G, Comandé G (2017) Why a right to legibility of automated decision-making exists in the general data protection regulation. International Data Privacy Law 7(6):243–265

Merkel A, Frederiksen M, Kaja Kallas K, Marin S (2021) Appell von vier Regierungschefinnen an die EU: "Europa muss seine digitale Souveränität stärken". Handelsblatt 02.03.2021. https://app.handelsblatt.com/meinung/gastbeitraege/digitalisierung-appell-von-vier-regierungschefinnen-an-die-eu-europa-muss-seine-digitale-souveraenitaet-staerken/26962398.html?ticket=ST-9074674-5C7wueNrsYvF7keg3bvY-ap2. Accessed 07 Mar 2021

Meszaros J, Corrales Compagnucci M, Minssen T (2021) The interaction of the medical device regulation and the GDPR—do European rules on privacy and scientific research impair the safety & performance of AI medical devices? 1-11, bevorstehende Publikation. In: Cohen IG, Minssen T, Price WN II, Robertson C, Shachar C (eds) The future of medical device regulation: innovation and protection. University Press, Cambridge

Minssen T (2019) AI in the Health & Life Sciences & the Medicus L(ex) Machina. Setterwalls Life Sciences Report. https://setterwalls.se/aktuellt/artikel/ai-health-life-sciences-medicus-lex-machina. Accessed 10 Feb 2021

Minssen T (2020) Cited in: Regulating digital health. Bull World Health Organ 98:235–236. https://doi.org/10.2471/BLT.20.020420. Accessed 04 Mar 2021

Minssen T, Pierce J (2018) Big data and intellectual property rights in the health and life sciences. In: Glenn CI, Fernandez Lynch H, Vayena F, Gasser U (eds) Big data, health law, and bioethics. Cambridge University Press, Cambridge, pp 311–323

Minssen T, Goldschmieding T, Sandfeld Jakobsen S (2020a) AI, big data & machine learning—2020a, 2nd edition- Chapter on DENMARK. In: AI, big data & machine learning—2020, 2nd edn. Global Legal Insights (GLI), London, pp 113–128

Minssen T, Gerke S, Aboy M, Price N, Cohen G (2020b) Regulatory responses to medical machine learning. J Law Biosci:lsaa002. https://doi.org/10.1093/jlb/lsaa002

Minssen T, Seitz C, Aboy M, Corrales Compagnucci M (2020c) The EU-US privacy shield regime for cross-border transfers of personal data under the GDPR. Eur Pharm Law Rev 4(1):34–50. https://doi.org/10.21552/eplr/2020/1/6

Minssen T, Outterson K, Van Katwyk SR, Batista PHD, Chandler C, Ciabuschi F, Harbarth S, Kesselheim A, Laxminarayan R, Liddell K, Osterholm MT, Price LB, Hoffman SJ (2020d) Preparing for antimicrobial resistance in the wake of the COVID-19 pandemic: the vision and "social science" mission of the INAMRSS network. Harvard Law School's Bill of Health blog. https://blog.petrieflom.law.harvard.edu/2020/12/11/antimicrobial-resistance-inamrss-network/#more-29568. Accessed 10 Feb 2021

Minssen T, Outterson K, Van Katwyk SR, Batista PHD, Chandler C, Ciabuschi F, Harbarth S, Kesselheim A, Laxminarayan R, Liddell K, Osterholm MT, Price L, Hoffman SJ (2020e) Social, cultural and economic aspects of antimicrobial resistance. Bull World Health Organ 98(12):823–824. https://doi.org/10.2471/BLT.20.275875

Minssen T, Mimler M, Mak V (2020f) When does stand-alone software qualify as a medical device in the European Union?—The CJEU's decision in Snitem and what it implies for the next generation of medical devices. Med Law Rev 28(3):615–624. https://doi.org/10.1093/medlaw/fwaa012. PMID: 32607541

Mirsky Y, Mahler T, Shelef I et al. (2019) CT-GAN: Malicious tampering of 3D medical imagery using deep learning. https://arxiv.org/pdf/1901.03597.pdf. Accessed 10 May 2019

Mittelstadt B, Allo P, Taddeo M, Wachter S, Floridi L (2016) The ethics of algorithms: mapping the debate. Big Data Soc 3(2). https://doi.org/10.1177/2053951716679679

Monroe C (2020) Quantum computing: how conditions created by the COVID-19 shutdown are delivering ‚the best data we have ever seen'. Nature 583:10. https://doi.org/10.1038/d41586-020-01937-x

Mori T, Uchihira N (2018) Balancing the trade-off between accuracy and interpretability in software defect prediction. Empir Softw Eng 24:1–47

Oduncu FS (2012) Verteilungsgerechtigkeit, Rationierung und Priorisierung—das Gesundheitswesen im Spannungsfeld zwischen Medizin, Ökonomie, Ethik und Recht. Medizinrecht 30:359–367. https://doi.org/10.1007/s00350-012-3162-x

O'Shea L (2020) Failed COVID-19 tracing apps must be abandoned to restore public trust. https://asia.nikkei.com/Opinion/Failed-COVID-19-tracing-apps-must-be-abandoned-to-restore-public-trust. Accessed 10 Feb 2021

Otto C (2020) KI und die geplante EU-Gefährdungshaftung. https://cot.legal/ki-und-die-geplante-eu-gefaehrdungshaftung. Accessed 02 Mar 2021

Pearce H (2018) Personality, property and other provocations: Exploring the conceptual muddle of data protection rights under EU law. Eur Data Prot L Rev 4(2): 190–208. https://doi.org/10.21552/edpl/2018/2/8

Preeti PK (2020) AI drug discovery: a key-player in finding cure for COVID-19. https://industrywired.com/ai-drug-discovery-a-key-player-in-finding-cure-for-covid-19/. Accessed 10 Feb 2021

Price WN II (2019) Medical AI and contextual bias. Harv J Law Technol 33:66. https://papers.ssrn.com/sol3/papers.cfm?abstract_id=3347890
Price WN II, Gerke S, Cohen IG (2019a) Potential liability for physicians using artificial intelligence. JAMA 322:1765–1766. doi:10.1001/jama.2019.15064
Price WN II, Kaminski ME, Minssen T, Spector-Bagdady K (2019b) Shadow health records meet new data privacy laws. Science 363(6426):448–450
Price WN II, Rai AK, Minssen T (2020) Knowledge transfer for large-scale vaccine manufacturing. Science 369(6506):912–914. https://doi.org/10.1126/science.abc9588
Price WN II, Gerke S, Cohen IG (2021) How much can potential jurors tell us about liability for medical artificial intelligence? J Nucl Med. 62(1):15–16. https://doi.org/10.2967/jnumed.120.257196
Price N (2017) Artificial intelligence in health care: applications and legal implications. SciTech Lawyer 14(1):10–13.
Price WN (2015) Black-box medicine. Harv J Law Technol 28:420–467
Purtova N (2015) The illusion of personal data as no one's property. Law Innov Technol 7(1):83–111. https://doi.org/10.1080/17579961.2015.1052646
Rahman M (2021) Here are the countries using Google and Apple's COVID-19 contact tracing API. https://www.xda-developers.com/google-apple-covid-19-contact-tracing-exposurenotifications-api-app-list-countries/. Accessed 10 Feb 2021
Rajkomar A, Dean J, Kohane I (2019) Machine learning in medicine. N Engl J Med 380:1347–1358. https://doi.org/10.1056/NEJMra1814259
Robert Koch Institut (2021) Kennzahlen zur Corona-Warn-App. https://www.rki.de/DE/Content/InfAZ/N/Neuartiges_Coronavirus/WarnApp/Archiv_Kennzahlen/Kennzahlen_08012021.pdf?__blob=publicationFile. Accessed 10 Feb 2021
Rudin C, Ustun B (2018) Optimized scoring systems: toward trust in machine learning for healthcare and criminal justice. Interfaces 48(5):449–466
Sava D (2020) Google Cloud AI and Harvard Global Health Institute Collaborate on new COVID-19 forecasting model. https://cloud.google.com/blog/products/ai-machine-learning/google-cloud-is-releasing-the-covid-19-public-forecasts. Accessed 10 Feb 2021
Schweda M, Schreiter FV (2021) The treasure hunt is on … Data access claims after the reform of German competition law. https://www.jdsupra.com/legalnews/the-treasure-hunt-is-on-data-access-1608194/. Accessed 10 Feb 2021
Scott C (2000) Why law prevades medicine: an essay on ethics in health care. Notre Dame J Law Ethics Public Policy 14(1):245–303. http://scholarship.law.nd.edu/ndjlepp/vol14/iss1/9
Selbst AD, Powles J (2017) Meaningful information and the right to explanation. Int Data Priv Law 7(4):233–242
Shachar C, Gerke S, Adashi EY (2020) AI surveillance during pandemics: ethical implementation imperatives. Hast Cent Rep 50(3):18–21. https://doi.org/10.1002/hast.1125
Sharkey N (2019) The impact of gender and race bias in AI. Humanit Law Policy. https://blogs.icrc.org/law-and-policy/2018/08/28/impact-gender-race-bias-ai/. Accessed 10 Mar 2021
Short E (2020) It turns out Amazon's AI hiring tool discriminated against women. Silicon Republic. https://www.siliconrepublic.com/careers/amazon-ai-hiring-tool-women-discrimination. Accessed 10 Feb 2021
Suchanek A, Lin-Hi N (2018) Revision von Ethik vom 19.02.2018. Gabler Wirtschaftslexikon. https://wirtschaftslexikon.gabler.de/definition/ethik-34332/version-257836. Accessed 10 Feb 2021
Szentesi S (2021) COVID-19: competition law implications of the coronavirus crisis. https://ca.practicallaw.thomsonreuters.com/w-024-8054?transitionType=Default&contextData=(sc.Default)&firstPage=true. Accessed 10 Feb 2021
Topol EJ (2019) High-performance medicine: the convergence of human and artificial intelligence. Nat Med 25:44–56. https://doi.org/10.1038/s41591-018-0300-7
Vamathevan J, Clark D, Czodrowski P et al (2019) Applications of machine learning in drug discovery and development. Nat Rev Drug Discov 18:463–477. https://doi.org/10.1038/s41573-019-0024-5

Van Dorpe S (2021) Germany shows EU the way in curbing Big Tech. https://www.politico.eu/article/germany-shows-eu-the-way-in-curbing-big-tech/. Accessed 10 Feb 2021

Vayena E (2021) Value from health data: European opportunity to catalyse progress in digital health. Lancet 397(10275):652–653. https://doi.org/10.1016/S0140-6736(21)00203-8

Verordnung (EU) 2016/679 (DSGVO) des Europäischen Parlaments und des Rates vom 27. April 2016 zum Schutz natürlicher Personen bei der Verarbeitung personenbezogener Daten, zum freien Datenverkehr und zur Aufhebung der Richtlinie 95/46/EG (Datenschutz-Grundverordnung) (Text von Bedeutung für den EWR), OJ L 119, 4.5.2016, pp 1–88. http://data.europa.eu/eli/reg/2016/679/oj

Verordnung (EU) 2017/745 des Europäischen Parlaments und des Rates vom 5. April 2017 über Medizinprodukte, zur Änderung der Richtlinie 2001/83/EG, der Verordnung (EG) Nr. 178/2002 und der Verordnung (EG) Nr. 1223/2009 und zur Aufhebung der Richtlinien 90/385/EWG und 93/42/EWG des Rates (Text von Bedeutung für den EWR). http://data.europa.eu/eli/reg/2017/745/oj

Verordnung (EU) 2017/746 des Europäischen Parlaments und des Rates vom 5. April 2017 über In-vitro-Diagnostika und zur Aufhebung der Richtlinie 98/79/EG und des Beschlusses 2010/227/EU der Kommission (Text von Bedeutung für den EWR). https://eur-lex.europa.eu/eli/reg/2017/746/oj

Vorstand der Bundesärztekammer (2020) Digitale Transformation in der Medizin in Pandemiezeiten (Behandlung—Information—Kommunikation—BIK)—Erfahrungen und Perspektiven. https://www.bundesaerztekammer.de/fileadmin/user_upload/downloads/pdf-Ordner/Positionen/2020-05-20_Digitale_Transformation_in_der_Medizin_in_Pandemiezeiten-BIK.pdf. Accessed 10 Feb 2021

Wachter S, Mittelstadt B (2019) A right to reasonable inferences: re-thinking data protection law in the age of big data and AI. Columbia Bus Law Rev (2):494–620. https://ssrn.com/abstract=3248829

Wachter S, Mittelstadt B, Floridi L (2017) Why a right to explanation of automated decision-making does not exist in the general data protection regulation. Int Data Privady Law 7(2):76–99

Wachter S, Mittelstadt B, Russell C (2018) Counterfactual explanations without opening the black box: automated decisions and the GDPR. Harv J Law Technol 31(2):842–887

Wachter S, Mittelstadt B, Russell C (2020) Why fairness cannot be automated: bridging the gap between EU non-discrimination law and AI. https://doi.org/10.2139/ssrn.3547922

Wahl B, Cossy-Gantner A, Germann S et al (2018) Artificial intelligence (AI) and global health: how can AI contribute to health in resource-poor settings? BMJ Glob Health 3(4):1–7. https://doi.org/10.1136/bmjgh-2018-000798

Watson AR, Wah R, Thamman R (2020) The value of remote monitoring for the COVID-19 pandemic. Telemed e-Health 26(9):1110–1112. https://doi.org/10.1089/tmj.2020.0134

Whitelaw S, Mamas A, Topol E, Van Spall HGC (2020) Applications of digital technology in COVID-19 pandemic planning and response. Lancet Digital Health 2(8):E435–E440. https://doi.org/10.1016/S2589-7500(20)30142-4

Wieler H (2021) EU-Cybersecurity-Strategien: Europäische Kommission schlägt neue Security-Strategien vor. https://www.infopoint-security.de/europaeische-kommission-schlaegt-neue-security-strategien-vor/a26289/. Accessed 10 Feb 2021

Wischmeyer T (2018) Regulierung intelligenter Systeme. Archiv des öffentlichen Rechts 143(1):1–66

Wittbold KA et al (2020) How hospitals are using AI to battle Covid-19. Harvard Business Review. https://hbr.org/2020/04/how-hospitals-are-using-ai-to-battle-covid-19. Accessed 15 Feb 2021

World Health Organization (WHO) (2020). COVID-19 technology access pool. https://www.who.int/emergencies/diseases/novel-coronavirus-2019/global-research-on-novel-coronavirus-2019-ncov/covid-19-technology-access-pool. Accessed 10.02.2021

World Health Organization (WHO) (2021) Smart Vaccination Certificate Working Group. https://www.who.int/groups/smart-vaccination-certificate-working-group. Accessed 10 Feb 2021

Wu S (2020) Tracing AI decisions: AI explainability and the GDPR. https://www.airoboticslaw.com/blog/ai-explainability-gdpr. Accessed 15 Feb 2021

Yun LT (2020), in: Regulating digital health, Bulletin of the World Health Organization, 98:235–236. https://doi.org/10.2471/BLT.20.020420

Zame WR, Bica I, Shen C, Curth A, Lee HS, Bailey S, Weatherall J, Wright D, Bretz F, Schaar MVD (2020) Machine learning for clinical trials in the era of COVID-19. Stat Biopharm Res 12(4):506–517. https://doi.org/10.1080/19466315.2020.1797867

Zuboff S (2021) The coup we are not talking about. The New York Times. https://www.nytimes.com/2021/01/29/opinion/sunday/facebook-surveillance-society-technology.html. Accessed 10 Feb 2021

'Infodemics': Dealing with Information in Pandemic Times from an Ethical Perspective

Sebastian Wäscher, Tim Nguyen and Nikola Biller-Andorno

Contents

1 Introduction 203
2 Problem Description: Information Overload and the Reduction of Complexity 206
3 Scientific Evidence 208
4 Structural change in the media landscape 210
5 From Information to Appeal 211
6 Problem Solving 213
6.1 WHO 214
6.2 The 'PubliCo' Project 215
7 Conclusion 216
References 218

1 Introduction

Half-truths, misinformation, fake news, conspiracy theories. Keywords that have been on everyone's lips since the US presidential election in 2016 at the latest. In the context of the current Covid-19 pandemic, all of these terms have gained increased attention again. The World Health Organization (WHO) refers

S. Wäscher (✉) · N. Biller-Andorno
Institute of Biomedical Ethics and History of Medicine, University of Zurich, Zurich, Switzerland
e-mail: sebastian.waescher@ibme.uzh.ch

N. Biller-Andorno
e-mail: biller-andorno@ibme.uzh.ch

T. Nguyen
Health Ethics and Governance Unit, Department of Research for Health, WHO Health Emergencies Programme (WHE), Geneva, Switzerland
e-mail: nguyent@who.int

© The Author(s), under exclusive license to Springer-Verlag GmbH, DE, part of Springer Nature 2023

A. Reis et al. (eds.), *Pandemics and Ethics*,
https://doi.org/10.1007/978-3-662-66872-6_13

to the enormous amount of information of varying quality in this context as an "infodemic".

> "An infodemic is an overabundance of information—some accurate and some not—occurring during an epidemic. In a similar manner to an epidemic, it spreads between humans through digital and physical information systems. It makes it hard for people to find trustworthy sources and reliable guidance when they need it" (Tangcharoensathien et al. 2020, p. 2).

The WHO uses the term "infodemic" to draw attention to the fact that it is of utmost importance to distinguish between correct and false information as well as important and unimportant information in times of crisis. Communication in times of crisis is always given special importance, to enable citizens to gain a fact-based assessment of the situation and a solid basis for action. The most dominant theme of media coverage in 2020 was the Covid-19 pandemic, during which it became evident that the manifold information could not always be brought together to form a coherent overall picture. In particular, an often unclear, rapidly changing scientific data situation, the high-frequency dissemination of varying content through multiple channels, and attempts to influence the behaviour of vulnerable risk groups made it a challenge for all media users to gain an overview of the facts about Covid-19.

In increasingly complex societies, media play a central role in the (mass) dissemination of information. Complex, internationally oriented societies need a system to secure self-assurance. Media systems therefore have the function of self-observation of society (cf. Hoffjann and Arlt 2015), and thus establish public opinion. Niklas Luhmann already coined the phrase "What we know about our society, indeed about the world we live in, we know through the mass media" (Luhmann 1995, p. 5) 25 years ago. In general, it can be stated that, as soon as events exceed one's own verifiable experience horizon, actors are dependent on media conveyance of information. However, the media system, like the rest of society, has increasingly differentiated, which is often referred to as digitalization. A few years ago, it was still the traditional mass media that had a monopoly on the dissemination of socially relevant knowledge, but today increasingly digital platforms, such as social networks, are additional sources of information for many citizens (cf. Breuning et al. 2020; Kupferschmitt and Müller 2020). [1] What was once the exclusive task of traditional mass media is now extended to a large number of additional sources of information. However, the idea that media conveyed communication, regardless of the technical platform, can be seen as self-observation

[1] An overview of media usage in the USA can be found, for example, at the following Internet addresses:

https://www.pewresearch.org/internet/fact-sheet/social-media/

https://www.pewresearch.org/fact-tank/2019/04/10/share-of-u-s-adults-using-social-media-including-facebook-is-mostly-unchanged-since-2018/.

of society remains very plausible. It should be taken into consideration that the origins of most information can be traced back to a few sources, for example international press agencies or famous influencers.

In the course of societal differentiation (cf. Luhmann 2009a), various structures have developed in society that are supposed to guarantee a certain level of security with regard to the quality of information. Journalism and science are generally considered to be the institutions that are supposed to ensure reliable quality of information. These structures are represented in particular by specific codes and norms of the respective professions. For example, journalists are obliged to exercise due diligence in their reporting and with regard to truthfulness (cf. German Press Council 2019) or truth-seeking (cf. Swiss Press Council 2017). This is, for example, laid down in the respective press codes. Science, on the other hand, tries to provide systematically acquired knowledge that meets the standards of transparency, a basic intersubjective comprehensibility and verifiability; this is, for example, laid down in different documents on scientific integrity (cf. Swiss Academies of Arts and Sciences 2008; DFG 2020; All European Academies (ALLEA) 2017). Both institutions are dependent on the fundamental trust of citizens in the honesty of the information provided; this of course does not exclude a critical reading of the information provided, it is even expressly desired. However, a fundamental mistrust of science (cf. Luhmann 2009b) and journalism[2] would deprive them of their functionality.

The media landscape has been undergoing a structural change for some time now, which is not yet complete. It seems to be largely unclear how public communication and, with it, the public will develop further in the course of increasing digitalisation (cf. Altmeppen et al. 2019). New technologies offer opportunities for a public-oriented use, but also entail risks for the public good of a society. The rapid availability of information from the Internet poses challenges for the classical mass media, which they have not yet had to face. Journalism, which is generally seen as a source of reliable information for society as a whole through the production of public opinion, is now confronted with a diverse range of "influencers" who are not usually bound by the professional standards of journalism. In addition, science itself is struggling with the problems of information assessment. The emergence of so-called "predatory journals" may serve as an example, which offer to publish articles that would not be accepted in the classical specialist journals (cf. Darbyshire 2018). These developments in science intensify the fundamental problem of the so-called infodemic by making it possible for even apparently scientific results to lose their reliability and for the question of trust in information to become increasingly problematic. The publication of articles on preprint servers

[2] Communication science research is not unanimous about the functional role of journalism within society. There are various designs that, in the sense of Luhmann, try to describe journalism as a social system, whereas there are also attempts to locate journalism within a functional public sphere system (for a summary see Hoffjann and Arlt 2015). However, for the purposes of this article, this debate is not of further relevance.

also belongs to this field of activity, which are generally welcomed by scientists because they enable a rapid dissemination and an open discourse. However, the articles made public there have not yet undergone peer review, which is generally an important aspect of quality control in science (cf. Lachapelle 2020).

In a comment in The Lancet, one of the most respected medical journals, it says with regard to the Covid-19 infodemic: "The tidal wave of information on the internet concerning the COVID-19 pandemic has resulted in difficulties in discerning truth from fiction" (Lancet 2020, p. 291). Concerns about the assessment of the quality of information have increased steadily with digitalisation and the growing importance of social media. As early as 2018, Heidi J. Larson pointed out that social media must be seen as a global threat to public health (cf. Larson 2018). In the context of the debate about the vaccination readiness of society, she warns of the influence of false and/or misleading information on the vaccination readiness of citizens.

The problems associated with the term infodemic are, like most problems of modern societies, complex and cannot be viewed in isolation. The most important fields of activity are described and classified below in order to finally present two examples of how some of the challenges can be tackled.

2 Problem Description: Information Overload and the Reduction of Complexity

In order to understand which problems are addressed by the concept of infodemic, it is helpful to first clarify the terminology. First of all, the concept of information has to be clarified to grasp how certain problems arise in the context of information dissemination. In general, one could describe information as a data that has meaning for a recipient. This implicitly makes clear that classical information models, which deal with a sender, the information and a receiver, who simply receives the information, are too short-sighted (cf. Maletzke 1998). Information processing is a highly selective process in which the recipient interprets his environment according to his individual relevance structures (cf. Schmidt and Zurstiege 2007). Studies show that for actors information that corresponds to their own world view is more effective than information that questions their own opinion on a certain topic. However, the latter type of information is also critically questioned for its quality (cf. Lazer et al. 2018). The handling of information is therefore highly individual and dependent on many contextual factors. Nevertheless, it is helpful to distinguish between different types of information offerings (i.e. the "message" in the sender-receiver model).

In the current context of the Covid-19 pandemic, various terms of information are distinguished, which point to a problematic handling of the classification of information. Terms such as: misinformation, disinformation, fake news, conspiracy theory, facts, evidence and many more, which give the initially value-neutral term of information a certain value with regard to its quality. In general, these different terms refer to the truth content or the reliability that characterizes a certain information offer. In everyday language, the distinction between truth and lies would characterize the assessment of the information in such cases. In the context of this article, the term "truth content" should be understood as a statement (information) that can be empirically checked at all and then withstands a check. Problems can arise in principle if the empirical checking of statements is not possible without further ado. Such situations arise either if not enough has been observed, no observers were present, the checking of a statement is (too) complex or an empirical check is simply not possible. However, in a modern society the problem is that an independent check of a truth content can hardly take place unmediated. Luhmann's observation that the essential part of our knowledge about society is mediated by the media points to this fact (cf. Luhmann 1995).

For a basic classification, three types of information can be distinguished[3] (cf. Wardle and Hossein 2017):

1. Evidence: information that is empirically verified and documented; often also referred as facts.
2. Misinformation: information that, for example, has been taken out of its original context and embedded in a new context, making it doubtful. In contrast to false information, misinformation is not intentionally misleading.
3. False information (disinformation): information that is deliberately misleading and, on closer inspection (e.g. through a fact check), turns out to be empirically unverifiable or invented; this also includes so-called fake news.

In addition to this rough categorisation of information, the term conspiracy theory must be added. Conspiracy theories can be characterised as a bundle of information that has a certain coherence, but which is often not empirically verifiable in its entirety. Ted Goertzel sums up the problem of conspiracy theories: "Conspiracy theories are easy to propagate and difficult to refute" (Goertzel 2010, p. 493).

In today's world, it appears very plausible that social actors are exposed to an amount of information that they cannot process without further ado. Here too, a basic idea of Niklas Luhmann can be helpful in understanding why problems can arise solely from the sheer quantity of information. Luhmann emphasizes in his work that complexity must be reduced to a manageable level (cf. Baraldi et al. 2008). This means that social actors must select information to be able to process it at all and thus produce meaning. Conspiracy theories are probably particularly effective as a result of the combination of coherence and simplicity. They reduce the level of complexity to a level that is well processable and at the same time has enough internal complexity to appear credible. This is where the central problem in dealing with information becomes apparent: how can information be selected meaningfully? On the one hand, this is a quantitative question (What is

[3] For a further discussion of different types of information, see, for example, Posetti and Bontcheva 2020.

relevant?), But on the other hand also a qualitative question (How can the quality of the information be assessed?). If it is clear that complexity must be reduced, the question arises immediately how information should be selected. Modern societies have—as already mentioned—developed two central structures that are generally regarded as indicators of high-quality information: science and journalism. Both social sub-areas will be discussed in more detail below with a view to their role in the Covid-19 pandemic.

3 Scientific Evidence

Basically, the problem with the Covid-19 pandemic is that the information situation, especially at the beginning of the outbreak, was not very certain—in the sense of empirical evidence. Different factors, all of which were relevant for assessing the overall situation and still are, were either not known or only known from estimates. This is generally to be expected in such a situation. Knowledge about a new virus must first be collected through many elaborate procedures (which ultimately ensure the quality of scientific information), in order to provide solid evidence.

The WHO calls for information and interventions on epidemics to be disseminated or created on the basis of scientific evidence (see Tangcharoensathien et al. 2020). The scientificity of data and information is generally (and rightly) considered a criterion of quality for information. Scientific knowledge is gained on the basis of systematic methodological approaches, and for this reason it is ascribed a higher quality than other forms of knowledge (see Mittelstrass et al. 2004). However, scientific knowledge is not unshakeable knowledge; on the contrary, a typical process that characterizes the generation of scientific knowledge is falsification (see Albert 1960). This means that scientific knowledge must be understood as provisional, namely as long as it withstands empirical testing. In particular, when phenomena occur for the first time, it is typical in the course of scientific discovery that certain results of scientific research turn out to be not entirely tenable or even false. For scientific procedure, this is no problem, it is even quite typical. In principle, the scientific research process works through a systematic process of trial and error. Scientists rely on empirical evidence and are (usually) willing to change their conclusions on the basis of new evidence (Goertzel 2010). Over time, certain research results stabilize and can thus serve as a basis for further research. In many cases, science is thus a slow process that builds on constantly increasing knowledge.[4]

[4] We are aware that this portrayal is a strong simplification of the process of scientific discovery.

However, in many cases, quick action is required in crisis situations. This need can stand in contrast to the typical scientific approach, especially when there are few reliable findings about the causes of the crisis so far. In the case of the Covid-19 pandemic, such a situation has arisen.[5] It turns out that the term scientific evidence is not unproblematic in such circumstances. Since the data situation is constantly changing during the pandemic, but research is still required to carry out a kind of "real-time analysis", sometimes contradictory results arise which ultimately do not allow any final conclusions. Only one example should be given here to illustrate the problem. Flaxman et al. showed by means of a modeling of the course of the Covid-19 pandemic that non-pharmaceutical measures had a very pronounced effect on containing the pandemic (cf. Flaxman et al. 2020). Almost at the same time, however, statements can also be found from renowned researchers who advocate not using non-pharmaceutical interventions, as the social consequences, for example of a lockdown, would have far-reaching consequences that would ultimately do more harm to society as a whole than the targeted infection of non-risk groups. For example, the "Network for Evidence-Based Medicine" points out that the psychological stress caused by a lockdown situation would overall possibly bring much more problems with it than the Covid-19 virus itself (cf. EbM-Network 2020). In a similar direction is the Great Barrington Declaration (cf. Kulldorff et al. 2020). The goal of this declaration is to forego non-pharmaceutical interventions to the greatest possible extent in order to gradually come closer to a herd immunity, which would overall reduce the threat situation. However, recently there have been more and more indications for possible secondary infections (cf. Parry 2020), which would call the entire concept of herd immunity into question.

Independent of the positions represented, such discussions make it difficult to establish an evidence-based opinion, especially for people outside of science. The data basis in the case of the Covid-19 pandemic is now relatively large, but still not comprehensive and solid enough. The statistical evaluation of the data is also highly problematic and associated with many uncertainties. Scientific knowledge has developed such complexity today that it is also virtually impossible for researchers themselves to gain an overview. However, researchers are, by virtue of their professional training, able to deal with uncertainty, over-complexity and change. They are also usually aware of the provisional nature of scientific knowledge and that complexity sometimes has to be "held" in its entirety. Furthermore, researchers are aware of the methods and backgrounds of the practice of scientific research and therefore have confidence in the basic processes within science that produce certain—namely scientific—knowledge. [6] Basically, research is often

[5] For an overview of publications on Covid-19, see, for example: https://www.natureindex.com/news-blog/how-coronavirus-is-changing-research-practices-and-publishing.

[6] This does not mean that there are not also a number of problems within science that are related to the acquisition of knowledge. However, it seems relatively unproblematic to claim that scientific knowledge (with all its weaknesses) is the most stable and reliable knowledge that we are able to generate (cf. Douglas 2009).

faced with similar problems, but the scientific discourse has rarely been under such public scrutiny as in the case of the Covid-19 pandemic.

4 Structural change in the media landscape

Until a few years ago, the traditional mass media (print, TV and radio) were the most important instruments for informing the general public, but this dominance has gradually dissolved in recent years, although the traditional media still have the highest usage in terms of the total population (cf. Kupferschmitt and Müller 2020). The Internet has opened up the possibility of directing information to a wider audience to a large extent unregulated. The access barriers of the traditional media, both in terms of technology and in terms of education, are circumvented by the Internet. In particular, technical developments (in addition to the everyday use of computers, in particular film and photography technologies) have greatly simplified it for users to provide content. The consequences of this development have been discussed for years, prominently, for example, in relation to the question of the democratic potential of the Internet (cf. Dahinden 2000; Gerhards and Schäfer 2007). Today, the question of the relevance and, in particular, the accuracy of the information exchanged on the Internet is the subject of debate between different parties (cf. Bechmann 2020; Emanuelson 2018; Fischer 2019).

Altmeppen et al. point to a structural change in the public, which is essentially determined by digital technologies (Altmeppen et al. 2019). Social media have torn down or at least reduced further access barriers and thus contributed decisively to the currently observable structural change. In communication research, the public is the central point of reference under which all relevant aspects of public communication are discussed (cf. Hoffjann and Arlt 2015), such as the use of social media or the change in journalistic profession. Altmeppen et al. describe the public as an arena of public discourse in which the orientation towards the common good of society is negotiated (cf. Altmeppen et al. 2019). They refer to the close connection between public, common good and responsibility. The common good can only be realized through the responsible action of all relevant actors in the public. An attempt to institutionalize responsible action are the establishment of different rules. While the classical mass media were relatively well regulated, for example by codes, legislation and those mentioned technical and professional access barriers, different Internet platforms and social media are considered to be largely unregulated (cf. Allington et al. 2020).[7] Without clear normative references, such as laws or codes, it is difficult to characterize responsible action

[7] The classical media have also been criticized for the fact that they largely reported in conformity and left little room for divergent opinions (cf. e.g. https://vimeo.com/471959768, https://www.corona-in-der-schweiz.ch).

intersubjectively, as responsibility always presupposes a normative framework (cf. Loh 2017; Wäscher et al. 2020; Werner 2011). At most, a general media ethics could still provide a reference framework—far from clearly institutionalized rules—but research in this area is also still consolidating (cf. Altmeppen et al. 2019). A consequence of the current discussion about social media and the general flow of information within a society is that structures are needed (cf. Bechmann2020), which enable reliable information. A media system that is stable in itself and has clearly represented values is essential for democratic societies. The means of dissemination play only a secondary role. However, the "institutionalized research [...] hardly keeps up with the enormous dynamic development of digital applications, also because even basic concepts have to be reconsidered" (Altmeppen et al. 2019, p. 72).

However, social media play a central role in public communication today. First and foremost, they have to be regarded as communication platforms that provide a 'virtual space' that allows users to publish and consume content. The use of social media is as diverse as human actions in general (cf. Coiera 2013). However, for example, Brennen et al. show in an exploratory study that the majority of false and/or incorrect information is to be found on social media platforms (88 % of the sample) and only a small part in traditional media, such as TV (9 %) and print (8 %) (cf. Brennen et al. 2020). The handling of social media as a virtual place of unregulated information exchange thus represents a central point of reference for the problem of infodemics.

5 From Information to Appeal

Under the described current conditions, it is understandable that citizens are confronted with a challenge in dealing with information that is not easy to overcome. In addition, a number of measures had to be implemented in the course of the Covid-19 pandemic, which restricted some fundamental democratic rights, such as the right to assembly.[8]

As uncertain as the data situation is, the first experiences and the extremely rapid spread of the Covid-19 virus necessitated the taking of certain public health measures in order to halt the too rapid progress of the pandemic. Accordingly, governments and authorities had to make decisions under uncertainty in order to contain the anticipated damage in the sense of a precautionary principle as much

[8] It also seems that a number of other fundamental questions remain unanswered: Who, for example, determines the proportionality of measures and on the basis of which criteria? Can the proportionality be announced by the executive, is it determined by the courts and what role should citizens play in this process? At the latest when the entire Covid-19 pandemic is under control, these and other questions must be clarified in a discourse with the entire public in order to act more sovereignly in future scenarios than was the case in many countries at times.

as possible. This means, for example, that measures such as the wearing of masks were made compulsory, even though the data situation with regard to the effectiveness of the measure is not yet conclusive and unambiguous (cf. EbM network 2020). However, even if the evidence is not 100% clear in this case, the expected risk of wearing masks is negligible. As a pure risk-benefit calculation, according to the current state of knowledge, there is therefore nothing against wearing masks, especially when the very low effort of this measure is taken into account.

Public health measures not only aim to disseminate and make certain information accessible, but also to evoke actions on the basis of the information which serve the general welfare of society. Wakefield et al. show in relation to different health-related fields, such as tobacco consumption, alcohol abuse or cancer prevention, that mass media information campaigns can change the behaviour of citizens, although the evidence is mostly moderate (cf. Wakefield et al. 2010). They emphasise that often a combination of different measures is more effective than a pure mass media campaign.

The fact that social media have a strong influence on the course of an infodemic has already been shown in this article on the basis of different studies. However, social media also have a potential that has so far been used to a limited extent, for example to support public health measures and to make them effective (cf. Coiera 2013). In this sense, it is logical to increasingly rely on social media in order to reach a wider public. Targeted communication on social media that provides relevant high-quality information could function as a counterweight to the false and misleading information on the different Internet platforms.

In general, it can be stated that in many European countries[9] the measures taken by the respective governments were followed well. For example, Flaxmann et al. show in a study published in 'Nature' that the non-pharmaceutical interventions of the respective governments were able to reduce the assumed reproduction rate of the Covid-19 virus from an original 3.8 (on average) to 0.66. They make it clear that the effects of the individual measures cannot be exactly identified, with the exception of the lockdown, which contributed to around 81% of the reduction in the reproduction rate (cf. Flaxmann et al. 2020).

Despite a relatively good 'compliance' at the societal level, some critical voices can be heard with regard to the measures. As already discussed earlier, reliable health-related information is in competition with information of all conceivable quality. Prominent are currently conspiracy theories,[10] which can have a relatively strong influence on action. Freedom of opinion is a central good of democratic societies and accordingly democratic societies have to find an appropriate way to deal with critical or even unusual voices. This means that the belief in conspiracy theories and the advocacy thereof is, in the first instance, a central right of

[9] Eleven European countries were examined: Belgium, Denmark, Germany, France, Great Britain, Italy, Norway, Austria, Sweden, Spain and Switzerland.

[10] It should be noted at this point that the term "conspiracy theory" is sometimes used as a kind of argument of last resort to deprive positions of their argumentative basis.

citizens of democratic societies. However, the problem becomes virulent when the societal influence of such views becomes so great that the general welfare of society is endangered. At present, one can increasingly hear the concern that conspiracy theories have a not inconsiderable negative impact on social cohesion. Not surprisingly, various studies on conspiracy theories can be found, for example by the Konrad Adenauer Foundation, which shows that approximately one third of Germans potentially believe in conspiracy theories (see Roose 2020). At the same time, other international studies show a connection between conspiracy theories and the refusal of health-promoting measures (see Allington et al. 2020). This connection has been shown in different contexts, for example with vaccinations (see Jolley and Douglas 2014), HIV (see Grebe and Nattrass 2012) or contraception (see Thorburn and Bogart 2005). Allington et al. show that a similar connection can also be seen in the Covid-19 pandemic. Based on three different studies, they illustrate that there is a connection between the belief in conspiracy theories and the use of social media, and also a connection between the non-compliance with protective measures and the use of social media as an information source (see Allington et al. 2020).

However great the anticipated danger of conspiracy theories, misinformation and disinformation may be, the fundamental right to freedom of expression as a foundation of democratic societies must not be restricted. Similarly, the media user should be able to clearly distinguish between information and appeal. Public health information is thus faced with the challenge of asserting itself against other information as more useful, credible, correct or simply better in order to convince citizens of the usefulness of public health interventions. This can only succeed if complex problem-solving strategies are envisaged that act at different levels in order to strengthen confidence in public health communication and the resulting measures.

6 Problem Solving

With regard to the handling of the problems described, two areas can be distinguished from each other. First, the question arises of an appropriate handling of information and its selection. Second, the question arises of appropriate actions based on this information. With regard to the second problem area—the guidance of appropriate actions—public health actors must find creative ways to convince citizens of the correctness of the measures envisaged. Furthermore, reference will primarily be made to the first problem area, the handling of information in general. With regard to this problem area, Lazer et al. distinguish between two basic strategies. One is aimed at supporting actors in evaluating false information, in the sense of strengthening media and digital competence (empowerment). The other intends to change the structures of the media offerings in such a way that actors are exposed to less fake news overall, which is problematic in so far as this is a paternalistic approach that certainly requires a special justification (cf. Lazer et al.

2018). However, both solutions are based on a structural level in order to improve the general handling of information.

At the end of this article, two initiatives will be presented that address the described problems from different perspectives. First, an ad-hoc framework of the WHO will be presented, which primarily tries to sort the different problem areas and bring them into a common context. Subsequently, "PubliCo", a project of the University of Zurich, will be presented, which serves to improve communication in crisis situations and thus has a practical reference in dealing with an infodemic.

6.1 WHO

The WHO Information Network for Epidemics held a virtual workshop in spring 2020 to develop a framework for managing the COVID-19 infodemic. Based on presentations on different topics and structured discussions, topic areas were identified that were considered particularly relevant by the participants. With the help of a narrative analysis, a fifty-point action plan was distilled into five areas that have been included in the framework.

1. **Identification of evidence**

   Public health interventions and their recommendations must be based on current scientific knowledge. The comprehensible communication of these recommendations is necessary in order to reach as many people as possible and to enable them to make informed decisions in order to protect themselves and their relatives.
2. **Translation of scientific knowledge into actionable steps**
   Scientific knowledge should be transformed into actionable steps in order to reach all groups of people within society. To disseminate the recommendations, all possible communication platforms should be used, in addition to digital media, also and especially analogue ways. A coordinated approach in partnership with a variety of stakeholders, including civil society, is necessary to ensure that the information is understood and that availability is ensured for vulnerable or hard-to-reach population groups.
3. **Promoting action-oriented initiatives**
   Governments and authorities should develop initiatives to understand the concerns of citizens and their information needs. Recommendations and information should be processed specifically for different target groups in society.
4. **Analysis of the impact of an infodemic**
   Strategic partnerships with all relevant sectors should be strengthened in order to carry out a comprehensive analysis of the infodemic. This includes, for example, social media providers, the technology sector, science, health authorities and civil society. Through strategic partnerships, all relevant information can be brought together more effectively and processed together in a target group-oriented manner. Various tools can help, for example, to check facts and

track the development of the infodemic. These include trend observations and the analysis of the impact of information and interventions on the behaviour of the population.

5. **Coordinating and implementing political decisions**
   The systematic capture and analysis of communication in social media, television and radio broadcasts, combined with surveys on knowledge, risk perception and trust, help to set political action in a context. Authorities should use these analyses to understand the communication changes of citizens, as well as their questions in relation to the pandemic, and to anticipate the possible occurrence of misinformation.

WHO is working with a large number of partners on the implementation of the fifty-point framework. Numerous initiatives are described on their website (see www.who.int).

6.2 The 'PubliCo' Project

'PubliCo' is a project initiated by the University of Zurich, which takes up some of the aspects identified by WHO and the concept of an online platform.[11] The potential benefits of an interactive citizen platform in times of crisis are referred to in current literature.

> The creation of an interactive platform and dashboard to provide real-time alerts of rumours and concerns about coronavirus spreading globally would enable public health officials and relevant stakeholders to respond rapidly with a proactive and engaging narrative that can mitigate misinformation. (Depoux et al. 2020, p. 1)

However, 'PubliCo' does not focus on warnings of false reports, but rather tries to enable the exchange between citizens and political decision-makers. The goal of 'PubliCo' is to creatively take up the described problems of the infodemic and to solve them. The focus is on a deep and differentiated understanding of the public perception of the Covid-19 virus and psycho-social stressors associated with the different interventions for prevention, control and containment. In order to achieve this goal, targeted risk and crisis communication is envisaged using an online platform.

'PubliCo' is aimed at political decision-makers on the one hand and the general public on the other. The aim is to establish (indirect) two-way communication which is made possible by the online platform 'PubliCo'. The focus is on communication which supplies both sides with the relevant information. On the one hand, political decision-makers should be informed in real time about the emotional state ('Corona barometer'), moral preferences, dispositions to action, but also the knowledge ('Corona quiz') of the general public, on the other hand, the respective

[11] https://publico.community/

users of 'PubliCo' should be supplied with the information relevant to them, such as current measures or the latest empirical evidence on Covid-19.

In order to provide citizens with the information that is individually important to them, some data about the respective persons is first required. 'PubliCo' is designed as a complex tool that uses different methods of data collection to arrive at the most differentiated picture of the different perspectives in the population. For this purpose, three methods are used in the core:

1. An (quantitative) online survey ('Corona quiz')
2. 'Corona diaries', which are evaluated using a qualitative analysis
3. Qualitative interviews

Of central importance for the concept is the so-called 'Corona quiz'. The respective results of this quiz serve as the decisive source of information for the users. Citizens can—based on the very intensively used platform "moral machine" (Awad et al. 2018; Awad et al. 2020) —playfully test their knowledge and at the same time communicate their preferences. These playful elements ('gamification') are to be used to keep participation barriers as low as possible and to generate a high level of participation readiness among citizens. The qualitative data collection serves primarily to provide deeper data from the 'Corona Quiz' and to also reach population groups that are difficult to access for a digital survey. A conscious decision is made to set up a method triangulation in order to gain the broadest possible understanding of the perspective of citizens (cf. Wäscher et al. 2014).

Based on these data, it is then possible in a second step to provide the users with individually tailored information that meets their current needs. Likewise, these data serve political decision-makers as an information source for the current state of the population as a whole. In addition to the current knowledge of measures and the latest evidence, the data on the psychosocial state of the population are of particular relevance, as these are usually difficult to access. Figure 1 shows schematically how the described approach can be realized.

If the implementation of 'PubliCo' proves to be successful—which is also largely dependent on the willingness to use the platform—it could make a decisive contribution to alleviating the problems of the infodemic and providing a tool in the long term that offers citizens valuable support in times of crisis in times of crisis.

7 Conclusion

Dealing with information in pandemic times poses great challenges for society as a whole. Journalists and scientists must find ways to process complex information so that citizens are comprehensively informed but do not feel overwhelmed at the same time. Political decision-makers must justify and implement the measures taken for the whole society on the basis of reliable information. In addition, the media should provide space for a social discourse that helps to critically examine

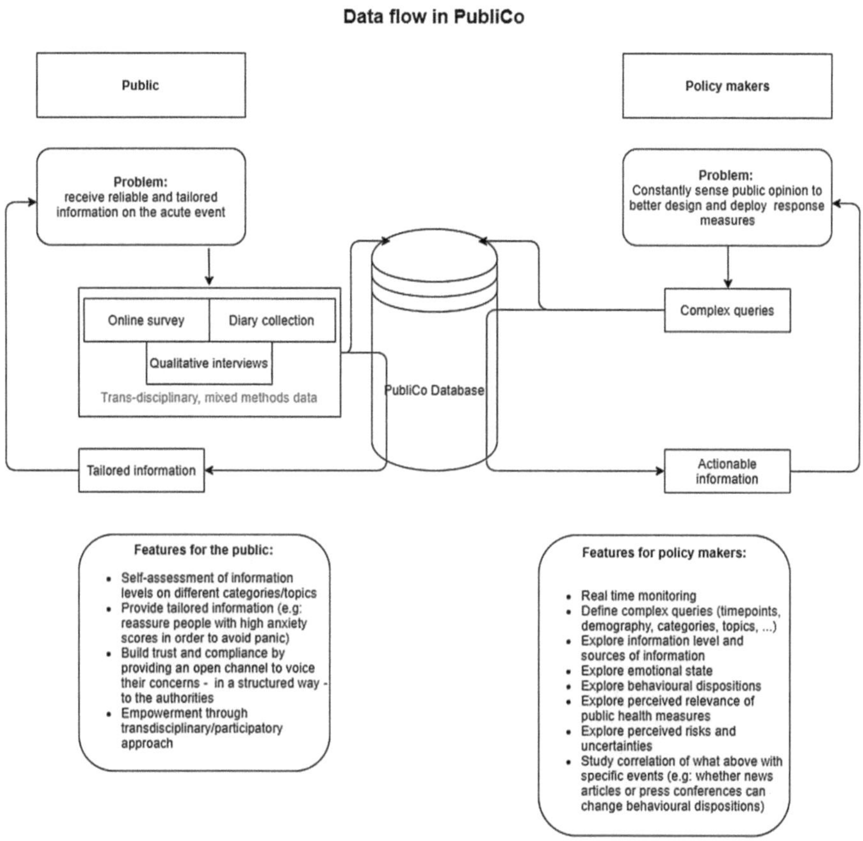

Fig. 1 Schematic representation of the online platform 'PubliCo' (cf. Spitale et al. 2021)

and discuss the proportionality of measures and the empirical and normative premises on which decisions are made from different perspectives. In this way, the trust of citizens in the behavior of journalists, scientists and political decision-makers in crisis situations can be strengthened. On the one hand, this refers to the trust in individual actors, but on the other hand—and this seems to be more important at the moment—it is about strengthening the trust in established social structures. It is important to ensure that conflicting statements and positions within science and journalism are not interpreted as an occasion for mistrust, but on the contrary for transparency and trustworthiness. A general trust that both are basically interested in the common good facilitates such an interpretation. This also means that every single person is called upon to assume their responsibility and to act responsibly in their respective (professional) field (cf. Altmeppen et al. 2019). Only with the help of a shared understanding of co-responsibility can complex problems be solved together (cf. Wäscher et al. 2020; Apel 1993; Council of Europe 2011).

Social media are currently pointing to a tension between freedom of opinion on the one hand and the problematic influence of misinformation on the other hand on a rational approach to health-promoting measures. The great challenge facing democratic societies is the assessment of information, the admission of freedom of opinion—even though damage can be caused here—and the containment of verifiable misinformation. In principle, a robust democracy must be able to deal with such a tension and sometimes—in the sense of complex plurality—also endure it.

The question of whether there is an "infodemic"—in the sense of an information overload—in the context of Covid-19 appears to be secondary on closer inspection. There is no doubt that there is an information overload in almost all social issues, this seems to be an integral part of modern information societies. Much more relevant is the question of how the quality of information can be assessed and verified and who is to be entrusted with this task on the basis of which legitimacy. In a second step, it must then be clarified how clearly false information can be dealt with in order to deprive it of its (potential) effectiveness. At the same time, a spectrum of opinion must be maintained in the interpretation and classification of facts.

The approaches presented in this article show by way of example how attempts are currently being made to solve the problems described. The WHO is trying to use different programmes to analyse the complex relationships of the infodemic globally in order to provide high-quality and reliable information based on facts. The online platform "PubliCo" helps to process information in the sense of an immediate and individually tailored two-way communication between citizens and political decision-makers.

It is to be expected that further solutions will be developed and critically discussed in the near future. One of the great challenges at present is to contain the potential damage caused by the pandemic and the measures taken to combat it at health, socio-economic and psycho-social levels. In doing so, basic democratic rights, such as freedom of opinion, must not be undermined. This means that the focus should initially be on enlightenment and self-responsibility and a paternalistic approach should be avoided whenever possible. In this way, the social resilience to the current pandemic and to future crises can be strengthened.

References

Akademien der Wissenschaften Schweiz (2008) Wissenschaftliche Integrität. Grundsätze und Verfahrensregeln. Akademien der Wissenschaften Schweiz, Bern

Albert H (1960) Der Kritische Rationalismus Karl Poppers. Arch Rechts Sozialphilosophie 46(3):391–415. http://www.jstor.org/stable/23678152

All European Academies (ALLEA) (2017) The European code of conduct for research integrity. https://www.allea.org/wp-content/uploads/2017/05/ALLEA-European-Code-of-Conduct-for-Research-Integrity-2017.pdf. Accessed 29 Jan 2021

Allington D, Duffy B, Wessely S, Dhavan N, Rubin J (2020) Health-protective behaviour, social media usage and conspiracy belief during the COVID-19 public health emergency. Psychol Med:1–7. https://doi.org/10.1017/S003329172000224X

Altmeppen K-D, Bieber C, Filipović A, Heesen J, Neuberger C, Röttger U et al (2019) Öffentlichkeit, Verantwortung und Gemeinwohl im digitalen Zeitalter. Publizistik 64(1):59–77. https://doi.org/10.1007/s11616-018-00463-1

Apel K-O (1993) How to ground a universalistic ethics of co-responsibility for the effects of collective actions and activities? Philosophica 52(2):9–29

Awad E, Dsouza S, Kim R, Schulz J, Henrich J, Shariff A et al (2018) The moral machine experiment. Nature 563(7729):59–64. https://doi.org/10.1038/s41586-018-0637-6

Awad E, Dsouza S, Shariff A, Rahwan I, Bonnefon J-F (2020) Universals and variations in moral decisions made in 42 countries by 70,000 participants. Proc Natl Acad Sci U S A. https://doi.org/10.1073/pnas.1911517117

Baraldi C, Corsi G, Esposito E (2008) GLU. Glossar zu Niklas Luhmanns Theorie sozialer Systeme, 1 edn. Suhrkamp, Frankfurt am Main

Bechmann A (2020) Tackling disinformation and infodemics demands media policy changes. Digit J 8(6):855–863. https://doi.org/10.1080/21670811.2020.1773887

Brennen J S, Simon F, Howard PN, Nielsen RK (2020) Types, sources, and claims of COVID-19 misinformation. https://reutersinstitute.politics.ox.ac.uk/types-sources-and-claims-covid-19-misinformation. Accessed 05 Oct 2020

Breuning C, Handel M, Kessler B (2020) Massenkommunikation 1964-2020: Mediennutzung im Langzeitvergleich. Ergebnisse der ARD/ZDF-Langzeitstudie. Media Perspektiven (7–8):410–432

Coiera E (2013) Social networks, social media, and social diseases. BMJ 346:f3007. https://doi.org/10.1136/bmj.f3007

Dahinden U (2000) Demokratisierung dank Internet? – Zum Austauschverhältnis zwischen neuen elektronischen und traditionellen massenmedialen Öffentlichkeiten. In: Jarren O, Imhof K, Blum R (eds) Zerfall der Öffentlichkeit?. VS Verlag, Wiesbaden, p 240–254

Darbyshire, P (2018) Fake news. Fake journals. Fake conferences. What we can do. In: Journal of clinical nursing 27 (9–10), S 1727–1729. https://doi.org/10.1111/jocn.14214

Depoux A, Martin S, Karafillakis E, Preet R, Wilder-Smith A, Larson H (2020) The pandemic of social media panic travels faster than the COVID-19 outbreak. J Travel Med 27(3). https://doi.org/10.1093/jtm/taaa031

Deutscher Presserat (2019) Pressekodex. https://www.presserat.de/pressekodex.html. Accessed 09 Nov 2020

DFG, Deutsche Forschungsgemeinschaft (2020) Verfahrensleitfaden zur guten wissenschaftlichen Praxis. Deutsche Forschungsgemeinschaft DFG (ed). https://www.dfg.de/download/pdf/foerderung/rechtliche_rahmenbedingungen/gute_wissenschaftliche_praxis/verfahrensleitfaden_gwp.pdf

Douglas HE (2009) Science, policy, and the value-free ideal. University of Pittsburgh Press, Pittsburgh

EbM-Netzwerk (2020) Stellungnahme COVID-19. https://www.ebm-netzwerk.de/de/veroeffentlichungen/pdf/stn-20200903-covid19-update.pdf. Accessed 16 Sept 2020

Emanuelson EJR (2018) Fake left, fake right: promoting an informed public in the era of alternative facts. Administrative Law Review 70(1):209–232

Europarat (2011) Towards a Europe of shared social responsibilities. Challenges and strategies. Trends in social cohesion 23. Council of Europe Publishing, Strasbourg

Fischer F (2019) Knowledge politics and post-truth in climate denial: on the social construction of alternative facts. Crit Policy Stud 13(2):133–152. https://doi.org/10.1080/19460171.2019.1602067

Flaxman S, Mishra S, Gandy A, Unwin HJT, Mellan TA, Coupland H et al (2020) Estimating the effects of non-pharmaceutical interventions on COVID-19 in Europe. Nature 584(7820):257–261. https://doi.org/10.1038/s41586-020-2405-7

Gerhards J, Schäfer MS (2007) Demokratische Internet-Öffentlichkeit? Ein Vergleich der öffentlichen Kommunikation im Internet und in den Printmedien am Beispiel der Humangenomforschung. Pub 52(2):210–228. https://doi.org/10.1007/s11616-007-0084-0

Goertzel T (2010) Conspiracy theories in science. EMBO Rep 11(7):493–499. https://doi.org/10.1038/embor.2010.84

Grebe E, Nattrass N (2012) AIDS conspiracy beliefs and unsafe sex in Cape Town. AIDS Behav 16(3). https://doi.org/10.1007/s10461-011-9958-2

Hoffjann O, Arlt H-J (2015) Die nächste Öffentlichkeit: Theorieentwurf und Szenarien. Springer Fachmedien, Wiesbaden

Jolley D, Douglas KM (2014) The effects of anti-vaccine conspiracy theories on vaccination intentions. PLoS One 9(2):e89177. https://doi.org/10.1371/journal.pone.0089177

Kulldorff M, Gupta S, Bhattacharya J (2020) Great Barrington Declaration. https://gbdeclaration.org/. Accessed 29 Jan 2021

Kupferschmitt T, Müller T (2020) ARD/ZDF-Massenkommunikation 2020: Mediennutzung im Intermediavergleich. Aktuelle Ergebnisse der repräsentativen Langzeitstudie. Media Perspektiven (7–8):390–409

Lachapelle F (2020) COVID-19 preprints and their publishing rate: an improved method. https://doi.org/10.1101/2020.09.04.20188771

Lancet T (2020) The truth is out there, somewhere. Lancet 396(10247):291. https://doi.org/10.1016/S0140-6736(20)31678-0

Larson HJ (2018) The biggest pandemic risk? Viral misinformation. Nature 562(7727):309. https://doi.org/10.1038/d41586-018-07034-4

Lazer DMJ, Baum MA, Benkler Y, Berinsky AJ, Greenhill KM, Menczer F et al (2018) The science of fake news. Science 359(6380):1094–1096. https://doi.org/10.1126/science.aao2998

Loh J (2017) Strukturen und Relata der Verantwortung. In: Heidbrink L, Langbehn C, Loh J (eds) Handbuch Verantwortung. Springer Fachmedien, Wiesbaden, pp 35–56

Luhmann N (1995) Die Realität der Massenmedien. Nordrhein-Westfälische Akademie der Wissenschaften, Geisteswissenschaften. Vorträge, 333. VS Verlag, Wiesbaden. https://doi.org/10.1007/978-3-663-16287-2

Luhmann N (2009a) Die Gesellschaft der Gesellschaft, 1 edn. Suhrkamp, Frankfurt am Main. http://www.gbv.de/dms/faz-rez/F19971014SCHWANI100.pdf

Luhmann N (2009b) Die Wissenschaft der Gesellschaft. Suhrkamp, Frankfurt am Main

Maletzke G (1998) Kommunikationswissenschaft im Überblick. VS Verlag, Wiesbaden

Mittelstraß J, Blasche S, Wolters G, Carrier M (eds) (2004) Enzyklopädie Philosophie und Wissenschaftstheorie. Unveränderte Sonderausgabe. Metzler, Stuttgart

Parry J (2020) Covid-19: Hong Kong scientists report first confirmed case of reinfection. BMJ 370:m3340. https://doi.org/10.1136/bmj.m3340

Posetti J, Bontcheva K (2020): Disinfodemic. Deciphering COVID-19 disinformation. United Nations. https://en.unesco.org/sites/default/files/disinfodemic_deciphering_covid19_disinformation.pdf. Accessed 29 Jan 2021

Roose J (2020) Sie sind überall. Eine repräsentative Umfrage zu Verschwörungstheorien. Konrad-Adenauer-Stiftung (ed), Berlin. https://www.kas.de/documents/252038/7995358/Eine+repr%C3%A4sentative+Umfrage+zu+Verschw%C3%B6rungstheorien.pdf/0f422364-9ff1-b058-9b02-617e15f8bbd8?version=1.0&t=1599144843148. Accessed 20 Oct 2020

Schmidt SJ, Zurstiege G (2007) Kommunikationswissenschaft. Systematik und Ziele. Rororo Enzyklopädie, 55697. Rowohlt Taschenbuch Verlag, Reinbek bei Hamburg

Schweizer Presserat (2017) Journalistenkodex. https://presserat.ch/. Accessed 09 Nov 2020

Spitale G, Merten S, Jafflin K, Kaiser-Grolimund A, Biller-Andorno N (2021): PubliCo. A new risk and crisis communication platform to bridge the gap between policy makers and the public in the context of the COVID-19 crisis. JMIR Res Protoc. https://doi.org/10.2196/33653

Tangcharoensathien V, Calleja N, Nguyen T, Purnat T, D'Agostino M, Garcia-Saiso S et al (2020) Framework for managing the COVID-19 infodemic: methods and results of an online, crowdsourced WHO technical consultation. J Med Internet Res 22(6):e19659. https://doi.org/10.2196/19659

Thorburn S, Bogart LM (2005) Conspiracy beliefs about birth control: barriers to pregnancy prevention among African Americans of reproductive age. Health Educ Behav 32(4):474–487. https://doi.org/10.1177/1090198105276220

Wakefield MA, Loken B, Hornik RC (2010) Use of mass media campaigns to change health behaviour. Lancet 376(9748):12611271. https://doi.org/10.1016/S0140-6736(10)60809-4

Wardle C, Hossein D (2017) Information Disorder. Toward an interdisciplinary framework for research and policymaking. Council of Europe. https://rm.coe.int/information-disorder-toward-an-interdisciplinary-framework-for-researc/168076277c. Accessed 12 Jan 2021

Wäscher S, Salloch S, Ritter P, Vollmann J, Schildmann J (2014) Triangulation in der empirischen Medizinethik am Beispiel des ETHICO-Projektes („Empirical-Ethical Interventions in Oncology"). Bioethica Forum 7(4):121–130

Wäscher S, Biller-Andorno N, Deplazes-Zemp A (2020) "I don't want to do anything bad." Perspectives on scientific responsibility: results from a qualitative interview study with senior Scientists. NanoEthics 15(2):100. https://doi.org/10.1007/s11569-020-00365-5

Werner MH (2011) Verantwortung. In: Düwell M, Hübenthal C, Werner MH (eds) Handbuch Ethik, 3rd edn. JB Metzler, Stuttgart, pp 541–548

Ethics and Old Age in the Covid-19 Pandemic

Hans-Jörg Ehni and Hans-Werner Wahl

Contents

1 Introduction 223
2 On the Situation of Older People in Nursing Homes During the Covid-19 Crisis 225
3 Self-Determination and Advance Directives 226
4 Social Contacts and Digitalization 228
5 Age Limits in Intensive Care 229
6 Age Discrimination: Heterogeneity of Older People 231
7 Against Ageism and for Intergenerational Solidarity 232
8 Tasks of Gerontological Research and an Ethics of Aging 233
References 234

1 Introduction

Older adults were and are particularly hard hit by the Covid-19 pandemic. The reason for this is initially a statistical correlation: Already at the beginning of the pandemic it became clear that the risks for a severe or fatal course of Covid-19 increase with chronological age (Grasselli et al. 2020; Richardson et al. 2020; Liu et al. 2020). A difficulty here is to assess the risks precisely in view of unclear data on infections with SARS-COV-2 and the associated deaths. The meta-analysis of an interdisciplinary working group around the economist Andrew Levin selected epidemiological studies on mortality due to Covid-19 according to their statistical and scientific quality. The working group came to the following result with regard

H.-J. Ehni (✉)
University of Tübingen, Tübingen, Germany
e-mail: hans-joerg.ehni@uni-tuebingen.de

H.-W. Wahl
Heidelberg University, Heidelberg, Germany
e-mail: wahl@nar.uni-heidelberg.de

© The Author(s), under exclusive license to Springer-Verlag GmbH, DE, part of Springer Nature 2023

A. Reis et al. (eds.), *Pandemics and Ethics*,
https://doi.org/10.1007/978-3-662-66872-6_14

to the Infection Fatality Ratio (IFR), that is, the number of deaths in relation to the estimated total number of infections from epidemiological projections: "The IFR is very low for children and young adults but rises to 0.4% at age 55, 1.3% at age 65, 4.2% at age 75, 14% at age 85, and exceeds 25% for ages 90 and above" (Levin et al. 2020, p. 7).

Data from the WHO from 71 countries confirm this assessment (cf. https://www.who.int/data/maternal-newborn-child-adolescent-ageing/covid-19-data, accessed 01.10.2020). The data in the following are based on these findings. These data are referring to deaths in confirmed infections (Reported Cases) as opposed to the estimated total number of infections, that is, the Case Fatality Ratio (CFR). Accordingly, the proportion of fatal courses (CFR) already increases from the age of 40. This proportion rises from about 1.3% for men and 0.6% for women in the 40 to 44 year age group to 7.32% and 4.25% for the 60 to 64 year olds. Only a statistical correlation with chronological age is noted here. Other factors that contribute causally to a severe course are left out.

After the age of 65, this increase is approximately 5% for men and 3% for women in each age group (always five years combined) until the mortality rate for 85-year-olds is 34.75% (men) and 22.45% (women). Based on the data from the WHO, it can be calculated that 70% of all Covid-19 deaths occur in the over-65 age group and 91% in the over-50 age group. According to WHO data, residents of long-term care facilities also bear a particularly large share of the burden of deaths. However, these figures vary greatly, ranging from 8% of all deaths in Singapore to 39% to over 80% in Slovenia and Canada. In Germany, 60% of the deceased were either in outpatient care or in nursing homes (see Wolf-Ostermann et al. 2020). This shows deficiencies in the protection of these groups in some countries, which requires a search for the reasons (see Stall et al. 2020).

The protection of health and life justifies the restriction of other fundamental rights (see European Group on Ethics in Science and Technology 2020). In order to protect those who, if they are attributed an increased risk, are classified as particularly vulnerable, special measures have also been decided, such as restrictions on visits to nursing homes (see Fischer et al. 2020). In addition to these legally sanctioned rules, social solidarity with vulnerable groups is necessary, which bears these rules and provides additional support (see German Ethics Council 2020). While the welfare of vulnerable groups, including older adults, has often been highlighted, measures are also being discussed and proposed in the course of the pandemic that, in weighing up with the alleged interests of the general public, would entail a special burden on these groups. It was considered whether it would not be better to isolate only the risk groups and, in particular, older adults with pre-existing conditions instead of demanding social distancing from the entire population (see Brooke and Jackson 2020). Some politicians generally doubted whether the protection of older age groups would outweigh the economic costs of the pandemic measures. In a questionable argument, the deputy Texas governor Dan Patrick demanded that older adults sacrifice their lives for the sake of economic well-being. Fortunately, these statements met with a resolute rejection (see Barrett et al. 2020). However, other negative comments and derogatory remarks about older people found an echo that was amplified in many ways in online comments and social media (see Jimenez-Sotomayor et al. 2020).

The Covid-19 pandemic thus causes very different damage such as burdens, which must be ethically responded to in an appropriate manner (see also D'Cruz and Banerjee 2020). One can firstly distinguish between the direct and indirect consequences. The direct consequences of the disease include mortality, permanent health damage and the burden of the disease itself as well as the treatment, such as invasive ventilation or side effects of medication. These burdens increase on average with age (see above). The indirect consequences arise firstly from the measures themselves, which are intended to contain the pandemic. Here, restricted freedom and social isolation play a special role, as basic values such as freedom and social participation are affected. Finally, the special situation of older adults draws the attention to another phenomenon: ageism, which is partly expressed in the measures against the pandemic and partly in the debates about it (see Ehni 2017). It is important to note here that negative evaluations on the basis of age also lead to impairments of physical, mental and cognitive health (see Ayalon et al. 2020; Levy et al. 2020).

According to this differentiation between direct and indirect consequences, we first consider the situation in nursing homes and possible measures to limit damage (see Fischer et al. 2020). We then explain the role of self-determination and advance directives in the current situation. After that, we discuss the consequences of social isolation and how improved access to digital technologies can provide relief. A special role in age discrimination in this context of health care are individual recommendations for triage. Even more direct derogatory statements, in which a negative evaluation of age and older people is expressed, take a step further. The heterogeneity of older people is to be highlighted against such stereotypes and the fact that they are generally attributed an increased risk (see Ayalon et al. 2020; Ng et al. 2015). In this way, ageism comes to light in the tense situation of the pandemic, which threatens to further fuel smoldering generational conflicts and has particularly damaging effects in the current situation. Finally, to conclude this overview of the central ethical challenges of the Covid-19 pandemic, we want to give a first answer to the question of what lessons can be learned from the current situation.

2 On the Situation of Older People in Nursing Homes During the Covid-19 Crisis

Nursing home residents are among the groups that on average are exposed to a higher risk of a severe course of Covid-19. In some countries, such as Canada, Slovenia, Belgium and Great Britain, the majority of all deaths in nursing homes occurred, according to the above-mentioned WHO statistics. Contributing factors to this situation were also shortages in infection protection—that is, disinfectants, protective clothing and masks—as well as a shortage of staff. This situation was further exacerbated by an increase in abuse against older adults, which the WHO has drawn attention to (see World Health Organization 2020). These abuses range from neglect, fraud and psychological violence to physical violence, which the residents of nursing homes are particularly affected by; but according to the WHO they have also increased in home care. The residents particularly affected by severe cases of abuse included, among others, those in Spanish nursing homes, where there were deaths because they were left to their own devices (see Rada 2020). This reflects fundamental and severe deficiencies in both the provision and equipment as well as the supervision and control of nursing homes, which must be remedied in the future (see American Geriatrics Society 2020; Fischer et al. 2020; Stall et al. 2020; Szczerbińska 2020).

Even if there were not such extreme cases everywhere, nursing homes in many countries were subject to special restrictions. In Germany, the federal states decided in March 2020 on visiting regulations or bans for nursing homes, which were in force until mid-May. A review of publications from nursing science on Covid-19 highlights above all isolation and possible measures against its negative consequences, which have been dealt with in many articles (see Fischer et al. 2020). The negative health consequences of isolation and the resulting feeling of loneliness are therefore sufficiently documented, although corresponding helpful interventions are less well researched. Various digital technologies for communication were considered, although here too the corresponding equipment and support are often lacking (see Sect. 3 and Wolf-Ostermann et al. 2020). However, Fischer et al. (2020) emphasize how important the personal visits of relatives and other close people are and that the contact with the nursing staff can be impaired by protective clothing. Fischer and colleagues also emphasize that there should be no general and patronizing restrictions, but that a weighing of safety and the negative consequences of isolation and loneliness should also be the subject of self-determined decisions.

3 Self-Determination and Advance Directives

Respect for self-determination also plays a central role in special measures that are limited to groups. This is the case, for example, when "social distancing" is simply limited to one age group, as has been partly discussed. This approach is based on the idea of achieving so-called "herd immunity" on the way to a natural infection of a correspondingly large part of the population (cf. Fine et al. 2011). In this case, the majority of the population leads a largely normal everyday life, while only those who are at increased risk of a severe course of Covid-19 are to be isolated, for example the residents of nursing homes through strict contact restrictions (cf. Armitage and Nellums 2020). Epidemiological calculations have already shown early on that isolating risk groups alone is not effective in containing the spread of the pandemic (cf. Ferguson et al. 2020). Recently, experts from virology and epidemiology have once again turned against this strategy, as it would extend over a very long period of time and require numerous victims. There are too many different risk groups that cannot be protected in the event of an uncontrolled spread of Covid-19 (cf. Omer et al. 2020; Deutsche Gesellschaft für Virologie 2020). From an ethical point of view, such a procedure is also discriminatory and an expression of a paternalistic attitude (cf. Ayalon et al. 2020; Morrow-Howell et al. 2020; D'Cruz and Banerjee 2020). Not all older people are to be considered a risk group in a general way. Such an approach reflects the idea that older adults are health-impaired in a uniform way. The opposite is the case (see also Sect. 6 below). The fact that there is a statistical correlation between age and the risks of a Covid-19 infection must not lead to the conclusion that older adults are to be supervised. There is no reason to trust older adults less than others to assess their own risks, to deal with them responsibly and to protect themselves within their own means. Unless general restrictions on individual freedom are decided by the responsible decision-makers in order to contain the pandemic, special restrictions should not be required of older adults. Within the framework of what is allowed to everyone, older adults should of course, like everyone else, weigh up their own needs and their safety. For example, when it comes to visits from friends or relatives.

Those who see older adults merely as recipients of regulations and advice not only disregard their autonomy, but also fail to recognize their potential. The current older generations have, in historical comparison, the best physical and physical functional ability as well as the relatively highest level of education (cf. Carstensen 2009; Diehl and Wahl 2020). These are the best conditions for involving them in communication about strategies in the pandemic. Based on their life experience, they remember other crises and hardships. Although older adults are exposed to a higher physical risk, there are also indications that many of them cope very well and better with the psychological stress of the pandemic in terms of subjective well-being and stress than younger age groups (cf. Knepple Carney et al. 2020; Lekamwasam and Lekamwasam 2020). Instead of simply classifying older adults as vulnerable and making corresponding regulations for them, their strengths should be used, their advice should be heard and they should be involved in the corresponding discussions (cf. Lind et al. 2020). Both are hardly the case.

In medical care, advance directives or advance care planning are supposed to ensure that the patient's will is respected even if patients are no longer able to express it. Among other things, invasive and burdensome medical measures, including resuscitation in the event of cardiac arrest, which someone with an advanced illness rejects, are to be avoided. Although advance directives are becoming increasingly common, a majority of the population in Germany and the USA does not have such a document (cf. Anonymus 2017; Farrell et al. 2020). Avoiding unwanted treatment and preserving the corresponding patient's will became particularly urgent in the event of a possible shortage of intensive medical care (cf. Farrell et al. 2020; Deutsche Interdisziplinäre Vereinigung für Intensiv- und Notfallmedizin (DIVI) et al. 2020). In the extreme case, a patient could die for whom no ventilator is available, while someone else is receiving treatment that he or she rejects. However, according to these recommendations, the instrument of the advance directive may not be used to give effect to the patient's will. This could happen by exerting pressure so that certain groups waive treatment of their own accord. Nor may a shortage situation lead to advance directives not being read and observed carefully. Thus, the rejection of resuscitative measures does not imply that an invasive ventilation is not desired. What is decisive is therefore precisely in the current situation to discuss therapies and their individual benefits as well as risks and burdens at an early stage, especially for those who reject invasive treatment.

4 Social Contacts and Digitalization

Information technologies, digital communication and social media shape everyday life during the pandemic and in social distancing more than is usually the case. They create opportunities to network and exchange when physical contact has to be avoided. In this way, they can at least partially compensate for losses in social exchange and the associated mental and physical stress. In part, older adults are assumed to have a low level of competence in the acquisition and use of new technologies. However, studies show a more differentiated picture. For example, currently about 77% of people over 65 own a desktop PC and 52% own a laptop (see Doh 2019). 28% of older adults own a tablet PC. Smartphones are used by 46% of older adults, which means that almost half of all people over 65 can potentially access the full range of functions of these devices. The proportion of internet users has now reached 75% in the over-65 age group. In other countries (e.g. Denmark) new developments are even more promising (see Doh 2019). The preconditions for an increased use of information and communication technologies by older adults during the pandemic are therefore available. However, there is still a so-called "digital divide" in the participation in these technologies, which is exacerbated by educational effects and increases in old age (see Doh 2019). In nursing homes in particular, there is a high need to counteract the negative effects of "social distancing" and isolation.

In the Covid-19 crisis, the digitalization of schools is being promoted and their technological equipment is being improved. However, it remains merely a desideratum that the equipment of nursing homes and the technical access of needy older adults is improved in the same way (see Berg-Weger and Morley 2020; Marston et al. 2020). In addition, debates should take place about how not only digital participation, but also social participation of older adults in general can be guaranteed in the current situation (see Czaja 2017; Czaja et al. 2018). These include physical and mental training, which can also be offered digitally. In general, different forms of activity, participation and engagement are beneficial as new stimuli for the well-being of older adults. Therefore, they are exposed to a higher risk of suffering from the negative consequences of inactivity and lack of participation during the current restrictions. Timely action not only prevents negative long-term consequences, but can also create better conditions for digital participation, social interaction and social participation of older adults in the long term after the pandemic (see also Wahl et al. 2021).

5 Age Limits in Intensive Care

In March and April 2020, intensive care units in several European countries were overwhelmed by the exponential increase in Covid-19 cases. First in Italy, then in Spain and France, the capacity for artificial ventilation was exhausted or exceeded. In this dramatic situation, doctors had to make tragic decisions about which patients to treat and which not to treat. In order to avoid arbitrariness and provide orientation based on uniform and well-founded criteria, several medical societies issued statements during this period on how to deal with the situation. The corresponding recommendations apply methods from triage in disaster medicine to the current problem of the pandemic. It is proposed which patients should be given priority treatment, which treatments should be discontinued and possibly also which patients should be excluded from treatment. Chronological age is one of the exclusion criteria that has been proposed in this context. Among other things, the recommendations of the Italian Society for Anesthesia, Analgesia, Resuscitation and Intensive Care Medicine (see Vergano et al. 2020) suggested such an exclusion criterion. Under aggravated scarcity conditions, it may be necessary to set an age limit for access to intensive care, without giving a specific number. The Swiss recommendations (see Scheidegger et al. 2020) take a similar approach. They state at the outset that age should not be the only criterion. However, these recommendations distinguish between two stages of resource scarcity. In stage A, there are still intensive care beds available, but the remaining available capacities are limited. In stage B, all beds are already occupied. The criteria for aggravated scarcity conditions formulated in the following contain an age limit of 85 years as an exclusion criterion. In a footnote, this is justified with a reference to the increased mortality risk of hospital patients in relation to age, which is confirmed by a Chinese study (see Scheidegger et al. 2020, p. 5). However, the data basis for this argumentation is very problematic. Because data are used here that were collected in another health care system at the beginning of a pandemic with an unknown disease. Whether there is comparability is unclear. It is to be expected that with more experience the treatment results will get better. But by excluding such treatment because of the mortality risk, exactly prevents doctors from gaining the experience for those who are most affected.

In general, the Swiss approach is contradictory, first rejecting age as an alleged placeholder for a state of health, only to reintroduce it again. If chronological age were to provide a reliable indication of health and chances of success, it would not have had to be rejected as a criterion from the outset. In contrast, the joint recommendations of seven medical societies and the Academy of Ethics in Medicine in Germany proceed differently. Here, only the individual state of health and the resulting prospects for intensive medical treatment are held as prioritization criteria, but not as exclusion criteria. In other words, no patients are a priori excluded by clearly defined criteria under conditions of scarcity, but only how the priority of patients is determined in treatment is specified. Chronological age is rejected as an exclusion criterion with reference to the principle of equality (cf. Deutsche Interdisziplinäre Vereinigung für Intensiv- und Notfallmedizin (DIVI) et al. 2020, p. 4).

Two of the Italian authors together with bioethicists have jointly defended the recommendations of SIAARTI against attacks that they express ageism (cf. Craxì et al. 2020). The chronological age was not meant as an exclusion criterion, but the "biological", that is a measure that also takes into account comorbidities and functional ability (cf. Craxì et al. 2020, p. 327). In addition, the preference for younger patients was justified by the generally accepted goal of saving the maximum number of life years. Both arguments are not very convincing. Even if one were to accept with a lot of goodwill that the original recommendations had meant the biological age, there is no generally accepted and simple measure for it, which would be applicable in the given situation (cf. Arking 2018, p. 95). The goal assumed here, to save the maximum number of life years, also contradicts the generally accepted procedures of triage according to Weyma Lübbe (cf. Lübbe 2020). Whoever advocates this goal can neither rely on coherence with accepted procedures nor on consensus in the respective expert debate. In part, arguments from the debate on age rationing are brought up in this context, such as the observation that older adults have already gone through more life phases with the corresponding chances (cf. Savulescu et al. 2020, p. 257). This is reminiscent of the so-called "Fair Innings" argument, which originally comes from the English bioethicist John Harris. According to this, people over a certain age have already enjoyed their fair share of life (cf. Harris 1985, pp. 91 ff.). The debate on age rationing exceeds the scope of this article. However, it should be noted that neither the "Fair Innings" argument nor other arguments that are supposed to support age rationing have prevailed in the ethical debate (cf. Farrell et al. 2020). With Weyma Lübbe one can state that there is only consensus with regard to the goal of saving the maximum number of human lives with the available resources (cf. Lübbe 2020). This goal can be achieved if, as in the German recommendations, one tries to give priority to those for whom the necessary intensive treatment has the best prospects for success. Chronological age alone does not play a role here, but first the available experiences from intensive medicine in relation to the health status of patients. This evidence must be systematically collected and evaluated for the severe courses of Covid-19 before it is suitable for action instructions (cf. Deutsche Interdisziplinäre Vereinigung für Intensiv- und Notfallmedizin (DIVI) et al. 2020, p. 7).

6 Age Discrimination: Heterogeneity of Older People

The harmful effects of age stereotypes have been shown in all the contexts of the pandemic discussed here: in the situation in nursing homes, in the isolation of risk groups, in access to information and communication technologies, and in the recommendations for triage. In particular, the stereotype plays a role that older adults are generally restricted in their physical and mental functional ability and therefore dependent on help, support and instructions. In contrast to such stereotypical ideas, however, people over the age of 65 are a group that is more heterogeneous than any other age group. This is true, for example, of the inter-individual variability in psychological properties, social needs and personality as well as in health-related key indicators such as physical functional ability, chronic diseases and self-assessment of health (cf. Lindenberger and Reischies 1999; Lowsky et al. 2014). Even among those over the age of 80, this heterogeneity is maintained despite significant biological ageing processes, for example with regard to mobility (cf. Mitnitski et al. 2017). Chronological age is therefore of little significance and cannot be used for accurate predictions with regard to needs, behaviour, functional impairment, diseases and pre-existing conditions (cf. Lowsky et al. 2014; Arking 2018). Chronological age and age limits are therefore just as unsuitable as merely age stereotypes suggest, to serve as criteria for special measures in the pandemic, such as the isolation of risk groups and other restrictions or the allocation of resources in the health care system and access to medical care, as envisaged in the above-mentioned recommendations for medical triage. Attributing an increased risk of a severe or fatal Covid-19 disease to all older adults may turn out to be just as wrong as attributing a low risk to all younger age groups. Risk factors for a severe course of this disease include male gender, obesity as well as other possible factors that are currently being discussed. These include, among other things, environmental pollution or genetic dispositions. During the course of the pandemic, it has also become apparent that the general risk assessment for older adults can lull younger people into a false sense of security. Because even younger people can have severe courses and also long-term effects that are not yet foreseeable, even without a severe course of the disease (cf. Levin et al. 2020).

Instead of simply assigning a high risk to older adults in general, the corresponding debates and measures adopted should take appropriate account of their heterogeneity. The same applies to the statements of politicians, scientists and journalists on the role of older adults in the Covid-19 pandemic. This heterogeneity should be just as much in evidence as stereotypes should be avoided. In response to the assessment of vulnerability, passivity and dependency, the responsible actors should make it clear that older people make significant contributions in voluntary work and support in childcare as grandparents (cf. Diehl and Wahl 2020). Protective measures should not restrict such activities across the board. Although the risk of contracting Covid-19 seriously or fatally increases with age, this is not the case to the same extent for all older adults. Those with pre-existing conditions or multimorbidity are at particular risk. For example, in the USA this subgroup makes up approximately 20% of the over-65s (cf. Sheehan et al. 2019). Although residents of nursing homes are, as noted above, a group particularly affected by the Covid-19 pandemic (cf. American Geriatrics Society 2020; Béland and Marier 2020), this group only makes up a relatively small proportion of the over-65s (e.g. 4% in Germany, Penger et al. 2019). If measures and communication in the Covid-19 pandemic avoid and counteract negative age stereotypes, they will also make a significant and important contribution to combating ageism, which is evident in this situation.

7 Against Ageism and for Intergenerational Solidarity

Research on age stereotypes has clearly shown that negative age stereotypes can be quickly triggered in older adults (see Wurm et al. 2017) and that they have about three times the impact of positive stereotypes (e.g. "all older people are wise") (see Meisner 2012). There is a lot of evidence that negative age stereotypes not only have an impact on a psychological level, but also lead to somatic diseases (see Wurm et al. 2017). However, during the pandemic, not only individual negative age stereotypes have played a role, but also general derogatory judgments about the value of the lives of older adults and the resulting discriminatory conclusions. Numerous authors have noted how often "ageism" has been expressed as a derogatory attitude and basis for discriminatory action in the pandemic (see Ayalon et al. 2020; Barrett et al. 2020; Brooke and Jackson 2020; Fraser et al. 2020). Corresponding statements come from politicians who express their indifference to the death of older adults or directly demand that they sacrifice their lives for the economic well-being of all (see D'Cruz and Banerjee 2020). Derogatory comments can be found in reader comments on the websites of print media and in social media, such as Twitter, where the cynical hashtag #boomerremover has experienced a sad boom (see Jimenez-Sotomayor et al. 2020). However, in our own study we found that the experience of age-discriminatory comments does not trigger feelings of stigmatization in all older adults, but does in significant subgroups (see Wahl et al. 2021).

Ageism, as a general negative and devaluing attitude towards older adults, according to which their lives are less valuable than others and altogether dispensable, can obviously have serious consequences in a situation like the Covid-19 pandemic, in addition to the documented harmful effects of internalized ageism on the mental and physical health of older people (see Levy et al. 2020). Such consequences include the already mentioned abuse of withholding medical care and nursing, exerted pressure to waive both of them voluntarily, neglect as reported from nursing homes in different countries with up to fatal consequences, abuse and violence (see Sect. 1). To counter ageism in words and deeds is a task for society as a whole. Policy and media have a duty not only to avoid such statements in communication about the pandemic, but to correct and criticize them. At the same time, intergenerational solidarity should be supported and corresponding civil society activities should be supported as a countermeasure. Only in this way can a humane society be guaranteed that is based on cooperation and social cohesion and in which vulnerable groups and individuals of all ages are protected from avoidable damage.

8 Tasks of Gerontological Research and an Ethics of Aging

Virology has been and remains at the center of the pandemic. Virologists have made a valuable contribution to the current situation with their expertise, recommendations and guidance. Other scientific disciplines are facing similar challenges. Gerontology can play a decisive role in ensuring that the health and well-being of all are taken into account equally in the current crisis. Accordingly, gerontological expertise was in demand when approaches were to be developed as to how the needs of older adults could be met. Estimates suggest that approximately 15–25% of people over the age of 80 have difficulty coping with social isolation and contact restrictions (see De Jong Gierveld and Van Tilburg 2010)—which by no means is limited to nursing homes! The responsible political decision-makers are dependent on the precautionary advice and recommendations for supportive measures from gerontologists. Most likely, this crisis will change the way many people experience their age in a fundamental way. Many opportunities for social interaction and participation have been limited or non-existent. New ways to create such opportunities must be found and supported. Gerontological research plays a key role in investigating the various consequences of the pandemic and relevant (counter-)measures. It can thus contribute not only to a urgently needed differentiated image of aging, but also give older adults a voice themselves. Extensive and time-consuming studies, e.g. the Berlin Aging Study, document the willingness of older adults to participate in the corresponding research (see Lindenberger and Delius 2010). Their results are then of course to be implemented. Older adults not only have a claim to virological studies, but also to gerontological research, which can just as well avert damage from them and improve their quality of life.

The crisis also offers the opportunity to better meet ethical requirements in connection with the life phase of old age. This includes a better understanding of the living conditions of older adults and how to counteract problems that affect them. Older adults have special strengths and can make a important contribution to coping with a difficult situation like the present one. Such a perspective was probably lacking in the relevant debates as well as in media reports, despite contrary gerontological evidence (see, for example, Diehl and Wahl 2020). Age stereotypes and ageism contribute significantly to the negative consequences of the pandemic, not only for older adults. Now is the time to take a stand against them by creating a better awareness of one-sided judgments and age discrimination as well as the strengths of older adults.

During the pandemic we have been experiencing a situation with numerous conflicts and moral dilemmas, in which weighing is difficult to carry out. In one way or another, in such weighing, the life of older adults is given less value, either because they are less productive, because they have already lived their life, because they have less life to lose, or because they are going to die soon anyway (see Farrell et al. 2020). Such arguments can be found in everyday discussions as well as in the opinions of ethicists and other experts. They undermine attitudes such as the joy of saving 100-year-old patients or the willingness to risk one's own health for the care of people with dementia. In extreme cases, such views can lead to civilization breaks, such as the deaths in Spanish nursing homes, where needy people were simply left to fend for themselves (see Rada 2020). When the consequences of different courses of action and measures are weighed against each other, an aggregation of interests, damages and benefits can be inevitable. So in triage, a procedure is undisputed and ethically justifiable, which aims to save the maximum number of human lives. This can mean prioritizing those who have the best chance of surviving a necessary intensive medical treatment. However, this does not mean that in such a situation, individual social groups are systematically disadvantaged and their rights violated by attributing less value to their lives than to those of others. Such views fundamentally contradict basic social values, as expressed in the idea of human rights. This is especially true of the same value and the same respect that should be accorded to every human being and the right of no one to be discriminated against on the basis of characteristics such as ethnic origin, gender, disability or age (see Gosepath 2011; Nickel 2019). Especially in times of crisis like in a pandemic, it is particularly important to uphold social values and protect individual rights that can easily fall victim to the alleged common good. This is especially true for the rights of those who cannot defend themselves without further ado and have few advocates. At the same time, this situation reminds us of our fundamental human vulnerability, which precisely in the pandemic requires mutual protection, care and solidarity.

References

American Geriatrics Society (2020) American Geriatrics Society policy brief: COVID-19 and nursing homes. J Am Geriatr Soc 68(5):908–911. https://doi.org/10.1111/jgs.16477

Anonymus (2017) Zahl der Patientenverfügungen gestiegen. Deutsches Ärzteblatt. https://www.aerzteblatt.de/nachrichten/81737/Zahl-der-Patientenverfuegungen-gestiegen. Accessed 11 Jan 2021

Arking R (2018) Biology of longevity and aging: pathways and prospects, 4th edn. Oxford University Press, New York

Armitage R, Nellums LB (2020) COVID-19 and the consequences of isolating the elderly. Lancet Public Health 5(5):e256. https://doi.org/10.1016/S2468-2667(20)30061-X

Ayalon L, Chasteen A, Diehl M, Levy B, Neupert SD, Rothermund K, Tesch-Romer C, Wahl H-W (2020) Aging in times of the COVID-19 pandemic: avoiding ageism and fostering intergenerational solidarity. J Gerontol Bio Sci. https://doi.org/10.1093/geronb/gbaa051

Barrett AE, Michael C, Padavic I (2020) Calculated ageism: generational sacrifice as a response to the COVID-19 pandemic. J Gerontol B Psychol Sci Soc Sci. https://doi.org/10.1093/geronb/gbaa132

Béland D, Marier P (2020) COVID-19 and long-term care policy for older people in Canada. J Aging Soc Policy 32:358–364. https://doi.org/10.1080/08959420.2020.1764319

Berg-Weger M, Morley JE (2020) Editorial: loneliness and social isolation in older adults during the COVID-19 pandemic: implications for gerontological social work. J Nutr Health Aging 24(5):456–458. https://doi.org/10.1007/s12603-020-1366-8

Brooke J, Jackson D (2020) Older people and COVID-19: isolation, risk and ageism. J Clin Nurs. https://doi.org/10.1111/jocn.15274

Carstensen LL (2009) A long and bright future. Broadway Books, New York

Craxì L, Vergano M, Savulescu J, Wilkinson D (2020) Rationing in a pandemic: lessons from Italy. Asian Bioeth Rev 12(3):1–6. https://doi.org/10.1007/s41649-020-00127-1

Czaja SJ (2017) The role of technology in supporting social engagement among older adults. Public Policy Aging Rep 27(4):145–148. https://doi.org/10.1093/ppar/prx034

Czaja SJ, Boot WR, Charness N, Rogers WA, Sharit J (2018) Improving social support for older adults through technology: findings from the PRISM randomized controlled trial. The Gerontologist 58(3):467–477. https://doi.org/10.1093/geront/gnw249

D'Cruz M, Banerjee D (2020) 'An invisible human rights crisis': the marginalization of older adults during the COVID-19 pandemic – an advocacy review. J Psychiatry Res 292:113369. https://doi.org/10.1016/j.psychres.2020.113369

De Jong Gierveld J, Van Tilburg T (2010) The De Jong Gierveld short scales for emotional and social loneliness: tested on data from 7 countries in the UN generations and gender surveys. Eur J Ageing 7(2):121–130. https://doi.org/10.1007/s10433-010-0144-6

Deutsche Gesellschaft für Virologie (2020) Stellungnahme der Gesellschaft für Virologie zu einem wissenschaftlich begründeten Vorgehen gegen die Covid-19 Pandemie. https://www.g-f-v.org/node/1358. Accessed 11 Jan 2021

Deutsche Interdisziplinäre Vereinigung für Intensiv- und Notfallmedizin (DIVI), Deutsche Gesellschaft für Interdisziplinäre Notfall- und Akutmedizin (DGINA), Deutsche Gesellschaft für Anästhesiologie und Intensivmedizin (DGAI), Deutsche Gesellschaft für Internistische Intensivmedizin und Notfallmedizin (DGIIN), Deutsche Gesellschaft für Pneumologie und Beatmungsmedizin (DGP), der Deutschen Gesellschaft für Palliativmedizin (DGP), und der Akademie für Ethik in der Medizin (AEM) (2020) Entscheidungen über die Zuteilung von Ressourcen in der Notfall und der Intensivmedizin im Kontext der COVID-19-Pandemie – Klinisch-ethische Empfehlungen. Version 2. https://www.awmf.org/leitlinien/detail/ll/040-013.html. Accessed 11 Jan 2021

Deutscher Ethikrat (2020) Solidarität und Verantwortung in der Corona-Krise. Ad hoc Empfehlung. https://www.ethikrat.org/fileadmin/Publikationen/Ad-hoc-Empfehlungen/deutsch/ad-hoc-empfehlung-corona-krise.pdf. Accessed 11 Jan 2021

Diehl M, Wahl H-W (2020) The psychology of later life: a contextual perspective. American Psychological Association, Washington

Doh M (2019) Auswertung von empirischen Studien zur Nutzung von Internet, digitalen Medien und Informations- und Kommunikations-Technologien bei älteren Menschen. Expertisen zum Achten Altersbericht der Bundesregierung. https://www.achter-altersbericht.de/fileadmin/altersbericht/pdf/Expertisen/Expertise_Doh.pdf. Accessed 11 Jan 2021

Ehni HJ (2017) Ageism. In: ten Have H (Hrsg) Encyclopedia of global bioethics. Springer International Publishing, Cham. https://doi.org/10.1007/978-3-319-05544-2_13-1

European Group on Ethics in Science and Technology (2020) Statement on European Solidarity and the Protection of Fundamental Rights in the COVID-19 Pandemic. https://ec.europa.eu/info/research-and-innovation/strategy/support-policy-making/scientific-support-eu-policies/ege_en#members. Accessed 11 Jan 2021

Farrell TW, Francis L, Brown T, Ferrante LE, Widera E, Rhodes R, Rosen T, Hwang U, Witt LJ, Thothala N, Liu SW, Vitale CA, Braun UK, Stephens C, Saliba D (2020) Rationing limited health care resources in the COVID-19 era and beyond: ethical considerations regarding older adults. J Am Geriatr Soc 68:1143–1149. https://doi.org/10.1111/jgs.16539

Ferguson N, Laydon D, Nedjati-Gilani G, Imai N, Ainslie K, Baguelin M, Bhatia S, Boonyasiri A, Cucunubá Z, Cuomo-Dannenburg G, Dighe A (2020) Impact of non-pharmaceutical interventions (NPIs) to reduce COVID-19 mortality and healthcare demand. Imperial College COVID-19 Response Team, London. https://www.imperial.ac.uk/media/imperial-college/medicine/sph/ide/gida-fellowships/Imperial-College-COVID19-NPI-modelling-16-03-2020.pdf. Accessed 11 Jan 2021

Fine P, Eames K, Heymann DL (2011) „Herd immunity": a rough guide. Clin Infect Dis 52(7):911–916. https://doi.org/10.1093/cid/cir007

Fischer F, Raiber L, Boscher C, Winter MH (2020) COVID-19-Schutzmaßnahmen in der stationären Altenpflege. Pflege 33(4):199–206. https://doi.org/10.1024/1012-5302/a000745

Fraser S, Lagace M, Bongue B, Ndeye N, Guyot J, Bechard L, Garcia L, Taler V, Adam S, Beaulieu M, Bergeron CD, Boudjemadi V, Desmette D, Donizzetti AR, Ethier S, Garon S, Gillis M, Levasseur M, Lortie-Lussier M, Marier P, Robitaille A, Sawchuk K, Lafontaine C, Tougas F (2020) Ageism and COVID-19: what does our society's response say about us? Age Ageing. https://doi.org/10.1093/ageing/afaa097

Gosepath S (2011) Equality. https://plato.stanford.edu/archives/spr2011/entries/equality/. Accessed 11 Jan 2021

Grasselli G, Zangrillo A, Zanella A, Antonelli M, Cabrini L, Castelli A, Cereda D, Coluccello A, Foti G, Fumagalli R, Iotti G, Latronico N, Lorini L, Merler S, Natalini G, Piatti A, Ranieri MV, Scandroglio AM, Storti E, Cecconi M, Pesenti A, for the Covid Lombardy ICU Network (2020) Baseline characteristics and outcomes of 1591 patients infected with SARS-CoV-2 admitted to ICUs of the Lombardy Region, Italy. J Am Med Assoc. https://doi.org/10.1001/jama.2020.5394

Harris J (1985) The value of life. Routledge & Kegan Paul, London

Jimenez-Sotomayor MR, Gomez-Moreno C, Soto-Perez-de-Celis E (2020) Coronavirus, ageism, and Twitter: an evaluation of tweets about older adults and COVID-19. J Am Geriatr Soc. https://doi.org/10.1111/jgs.16508

Knepple Carney A, Graf AS, Hudson G, Wilson E (2020) Age moderates perceived COVID-19 disruption on well-being. Gerontologist. https://doi.org/10.1093/geront/gnaa106

Lekamwasam R, Lekamwasam S (2020) Effects of COVID-19 pandemic on health and wellbeing of older people: a comprehensive review. Ann Geriatr Med Res. https://doi.org/10.4235/agmr.20.0027

Levin AT, Hanage W, Owusu-Boaitey N, Cochran K, Walsh S, Meyerowitz-Katz G (2020) Assessing the age specificity of infection fatality rates for COVID-19: systematic review, meta-analysis, and public policy implications. Eur J Epidemiol 35:1123–1138

Levy BR, Slade MD, Chang ES, Kannoth S, Wang SY (2020) Ageism amplifies cost and prevalence of health conditions. Gerontologist 60(1):174–181. https://doi.org/10.1093/geront/gny131

Lind M, Bluck S, McAdams DP (2020) More vulnerable? The life story approach highlights older people's' potential for strength during the pandemic. J Gerontol B Psychol Sci Soc Sci. https://doi.org/10.1093/geronb/gbaa105

Lindenberger U, Delius JAM (2010) Die Berliner Altersstudie. Forschungsberichte der interdisziplinären Arbeitsgruppen der Berlin-Brandenburgischen Akademie der Wissenschaften, vol 3, 3rd edn. Akademie, Berlin

Lindenberger U, Reischies F (1999) Limits and potential of intellectual functioning in old age. In: Baltes PB, Mayer KU (Hrsg) The Berlin aging study: aging from 70 to 100. Cambridge University Press, Cambridge, S 329–359

Liu K, Chen Y, Lin R, Han K (2020) Clinical features of COVID-19 in elderly patients: a comparison with young and middle-aged patients. J Infect 80(6):e14–e18. https://doi.org/10.1016/j.jinf.2020.03.005

Lowsky DJ, Olshansky SJ, Bhattacharya J, Goldman DP (2014) Heterogeneity in healthy aging. J Gerontol Biol Sci 69(6):640–649. https://doi.org/10.1093/gerona/glt162

Lübbe W (2020) Corona-Triage. Verfassungsblog, Bd 2020. https://verfassungsblog.de/corona-triage/. Accessed 11 Jan 2021

Marston HR, Musselwhite C, Robin Hadley R (2020) COVID-19 vs social isolation: the impact technology can have on communities, social connections and citizens. ageing issues. British Society of Gerontology. https://www.researchgate.net/publication/340081894_COVID-19_vs_Social_Isolation_the_Impact_Technology_can_have_on_Communities_Social_Connections_and_Citizens. Accessed 11 Jan 2021

Meisner BA (2012) A meta-analysis of positive and negative age stereotype priming effects on behavior among older adults. J Gerontol B 67B(1):13–17. https://doi.org/10.1093/geronb/gbr062

Mitnitski A, Howlett SE, Rockwood K (2017) Heterogeneity of human aging and its assessment. J Gerontol Biol Sci 72(7):877–884. https://doi.org/10.1093/gerona/glw089

Morrow-Howell N, Galucia N, Swinford E (2020) Recovering from the COVID-19 pandemic: a focus on older adults. J Aging Soc Policy. https://doi.org/10.1080/08959420.2020.1759758

Ng R, Allore HG, Trentalange M, Monin JK, Levy BR (2015) Increasing negativity of age stereotypes across 200 years: evidence from a database of 400 million words. PLOS ONE 10(2):e0117086. https://doi.org/10.1371/journal.pone.0117086

Nickel J (2019) Human Rights. https://plato.stanford.edu/archives/sum2019/entries/rights-human/. Accessed 11 Jan 2021

Omer SB, Yildirim I, Forman HP (2020) Herd immunity and implications for SARS-CoV-2 control. J Am Med Assoc. https://doi.org/10.1001/jama.2020.20892

Penger S, Oswald F, Wahl H-W (2019) Altern im Raum am Beispiel von Wohnen und Mobilität. In: Hank K, Schulz-Nieswandt F, Wagner M, Zank S (Hrsg) Alternsforschung: Handbuch für Wissenschaft und Praxis, 1st edn. Nomos Verlag, Baden-Baden, p 413–444. https://doi.org/10.5771/9783845276687-413

Rada AG (2020) Covid-19: the precarious position of Spain's nursing homes. BMJ 369:m1554. https://doi.org/10.1136/bmj.m1554

Richardson S, Hirsch JS, Narasimhan M, Crawford JM, McGinn T, Davidson KW, The Northwell Covid-19 Research Consortium (2020) Presenting characteristics, comorbidities, and outcomes among 5700 patients hospitalized with COVID-19 in the New York City area. J Am Med Assoc. https://doi.org/10.1001/jama.2020.6775

Savulescu J, Vergano M, Craxì L, Wilkinson D (2020) An ethical algorithm for rationing life-sustaining treatment during the COVID-19 pandemic. Br J Anaesth 125(3):253–258. https://doi.org/10.1016/j.bja.2020.05.028

Scheidegger D, Fumeaux T, Hurst S, Salathé M (2020) Covid-19-Pandemie: Triage von intensivmedizinischen Behandlungen bei Ressourcenknappheit. SAMW/SGI, Bern

Sheehan C, Domingue BW, Crimmins E (2019) Cohort trends in the gender distribution of household tasks in the United States and the implications for understanding disability. J Aging Health 31(10):1748–1769. https://doi.org/10.1177/0898264318793469

Stall NM, Jones A, Brown KA, Rochon PA, Costa AP (2020) For-profit long-term care homes and the risk of COVID-19 outbreaks and resident deaths. Can Med Assoc J 192(33):E946–E955. https://doi.org/10.1503/cmaj.201197

Szczerbińska K (2020) Could we have done better with COVID-19 in nursing homes? Eur Geriatr Med 11(4):639–643. https://doi.org/10.1007/s41999-020-00362-7

Vergano M, Bertolini G, Giannini A, Gristina GR, Livigni S, Mistraletti G, Riccioni L, Petrini F (2020) Clinical ethics recommendations for the allocation of intensive care treatments in exceptional, resource-limited circumstances: the Italian perspective during the COVID-19 epidemic. Crit Care 24(1). https://doi.org/10.1186/s13054-020-02891-w

Wahl H-W, Wurm S, Schlomann A, Ehni HJ (2021). Ältere Menschen in der Zeit der Corona-Pandemie: Theoretische Konzepte und eigene Studienergebnisse. Medien & Alter 17:9–24

Wolf-Ostermann K, Rothgang H, Domhoff D, Friedrich A-C, Heinze F, Preuß B, Schmidt A, Seibert K, Stolle C (2020) Zur Situation der Langzeitpflege in Deutschland während der Corona-Pandemie. Ergebnisse einer Online-Befragung in Einrichtungen der (teil)stationären und ambulanten Langzeitpflege. https://doi.org/10.26092/elib/116

World Health Organisation (2020) COVID-19 and violence against older people. https://www.who.int/publications/m/item/covid-19-and-violence-against-older-people. Accessed 11 Jan 2021

Wurm S, Diehl M, Kornadt AE, Westerhof GJ, Wahl H-W (2017) How do views on aging affect health outcomes in adulthood and late life? Explanations for an established connection. Dev Rev 46:27–43. https://doi.org/10.1016/j.dr.2017.08.002

Covid-19 Pandemic and the Protection of Older People in International Comparison. Results of Comparative Research from an Ethical Perspective

Sophia Forster and Andreas Frewer

> *"Locking away is not a [good] option.*
> *Locking away makes you sick [...]."*
>
> *(U. Wenzel, see Engelbrecht 2020)*

Contents

1 Introduction—Infection Control and Risks ... 239
2 Germany in International Comparison—Pandemic Measures Since March 2020 ... 240
2.1 Special Precautions in Hospitals ... 242
2.2 Vaccinations—Mandatory Protection for the Elderly? ... 244
2.3 General or Selective Lockdown (Cocooning) with Age Discrimination? ... 246
2.4 Digital Covid-19-Fighting—Participation of All Age groups? ... 248
3 A Comparison of the Situation in Nursing Homes in Different Countries ... 249
3.1 Covid-19 Associated Mortality in Nursing Homes ... 250
3.2 Measures to Protect Residents ... 257
4 Public Health Ethics for the Elderly—Comprehensive Reflection ... 260
5 Summary—Final Considerations and Outlook ... 262
References ... 263

1 Introduction—Infection Control and Risks

In an article on Deutschlandfunk, 82-year-old senior representative Ursel Wenzel referred to the strict isolation and quarantine regulations in the Corona pandemic lockdown as "locking away" (of older people). The protection of the well-being

S. Forster (✉) · A. Frewer
Professorship for Ethics in Medicine, Erlangen-Nürnberg University, Erlangen, Germany
e-mail: sophia.forster@fau.de

A. Frewer
e-mail: andreas.frewer@fau.de

© The Author(s), under exclusive license to Springer-Verlag GmbH, DE, part of Springer Nature 2023

A. Reis et al. (eds.), *Pandemics and Ethics*,
https://doi.org/10.1007/978-3-662-66872-6_15

threatened by a Covid-19 virus infection is to be ensured above all by restricting social contacts. However, regular interpersonal meetings are also a relevant protective factor for mental and physical health (Richter-Kuhlmann 2021). So by the end of March 2020, shortly after the start of the complete lockdown, Ursel Wenzel turned to society in an open letter. Her goal was to raise awareness of the critical situation of older people, who are categorically referred to as a "risk group" and are therefore to be isolated consistently. This was particularly true for residents of nursing homes, for whom the mandatory strict visiting ban was an extreme psychological burden, especially since the affected people were neither involved in the decision-making process underlying it, nor were they able to resist the resulting regulations. Therefore many residents reacted to the measures taken with incomprehension and rejection. Just two weeks after the start of the lockdown, the committed advocate of the elderly's rights revealed its "catastrophic consequences" on health and now demanded alternative solutions for "sufficient contact opportunities in a reasonable range" (Engelbrecht 2020). In disaster ethics, new decisions have to be made "in real time" and continuously adapted to the current situation, despite limited data sets. In addition, a weighing up of the proportionality of a measure taken to the resulting consequences in terms of justice and risk hedging is always required. To what extent previously taken decisions were justified and effective at the respective time—such as the strict quarantine measures in March and December 2020—can now be retrospectively analyzed successively. Especially in view of a global crisis, comparisons and reflections should definitely also be made at an international level. "Because whoever only learns from their own mistakes, learns little—too little" (Mukerji and Mannino 2020, p. 12).

The article first relates the pandemic dynamics in Germany to a global context (2). Subsequently, central topics are illuminated, which include special ethical relevance in the question of protection older generations (2.1–2.4). This will be followed by a detailed comparison of the situation in nursing and old people's homes in different countries in order to gain orientation about the local situation there (3.1–3.2). Secondarily, the results of the analysis should reveal potential sources of error of international comparisons. Finally, a comprehensive principles reflection concludes the article (4) and central final considerations give an outlook on the current dynamic course of events (5).

2 Germany in International Comparison—Pandemic Measures Since March 2020

In December 2019, "cases of pneumonia of unknown etiology" caused a stir in the metropolis of Wuhan of which the WHO Country Office in China was officially informed on December 31, 2019. On January 7, the new coronavirus SARS-CoV-2 was identified and described as the cause. Within two weeks, the first infections occurred in neighboring Asian countries: Thailand, Japan, South Korea, Singapore, Vietnam, Taiwan, Nepal and Malaysia. At the same time, the virus had already spread intercontinentally to France and Australia (Kamps and Hoffmann 2020, pp. 431–433). While Europe showed no reaction to the developments at that time, Taiwan and South Korea already imposed travel bans on people from the hotspot province of Hubei, introduced a mask requirement in public places and prevented the export of disinfectants or masks (Mukerji and Mannino 2020, pp. 38 ff.). Even if the infection figures reported from the People's Republic of China are to be viewed very critically, the extremely costly and radical quarantine measures aiming at containing the spread of the virus taken by the Chinese government at the end of January speak for themselves (ibid., p. 36). The combination of indirect warning due to the precedent of Wuhan and the rapid global spread could have moved Germany to take faster action in the form of prevention work to hedge risks.

The first Corona infected person in Germany was reported to the health department in Munich on January 27, 2020. While China published declining numbers for the first time in mid-February, the number of Covid cases in Europe continued to rise—especially rapidly in northern Italy and Spain. The exponential increase in the number of cases, especially in Lombardy, caused an overload of the healthcare system in early March. Italy sent catastrophic images of massively overcrowded intensive care units and extensive nighttime corpse transport, accompanied by clear warnings from its medical professionals to the rest of the world. On March 08, 2020, the government in Rome declared the first nationwide European shutdown. Shortly thereafter, the WHO declared the outbreak of the Corona virus as a pandemic (Kamps and Hoffmann 2020, pp. 436–441). In view of the l threateningly rising numbers in this country, on March 18, 2020, the German Chancellor addressed the population on television. She described the Corona crisis as the greatest challenge since the Second World War and classified the situation at that time as serious (2020). These impressive statements led to broad acceptance of the strict quarantine measures taken shortly after among the German population: a first nationwide lockdown (2020). On the contrary the course of events was problematic in countries such as the USA, Great Britain or Brazil, whose heads of state initially or permanently downplayed the pandemic despite the clear facts.

High age as a significant risk factor for a severe course of the disease was already apparent in the first statistics from the place of origin Wuhan (2020, pp. 436–441). Later findings of a German study by the Robert Koch Institute confirmed this correlation and added pre-existing conditions such as diabetes mellitus, cardiovascular and chronic lung diseases and cancer (2020, p. 6). (Kamps and Hoffmann 2020, p. 302). These relations were confirmed in the course of the pandemic in almost all studies worldwide. The authors Kamps and Hoffmann are convinced of the higher age as the most important risk factor for virus-associated mortality, based on the relationship of a high Case Fatality Rate (CFR)[1] among

[1] The "Case Fatality Rate" (CFR) in public health and infection epidemiology denotes the case-fatality ratio ("case fatality"). This proportion is to be calculated as a fraction: The numerator is the number of deaths from the disease among these cases, the denominator the total number of cases.

older people, as it was the case in Italy, Belgium or Sweden (ibid., p. 303).[2] In total, (as of December 8, 2020) 66.3% of virus deaths in Germany were over 80, 95.7% over 60 years old (Radtke 2020). At the beginning of the pandemic in March, few Covid-19 related deaths were recorded in Germany because of a high proportion of infected people from younger age groups, for example returnees from ski areas or carnivalists, who spread the virus mainly among peers (ibid., p. 39). In April, Covid-19 deaths also increased in Germany, which can be attributed to the transmission of the pathogen within older population groups, especially in the context of outbreaks in nursing homes (RKI 2020a). After summer months with little infection, Covid case numbers rose again in Germany. From September 2020, the relative proportion of elderly Corona patients also increased, which led to rising outbreak activity in nursing homes and a significantly higher number of Covid-19 patients treated in intensive care (in 75% of the cases successfully) exceeding the value from March by a wide margin (as of December 7, 2020) (DIVI (RKI 2020b) intensive care register and RKI 2020). Interpretations of the Federal Statistical Office on an excess mortality of the German population in 2020 compared to the years 2016–2019 led to the conclusion that the total mortality was influenced by the Covid-19 pandemic during the calendar weeks 14–19 (end of March to end of April) as well as again from 43 (beginning of November) to 45 (most recent status at time of going to press). The increasing curve of the number of deaths above the norm values also pointed to an excess mortality of unpredictable duration that would continue beyond the 45th calendar week (Zur Nieden et al. 2020).

2.1 *Special Precautions in Hospitals*

A severe case of Covid-19 infection usually means admission to a hospital, in severe cases even ventilation on an intensive care unit. Access to optimal medical care should be guaranteed for all groups of people at all times in order to prevent an disproportionate increase in deaths due to non-treatment and thus inhuman conditions in the sense of the right to health (Frewer and Bielefeldt 2016). So far, the German federal government has been able to ensure access to medical resources at all times for all people by means of financial support for clinics (Covid-19 Hospital Relief Act—27.03.2020, Future Program for Hospitals—03.06.2020), postponing elective procedures at the time of the first wave of infection, and

[2] Conclusions from the CFR on the Covid-19 lethality of a country were particularly difficult to draw at the beginning, as the CFR depends on the number of tests carried out. In addition, the estimated "dark figure" (undetected, asymptomatic cases) could only be estimated after the conduct of separate antibody studies. International comparisons were therefore almost impossible at the beginning of the pandemic, but also only partially possible later. Therefore, comparisons should always be critically questioned.

various other measures (Federal Ministry of Health 2020). In contrast, reports from the European neighboring countries of Spain, France and Italy claimed the situation of older patients, who were categorically denied medical care. Specifically, at the end of March 2020, the German Institute for Disaster Medicine reported that resuscitation attempts on patients over 80 years of age had been discontinued for six days at the University Hospital in Strasbourg; however, this accusation was denied by the hospital management there (Lemkemeyer 2020). In Bergamo, Italy, it is said that no corresponding ventilation therapy was carried out in the event of lung failure in patients over 80 years of age (Seisselberg 2020). In Germany, the "Air Security Act" passed by the Federal Constitutional Court in 2006 can ensure a fair distribution: This prohibits, in the event of a shortage of resources, categorically denying medical care to older people. If age were to play a primary or exclusive role in a triage situation, this would be discriminatory and prohibited (German Institute for Human Rights 2020, p. 8). From the examples of France and Italy described above, it can be deduced that written theoretical concepts of fair distribution are not sufficient for a correct practical implementation in a crisis situation. At the end of March, the Academy for Ethics in Medicine (AEM) demanded that ethicists should be involved in the planning and creation of clear instructions for action (so-called "Corona-Taskforces"). Formulated concepts should be passed on to potentially affected medical personnel via suitable information and training formats. In addition to regular trainings, ad hoc available consultation options for decision-making in the acute situation should be possible via video or telephone connection to ethicists in order to support the correct application in practice (AEM 2020). Scientists from Yale, London, Berlin and Essen focused their statement in the American Journal of Bioethics (13.12.2020) on difficult questions of triage in the context of international cooperation and extensive preventive measures (Cook 2020). Great efforts are requested, such as the transfer of seriously ill patients from crisis areas—if necessary also cross-border—to less affected regions in order to prevent a triage situation from arising in the first place (ibid.).

Particular attention should be paid to the observance of advance directives; on the one hand to safeguard the patient's will, but on the other hand also in times of crisis to ensure the fair distribution of scarce medical resources. In the event of a rejection of life-prolonging measures, these denied resources become available to other patients as quickly as possible (AEM 2020). An international comparison shows that the German health system has an above-average basic supply of hospital and intensive care beds. Accordingly, 34 intensive care beds and 6,000 hospital beds are available per 100,000 inhabitants, while other European countries such as Spain and Italy have less than ten intensive care beds per 100,000 inhabitants. The German Interdisciplinary Association for Intensive and Emergency Medicine (DIVI) introduced a nationwide network for the registration of free intensive care beds in order to keep track of the distribution of occupancy and to prevent a triage in critical situations by transferring patients. In addition, new intensive care beds with ventilation facilities were made attractive to clinics by financial incentives and more than half of the intensive care beds were "reserved" for Covid-19 cases, which also raises some moral questions.[3]

2.2 *Vaccinations—Mandatory Protection for the Elderly?*

The immunity achieved through a Covid-19 vaccine should primarily serve to protect "people at high risk of severe and fatal course" (Deutsches Ärzteblatt 2020). For this purpose, vulnerable groups of people must be precisely defined and prioritized including those who are in direct contact with them and thus represent a potential infection risk. Based on a clear concept for the allocation of scarce vaccine doses, it should be decided who will be vaccinated at the beginning. To this question of distributional justice, the Standing Committee on Vaccination (STIKO), the German Ethics Council (DER) and the National Academy of Sciences Leopoldina published their jointly developed position paper on 09.11.2020. "This emphasizes the double vulnerability of people in need of protection who are dependent on constant contact (e.g. residents in nursing homes [...])" (STIKO et al. 2020, p. 2). The experts also explicitly stated that "the mere fact of a person's age [...] does not automatically make them a member of a high-risk group" (ibid.)—because that would be age discrimination. Nevertheless, it is necessary, for reasons of time and practicality, to also base the definition of such a risk group on generalizations. Since, in the case of an effective and safe vaccine, it is an additional protective measure that can be voluntarily accepted, but which is not associated with any obligation or disadvantage for the affected group of people, a more precise determination of individual urgency is not necessary (ibid., pp. 2 f.). STIKO laid down more detailed guidelines and concrete definitions in its recommendation draft of 07.12.2020. It distinguishes between "very high", "high", "moderate" and "increased" priority, which is attributed to the different groups of people (Deutsches Ärzteblatt 2020). In general, all "people aged ≥80 years" as well as all "residents of nursing homes for the elderly" belong to the highest ("very high") priority. This also includes all employees in direct contact with the residents as well as all those working in outpatient or inpatient care for the elderly. "Personnel in medical facilities" are only classified in the highest priority group if certain sub-criteria are met (Deutsches Ärzteblatt 2020). The most vulnerable are those who are "exposed to a particularly high exposure risk"—primarily due to self-endangerment—and those "in close contact with vulnerable groups" (Deutsches Ärzteblatt 2020). It is planned to anchor of STIKO's final recommendations in the Vaccination Ordinance of

[3] How can a fair treatment of intensive care beds reserved for Covid-19 be regulated if acutely life-threatening Covid-19 negative patients urgently need this space? Would economically and personnel-wise poorly equipped hospitals create new intensive care beds by financial incentives, but possibly not be able to care for them sufficiently due to a lack of qualified personnel?

the Federal Ministry of Health—but its application would remain not mandatory (ibid.). This was followed by criticism from the Scientific Service of the German Bundestag, which called for a binding legal anchoring of the guidelines for vaccine allocation—because vaccination in the case of the Covid-19 pandemic has a high general fundamental rights relevance for all due to the existing, far-reaching restrictions on everyday life. This assumption is considered decisive for the Federal Constitutional Court to determine whether a measure requires a legal regulation or not (Kröger 2020).

Despite existing protective measures and regular testing, the residual risk of infection of patients by employees in medical and care facilities remains. In order to reduce this risk of infection from outside, employees would have to voluntarily agree to be vaccinated. Depending on the willingness to be vaccinated, it could therefore make sense to introduce a compulsory vaccination for certain occupational groups (Kröger 2020). There is a similar regulation in the context of proof of immunity against measles, mumps and rubella for employees in health services and communal facilities (Deutsches Grünes Kreuz 2020). Recommendations for certain occupational groups that are based on voluntary participation, as in the case of vaccination against influenza, have already shown that the actual vaccination rates of medical and nursing staff remained very low—for example 39% in the 2017/18 season (Bödeker et al. 2020). In the "Initiative against Flu" project of the OKaPII study, alternative incentives such as attractive bonuses[4] for those vaccinated, vaccinations organized and carried out on site by the employer or information events that have been shown an increase in influenza vaccination rate among the affected occupational groups (Bödeker et al. 2020). Similar measures could possibly achieve sufficiently high vaccination rates among the affected staff without restrictions on freedom by introducing a compulsory Covid-19 vaccination.

In the long term, the goal of vaccination is to achieve "herd immunity". For this purpose, in the case of the Covid-19 pandemic, immunization of approximately 50–70% (possibly also higher) of the population is necessary, which can only be achieved, inter alia, by high vaccination rates among people. However, studies on vaccination rates in the population yielded alarmingly low values, as confirmed at the end of November by the Barmer survey (2020), in which only 53% expressed a willingness to be vaccinated. Differences could also be observed among the various age groups: only 22% of younger respondents between the ages of 16 and 39 would have accepted to get vaccinated at the time—compared to 66% of older respondents over the age of 60 (Deutsche Apotheker Zeitung 2020). According to an international study by the Barcelona Institute for Global Health (June 2020), there were also significant differences in the acceptability of a Covid-19 vaccine

[4] By taking part in competitions or free loading of the canteen chip, the interest of the employees could be gained (Bödeker et al. 2020). Of course, discounts are also conceivable for Covid-19 vaccinations, such as access to cultural events or (flight) travel only with vaccination pass, which raises questions of fairness (see below, footnote 5).

among the 17 countries surveyed. China was the most willing country to be vaccinated with 89%, Germany achieved a value in the lower middle range with 68%. The country with the lowest acceptability was Russia (Hüttemann 2020). According to the respondents, transparent vaccine communication and trust in the government as well as voluntary vaccination could lead to higher willingness (ibid.). Discussions on the topic of herd immunity through immunization of the population are indicated in detail due to the far-reaching consequences.[5]

Russia began to vaccinate teachers and doctors on 05.12.2020, although the vaccine's acceptance among the population was low even among the national medical profession (7%). The government hoped for a quick improvement in the critical situation through mass vaccinations in order to avoid a further lockdown (Lokshin 2020). In Great Britain, the vaccination programme started on 08.12.2020 with 800,000 doses of the BNT162b vaccine from the German-American company consortium BioNTech and Pfizer, which were initially administered to residents and employees in nursing homes and to people over the age of 80 (Tagesschau 2020a). Canada and the USA also granted emergency approval for the BioNTech and Pfizer vaccine starting to vaccinate on 14.12.2020. In Canada, the ten provinces each opted for their own allocation rules. For example, Ontario announced primarily vaccinations in hospitals in Toronto and Ottawa, while in Québec vaccinations should initially be given to residents of nursing homes (CBC News 2020a). In the USA, according to the CDC, employees in health facilities and residents of nursing homes were vaccinated first (Ärztezeitung 2020).

2.3 *General or Selective Lockdown (Cocooning) with Age Discrimination?*

In Germany, the first so-called "hard" lockdown crystallised out as an effective measure to break the exponential increase in infection rates and thus prevent the impending overload of the healthcare system. The summer months were manageable, so that normal operation could be temporarily resumed in some areas. The rapid increase in case numbers in autumn 2020 forced the government to take radical action again. So on 09.11.2020 a further, less strict "partial lockdown" began with the aim of quickly flattening the infection curve as a "wavebreaker"—but without success by the end of December 2020. Although these two shutdowns differed in the severity of the measures between the different federal states, they had to be adhered to by all in the same way. The discourse about ways out of the

[5] For example, considerations should be made with regard to regulations for the phase of a partially immune society. This also raises the question of whether vaccinated people could receive more civil liberties during this period than people who have not yet been vaccinated. On December 28, 2020, Federal Health Minister Spahn pleaded for solidarity within society as a whole and no additional granting of privileges to vaccinated people (Tagesschau 2020b).

lockdown towards alternative concepts for the controlled bridging of the time until herd immunity was highly topical in Germany as early as May 2020 and was so again at the end of November 2020 during the partial lockdown. The so-called "cocooning" strategy represents one of these possibilities for loosening a complete shutdown. It first divides the population into "risk group", estimated at 1/3 of the population, and "non-risk group" according to the probability assigned to them statistically of suffering a severe course of Covid-19 (Mukerji and Mannino2020, pp. 78–81). The isolation measures should only apply selectively to the risk group here. On the one hand, these people could be protected from infection, on the other hand, the entire society would also benefit from a lower burden on the health care system through a lower number of hospitalizations. Both goals of a shutdown—minimizing deaths and preventing an overloaded healthcare system—would be achieved (Savulescu and Cameron 2020). The remaining 2/3 of society could thus return to everyday life. Additional advantages would be less severe economic consequences and a reduction in the restriction of basic and civil rights for the non-risk group (ibid.). However, the approach is to be viewed very critically. Since 2/3 of society generally cause higher infection rates through increased contacts and a complete isolation of the risk group is practically impossible, this in turn increases the risk of infection for those in need of protection, especially those who rely on essential contacts such as in nursing homes (Frith 2020). In addition, an infection can also lead to severe course or long-term consequences in the non-risk group. In reverse, the infection rates could be lowered more quickly by a slightly longer, general lockdown, thus the regulations could be lifted earlier for everyone at the same time (ibid.). Furthermore, additional disadvantages arise for the risk group, for example through social isolation. The boundary—vulnerable or not—would fall on a certain number on the basis of a statistical determination at the factor "age" (ibid.) and thus wrongly designate this group as homogeneous in need of care and protection. But precisely the factor "old age" cannot be automatically attributed to vulnerability (see also Kruse 2017 as well as Bergemann and Frewer 2018). "Measures must never lead to inhuman treatment in their interaction, for example, the total isolation of healthy people without their consent or against their will" (German Institute for Human Rights 2020, p. 4). Such a regulation would thus cause age discrimination (ageism), which in turn, according to behavior researchers at the University of Luxembourg, could lead to a 20% worse health and life satisfaction of those affected (Heinrich 2020). Critics warn of such special restrictions for older people leading to a division of society (Savulescu and Cameron 2020). The obligation of each group of persons to comply with the regulation assigned to it is also problematic. Ethically highly questionable solutions are discussed, such as withholding access to healthcare for people from the risk group who resist social isolation (ibid.). As already mentioned above, great injustice would arise and contradict the ethical principles justice and equality. Although both groups suffer disadvantages, the main burden still lies with the risk group. Derek Parfit's concept of the "Priority View", which provides for preferential protection of the weakest, underlines the importance of not imposing additional burdens on risk groups, as they are inherently in a worse position being vulnerable

(Frith 2020). According to the German Institute for Human Rights, the conditions for a selective lockdown are its temporal limitation and accompanying measures to mitigate the effects of isolation, for example by promoting alternative digital contact options (German Institute for Human Rights 2020, p. 5). A slightly modified form would be the "Cocooning Plus" strategy aiming at a low level of infection (with a reproduction factor of less than one being referred to as a reference value) by means of so-called "containment" measures that affect the entire population. In addition, special protection measures apply explicitly only to risk groups (Mukerji and Mannino 2020, pp. 89–92).

2.4 Digital Covid-19-Fighting—Participation of All Age groups?

The Covid 19 pandemic led to an abrupt change and entry into the virtual world, which opened up a whole new range of possibilities—without the risk of contagion. These included maintaining social contacts via video calls, working remotely or combating the pandemic by generating data for dissemination and research purposes. Digital measures to monitor the spread of infection were implemented at several levels including the introduction of a so called "Corona application" to track contacts via "contact tracing". Since April 2020, health data from fitness watches etc. can be voluntarily made available to research. Vital signs and exercise logs are collected in order to trace the local spread of infection and to gain new insights into the course of the disease. At that time, more than 500,000 data donors were already registered. On 3 July 2020, the demographic distribution of the data donors was published in a science blog. It is described that the average age of the participants was about 3.6 years higher than the census of the German population. It should be noted, however, that only 10% of the donors gave any information at all about their age, which does not allow for a representative statement about the population as a whole. The higher average age can in turn be attributed to an above-average proportion of 45- to 60-year-olds. From a higher age (>70 years), there are significantly fewer or even no data donors (Corona Data Donation 2020). This distribution should be viewed critically, as special focus must be placed on the spread of infection in older higher vulnerable people. In addition, it is known that geriatric patients show symptoms in a modified form in many clinical pictures. Therefore Covid-19-specific symptoms among elderly patients need to be researched separately. For example, 31% of those infected with Covid-19 suffer from fever (RKI 2020c). It is known that other infectious diseases generally manifest themselves in old age without this warning signal (Hohmann-Jeddi 2019). A representation of the occurrence of infections on the basis of a "fever curve" is therefore probably only reliable to a limited extent for all age groups. In order to guarantee the basic principle of access to optimal diagnostic and therapeutic resources for vulnerable groups, sufficient data from these groups must be made available for research (OECD 2020). Likewise, in the example of serological studies carried out on blood donors, older people are not adequately represented due to their frequent previous illnesses. Overall, the issue of digital solutions raises the question of participation, since older people have less technical equipment and less previous knowledge to be able to use these newly introduced methods to cope with the pandemic.

3 A Comparison of the Situation in Nursing Homes in Different Countries

At the outset, it must be mentioned that, so far, not only in nursing homes has the combination of increased infection rates due to numerous contacts within a cohort of many multimorbid people led to high death rates; outpatient care services or partial hospitalization facilities also record a high proportion of vulnerable people, have been and are still strongly affected by the pandemic, but have so far not been recorded in any statistics, let alone been considered separately by politics. In Germany, for example, more than one in ten Covid-19 deaths is attributable to a person cared for by an outpatient care service, although they only make up 1.5% of the total population; nevertheless, the Robert Koch Institute does not record any separate data on this (Wolf-Ostermann et al. 2020, pp. 8–10). On an international level, evidence on care situations outside of inpatient care is only very limited. The few existing data are so far not sufficiently comparable globally due to the many different forms of alternative care options (Comas-Herrera et al. 2020, p. 2). In addition, inpatient care facilities have a significantly larger share of Covid-19 deaths (49% in Germany) than outpatient care arrangements. Besides they are also more widely represented in society accounting for 7% of the population (Wolf-Ostermann et al. 2020, pp. 8 f.). In international comparison, it becomes clear that a focus of Covid-19 deaths on nursing homes can be observed in all countries with fatal outbreak events. Thus, they are the most important place in terms of Covid-19 mortality (Comas-Herrera et al. 2020, p. 2). In the present work, only the situation in inpatient care facilities is to be considered due to the high relevance, the global nature and the better comparability. Infection events of employees and residents correlate with each other, but nevertheless the nursing staff in Germany has a Covid-19 mortality rate similar to that of the general population[6] (RKI 2020e). Therefore, the deaths of the residents will be primarily addressed and employees will initially be left out when identifying mortality in nursing homes. It is also important to differentiate between age and dependency; for example, in 2017 only

[6] 25,469 employees of the institutions listed in § became infected with Covid-19, 69 of whom died. This results in a case fatality ratio of 0.27%. In all of Germany there were 1,351,510 Covid-19 cases, 22,475 of which were fatal, resulting in a CFR of 1.66%. In comparison, the CFR of residents was 6721 deaths out of 49,272 infected, or 13.6% (RKI 2020e).

4.3% of people over the age of 65 lived in a nursing home in Germany. The cohort of residents considered here consists of older, dependent and often multimorbid people who should be taken into account as a particularly vulnerable group.

3.1 Covid-19 Associated Mortality in Nursing Homes

3.1.1 Data and Methods for Quantifying Covid-19 Deaths

The international experts of the Comas-Herrera study group intensively researched the effects of the Covid-19 pandemic on mortality in nursing homes. Among other things, three methods for quantifying the number of cases were elaborated, which should also be included in the following section. On the one hand, a Covid-19 death can be proven by a positive test result and recorded internationally in a uniform manner with the emergency code U07.1 (ICD-10) (German Institute for Medical Documentation and Information 2020). The strong dependence of this method on the total number of tests carried out has to be seen critically. Initially, sufficient medical resources were not available in many countries in this respect. So especially at the beginning of the pandemic, false low case numbers were published. But even at later stages, the test rate varies greatly from country to country, which in turn makes international comparisons more difficult. Nursing homes also naturally have a very high proportion of geriatric patients, who often show atypical symptoms such as delirium or even asymptomatic course in case of infection.[7] Both cases lead to no suspicion testing (Comas-Herrera et al. 2020, pp. 3 f.). So the Covid-19 mortality could be underestimated especially in nursing homes. It is also critical that indirect[8] deaths are not included in this method (ibid., p. 4).

Another possibility is the association of a death with Covid-19 on the basis of clinical or epidemiological suspicion. If a test is not possible or the result is invalid, the Covid-19 classification code U07.2 may be used here (Deutsches Institut für Medizinische Dokumentation und Information 2020). This variant is only counted in addition to the statistics of confirmed Covid-19 cases by test. The problem with this method could be an overestimation[9] of the Covid-19 death rate due to misclassification. In general, it must be taken into account that countries that use different methods of data aggregation and quantification can only be

---

[7] About half of all residents of nursing homes in Germany showed no symptoms at all (Wolf-Ostermann et al. 2020).

[8] Deaths without direct connection to an infection with SARS-CoV-2, which, nevertheless, occur as a result of the pandemic—for example, by not treating acute, severe illnesses due to overcrowding in emergency rooms and intensive care units.

[9] This relationship can also be observed in the published statistics of countries such as the USA, Canada, France, Great Britain and Ireland. These five nations aggregated confirmed and suspected deaths in their data and published all above-average high case numbers (Comas-Herrera et al. 2020, p. 4).

compared to a very limited extent. The third option is the consideration of excess mortality. This measures the increase in all deaths during the pandemic relative to an average value from the death rates of previous years. In this way, all deaths above the expected value correspond to the direct and indirect deaths of the pandemic (Comas-Herrera et al. 2020, p. 4). In order to represent the Covid-19-related mortality in nursing homes appropriately, two ratios can be formed: On the one hand, all Covid-19 deaths of residents should be related to the total number of residents (ibid., p. 2). This percentage correlates strongly with the number of Covid-19 deaths in the rest of the population. On the other hand, the denominator can be changed to the total number of virus-associated deaths. Both ratios give insights into how much nursing homes are affected by the pandemic.

As an example, in addition to Germany, four other countries were analyzed in more detail here. On the one hand, similarly populous and developed industrial nations should be examined, on the other hand countries on different continents should be analyzed in more detail. Furthermore, comparative contrast effects are interesting, shown within countries presenting particularly high or low values in the two above-mentioned ratios. In this way, explanations should be found for these exceptional peaks of the parameters as well as trends for further development.

3.1.2 Germany

The Robert Koch Institute publishes a daily situation report on the course of the infection. However, the situation in nursing and old people's homes is not (sufficiently) differentiated in this country as they are covered by § 36 of the Infection Protection Act which also includes homes for asylum seekers, homeless shelters and prisons. It must be assumed that, due to the age distribution of the aforementioned facilities, the majority of Covid-19 deaths occurring in the cohort are attributable to nursing homes (Wolf-Ostermann et al. 2020, p. 11). However, explicit data for nursing homes are not available.[10] There are still "no details on care, accommodation and activity in many[11] cases […]", which is why their number is to be understood as a minimum (RKI 2020e). In addition, a time lag between the time of death and its occurrence in the statistics was criticized.[12] In this way, a

[10] Starting from 08.01.2021, the RKI has now also made available differentiated information on Covid-19 cases in facilities pursuant to § 36 in its daily situation reports. The new subdivision is divided into nursing homes, outpatient nursing services, communal accommodation for asylum seekers and others. These detailed data have been collected since the autumn months of 2020 (RKI 2021). Despite several inquiries (most recently on January 29, 2021), no further information was available from the RKI; of course, the RKI is currently extremely busy.

[11] On May 5, 2020, the proportion of these missing notifications was as high as 36% (Wolf-Ostermann et al. 2020, p. 19).

[12] First, the local health department is informed in Germany, which in turn subsequently forwards it to the respective authority at the state level. They finally pass on the information to the Robert Koch Institute, which includes the data in the daily statistics (Comas-Herrera et al. 2020, p. 9).

rapid, exponential increase in infections could have been distorted, which, among other things, also made comparisons of the excess mortality of individual calendar weeks inaccurate. In Germany, only Covid-19 deaths confirmed by test results were counted. Due to an established system with high test capacity[13]including regular testing on residents and employees of nursing homes, the data collected were representative (RKI 2020d). Compared to countries with similar high Covid-19 death rates, Germany as a whole had a lower mortality rate in nursing homes (Comas-Herrera et al.2020, p. 9). This could be an indication of the effectiveness of the protective measures in these facilities.

6,721 people died "from or with" Covid-19 according to § 36 which represents 30% of the total number of Covid-19 deaths at that time. This number has to be seen as a minimum value due to broadly missing data on accommodation. In contrast, the online survey of numerous nursing homes carried out by the University of Bremen in May 2020 resulted in a much higher focus of mortality in nursing homes of over 50%. This value was similar to the one of other European countries such as Italy, France, Ireland and Belgium (Wolf-Ostermann et al. 2020, pp. 54–55). It can therefore be assumed for Germany that the true proportion of Covid-19 deaths in nursing homes was much higher than the values assumed by the Robert Koch Institute. In 2017, 818,000 people lived in nursing homes in Germany (Comas-Herrera et al. 2020, p. 9). According to the Robert Koch Institute, 0.82% of those in care had died from or with Covid-19 by December 15, 2020 (RKI 2020e) whereas the team around Comas-Herrera et al. determined a comparatively low percentage of 0.05% in September (ibid., p. 9). The value has therefore increased sixteenfold within a quarter of a year. The nationwide increase in Covid-19 deaths[14] and the relative increase in older people infected since September are reflected in this percentage, the extent of which is clearly shown in the serious consequences for nursing homes.

On average, 6.4 residents of each nursing home died from or with Covid-19 according to the Bremen study. Nevertheless, in about 25% of the affected nursing homes, a severe outbreak occurred with at least eight Covid-19 deaths, which highlights the dangers of a rapid spread of infection in a nursing home (Wolf-Ostermann et al. 2020, p. 19). In addition, smaller nursing homes were more affected than larger ones (ibid.). Within Germany, clear regional differences could also be observed. For example, there was a high incidence of infection with high death rates in nursing homes in Bavaria and Baden-Württemberg, while Hamburg and Hesse only showed high infection rates without increased mortality. In Berlin and Lower Saxony, a large number of Covid-19 deaths occurred with a lower

[13] In Germany, an average of 1.6% of the population was tested in week 49, which was above average in international comparison (RKI 2020f).

[14] Since October, the general infection situation has been increasing exponentially in a second wave in Germany. On November 11, there were 11,767 deaths in total, but within a month (as of December 15, 2020) this number had almost doubled to 22,475 (RKI 2020b/2020e).

incidence of infection (ibid., pp. 20–21). Here, particular attention must be paid to possible omissions and suggestions for improvement.

3.1.3 Spain

In Spain, two methods for assessing Covid-19 mortality in nursing homes and care homes were applied in parallel. On the one hand, regional authorities were required to regularly report the number of suspected and confirmed Covid-19 deaths in care homes together with the total number of deaths that have occurred there. In addition, a system for monitoring monthly mortality (Sistema de de Monitorización de la Mortalidad mensual, MoMo) was introduced (Instituto de Mayores y Servicios Sociales 2020). This makes it possible to analyze excess mortality among registered residents of the national long-term care system (Sistema para la Autonomía y Atención a la Dependencia = SAAD) on the basis of information from this institute. These figures also include people receiving home care and are partly mixed with information on facilities for people with mental illness or disabilities (Comas-Herrera et al. 2020, pp. 13 ff.). According to this, the data are not entirely comparable due to the many differences between the groups of people included. On October 7, 2020, 20,649 Covid-19 deaths were recorded among residents of care homes. This represents 63% of all positive Covid-19 deaths among 32,929 such deaths. Of a total of 333,920 residents, 6.18% have died by October (ibid., p. 14). By December 15, 2020, the number of Covid-19 deaths had risen to 48,401 (Corporación de Radio y Televisión Española 2020a). Of these, 24,372 of the deceased[15] were in care homes (ibid. 2020b). This results in percentages of 50.3% for the proportion of residents to the total number of deaths and 7.3% as the ratio of those who have died of or from Covid-19 in hospital to all residents. The data from the Instituto de Mayores y Servicios Sociales show an absolute excess mortality in care homes[16] of 18,911 from March to the end of July 2020. This increase in mortality was 50% based on the average mortality in care homes in previous years. Based on the excess mortality of the entire population, 53% of the above-average Covid-19 deaths were concentrated in nursing and care homes, although they only represented 7.6% of the national population (Comas-Herrera et al. 2020, p. 14). Another report, which looked at the period from March to the end of November, found an absolute excess mortality of 21,513 among residents. 8.6% of the total population had died as a result of the pandemic (Instituto de Mayores y Servicios Sociales 2020).

[15] This also includes people who have tested positive and those who are suspected.

[16] Only residents of care and nursing homes registered in the national long-term care programme are considered.

3.1.4 Canada

At the time of data collection (December 15, 2020), the country did not publish any overall Canadian statistics on case and death numbers in nursing homes. The individual provinces reported this in part in their own statistics, which makes research more difficult for values related to the whole country, but also focuses on strong regional differences in the course of infection (Comas-Herrera et al. 2020, p. 7). The country adds in its statistics Covid-19 cases confirmed by test to the clinically and epidemiologically suspected cases (ibid., p. 4). In addition, many nursing and old people's homes initially reported Covid-19 cases to the authorities even with very little suspicion[17] (ibid., p. 7). From the data, probably too high percentages were thus determined. This is also reflected in the country-wide statistics of the WHO on the proportion of fatal Covid-19 cases in nursing homes based on the total number of deaths in a nation, in which Canada recorded the highest value of 85% in June 2020 (WHO 2020). The international research group around Comas-Herrera referred to the situation at the beginning of October 2020. At that time, 7,411 of the 425,755 residents had died (1.7% of all residents). Based on all 9,318 Covid-19 deaths at that time, 80% were associated with a nursing home—already 5% less than a quarter of a year earlier (Comas-Herrera et al. 2020, p. 7). The time course of the deaths showed a much lower percentage increase in the months of November and December 2020 than, for example, in Germany; on December 15, 2020, there were 13,658 confirmed Covid-19 deaths (CBC News 2020b). No data on deaths in nursing homes for the whole of Canada could be found on the official websites of the authorities for December 15, 2020. For this reason, values from three of the most affected provinces[18]—Québec, Ontario and British Columbia—are to be considered as an example. For example, British Columbia reported in the 50th calendar week a proportion of 71% Covid-19 associated deaths among residents based on the total number of deaths during these seven days (British Columbia Centre for Disease Control 2020). In Québec, the province most affected in the middle of December, the described quotient was similarly high at that time and remained constant in the calendar weeks 49 and 50 at 74% (Gouvernement du Québec 2020). In Ontario, it was only 63% in the middle of December (Public Health Ontario2020). These overall declining percentages of Covid-19 deaths to total virus-associated deaths could mean an improvement in the situation in nursing homes. It is also conceivable that only the initially too high values have been replaced by now more realistic, lower numbers. The example of Canada shows how great regional differences in procedures and infection course can be within a country strongly shaped by federalism and how complex it is therefore to compare internationally.

[17] In some institutions, all deaths of the institution were even reported (Comas-Herrera et al. 2020, p. 7)

[18] The total number of Covid-19 deaths in Québec, British Columbia and Ontario corresponded to around 90% of the total number of deaths in Canada on December 15, 2020 (CBC News 2020b).

3.1.5 Australia

The Australian government published all data collected, including special data on infection, death and recovery rates of recipients of outpatient care and residents of nursing homes, in daily reports (Australian Government Department of Health 2020a). Only when a positive test result was available infection and death cases were included in the official Covid-19 statistics (Comas-Herrera et al. 2020, p. 5). So on October 11, 2020, 677 deaths among the positive tested residents were recorded as part of the 898 Covid-19 deaths in total—which is a percentage of 75%. In the winter months of 2020, a large pandemic wave[19] with infection hotspots in the state of Victoria rapidly spread to local nursing homes. So 90% of all deaths in nursing homes were concentrated in facilities in Victoria (Charlesworth and Low 2020, p. 4).

Up to and including 15.12.2020, the number of Covid-19 deaths in nursing homes has only slightly increased to 685—the total number of deaths to 908—resulting in a ratio of 75% since October 2020. The basis for this was a lack of new outbreaks of infection in nursing homes since September 27, 2020 (Australian Government Department of Health 2020a). As a result, up to December 15, 0.33% of the 208,500 residents died of Covid-19 (Comas-Herrera et al. 2020, p. 5). Despite the Covid-19 pandemic, a "lower mortality" was recorded in nursing homes for the first half of the year. Up to July 31, 2020, a total of 32,398 residents died; 3% fewer than in the previous year (Australian Government Department of Health 2020a). Suspected reasons therefore are the significantly lower death rates of the elderly due to the influenza virus[20] and the introduction of monitored Corona infection protocols (Australian Government Department of Health 2020a). Nevertheless, with a ratio of three Covid-19 deaths in nursing homes to four total deaths, Australia was one of the countries with the relatively most affected facilities.

3.1.6 South Korea

Data from the Ministry of Health and Welfare and the Korea Centers for Disease Control and Prevention reported on September 7, 2020 a total of 336 confirmed Covid-19 deaths. Of these, 27 (8%) lived in nursing homes and another 76 (22.6%) in long-term care hospitals. Both forms of institutional care thus

[19] Due to the properties of the Corona virus, seasonal outbreaks of infection can be recorded in the winter months, which in Australia resulted in a second wave of infection from mid-June to mid-September (Australian Government Department of Health 2020b).

[20] In the pandemic year 2020, more residents were vaccinated against the influenza virus preventively. While 834 people over the age of 64 died of influenza in the previous year, only 28 died in 2020 (Australian Government Department of Health 2020a).

accounted for a total of 31% of Covid-19's overall death toll.[21] Based on a total of 177,318 beds (as of 2018) in care facilities, the Covid-19 mortality rate was 0.01% (Comas-Herrera et al. 2020, p. 13). This proportion represented the lowest value measured internationally (ibid., p. 2). It should be noted that this figure refers to the maximum possible number of residents and could therefore be falsely low due to a lower occupancy in reality. No exact figures on the actual number of institutionalized people were published. On December 15, 2020 there were a total of 600 deaths (Korea Disease Control and Prevention Agency 2020). Due to the lack of differentiation between residents of care facilities and non-residents, it must be assumed that the percentage of measurement in September 2020 of 31% approached the value at the time of mid-December. This results in a number of 180 deaths of residents which means, based on all beds, an unchanged percentage of 0.1%.

3.1.7 Synoptic Comparison of the Countries

In general, it can be concluded that international comparisons can only be represented to a limited extent in quotients and statistics due to the large discrepancies in different methods of data collection, but require detailed background knowledge. Nevertheless, the following two tables should provide an overview of data from the five countries studied (Table 1 and 2).

Globally, no country with widespread infection could prevent outbreaks in nursing homes (Australian Government Department of Health 2020a). In all 21 countries with pandemic outbreak and resulting deaths, a high relative proportion of Covid-19 deaths was also found in facilities in relation to all deaths, which also represents the arithmetic mean of 46% (Comas-Herrera et al. 2020, p. 30). This value also illustrates the global relevance of the topic. However, it should be noted that international comparisons are very difficult to make and only partially valid, as they are, as already described, influenced by many factors.[22] Published comparisons of data from several countries should therefore always be critically questioned. Nevertheless, they serve the purpose of finding appropriate political guidelines in the global pandemic course and should therefore be part of the daily discourse.

---

[21] All infected residents were transferred to hospitals, so that no deaths from or with Covid-19 occurred within any nursing homes (Comas-Herrera et al. 2020, p. 13).

[22] In addition to the already mentioned difficulties in the Covid-19 country comparison—different procedures for data aggregation and quantification, different definitions of the analyzed cohorts, etc.—further problems should be listed here. On the one hand, the country-specific age distribution, which must be given special attention with regard to the accumulation of lethal Covid-19 disease courses, plays a decisive role. This results in many sources of error, such as also deaths with exclusive indication of death instead of place of residence, which can contribute to distortions when dying in hospital after previous transfer from a nursing home (Comas-Herrera et al. 2020, p. 2).

Table 1 Confirmed (and suspected) Covid-19 deaths among residents relative to all deaths, beds and residents of care facilities, as well as excess mortality

		Australia	Germany *here: residents of facilities according to § 36 IfSG*	Canada *here: British Columbia (BC), Québec (Q) and Ontario (O)*	Spain	South Korea
Assumed/ Confirmed		C	C	A+C	A+C	C
Excess mortality (period)		−3% (01.01.–31.07.2020)			8.6% (March-Nov. 2020)	
	… total deaths	75%	30.0%	BC: 71% Q: 74% O: 63%	50.3%	
Covid-19 deaths among residents based on … (as of 15.12.2020)	… total number of residents	0.33%	0.82%		6.2%	
	… number of beds		0.71%		7.3%	0.01%

This hypothetical ratio is created in order to make a comparison to the data from South Korea, which always refers to the number of beds (Comas-Herrera et al. 2020, p. 13). In 2017, there were 952,367 nursing places available in Germany. For Australia, this additional comparison can be dispensed with, as no data on the number of beds in 2020 can be found and the last recorded number of beds from 2019 is smaller than the number of residents described by Comas-Herrara. Therefore, in the case of Australia, no meaningful calculation of this ratio is possible. In Canada, the data of some provinces are determined by the number of beds, others by the number of residents, so that no determination of uniform data is possible here (OECD Statistics 2020).

3.2 *Measures to Protect Residents*

3.2.1 Causes and Objectives

All introduced regulations serve to ensure the protection of health. Special measures are therefore required for particularly vulnerable groups. However, a constant weighing up must also take place here. In the pandemic, safety from infection can mainly be achieved through contact reduction and isolation. But this is impossible in nursing due to necessary direct contact. At the same time, the negative consequences of social isolation on health are particularly pronounced in this vulnerable group of people. In addition, other important goods such as the right to participation or freedom must also be taken into account. In the last six months, numerous

Table 2 Course of Covid-19 deaths among residents in calendar week 25, 42 and 50 (2020)

	Covid-19 deaths among residents up to and including calendar week 25	Covid-19 deaths among residents up to and including calendar week 42 (percentage increase since week 25)	Covid-19 deaths among residents up to and including calendar week 50 (percentage increase since week 42)
Australia	29	677 (2234%)	678 (0.1%)
Germany	3,491	3,752 (7%)	6,532 (174%)
Canada	6,236	7,411 (19%)	(no data)
Spain	19,553	20,649 (6%)	24,372 (18%)

The values for calendar weeks 25 and 42 were taken from the overview of the research team around Comas-Herrera et al. (2020). The latest figures for calendar week 50 are from information from the national authorities of the respective countries. Essential data are missing for South Korean deaths in nursing homes, so that no valid data are available for the individual points in time and therefore no comparison can be made within the table.

statements, recommendations, guidelines and laws have been drawn up for the use in stationary nursing homes, which precisely addressed these considerations and published resulting recommendations. Especially in the case of methods to protect residents, global comparisions allow learning from other countries. For example, effective protection measures could be taken over from countries with little infection in nursing homes as well as triggers of infection outbreaks could be analyzed and prevented.

A European-wide analysis by the European Centre for Disease Prevention and Control (ECDC) worked out causes of increased infection in nursing homes such as lack of medical resources (protective equipment, testing, staff), infection through contagious staff[23] or incorrect handling of the crisis situation (ECDC 2020a). This results in measures for the identification, monitoring and control of the infection process (see below).

3.2.2 Five Countries on Four Continents Compared[24]

In Germany, the Infection Protection Act requires the reporting of confirmed and suspected cases of Covid-19 to the local health department. From there, this information is forwarded to the competent authority of the federal state and finally to

[23] It should be mentioned here that infected staff with asymptomatic course of the disease caused high infection rates due to lack of suspicion-independent testing.

[24] To select the countries, it should be added that, in addition to Germany (83 million inhabitants), another European country, Spain (47 million inhabitants), as well as a nation from each of the continents of America (Canada: 38), Asia (South Korea: 52) and Australia (25) should be represented. The situation in Africa is fundamentally different on the one hand and, on the other hand, difficult to compare in terms of the data available. In total, of course, only brief highlights can be given here with a view to individual characteristic developments due to space constraints.

the national level (ECDC 2020b). The many different steps in data transmission can only be carried out with many new employees, enormous time and effort due to the complex federal structure and apparently outdated technical means such as fax and scanner in some places. Instead, uniform digital systems such as the "Sormas" program developed for Ebola could carry out this work automatically (Klauth 2020). In guidelines for the prevention and management of Covid-19 in nursing homes, the Robert Koch Institute recommends local, daily symptom monitoring of residents and employees, including case-specific disease course, test results, protective measures taken and all reported infection numbers (RKI 2020d). The national test strategy—"Who will be tested for the presence of SARS-CoV-2 infection in Germany?"—provides for a prioritized distribution of serial rapid tests for employees and residents (RKI 2020d). Thus, the Federal Government ordered the use and cost-coverage of SARS-CoV2 rapid tests for stationary facilities (The Federal Government 2020). Overall, the test capacities were increased, so that in the 49th calendar week 1.6% of the population were tested per day (RKI 2020f). Regulations on admission stops as well as bans and restrictions on visits vary greatly between the individual federal states.[25] However, visiting of the dying was and is always allowed (Federal Ministry of Health 2020). Apart from that, each facility is obliged to develop its own hygiene concept according to the guidelines of the respective federal state. As reported by an online survey by the University of Bremen, German nursing home employees would prefer a uniform national regulation of the measures (Wolf-Ostermann et al. 2020, p. 30). In addition, special crisis teams, so-called "long term care task forces", were introduced (Curry and Langins 2020). Fair distribution of protective equipment is ensured by a central organization and new staff were hired and transferred to areas with strong impact according to the current situation (ibid.). Another demand of the nursing staff is the increase in remuneration, which has not yet been taken into account by mid-December 2020 (Wolf-Ostermann et al. 2020, p. 59).

At this point, the spotlight should be briefly shone on the structural and specific problems of the other countries. Spain's government(s) analyzed the problems in nursing homes particularly intensively. The country's own research into the causes of serious outbreak situations revealed a high local infection rate in the public, a high number of residents per facility, many visitors in the week before the outbreak of infection, a large number of infected or absent staff, little availability of protective equipment, low test capacity and the inadequate implementation of disinfection measures (García et al. 2020). With 1.7% of the population tested per day, the country has an extremely high test rate (ECDC 2020c). Canada initially struggled with the problem of providing sufficient test resources. By mid-December 2020, this deficit could be made up for, so that 0.22% of the population could be tested per day at that time (ibid.). In Australia, the test rate at that time was

[25] So there was never an official visiting ban in Berlin, but only restrictions. Individual home management could still cause complete bans. However, the Bavarian government issued visiting bans and admission stops during the first wave of infection.

0.1% and in South Korea, by comparison, 0.6% (ibid.). The country provided for strict rules on social distancing as well as extensive opportunities for testing and treatment. Precautions were particularly strict in nursing homes. So quarantine and isolation measures were imposed on entire facilities. Residents were already transferred to a hospital at the suspicion of infection (Kim 2020). Overall, a widespread outbreak of infection in homes could be prevented.

The authors Comas-Herras et al. suspect further, far-reaching changes in the sector of stationary nursing facilities. They speak of an increased public awareness of the elevated risk of infection for residents in nursing homes, so that relatives could tend to rely more on alternative care options. In addition, due to the excess mortality during the pandemic, there were already fewer residents in nursing homes at the time. Furthermore, new government regulations on extended infection control measures are feared. For example, prescribed, increased staff numbers or additional training could lead to overall increased costs for residents and ultimately result in fewer admissions for financial reasons (Comas-Herrera et al. 2020, p. 30).

4 Public Health Ethics for the Elderly—Comprehensive Reflection

The Covid-19 pandemic has brought ethical and human rights issues in the treatment of older people into the focus of national and global considerations in a special way. Basic and human rights had to be temporarily restricted to a great extent—the Corona crisis thus affects several civil rights: the right to freedom of assembly because of the danger of infection in crowds, the right to freedom of religion in the practice of church pastoral care in clinics and nursing homes up to the cancellation of church services, but also alleged violations of the right to freedom of expression at forbidden demonstrations by Corona deniers and conspiracy theorists. These measures make use of a tightened Infection Control Act (IfSG) in Germany, which must ensure the functioning of fully occupied intensive care units and prevent the entire society from an overloaded health care system. In all the restrictions mentioned, difficult decisions have to be made politically and legally as well as ethically, which are of an particular moral relevance and aim at a balance between self-determination (autonomy) of the individual and non-harm or beneficence for the collective. The respect for the dignity of all people affected in the health care system is to be striven for. Of course, human lives cannot be weighed against each other, but the protection of the elderly has also been given priority, whether in measures to prevent infection or social solidarity for care services and the medical system. Despite all the personal demands and social challenges, it is also a positive aspect that a clear political and social majority supports the measures with the "shutdown" of economic and social life to protect the elderly as a particularly vulnerable group. With the exception of a few will-o'-the-wisps in the discourse with positions to unnecessarily save lives here, which would die in a few months anyway (such as the quotation from the mayor of Tübingen) or worrying trends with anti-democratic and irrational currents of "lateral thinkers", the broad consensus is remarkable. Social consensus for the differentiated protection of older people is a positive result despite all the problems in the pandemic. This should not, however, obscure the fact that Covid-19 has mercilessly exposed a number of weaknesses in health systems worldwide. This affects basic hygiene requirements such as capacity in intensive care beds or the infrastructure of health departments, as well as the implementation of public health measures in the field. In the latter case, several problems are to be diagnosed in a comparative study such as the present one: While the federalist structure in Germany has repeatedly caused difficulties in the coordination and synchronization of protection measures for quick and uniform regulations at the national level, a comparative article such as this one obviously puts the finger much more strongly on the sore spot of numerous European heterogeneities in data collection, statistical recording and health consequences in a multi-layered continent, in which the political achievement of open borders can cause uncontrolled spread. The parallel action of quite different public health institutions also makes it more difficult to compare data or measures, as has become clear again and again from the results of this contribution. In Germany, great importance has been attached to the protection of older people since the beginning of the pandemic—through strict measures, but also through the political accommodation of criticism of too much social isolation of older people or, for example, the relaxation of the rules of visits to dying people. Between the individual micro level in clinics or nursing homes and the macro level of the health system, gaps become apparent. In addition to the "Clinical Ethics Committees" (CEC), which are increasingly common in hospitals, there could be many more committees in old people's and nursing homes, as well as a link to the German Ethics Council (DER) at the national level, such as "Committees for Ethics in Healthcare" (KEG), for example at the level of the respective government districts or at least the federal states. Here there are still vacant interfaces and painful gaps between politics, science and society, which could be filled by good organizational ethics and active committees also for the implementation in the field. The "Academy for Ethics in Medicine" (AEM) as a professional society also sees a greater need for regional exchange, has founded new working groups and initiated internet forums in the German-speaking world; the differentiated documentation of treatment methods and a reflective exchange of experience on quality assurance and the increase of justice in healthcare are important desiderata. The recurring problem of whether necessary measures are a matter of state or federal government should be better anticipated and structured in the interests of tighter pandemic management. This is also a necessity in the tension field of ethics and efficiency. Especially in the field of protection of older people, there is still a lot to be done here guaranteeing the participation of those affected, for example by senior citizens' councils, etc.

5 Summary—Final Considerations and Outlook

The analyses of the European Centre for Disease Prevention and Control (ECDC) offer some groundbreaking perspectives (ECDC 2020a). The mandatory implementation of a national Covid-19 surveillance system in nursing homes is necessary, which reports daily on the symptoms of the residents as well as possible, probable and confirmed cases. Electronic systems should forward this information immediately to local, regional and finally national and European or global authorities. Through regular series testing of all residents and staff, as well as a mandatory negative test result of the visitors, infections could be detected early(er). Subsequently, the spread of infections should be avoided by means of contact tracing and immediate strict protection and isolation measures. Much more extensive exercising with practical training units on hygiene and dealing with pandemics is essential for good implementation of prevention (ECDC 2020a). In addition, the European cooperation "Covid-19 Health System Response Monitor" demands financial and personnel support for nursing staff, personnel planning that reduces contacts, guidelines and concepts for isolation and quarantine measures as well as visiting regulations and procedures for the distribution of scarce medical supplies (Curry and Langins 2020). A European-wide register for better recording of occupied and vacant intensive care beds would also be a useful public health instrument.

A low incidence of infection outside of nursing homes is decisive for a low incidence of infection in nursing homes. Measures to combat the pandemic in general can already be very well compared internationally through the Covid-19 Health System Response Monitor (Covid-19 Health System Response Monitor 2020). However, this concept lacks the subcategory "nursing home", which could enable a separate consideration of this important aspect. But on every level, the effects on affected older people and the possibilities of compensation have to be considered in medical ethical terms as well. More than half a year after the outbreak of the pandemic, the Berlin senior representative Wenzel mentioned at the beginning, out of concern for new strict isolation measures like during the first lockdown, sought contact with the public in an appeal (Rundfunk Berlin-Brandenburg 2020). She spoke out again against an absolute ban on visits. It is important to have the opportunity to decide as an older person which personal risk one is willing to take. "Life time […] is not more important than life quality—for [them] the latter is more important" (ibid.). The fears of concerned seniors and relatives of residents should be taken more seriously. Participation is an essential social element from an ethical and human rights perspective and is particularly important for the implementation of justice in the entire population (Fritsch 2020). Thus, as the Chancellor Angela Merkel rightly emphasized in a video conference on October 28, 2020, "complete social isolation" should be avoided by individual decisions (The Federal Government 2020). In addition, the legislator anchored in the Infection Protection Act under § 28 a "minimum of social contacts". How exactly the implementation[26] of this formulation should be made, the German Ethics Council describes in its Ad-hoc Recommendation published on December 18, 2020. Finally, for example, the Red Cross also organized special actions for those in care together with other relief organizations as the free testing of visitors to nursing homes that made it possible for all residents to have a safe Christmas visit (exemplary: Bayerisches Staatsministerium für Gesundheit und Pflege 2020). A number of other measures are necessary in the course of the pandemic—and should be professionally accompanied in terms of medical ethics and human rights (see, for example, Bielefeldt 2017; Frewer et al. 2019; Frewer et al. 2020; Mahler et al. 2020). In a comparative perspective, there is certainly much to be learned from successful measures in other (federal) states.

Note

This work was created in the context of a cumulative dissertation for the medical doctorate ("Dr. med.") by the first author under the supervision of the last author at the Friedrich-Alexander-Universität Erlangen-Nürnberg (FAU). We would like to thank the scholarship holders of the Graduate School "Human Rights and Ethics in Medicine for the Elderly" with funding from the Josef and Luise Kraft Foundation (Munich) for the interesting scientific exchange and the support.

References

Akademie für Ethik in der Medizin (AEM) (2020) Möglichkeiten und Grenzen von Ethikberatung im Rahmen der COVID-19-Pandemie (31.03.2020). Ein Diskussionspapier der Akademie für Ethik in der Medizin. Göttingen. https://www.aem-online.de/fileadmin/user_upload/AEM_Ethikberatung_im_Rahmen_von_COVID-19_2020-03-31.pdf. Accessed 09 Dec 2020

Ärztezeitung (2020) Vakzine von BioNTech/Pfizer zugelassen. Corona-Impfung in den USA ab Montag geplant (13.12.2020). Springer Medizin, Berlin. https://www.aerztezeitung.de/Nachrichten/Corona-Impfung-in-den-USA-ab-Montag-geplant-415546.html?bPrint=true. Accessed 14 Dec 2020

[26] Social contacts in nursing homes are divided into external and internal. Within the nursing home, for example, more qualified personnel could be hired through financial support. The activities of volunteers in the facilities should also be made more attractive in this crisis situation. Visits from outside should also be allowed after consultation with all parties involved. If there are no trusted persons, efforts should be made to engage citizens who voluntarily seek contact with seniors in nursing homes. Important in the design of social contacts is to take into account the wishes of the person being cared for, because in the end it is the quality of the meetings that counts—not just their frequency. Of course, such contact possibilities require the observance of strict safety precautions, which should be obtained through additional financial resources for sufficient protective equipment and testing (German Ethics Council 2020).

Australian Government Department of Health (2020a) COVID-19 outbreaks in Australian residential aged care facilities (11.12.2020). Canberra. https://www.health.gov.au/sites/default/files/documents/2020/12/covid-19-outbreaks-in-australian-residential-aged-care-facilities-11-december-2020_0.pdf. Accessed 14 Dec 2020

Australian Government Department of Health (2020b) Coronavirus (COVID-19) at a glance (15.12.2020). Canberra. https://www.health.gov.au/sites/default/files/documents/2020/12/coronavirus-covid-19-at-a-glance-15-december-2020_0.pdf. Accessed 21 Dec 2020

Barmer (2020) BARMER-Umfrage zur Corona-Impfbereitschaft – Mehrheit will sich und eigene Kinder impfen lassen (30.11.2020). Berlin. https://www.barmer.de/presse/presseinformationen/pressemitteilungen/corona-impfbereitschaft-269498. Accessed 09 Dec 2020

Bayerisches Staatsministerium für Gesundheit und Pflege (2020) Pressemitteilung. Huml: BRK und weitere Hilfsorganisationen bieten für Angehörige von Pflegebedürftigen und von Menschen mit Behinderung über Weihnachten kostenfreie Corona-Tests an. München. https://www.stmgp.bayern.de/presse/huml-brk-und-weitere-hilfsorganisationen-bieten-fuer-angehoerige-von-pflegebeduerftigen/?output=pdf. Accessed 18 Dec 2020

Bergemann L, Frewer A (eds) (2018) Vulnerabilität und Autonomie in der Medizin. Menschenrechte – Ethik – Empowerment. transcript, Bielefeld

Bielefeldt H (2017) Menschenwürde und Autonomie am Lebensende. Perspektiven der internationalen Menschenrechte. In: Welsh C, Ostgathe C, Frewer A, Bielefeldt H (eds) Autonomie und Menschenrechte am Lebensende. Grundlagen, Reflexionen, Erfahrungen aus der Praxis. transcript, Bielefeld, pp 45–66

Blom AG (2020) Zum gesellschaftlichen Umgang mit der Corona-Pandemie. Ergebnisse der Mannheimer Corona-Studie (21.08.2020). Bundeszentrale für politische Bildung, Berlin. https://www.bpb.de/apuz/314345/zum-gesellschaftlichen-umgang-mit-der-corona-pandemie. Accessed 09 Dec 2020

Bödeker B., Neufeind J, von der Haar A, Mehlitz D, Bichel Y (2020) Initiativen gegen Grippe. Was machen Krankenhäuser zur Steigerung von Influenza-Impfquoten? (19.11.2020) Berlin. https://www.rki.de/DE/Content/Infekt/Impfen/Forschungsprojekte/OKaPII/OKaPII-Broschuere.pdf?__blob=publicationFile. Accessed 09 Dec 2020

British Columbia Centre for Disease Control (2020) British Columbia (BC) COVID-19 situation report (18.12.2020). Vancouver. http://www.bccdc.ca/Health-Info-Site/Documents/COVID_sitrep/Week_50_BC_COVID-19_Situation_Report.pdf. Accessed 21 Dec 2020

Bundesministerium für Gesundheit (2020) Meldungen. Coronavirus SARS-CoV-2: Chronik der bisherigen Maßnahmen. Bundesministerium für Gesundheit, Berlin. https://www.bundesgesundheitsministerium.de/coronavirus/chronik-coronavirus.html. Accessed 09 Dec 2020

CBC News (2020a) Coronavirus: what's happening in Canada and around the world on Monday (14.12.2020). https://www.cbc.ca/news/canada/coronavirus-covid19-canada-world-december-14-1.5840052. Accessed 14 Dec 2020

CBC News (2020b) Tracking the coronavirus (15.12.2020). CBC. https://newsinteractives.cbc.ca/coronavirustracker/. Accessed 15 Dec 2020

Charlesworth S, Low LF (2020) The long-term care COVID-19 situation in Australia (13.12.2020). International Long Term Care Policy Network. https://ltccovid.org/wp-content/uploads/2020/10/Australia-LTC-COVID19-situation-12-October-2020-1-2.pdf. Accessed 14 Dec 2020

Comas-Herrera A, Zalakaín E, Lemmon E, Henderson D, Liwin C, Hsu AT, Schmidt AE, Arling G, Fernández J-L (2020) Mortality associated with COVID-19 in care homes: international evidence (14.10.2020). International long term care policy network. https://ltccovid.org/wp-content/uploads/2020/10/Mortality-associated-with-COVID-among-people-living-in-care-homes-14-October-2020-5.pdf. Accessed 14 Dec 2020

Cook M (2020) Ethicists propose standards for Covid-19 triage (13.12.2020). BioEdge. https://www.bioedge.org/bioethics/ethicists-propose-standards-for-covid-19-triage/13656?utm_source=BioEdge&utm_campaign=7e85e61b71-EMAIL_CAMPAIGN_2020_12_13_05_06&utm_medium=email&utm_term=0_76ab23e62c-7e85e61b71-124717655. Accessed 13 Dec 2020

Corona-Datenspende (2020) Demographie der Spender*innen (03.07.2020). Robert Koch-Institut, Berlin. https://corona-datenspende.de/science/reports/demographie/. Accessed 04 Dec 2020

Corporación de Radio y Televisión Española (2020a) Coronavirus. El mapa del coronavirus en España: 48.401 muertos y más de 1,7 millones de contagiados (15.12.2020). https://www.rtve.es/noticias/20201215/mapa-del-coronavirus-espana/2004681.shtml. Accessed 16 Dec 2020

Corporación de Radio y Televisión Española (2020b) Coronavirus. Radiografía del coronavirus en residencias de ancianos: más de 24.300 muertos con COVID-19 o síntomas compatibles (15.12.2020). https://www.rtve.es/noticias/20201215/radiografia-del-coronavirus-residencias-ancianos-espana/2011609.shtml. Accessed 16 Dec 2020

Covid-19 Health System Response Monitor (2020) World Health Organization, European Commission, European Observatory on Health Systems and Policies. https://www.covid-19healthsystem.org/searchandcompare.aspx. Accessed 15 Dec 2020

Curry N, Langins M (2020) Cross-country analysis. What measures have been taken to protect care homes during Covid-19 crisis? (08.06.2020) World Health Organization Europe, European Commission, European Observatory on Health System and Policies. Covid-19 Health System Response Monitor. https://analysis.covid19healthsystem.org/index.php/2020/06/08/what-measures-have-been-taken-to-protect-care-homes-during-the-covid-19-crisis/. Accessed 07 Dec 2020

Deutsche Interdisziplinäre Vereinigung für Intensiv- und Notfallmedizin (DIVI)/Robert Koch-Institut (RKI) (2020) DIVI-Intensivregister. Tagesreport vom 09.12.2020. Berlin. https://www.intensivregister.de/#/aktuelle-lage/reports. Accessed 09 Dec 0202

Deutscher Ethikrat (2020) Mindestmaß an sozialen Kontakten in der Langzeitpflege während der Covid-19-Pandemie. Berlin. https://www.ethikrat.org/fileadmin/Publikationen/Ad-hoc-Empfehlungen/deutsch/ad-hoc-empfehlung-langzeitpflege.pdf. Accessed 21 Dec 2020

Deutsches Ärzteblatt (2020) STIKO-Impfempfehlungen liegen vor: Medizinisches Personal wird nicht gleichermaßen priorisiert (07.12.2020). Ärzteblatt, Berlin. https://www.aerzteblatt.de/nachrichten/119116/STIKO-Impfempfehlungen-liegen-vor-Medizinisches-Personal-wird-nicht-gleichermassen-priorisiert. Accessed 10 Dec 2020

Deutsches Grünes Kreuz (2020) Impfungen für bestimmte Berufsgruppen nach den Empfehlungen der STIKO 2020/2021. Deutsches Grünes Kreuz, Marburg. https://dgk.de/fileadmin/user_upload/impfen/vortraege/6_Berufsimpfungen_09_2020.pdf. Accessed 09 Dec 2020

Deutsches Institut für Menschenrechte (2020) Stellungnahme. Menschenrechte Älterer auch in der Corona-Pandemie wirksam schützen (09.04.2020). Deutsches Institut für Menschenrechte, Berlin. https://www.institut-fuer-menschenrechte.de/fileadmin/user_upload/Publikationen/Stellungnahmen/Stellungnahme_Menschenrechte_AElterer_auch_in_der_Corona-Pandemie_wirksam_schuetzen.pdf. Accessed 01 Dec 2020

Die Bundesregierung (2020) Videokonferenz der Bundeskanzlerin mit den Regierungschefinnen und Regierungschefs der Länder am 28. Oktober 2020. TOP Bekämpfung der SARS-Cov2-Pandemie. Presse- und Informationsamt der Bundesregierung, Berlin. https://www.bundesregierung.de/breg-de/suche/videokonferenz-der-bundeskanzlerin-mit-den-regierungschefinnen-und-regierungschefs-der-laender-am-28-oktober-2020-1805248. Accessed 18 Dec 2020

Engelbrecht S (2020) Senioren und das Coronavirus. „Wegsperren macht krank". Köln: Deutschlandfunk (30.03.2020). https://www.deutschlandfunk.de/senioren-und-das-coronavirus-wegsperren-macht-krank.1773.de.html?dram:article_id=473575. Accessed 29 Nov 2020

European Centre for Disease Prevention and Control (ECDC) (2020a) Surveillance of COVID-19 in long-term care facilities in the EU/EEA (19.05.2020). Stockholm. https://www.ecdc.europa.eu/en/publications-data/surveillance-COVID-19-long-term-care-facilities-EU-EEA. Accessed 17 Dec 2020

European Centre for Disease Prevention and Control (ECDC) (2020b) Infection prevention and control and preparedness for COVID-19 in healthcare settings (06.10.2020). Stockholm. https://www.ecdc.europa.eu/sites/default/files/documents/Infection-prevention-and-control-in-healthcare-settings-COVID-19_5th_update.pdf. Accessed 17 Dec 2020

European Centre for Disease Prevention and Control (ECDC) (2020c) Data on testing for COVID-19 by week and country (07.01.2021). Stockholm. https://www.ecdc.europa.eu/en/publications-data/covid-19-testing. Accessed 08 Dec 2020

Frewer A, Bielefeldt H (eds) (2016) Das Menschenrecht auf Gesundheit. Normative Grundlagen und aktuelle Diskurse. transcript, Bielefeld

Frewer A, Giese C, Green C, Mahler C, Mosler H (eds) (2019) Menschenrechte und Ethik in der Medizin für Ältere. Beiträge des Preisträger-Forums in München mit Projekten aus Basel und Frankfurt/M. MEM 1 (2019). K & N, Würzburg

Frewer A, Klotz S, Herrler C, Bielefeldt H (eds) (2020) Gute Behandlung im Alter? Menschenrechte und Ethik zwischen Ideal und Realität. transcript, Bielefeld

Frith L (2020) Lockdown, public good and equality during COVID-19 (28.10.2020). J Med Ethics. https://jme.bmj.com/content/medethics/46/11/713.full.pdf. Accessed 21 Nov 2020

Fritsch J (2020) Pflegeheime und Corona. Verfassungsrechtler hält erneute Besuchsverbote für rechtswidrig (13.11.2020). Ärztezeitung/Springer Medizin, Berlin. https://www.aerztezeitung.de/Wirtschaft/Verfassungsrechtler-haelt-erneute-Besuchsverbote-fuer-rechtswidrig-414646.html. Accessed 18 Dec 2020

García JMF, Loreña LH, Villafranca RR, Puerta FA (2020) Auditoría de los centros residencias en Navarra ante la crisis de la Covid-19. Observatorio de la Realidad Social. https://www.navarra.es/documents/48192/5050746/Auditoria-Covid-Navarra-Residencias.pdf/203c9382-cb09-afe8-f790-0a6f47a3f70e?t=1600765656950. Accessed 14 Dec 2020

Gouvernement du Québec (2020) Data on COVID-19 in Québec (13.12.2020). Québec. https://www.quebec.ca/en/health/health-issues/a-z/2019-coronavirus/situation-coronavirus-in-quebec/#c53633. Accessed 14 Dec 2020

Heinrich C (2020) Wie geht es Älteren in Corona-Zeiten? (11.11.2020) Spektrum, Heidelberg. https://www.spektrum.de/news/wie-geht-es-den-aelteren-in-corona-zeiten/1792238. Accessed 29 Nov 2020

Hohmann-Jeddi C (2019) Infektionen bei Älteren. Fieber fehlt häufig (16.05.2019). Avoxa-Mediengruppe Deutscher Apotheker GmbH. Pharmazeutische Zeitung, Eschborn. https://www.pharmazeutische-zeitung.de/fieber-fehlt-haeufig/. Accessed 04 Dec 2020

Hüttemann D (2020) Covid-19-Impfungen. Impfbereitschaft schwankt zwischen 55 und 89 Prozent (20.10.2020). Pharmazeutische Zeitung, Eschborn. https://www.pharmazeutische-zeitung.de/impfbereitschaft-schwankt-zwischen-55-und-89-prozent-121263/. Accessed 06 Dec 2020

Instituto de Mayores y Servicios Sociales (2020) MoMo. En el sistema para la autonomía y atención a la dependencia (SAAD) (30.11.2020). https://sede.imserso.gob.es/InterPresent2/groups/imserso/documents/binario/momo_dep_202011.pdf. Accessed 16 Dec 2020

Kamps BS, Hoffmann C (2020) Covid reference, vol 5. Steinhäuser, Wuppertal. https://amedeo.com/CovidReference05.pdf. Accessed 09 Dec 2020

Kim H (2020) The impact of COVID-19 on long-term care in South Korea and measures to address it (07.05.2020). International Long Term Care Policy Network. https://ltccovid.org/wp-content/uploads/2020/05/The-Long-Term-Care-COVID19-situation-in-South-Korea-7-May-2020.pdf. Accessed 14 Dec 2020

Klauth J (2020) Faxgerät und Zettelwirtschaft – Gesundheitsbehörden irren durch die Pandemie (18.12.2020). Welt, Berlin. https://www.welt.de/wirtschaft/article222754040/Digitales-Versagen-Gesundheitsbehoerden-irren-durch-die-Pandemie.html. Accessed 18 Dec 2020

Korea Disease Control and Prevention Agency (2020) The updates on Covid-19 in Korea as of 15 December. http://www.kdca.go.kr/board/board.es?mid=a30402000000&bid=0030. Accessed 21 Dec 2020

Kröger M (2020) Covid-19. Experte hält Impfpflicht für denkbar (05.12.2020). Der Spiegel. Hamburg. https://www.spiegel.de/politik/covid-19-experten-fordern-gesetz-zur-regelung-der-impfstoff-verteilung-a-c88f1c7f-7b11-4108-b022-fb4b0e77b09d/ Accessed 05 Dec 2020

Kruse A (2017) Lebensphase hohes Alter. Verletzlichkeit und Reife. Springer, Berlin

Lemkemeyer S (2020) Patienten*innen über 80 Jahre werden nicht mehr beatmet. Deutsche Katastrophenärzte verfassen Alarmbericht über Straßburg (27.03.2020). Der Tagesspiegel. https://m.tagesspiegel.de/wissen/Patienten/innen-ueber-80-jahre-werden-nicht-mehr-beatmet-deutsche-katastrophenaerzte-verfassen-alarmbericht-ueber-strassburg/25682596.html. Accessed 02 Dec 2020

Lokshin P (2020) Eine Impfstrategie mit vielen Fragezeichen (08.12.2020). Welt. Berlin. https://www.welt.de/politik/ausland/article222090266/Russlands-Corona-Impfungen-Der-ueberraschende-Erste.html. Accessed 09 Dec 2020

Mahler C, Giese C, Green CEDA, Mosler H, Frewer A (eds) (2020) Unterstützung für ältere Menschen. Beratung – Digitalisierung – Pflegepraxis. Beiträge des Preisträger-Forums in Berlin mit Projekten aus Bochum, Greifswald und München. Menschenrechte und Ethik in der Medizin für Ältere, vol 2. K & N, Würzburg

Merkel A (2020) Fernsehansprache von Bundeskanzlerin Angela Merkel (18.03.2020). Die Bundesregierung, Berlin. https://www.bundesregierung.de/bregde/aktuelles/fernsehansprache-von-bundeskanzlerin-angela-merkel-1732134. Accessed 10 Dec 2020

Mukerji N, Mannino A (2020) Covid-19: Was in der Krise zählt. Über Philosophie in Echtzeit. Reclam, Stuttgart

Organisation for Economic Cooperation and Development (OECD) (2020) Beyond containment: health system responses to COVID-19 in the OECD (16.04.2020). https://www.oecd.org/coronavirus/policy-responses/beyond-containment-health-systems-responses-to-covid-19-in-the-oecd-6ab740c0/. Accessed 09 Dec 2020

Organisation for Economic Cooperation and Development (OECD) Statistics (2020) Long-term care resources and utilization: beds in residential long term-care facilities. https://stats.oecd.org/Index.aspx#. Accessed 16 Dec 2020

Public Health Ontario (2020) Weekly epidemiologie summary. Covid-19 in Ontario: focus on November 29, 2020 to December 5, 2020 (08.12.2020). Toronto. https://files.ontario.ca/moh-covid-19-weekly-epi-report-en-2020-12-05.pdf. Accessed 14 Dec 2020

Radtke R (2020) Todesfälle mit Coronavirus in Deutschland nach Alter und Geschlecht (09.12.2020). Statista, Berlin. https://de.statista.com/statistik/daten/studie/1104173/umfrage/todesfaelle-aufgrund-des-coronavirus-in-deutschland-nach-geschlecht/. Accessed 09 Dec 2020

Richter-Kuhlmann E (2021) Alten- und Pflegeheime. Kontakte trotz Pandemie. Deutsches Ärzteblatt 118 (11.01.2021). https://www.aerzteblatt.de/treffer?mode=s&wo=1041&typ=16&aid=217314&s=richter%2Dkuhlmann. Accessed 17 Jan 2020

Robert Koch Institut (RKI) (2021) Täglicher Lagebericht des RKI zur Coronavirus-Krankheit-2019 (COVID-19) (08.01.2021). Berlin. https://www.rki.de/DE/Content/InfAZ/N/Neuartiges_Coronavirus/Situationsberichte/Jan_2021/2021-01-08-de.pdf?__blob=publicationFile. Accessed 21 Febr 2021

Robert Koch-Institut (RKI) (2020a) Täglicher Lagebericht des RKI zur Coronavirus-Krankheit-2019 (COVID-19) (30.04.2020). Berlin. https://www.rki.de/DE/Content/InfAZ/N/Neuartiges_Coronavirus/Situationsberichte/2020-04-30-de.pdf?__blob=publicationFile. Accessed 09 Dec 2020

Robert Koch-Institut (RKI) (2020b) Täglicher Lagebericht des RKI zur Coronavirus-Krankheit-2019 (COVID-19) (11.11.2020). Berlin. https://www.rki.de/DE/Content/InfAZ/N/Neuartiges_Coronavirus/Situationsberichte/Nov_2020/2020-11-11-de.pdf?__blob=publicationFile. Accessed 09 Dec 2020

Robert Koch-Institut (RKI) (2020c) Epidemiologischer Steckbrief zu SARS-CoV-2 und COVID-19 (27.11.2020). Berlin. https://www.rki.de/DE/Content/InfAZ/N/Neuartiges_Coronavirus/Steckbrief.html;jsessionid=B55CACA13257C4BC9727EE9216A83F03.internet072#doc13776792bodyText8. Accessed 09 Dec 2020

Robert Koch-Institut (RKI) (2020d) Nationale Teststrategie – wer wird in Deutschland auf das Vorliegen einer SARS-CoV-2 Infektion getestet? (08.12.2020) Berlin. https://www.rki.de/DE/Content/InfAZ/N/Neuartiges_Coronavirus/Teststrategie/Nat-Teststrate.html. Accessed 13 Dec 2020

Robert Koch-Institut (RKI) (2020e) Täglicher Lagebericht des RKI zur Coronavirus-Krankheit-2019 (COVID-19) (15.12.2020). Berlin. https://www.rki.de/DE/Content/InfAZ/N/Neuartiges_Coronavirus/Situationsberichte/Dez_2020/2020-12-15-de.pdf?__blob= publicationFile. Accessed 21 Dec 2020

Robert Koch-Institut (RKI) (2020f) Täglicher Lagebericht des RKI zur Coronavirus-Krankheit-2019 (COVID-19) (16.12.2020). Berlin. https://www.rki.de/DE/Content/InfAZ/N/Neuartiges_Coronavirus/Situationsberichte/Dez_2020/2020-12-16-de.pdf?__blob=publicationFile. Accessed 17 Dec 2020

Rundfunk Berlin-Brandenburg (2020) Vis à Vis. „Alte Menschen wollen gefragt werden, welches Risiko sie eingehen wollen" (10.11.2020). Inforadio, Berlin. https://www.inforadio.de/programm/schema/sendungen/vis_a_vis/202011/10/vis-a-vis-coronavirus-senioren-ursel-wenzel-berlin.html. Accessed 09 Dec 2020

Savulescu J, Cameron J (2020) Why lockdown of the elderly is not ageist and why leveling down equality is wrong (19.06.2020). J Med Ethics. https://jme.bmj.com/content/medethics/46/11/717.full.pdf. Accessed 09 Dec 2020

Seisselberg J (2020) Italiens Kliniken unter Druck. „Immer mehr Fälle, ganz wenig Betten" (12.03.2020). Tagesschau ARD-Studio Rom. https://www.tagesschau.de/ausland/italien-kliniken-101.html. Accessed 02 Dec 2020

Ständige Impfkommission (STIKO) et al (2020) Positionspapier der gemeinsamen Arbeitsgruppe. Wie soll der Zugang zu einem COVID-19-Impfstoff geregelt werden? (09.11.2020) https://www.ethikrat.org/fileadmin/Publikationen/Ad-hoc-Empfehlungen/deutsch/gemeinsames-positionspapier-stiko-der-leopoldina-impfstoffpriorisierung.pdf. Accessed 10 Nov 2020

Tagesschau (2020a) Corona-Pandemie. Briten wollen von Dienstag an impfen (04.12.2020). Hamburg. https://www.tagesschau.de/ausland/coronavirus-grossbritannien-impfprogramm-101.html. Accessed 09 Dec 2020

Tagesschau (2020b) Corona-Pandemie. Spahn gegen Sonderrechte für Geimpfte (28.12.2020). Hamburg. https://www.tagesschau.de/inland/privilegien-geimpfte-101.html. Accessed 28 Dec 2020

Wolf-Ostermann K, Rothgang H, Domhoff D, Friedrich A-C, Heinze F, Preuß B, Schmidt A, Seibert K, Stolle C (2020) Zur Situation der Langzeitpflege in Deutschland während der Corona-Pandemie. Ergebnisse einer Online-Befragung in Einrichtungen der (teil)stationären und ambulanten Langzeitpflege. Institut für Public Health und Pflegeforschung (IPP)/SOCIUM Forschungszentrum Ungleichheit und Sozialpolitik, Bremen. https://www.uni-bremen.de/fileadmin/user_upload/fachbereiche/fb11/Aktuelles/Corona/Ergebnisbericht_Coronabefragung_Uni-Bremen_24062020.pdf. Accessed 12 Dec 2020

World Health Organization (WHO) (2020) Percent of total Covid-19 related deaths occurring in long-term-care facilities by country (26.06.2020). https://www.who.int/data/maternal-newborn-child-adolescent-ageing/static-visualizations/COVID-Deaths-LTCFs-percent. Accessed 14 Dec 2020

Zur Nieden F, Sommer B, Lüken S (2020) Wirtschaft und Statistik. Amtliche Statistik in Zeiten von Corona. Sonderauswertung der Sterbefallzahlen 2020 (18.12.2020). Statistisches Bundesamt (Destatis), Wiesbaden. https://www.destatis.de/DE/Methoden/WISTA-Wirtschaft-und-Statistik/2020/04/wista-042020.pdf;jsessionid=4135421161024CDBFF1FDC2C70AF7A08.internet8711?__blob=publicationFile. Accessed 21 Dec 2020

Pandemics and Gender—The Unequal Effects of a Pandemic on Gender Equality

Elena Jirovsky-Platter and Anita Rieder

Contents

1 Introduction ... 269
2 Gender-Specific Effects of Public Health Measures ... 271
2.1 Gender-Based Violence ... 271
2.2 Socio-Economic Impacts ... 272
3 Gender and Health ... 273
3.1 Risk of Infection ... 273
3.2 Sexual and Reproductive Health ... 274
4 Final Considerations ... 276
References ... 277

1 Introduction

Sociocultural norms shape the identities, relationships, behavior and social status of a person in society. Gender attributions and the corresponding social expectations, change over time and vary depending on the local context and prevailing power relations between the sexes. Regarding to gender and ethics in the context of an epidemic or pandemic, the ethical concerns are primarily issues of equality and justice, unequal opportunities and distribution of resources, and discrimination based on gender in connection with the outbreak of an infectious disease. In general, it can be said: Inequalities and resulting gender-specific risk factors play a central role regarding the spread of infectious diseases and the further social consequences of dealing with them (see, for example, Abramowitz et al. 2015;

E. Jirovsky-Platter (✉) · A. Rieder
Medical University of Vienna, Vienna, Austria
e-mail: elena.jirovsky-platter@meduniwien.ac.at

A. Rieder
e-mail: anita.rieder@meduniwien.ac.at

© The Author(s), under exclusive license to Springer-Verlag GmbH, DE, part of Springer Nature 2023

A. Reis et al. (eds.), *Pandemics and Ethics*,
https://doi.org/10.1007/978-3-662-66872-6_16

Harman 2016; Oertelt-Prigione 2020; United Nations Radio 2014). The resulting or increased inequalities have a negative effect on the health and well-being of affected persons in the sense of public health (see Raj et al. 2020).

When it comes to gender and inequality, the disadvantage of women is in the focus. Women are still disadvantaged in most societies and, more often than men, are affected by multiple, overlapping social attributions, also have a negative effect on health. Relevant ethical issues concern the distribution of resources, the maintenance of health care and protection facilities. If one wants to look at ethical aspects of a disease outbreak a central task is to recognize and understand the intersecting inequalities in health.

It is impossible to understand inequality without taking into account the different dimensions such as environment, economic conditions, social norms and vulnerabilities in an intersectional way (cf. Cielo and Coba 2018). The current Covid-19 pandemic is already exacerbating existing gender inequalities. This is not a new phenomenon, as has been shown time and again in past epidemics and pandemics (cf. e.g. Davies and Bennett 2016; United Nations Radio 2014; Wenham et al. 2019). Each pandemic is different, and even the local manifestations vary, but there are parallels in the social and economic implications. Crises in general have the effect of exacerbating existing forms of marginalization due to age, ethnicity, class, gender or sexuality (cf. Dowler 2020). For many people of both genders, the current Covid-19 pandemic is one of multiple, overlapping crises: the climate crisis, poverty or recession are already threatening their lives and livelihoods, thus exacerbating social inequalities (cf. Dowler 2020). Gender is one of many other social categories that make people even more vulnerable to certain problems and unequal treatment. Systemic inequality and racism, for example, impact on the African American population in the USA, which is much less likely to have health insurance and also has a higher health risk due to diabetes II and obesity (cf. Gray et al. 2020). In another country hard hit by the epidemic, Brazil, the pandemic's effects on Brazil's dark-skinned population, which is generally worse off socially, are much more severe than the effects on other Brazilian populations—here too, women are even more vulnerable due to their social position (cf. Baqui et al. 2020).

It is reasonable to assume that the human rights of women are particularly at risk in a pandemic (cf. Gulati and Kelly 2020). The crisis arising from the pandemic and the social and economic implications will have, and will continue to have, far more negative consequences for women than for men (cf. Blaskó et al. 2020; Wenham et al. 2020a).

It is often criticized that in most countries the Covid legislation and public health measures do not sufficiently take into account the gender-specific implications of Covid-19 (cf. Wenham et al. 2020b). In every country, certain restrictions are necessary due to the pandemic. However, the effects and inequalities in connection with Covid-19 are expressed differently worldwide and of course differently in poorer than in richer countries. In Europe and the United States, for example, it is home-schooling and the resulting additional burden on working women (cf. Blaskó et al. 2020) that exacerbate inequality. In African countries such as South Africa, the loss of livelihood through street vending prohibited by lockdown (cf. Melber 2020) causes existential issues for those mostly female street vendors.

This article sheds light on the ethical aspects of gender and pandemics by means of examples. We mainly refer to the current Covid-19 pandemic, but also repeatedly point to examples from epidemics of recent years, because in each local context the common public health measures, such as quarantine, are usually similar during an outbreak of disease and similar social and economic implications can be observed. Many ethical problems that were already known from the past (cf. e.g. Abramowitz et al. 2015; Harman 2016; Oertelt-Prigione 2020; United Nations Radio 2014) are repeated in the Covid-19 pandemic.

2 Gender-Specific Effects of Public Health Measures

2.1 Gender-Based Violence

In many countries, gender-based violence seems to be increasing as a result of quarantine measures (see John et al. 2020). Since the outbreak of the coronavirus pandemic, many authors have pointed out that necessary public health measures such as quarantine and lockdown, which reduce the risk of infection, can potentially lead to more violence in relationships, and are calling for better protection of women; after all, one can learn from the experiences of previous epidemics (see Kofman and Garfin 2020; Manrique De Lara and De Jesus Medina Arellano 2020; Roesch et al. 2020; Sanchez et al. 2020; van Gelder et al. 2020). Various factors, such as restricted access to shelters, dependence on an abusive partner from whom there is no escape, or alcohol abuse, intensify existing problems of violence against women (see Sanchez et al. 2020). For example, it is warned that in Mexico, where gender-based violence is already a big problem and on average eleven women are killed every day because of their gender, the lockdown makes it more difficult for women to leave the abusive men and to get to safety (see Manrique De Lara and De Jesus Medina Arellano 2020). In China, cases of domestic violence have tripled, and in Great Britain, deaths from domestic violence have doubled (see Roesch et al. 2020). In the current crisis, victims of domestic violence are also experiencing more mental health problems than other people (see Raj et al. 2020). Studies of the Ebola outbreak in 2014-2016 in West Africa have also shown that sexual violence increased during the epidemic and also in consequence of the epidemic: girls or women had no or very few protection options if their relatives had died, and in some cases had to prostitute themselves or enter into other, dangerous and exploitative situations in order to survive (see UNDP 2015a, b). An increase in sexual and domestic violence was also documented during the Ebola outbreak in North Kivu in DRC from 2018 to 2019 (see International Rescue Commitee 2019). Other forms of gender-based violence could also increase during the current Covid-19 pandemic: for example, UNICEF warns that as a result of the lockdown girls in many countries may drop out of the education system forever, will be married off at an early age, or that in countries where female genital mutilation is common, it may be easier to carry out the mutilations secretly under the current circumstances (see UNICEF 2020).

Different countries are putting very different emphases on getting a handle on these problems during the pandemic—of course depending on whether and how gender-based violence has been dealt with in the country in the past. Where domestic violence is not considered a criminal act, as in Hungary, there is little commitment to providing increased support to potential victims during this crisis (see Kováts 2020; Margolis 2020).

2.2 Socio-Economic Impacts

It becomes apparent that the pandemic is exacerbating existing gender roles, leading on the one hand to an even greater social burden on women (Covid), but also to a higher risk of disease. Certain occupations, which are particularly often carried out by women, such as paid or unpaid care, sales, food trade or nursing, are considered particularly important, but in many places they are among the occupations with the lowest incomes (see ILO 2018).

Pandemics or local epidemics such as Ebola Virus Disease, Influenza, Zika and currently also Covid-19 have a massive socio-economic impact on the population and impede ongoing development processes and the achievement of development goals in the long term (see UNDP 2017). Health or social inequalities are rather exacerbated; countries affected by an outbreak of an infectious disease have high direct and indirect costs, with poorer countries and their already vulnerable poorest population groups feeling the effects to a much greater extent (see UNDP 2017).

The different genders are differentially affected by an outbreak of an infectious disease and the associated public health measures on a socio-economic level. On the one hand, people experience different consequences due to their gender and their social roles (see below), on the other hand, existing economic imbalances are exacerbated by public health measures. Women are burdened solely by their gender, because they still bear the greater share of care tasks, because they work part-time more often and are therefore more quickly affected by unemployment (see Blaskó et al. 2020; Leuze and Strauß 2016). In this pandemic, women seem to be challenged by home office and home-schooling at the same time, even though all family members are challenged. If in addition the women are responsible for all chores, an even greater imbalance results. Unpaid work is still unevenly distributed in families and in many cases the women have already been much more burdened than their male counterparts under normal circumstances (see UN Economic and Social Council2016). In such contexts where informal economy, i.e. the "economic activities of people outside formal regulated sectors" (Klein 2018) prevails in many areas, it is also added that families can have less income from the outset and are therefore more vulnerable as a family. Again, however, women and men are differently affected by poverty, which is exacerbated or caused by the public health measures (cf. Manrique De Lara and De Jesus Medina Arellano 2020). Poverty and job loss (in informal work) of course affect both genders, but women are often in special and more vulnerable situations and have additional duties. In societies where daily life takes place mainly on the street and informal employment prevails, preventive isolation measures and lockdowns endanger the income and survival of many people (cf. Melber 2020). Crises such as epidemics and pandemics threaten women's participation in economic activities and increase gender differences in livelihoods (cf. Gender in Humanitarian Action Asia and the Pacific 2020). Closing markets or banning street vending can hinder access to cheap food (cf. Melber 2020). This puts people—and especially vulnerable groups—in precarious circumstances that make it impossible for them to comply with quarantine measures, as was the case, for example, during the Ebola epidemic in Liberia (cf. Kutalek et al. 2015). In local contexts where women are primarily responsible for food supply, a lockdown can prevent or at least make it more difficult to generate enough informal income to survive. In many countries, such as Burkina Faso or Uganda, women work as small traders and earn money in this way to buy food for their children or the family; either they trade in fruit or they sell snacks or whole meals by the roadside. Through a lockdown, these traders are prevented from generating income for their children. Women who are already affected by poverty therefore suffer particularly from the lockdown and cannot feed their families. Women in such countries are therefore even more vulnerable and affected by poverty if they cannot meet their daily duties and work needs. It may also be that this leads to more tension in families and in turn more violence occurs (see above).

3 Gender and Health

3.1 Risk of Infection

Different genders are at different risk of infection from infectious diseases. There are gender-related factors that favor infection with SARS-CoV-2 and disease with Covid-19: Women and men are exposed to the virus differently through their social roles, have different access to tests or protective equipment, or comply with preventive measures to different degrees (see Oertelt-Prigione 2020). For example, in connection with influenza outbreaks, it has been shown how much gender stereotypes shape our behavior: Women are more likely to be expected to control infection, while men are more likely to be expected to deal with illness stoically, not to care, which also significantly shapes the implementation of protective measures (see Davis et al. 2015). Special gender-specific risk factors for infection arise from the fact that women are more active in the service sector, including the health sector (see Oertelt-Prigione 2020). Worldwide, around 70% of health and social sector professionals are women (see Boniol et al. 2019). They are central key personnel for maintaining health and safety in the event of an outbreak of an infectious disease (see O'Donnell and Rick 2020). However, women are particularly at risk of infection through their work with infectious diseases. Gender norms often put women at risk because their social role exposes them to a higher risk of infection, while emergency response is often almost exclusively designed by men (see John et al. 2020). Women have more care responsibilities in the family to locally varying degrees. For example, the Ebola outbreak in West Africa in 2014-2016 showed how gender-specific norms led to women becoming more infected with Ebola because they were mainly the ones who took on the role of carertakers in families, but also because they made up the majority of front-line health workers (see Abramowitz et al. 2015; Davies and Bennett 2016; Menéndez et al. 2015). However, this remained almost invisible in international emergency response (see Harman 2016). Women who work in the informal sector, such as maids or cleaners, are also at increased risk of infection, especially if there is no or insufficient protection and control for workers. Women who work in such areas are usually from more vulnerable backgrounds, such as migrants (see Oertelt-Prigione 2020; Wenham et al. 2020b).

Other gender-specific differences in the health sector also relate to the fact that protective equipment is often not adapted to anatomical needs of women or smaller people in general (see Sutton et al. 2014). Poor fit can lead to higher infection rates among them. Although this is about physical characteristics, the reason for the exclusive presence of protective equipment in uniform size is the perpetuation of social norms and inequalities. Of course, men also work in occupational groups where mostly men are employed and where they have an increased health risk. In the case of Ebola, where a corpse remains infectious, male undertakers were also potentially at increased risk of infection. The loss of jobs due to the epidemic forced many men to take on this work (see BBC News Africa 2014). Undertakers are mainly men in many countries, and especially in countries with a large number of Covid-19 related deaths, they are exposed to a very high psychological stress through their work (see Hennigan 2020). These professional and private risks must be taken into account in public health strategies in the event of an outbreak of infectious diseases (see Oertelt-Prigione 2020).

3.2 Sexual and Reproductive Health

A topic that should be highlighted in the event of an outbreak of an infectious disease and the subsequent public health measures, in particular the lockdown, is the sexual- and reproductive health of women, the maintenance of adequate provision of sexual- and reproductive health care and the preservation of the dignity of women. Sexual and reproductive rights are currently particularly at risk (see De Zordo et al. 2020) and have also not been given sufficient attention in the past—for example, in the case of emergency response to the Zika outbreak in South America (see Wenham et al. 2019).

One must question what is happening with access to information on family planning and contraceptives, abortion options, high-risk pregnancies, screenings, but also normal pregnancies and births during an emergency such as the pandemic. Do women receive adequate care? Are victims of sexual violence of any gender adequately cared for? Do they have the opportunity to find the help they need during a lockdown?

What—at first glance—may appear less problematic in countries with a stable healthcare system, has far-reaching consequences for healthcare and further social development in poorer countries (see Hussein 2020; Thorne et al. 2020). Development programmes and humanitarian projects that specifically support women and girls often have to be interrupted during health crises (see CARE 2020). For example, there was an increase in deaths in childbirth in India during the current Covid-19 pandemic (see Kumari et al. 2020). In Nepal too, the rate of stillbirths and neonatal mortality increased because the quality of care deteriorated sharply (see Kc et al. 2020). During the Ebola virus outbreak in West Africa, the already poor access to healthcare for pregnant women and women in childbirth became dramatically worse during the epidemic (see Menéndez et al. 2015). The outbreak of Ebola virus disease also affected the provision and access to sexual and reproductive healthcare in North Kivu in the Democratic Republic of Congo (see McKay et al. 2019).

There are also critical aspects in richer countries that endanger the sexual and reproductive rights of women: In the USA, for example, there were unclear guidelines for the care of pregnant women; in addition, accompanying persons were not allowed during childbirth (see Davis-Floyd et al. 2020). In the EU country of Malta, it became apparent how problematic the existing legislation on sexual and reproductive healthcare can be in such a situation of exception. Even in normal times, Maltese women who are unintentionally pregnant have to travel abroad to have an abortion or order abortion pills online. During the lockdown in spring 2020, the fact that travel was not possible, for example, led to unintentionally pregnant women having suicidal thoughts because they had to wait too long for ordered abortion pills. Dangerous alternatives were considered in order to be able to abort anyway. Women in Malta also became unintentionally pregnant because they could not buy their usual contraceptives and were then, for example, raped by a violent partner. Birth control pills were not on the list of essential medications that the Maltese government stockpiled before the lockdown to ensure supply (see Caruana-Finkel 2020). In countries with very conservative governments and already strict abortion laws, abortions during the lockdown were defined as "optional procedures"; thus, relevant facilities could be closed. In the USA, Poland, Latin America and the Caribbean, there were further restrictive measures to make abortion more difficult (see Assis and Larrea 2020; Church et al. 2020; Thorne et al. 2020).

4 Final Considerations

The examples given above illustrate in a striking way that, due to gender, there can be unequal treatment and unequal burden during and after an infectious disease outbreak, which raises numerous ethical questions. However, it also becomes clear that the described inequalities already existed in a society before and that they are only made more visible by the pandemic or epidemic.

Women in particular are exposed to more gender-related violence due to their gender; their rights to health, dignity, security and autonomy are violated. This implies that everything should be done to protect people from violence and to ensure their physical integrity during a state of emergency such as a pandemic. Sexual and reproductive rights are only partially protected, as are rights to work and economic independence. However, gender and biological sex are particularly closely linked to questions of sexual and reproductive health. A person's right to health is linked to their right to life, to the free development of their personality, to their dignity and to the free decision about their sexuality and reproduction. The resulting ethical problems are manifold. It must be ensured that all people have equal access to health, justice and a life without violence despite the exceptional situation that a pandemic brings with it. As already mentioned at the beginning, however, gender aspects are paradoxically given too little attention in emergency situations such as the outbreak of an infectious disease (cf. Harman 2016; Purdie et al. 2020; Wenham et al. 2020a). This appears to be highly problematic in view of the examples given above.

Especially vulnerable groups that are exposed to additional stress due to their gender must be involved in decision-making and support must be created. The aftermath of an outbreak of an infectious disease and the associated public health measures must also be questioned from a gender perspective. In order to counteract the fact that the pandemic affects genders to a different extent, special measures must be designed and implemented that promote equality and equal opportunities and guarantee health care, otherwise the social and economic inequality between genders will be exacerbated for years to come. It must be ensured that everything possible is done so that all people can equally exercise their rights even in a pandemic. In the future, it must be ensured internationally that political decision-makers are advised by expert committees that take public health approaches and ethical questions into account and thus ensure that ethical principles are integrated into all processes of dealing with a pandemic and into necessary political decisions, especially when it comes to ensuring fair and equal treatment.

References

Abramowitz SA, McLean KE, McKune SL, Bardosh KL, Fallah M, Monger J, Tehoungue K, Omidian PA (2015) Community-centered responses to Ebola in urban Liberia: the view from below. PLOS Negl Trop Dis 9(4). https://doi.org/10.1371/journal.pntd.0003706

Assis MP, Larrea S (2020) Why self-managed abortion is so much more than a provisional solution for times of pandemic. Sex Reprod Health Matters 28(1):1779633. https://doi.org/10.1080/26410397.2020.1779633

Baqui P, Bica I, Marra V, Ercole A, van der Schaar M (2020) Ethnic and regional variations in hospital mortality from COVID-19 in Brazil: a cross-sectional observational study. Lancet Glob Health 8:e1018–e1026. https://doi.org/10.1016/S2214-109X(20)30285-0

BBC News Africa (2014) Dangerous job of grave digging in Ebola hit Sierra Leone. https://www.bbc.com/news/av/health-30273824. Accessed 04 Nov 2020

Blaskó Z, Papadimitriou E, Manca AR (2020) How will the COVID-19 crisis affect existing gender divides in Europe?. Publications Office of the European Union, Luxembourg

Boniol M, McIsaac M, Xu L, Wuliji T, Diallo K, Campbell J (2019) Gender equity in the health workforce: analysis of 104 countries. WHO. https://www.who.int/hrh/resources/gender_equity-health_workforce_analysis/en/. Accessed 15 Feb 2021

CARE (2020) Gender implications of COVID-19 outbreaks in development and humanitarian settings. https://www.care-international.org/files/files/Gendered_Implications_of_COVID-19_Full_Paper.pdf. Accessed 11 Feb 2021

Caruana-Finkel L (2020) Abortion in the time of COVID-19: perspectives from Malta. Sex Reprod Health Matters 28(1):1780679. https://doi.org/10.1080/26410397.2020.1780679

Church K, Gassner J, Elliott M (2020) Reproductive health under COVID-19 – challenges of responding in a global crisis. Sex Reprod Health Matters 28(1):1773163. https://doi.org/10.1080/26410397.2020.1773163

Cielo C, Coba L (2018) Extractivism, gender, and disease: an intersectional approach to inequalities. Ethics Int Aff 32(2):169–178. https://doi.org/10.1017/s0892679418000291

Davies SE, Bennett B (2016) A gendered human rights analysis of Ebola and Zika: locating gender in global health emergencies. Int Aff 92(5):1041–1060. https://doi.org/10.1111/1468-2346.12704

Davis MD, Stephenson N, Lohm D, Waller E, Flowers P (2015) Beyond resistance: social factors in the general public response to pandemic influenza. BMC Public Health 15:436. https://doi.org/10.1186/s12889-015-1756-8

Davis-Floyd R, Gutschow K, Schwartz DA (2020) Pregnancy, birth and the COVID-19 pandemic in the United States. Med Anthropol 39(5):413–427. https://doi.org/10.1080/01459740.2020.1761804

De Zordo S, Mishtal J, Zanini G, Gerdts C (2020) Consequences of gestational age limits for people needing abortion care during the COVID-19 pandemic. Sex Reprod Health Matters 28(1):1818377. https://doi.org/10.1080/26410397.2020.1818377

Dowler C (2020) Introduction: intersecting crises. In *Intersecting Crisis* edited by Dowler C. American Ethnologist Features. https://americanethnologist.org/panel/pages/features/pandemicdiaries. Accessed 04 June 2021

van Gelder N, Peterman A, Potts A, O'Donnell M, Thompson K, Shah N, Oertelt-Prigione S et al (2020) COVID-19: reducing the risk of infection might increase the risk of intimate partner violence. EClinicalMedicine 21:100348. https://doi.org/10.1016/j.eclinm.2020.100348

Gender in Humanitarian Action Asia and the Pacific (2020) The COVID-19 Outbreak and Gender: Key Advocacy Points from Asia and the Pacific. https://www2.unwomen.org/-/media/field%20office%20eseasia/docs/publications/2020/03/ap-giha-wg-advocacy.pdf?la=en&vs=2145. Accessed 11 Feb 2021

Gray DM 2nd, Anyane-Yeboa A, Balzora S, Issaka RB, May FP (2020) COVID-19 and the other pandemic: populations made vulnerable by systemic inequity. Nat Rev Gastroenterol Hepatol 17(9):520–522. https://doi.org/10.1038/s41575-020-0330-8

Gulati G, Kelly BD (2020) Domestic violence against women and the COVID-19 pandemic: what is the role of psychiatry? Int J Law Psychiatry 71:101594. https://doi.org/10.1016/j.ijlp.2020.101594

Harman S (2016) Ebola, gender and conspicuously invisible women in global health governance. Third World Q 37(3):524–541. https://doi.org/10.1080/01436597.2015.1108827

Hennigan WJ (2020) ‚We do this for the living.' Inside New York's citywide effort to bury its dead. Time Magazine, New York

Hussein J (2020) COVID-19: what implications for sexual and reproductive health and rights globally? Sex Reprod Health Matters 28(1):1746065. https://doi.org/10.1080/26410397.2020.1746065

ILO (2018) Care work and care jobs for the future of decent work. International Labour Office, Geneva. https://www.ilo.org/wcmsp5/groups/public/%2D%2D-dgreports/%2D%2D-dcomm/%2D%2D-publ/documents/publication/wcms_633135.pdf. Accessed 02 Feb 2020

International Rescue Commitee (2019) „Everything on her shoulders". Rapid assessment on gender and violence against women and girls in the Ebola outbreak in Beni, DRC. https://www.rescue.org/sites/default/files/document/3593/genderandgbvfindingsduringevdresponseindrc-final8march2019.pdf. Accessed 11 Feb 2021

John N, Casey SE, Carino G, McGovern T (2020) Lessons never learned: crisis and gender-based violence. Dev World Bioeth 20(2):65–68. https://doi.org/10.1111/dewb.12261

Kc A, Gurung R, Kinney MV, Sunny AK, Moinuddin M, Basnet O, Paudel P, Bhattarai P, Subedi K, Shrestha MP, Lawn JE, Målqvist M (2020) Effect of the COVID-19 pandemic response on intrapartum care, stillbirth, and neonatal mortality outcomes in Nepal: a prospective observational study. Lancet Glob Health 8(10):e1273–e1281. https://doi.org/10.1016/s2214-109x(20)30345-4

Klein M (2018) Informeller Sektor. In: Springer Gabler Wirtschaftslexikon. https://wirtschaftslexikon.gabler.de/definition/informeller-sektor-40129/version-263522

Kofman YB, Garfin DR (2020) Home is not always a haven: the domestic violence crisis amid the COVID-19 pandemic. J Psychol Trauma 12(S1):199–201. https://doi.org/10.1037/tra0000866

Kováts E (2020) Pandemic management on the backs of women in Hungary. https://eu.boell.org/en/2020/06/05/pandemic-management-backs-women-hungary. Accessed 02 Nov 2020

Kumari V, Mehta K, Choudhary R (2020) COVID-19 outbreak and decreased hospitalisation of pregnant women in labour. Lancet GlobHealth 8(9):e1116–e1117. https://doi.org/10.1016/s2214-109x(20)30319-3

Kutalek R, Wang S, Fallah M, Wesseh CS, Gilbert J (2015) Ebola interventions: listen to communities. Lancet Glob Health. https://doi.org/10.1016/S2214-109X(15)70010-0

Leuze K, Strauß S (2016) Why do occupations dominated by women pay less? How ‚female-typical' work tasks and working-time arrangements affect the gender wage gap among higher education graduates. Work Employ Soc 30(5):802–820. https://doi.org/10.1177/0950017015624402

Manrique De Lara A, De Jesus Medina Arellano M (2020) The COVID-19 pandemic and ethics in Mexico through a gender lens. J Bioeth Inquiry. https://doi.org/10.1007/s11673-020-10029-4

Margolis H (2020) Hungary rejects opportunity to protect women from violence. Human Rights Watch, New York. https://www.hrw.org/news/2020/05/08/hungary-rejects-opportunity-protect-women-violence. Accessed 02 Nov 2020

McKay G, Black B, Mbambu Kahamba S, Wheeler E, Mearns S, Janvrin A (2019) Not all that bleeds is Ebola. How has the DRC Ebola outbreak impacted sexual and reproductive health in North-Kivu? The International Rescue Committee, New York

Melber H (2020) Commentary. Africa needs tailored responses to coronavirus. The Nordic Africa Institute. https://nai.uu.se/news-and-events/news/2020-04-03-africa-needs-tailored-responses-to-coronavirus.html?utm_medium=email&utm_source=newsletter&utm_campaign=apr+20. Accessed 15 Oct 2020

Menéndez C, Lucas A, Munguambe K, Langer A (2015) Ebola crisis: the unequal impact on women and children's health. Lancet Glob Health 3(3). https://doi.org/10.1016/s2214-109x(15)70009-4

O'Donnell M, Rick S (2020) A gender lens on COVID-19: investing in nurses and other frontline health workers to improve health. Center for Global Development Blog. https://www.cgdev.org/blog/gender-lens-covid-19-investing-nurses-and-other-frontline-health-workers-improve-health-systems. Accessed 04 June 2021

Oertelt-Prigione S (2020) The impact of sex and gender in the COVID-19 pandemic. Case study. Publications Office of the European Union, Luxembourg

Purdie A, Hawkes S, Buse K, Onarheim K, Aftab W, Low N, Tanaka S (2020) Sex, gender and COVID-19: disaggregated data and health disparities. BMJ Global Health blog. https://blogs.bmj.com/bmjgh/2020/03/24/sex-gender-and-covid-19-disaggregated-data-and-health-disparities/. Accessed 19 Oct 2020

Raj A, Johns NE, Barker KM, Silverman JG (2020) Time from COVID-19 shutdown, gender-based violence exposure, and mental health outcomes among a state representative sample of California residents. EClinicalMedicine 26:100520. https://doi.org/10.1016/j.eclinm.2020.100520

Roesch E, Amin A, Gupta J, Garcia-Moreno C (2020) Violence against women during covid-19 pandemic restrictions. The BMJ 369:m1712. https://doi.org/10.1136/bmj.m1712

Sanchez OR, Vale DB, Rodrigues L, Surita FG (2020) Violence against women during the COVID-19 pandemic: an integrative review. Int J Gynecol Obst 151(2):180–187. https://doi.org/10.1002/ijgo.13365

Sutton E, Irvin M, Zeigler C, Lee G, Park A (2014) The ergonomics of women in surgery. Surg Endosc 28(4):1051–1055. https://doi.org/10.1007/s00464-013-3281-0

Thorne JG, Buitendyk M, Wawuda R, Lewis B, Bernard C, Spitzer RF (2020) The reproductive health fall-out of a global pandemic. Sex Reprod Health Matters 28(1):1763577. https://doi.org/10.1080/26410397.2020.1763577

UN Economic and Social Council (2016) Women's economic empowerment in the changing world of work. Report of the Secretary-General. United Nations Economic and Social Council. https://www.un.org/ga/search/view_doc.asp?symbol=E/CN.6/2017/3. Accessed 03 Nov 2020

UNDP (2015a) Assessing sexual and gender based violence during the Ebola Crisis in Sierra Leone. https://www.sl.undp.org/content/sierraleone/en/home/library/crisis_prevention_and_recovery/publication_1/assessing-sexual-and-gender-based-violence-during-the-ebola-cris.html. Accessed 20 Oct 2020

UNDP (2015b) Recovering from the Ebola crisis: submitted by the United Nations, the World Bank, European Union and African Development Bank as a contribution to the formulation of national Ebola recovery strategies in Liberia, Sierra Leone and Guinea. https://www.undp.org/content/dam/undp/library/crisis%20prevention/Recovering%20from%20the%20Ebola%20Crisis-Full-Report-Final_Eng-web-version.pdf. Accessed 20 Oct 2020

UNDP (2017) A socio-economic impact assessment of the Zika Virus in Latin America and the Caribbean: with a focus on Brazil, Colombia and Suriname. http://www.undp.org/content/dam/undp/library/HIV-AIDS/UNDP-Zika-04-03-2017-English-WEB.pdf. Accessed 27 Oct 2020

UNICEF (2020) COVID-19 disrupting SDG 5.3: eliminating female genital mutilation. Technical note. https://www.unicef.org/media/68786/file/External-Tehnical-Note-on-COVID-19-and-FGM.pdf. Accessed 19 Oct 2020

United Nations Radio (2014) UNICEF: women most affected by Ebola outbreak in W. Africa. https://news.un.org/en/audio/2014/07/590822. Accessed 19 Oct 2020

Wenham C, Arevalo A, Coast E, Corrêa S, Cuellar K, Leone T, Valongueiro S (2019) Zika, abortion and health emergencies: a review of contemporary debates. Glob Health 15(49). https://doi.org/10.1186/s12992-019-0489-3

Wenham C, Smith J, Davies SE, Feng H, Grépin KA, Harman S, Herten-Crabb A, Morgan R (2020a) Women are most affected by pandemics – lessons from past outbreaks. Nature 583(S):194–198

Wenham C, Smith J, Morgan R (2020b) COVID-19: the gendered impacts of the outbreak. Lancet 395(10227):846–848. https://doi.org/10.1016/S0140-6736(20)30526-2

The Roles of National Ethics Committees in Pandemics. Orientation in Times of Crisis

Patrik Hummel and Andreas Reis

Contents

1 Introduction 281
2 National Ethics Committees 282
3 Activities of National Ethics Committees on Infectious Diseases, Epidemics and Pandemics 285
3.1 HIV/AIDS 286
3.2 SARS 287
3.3 Pandemic Influenza 288
3.4 Ebola 288
4 National Ethics Committees and Covid-19 289
5 Summary and Outlook 297
References 298

1 Introduction

Pandemics such as SARS, pandemic influenza and Covid-19 raise a variety of ethical questions for policy-makers and societies as a whole. National Ethics Committees have been playing an increasingly important role in public discourse and policy advice in many countries since the 1990s. During the Covid-19 pandemic, these bodies have gained a new level of public attention.

P. Hummel (✉)
Eindhoven University of Technology, Philosophy & Ethics Group, DeZaale, Eindhoven, Netherlands
e-mail: p.a.hummel@tue.nl

A. Reis
Health Ethics and Governance Unit, Department of Research for Health, World Health Organization, Geneva, Switzerland
e-mail: reisa@who.int

© The Author(s), under exclusive license to Springer-Verlag GmbH, DE, part of Springer Nature 2023

A. Reis et al. (eds.), *Pandemics and Ethics*,
https://doi.org/10.1007/978-3-662-66872-6_17

To give a concrete example from Germany: in early May 2020, the German cabinet discussed the possibility of an immunity passport. If it turned out that a past Covid-19 infection protects against reinfection, it would be conceivable to issue a certificate of immunity to recovered individuals. This would allow them to return to everyday life. Federal Health Minister Jens Spahn announced in the media that it was "important to him that in the context of the application of the regulation, ethical aspects are given sufficient consideration" (Ärzte-Zeitung 2020; our translation). This announcement was preceded by reservations and skepticism against immunity certificates from representatives of the opposition, who feared incentives for misuse, loss of trust, and social division (Becker and Schmoll 2020). Spahn finally asked the German Ethics Council for its assessment of "how and in what context proof of immunity should be used" (Deutsches Ärzteblatt 2020; our translation). Similar questions were subsequently being discussed at the European level in debates about a Corona vaccination passport.

In the first part of this chapter, we will sketch the functions of National Ethics Committees. Against this background, we will then explain the roles that such Committees play during pandemics, in particular the Covid-19 pandemic. At the end of the chapter, we give an outlook on future developments and recommendations for action.

2 National Ethics Committees

The role of a National Ethics Committee is understood in different ways in different countries. The formal constitution, mandate, procedural aspects, and relationships to other stakeholders vary. Systematic studies distinguish between generalist and primarily research-based National Ethics Committees (Fuchs 2005; Köhler et al. 2021; Hummel et al. 2021). The former deal with the full range of bioethical issues and their normative foundations. In contrast to these generalist bodies, national research councils and commissions focus on biomedical research by formulating guidelines and accompanying research policy on the one hand, and by assessing specific research projects on the other.

Examples of generalist National Ethics Committees include the National and Presidential Commissions established in the United States since the 1970s (Capron 2017, p. 6), the French Comité Consultatif National d'Ethique (CCNE) founded in 1983, and the various national bioethics committees that are directly or indirectly inspired by UNESCO's Bioethics Programme (UNESCO 2010; Bagheri et al. 2016) and associated with its initiatives for capacity building at the national level (Langlois 2014; Gefenas and Lukaseviciene 2017, p. 11).

The most frequently described function of National Ethics Committees is the bundling of expertise and the advising of policy-makers on ethical aspects of science and responsible innovation (Mali et al. 2012). Ethics committees provide "judgment formation and advice to public decision-making bodies on moral issues of science and its application, in particular in the field of life sciences and medicine" (Fuchs 2005, p. 11; our translation). In addition to research itself, this also encompasses clinical issues and implications for public health.

The reference to processes of judgment formation indicates that National Ethics Committees do not only provide advice. They also often see themselves as platforms and catalysts for public discourse (Gefenas and Lukaseviciene 2017, p. 10; Siewert and Dabrock 2020). Bioethical issues and scientific innovation processes are often both impactful and controversial. Whether it is genetic engineering, reproductive technologies or pandemics, large parts of the population are affected and various stakeholders introduce distinctive and sometimes irrevocable attitudes and value judgements into debates. Here, Ethics Committees play a key role in mediating controversial positions. In this process, they facilitate the expression of diverse views, provide background information, and take the perspectives of both experts and laypeople seriously (Dodds and Thomson 2006, p. 327; for a recent example, see Archard et al. 2020). The different facets of this role have the consequence that in pluralistic societies, the "range of results achieved [...] can range from consensus to identification of ethical corridors or moral compasses to a reflective management of dissent" (Siewert and Dabrock 2020, p. 258; our translation).

Here and in policy advising, National Ethics Committees are thus confronted with various normative demands which impact the legitimacy and authority of these Committees and their statements. Montgomery (2017) speaks of quality criteria (in his words: *virtues*) which national ethics councils fulfil or *should* fulfil: he specifically mentions independence, courage, inclusion, openness, pragmatism, and integrity (cf. also Köhler et al. 2021). Furthermore, some authors point out that democratic institutions, principles, and ideals could be undermined if National Ethics Councils assume functions that go beyond consultation and end up constraining, preempting, or replacing political will-formation and parliamentary processes (Friele 2003). Further requirements concern, *inter alia*, conflicts of interest, impartiality, and meaningful dialogue with the public (Schüklenk and Lott 2005). Especially in the context of increased media attention to National Ethics Committees, e.g., since the beginning of the Covid-19 pandemic, the chairpersons of these committees figure more prominently in public perception. This offers opportunities for public communication, but also raises the risk of confusing the chairpersons or their positions with the respective committee as such (Siewert and Dabrock 2020, p. 251). Another complication can be that some of the sketched requirements at least partly relate to democratic standards (Dodds and Thomson 2006) which do not have the same importance for every country with a National Ethics Committee.

In contrast to generalist Committees, other National Ethics Committees focus on biomedical research. In research ethics, internationally recognized standards such as the Nuremberg Code, the Declaration of Helsinki, and guidelines such as the CIOMS Guidelines of the Council for International Organizations of Medicine (2016) provide orientation for ethics review processes. At the same time, these standards do not replace the involvement of national or local ethics committees in the review of specific research projects and the interpretation, concretization, and application of articulated standards in international research. National Ethics Committees have always been actively involved in these debates. In a statement from 1993, the French CCNE emphasizes that special precautions must be taken for research projects involving French scientists and scholars in developing countries in order to ensure the dignity and safety of participants (CCNE 1993). Since economic asymmetries generate or exacerbate vulnerability and risks of exploitation, the Comité demands from research consortia that they commit to partnership, safety of participants, and prior ethics review in the target country. In addition to risk-benefit considerations for individual research subjects, research projects in low-income countries should also examine how and to what extent the local population can later benefit from the results of the research and, e.g., have access to successfully tested interventions. National research ethics committees can contextually assess factors such as safety, scientific rigor, adequacy of the consent process, and other ethical issues. Considerations such as these have promoted the establishment of national research committees in the Global South, for example, at the beginning of the 2000s in a number of countries in the WHO African Region (Kirigia et al. 2005; Effa et al. 2007).

In November 2019, 47% of National Ethics Committees were located in countries classified by the World Bank as high-income countries, 10% were located in low-income countries. These Committees were geographically distributed across all WHO regions: 44% were located in Europe (EURO), 18% in the Americas (PAHO), 15% in Africa (AFRO), 11% in the Western Pacific (WPRO), 6% in the Eastern Mediterranean (EMRO) and 5% in the South-East Asia (SEARO) region (Hummel et al. 2021).

The formal and procedural codification of roles attributed to National Ethics Committees varies significantly. There is no such thing as the archetypical National Ethics Committee. In a number of countries, Committees are not external and neutral institutions, but part of the Ministry of Health, Education and/or Research. Bodies such as the British Nuffield Council of Bioethics are independent, nongovernmental institutions (Montgomery 2017). In some countries, Committees are not continuous and permanent institutions: in the United States, National Commissions on bioethics and research ethics have been set up and dissolved again at the end of legislative periods since the 1970s (Annas 1994; Fuchs 2005, pp. 65–69; Leinhos 2005; Capron 2017). The Trump administration refrained from establishing a National Commission. The methodological approaches also differ between National Ethics Committees, sometimes even between documents of the same Committee: some concentrate on the application of established values, principles and norms, others pursue a more flexible approach by taking specific, applied ethical issues as their starting points and deploying theoretical normative concepts only implicitly or as part of the focal framework (Schmidt and Schwartz 2016).

Common denominators between National Ethics Committees are less to be found on the formal level, but in the self-conception of Committees: "Despite the diversity of structure, composition, affiliation and tasks, similarities become apparent when comparing the founding documents in the way they refer to the rapid development of research, especially in the life sciences, and the suspected moral implications of its applications in medicine. This challenge is to be met by bringing together expertise and engaging in joint ethical judgment formation" (Fuchs 2005, p. 85; our translation).

National Ethics Committees deal with topics in their domain not only within, but also between countries. Montgomery (2017) speaks of three target groups of National Ethics Committees: in addition to governments and the public of the respective country, National Ethics Committees cater to the international community and seek to ameliorate deliberative processes. For example, the German Ethics Council describes its three core tasks as follows: in addition to informing the public and issuing recommendations, its goal is to engage in "cooperation with national ethics committees and similar institutions of other states and international organizations" (Ethikratgesetz 16 Juli 2007 (BGBl. I p. 1385), § 2 (1); our translation).

The Covid-19 pandemic once again highlights that bioethical challenges do not stop at national borders. The fact that research is not a purely national process has also become apparent during the pandemic, for example through vaccine studies with cohorts on all continents. Therefore, exchange and cooperation at the international level are essential. A central platform for deliberation between National Ethics Committees is the Global Summit of National Ethics Committees (Bouësseau et al. 2011; Ruiz de Chávez Guerrero und Pina 2015; Deutscher Ethikrat 2018). The Global Summit takes place every two years and is coordinated by WHO and UNESCO. In addition to networking and facilitating the exchange of experiences, the Summit is a platform for Committees to jointly identify global priority topics. For example, at the 12th Global Summit 2018 in Dakar, Senegal, participating countries adopted a "Call for Action" (Global Summit of National Ethics Committees 2018) highlighting the need for international attention and coordination with regard to ethical aspects of electronic processing of health-related data, social justice, civil society engagement, and the resilience of health systems during epidemics and natural disasters. Furthermore, the European Commission has been organizing the European Forum of National Ethics Committees for more than ten years. Meetings between National Ethics Committees of neighbouring countries (Deutscher Ethikrat 2020a, p. 18) also take place regularly. In recent years, regional summit meetings of National Ethics Committees from the respective WHO regions have also been established in other parts of the world (World Health Organization Regional Office for the Eastern Mediterranean 2017; World Health Organization Regional Office for the Western Pacific 2019).

3 Activities of National Ethics Committees on Infectious Diseases, Epidemics and Pandemics

National Ethics Committees influence public debate on bioethics and societal issues primarily through the publication of opinion documents and recommendations. The most common topics of these documents are research ethics, ethical aspects of genetic methods, organ transplantation, assisted reproductive technologies, and ethical challenges at the end of life (Hummel et al. 2021). National Ethics Committees have also worked and published on particular infectious diseases such as HIV and tuberculosis as well as epidemics and pandemics in general, although to a lesser extent than on aforementioned topics. This might constitute a parallel to the academic bioethics discourse, in which, according to some (Selgelid 2005), the ethics of infectious diseases has received relatively little attention. However, it should be emphasized that the mere number of opinion documents and recommendations does not necessarily reflect the level of priority of these topics for individual countries and the international community, but only that the publications of National Ethics Committees more often concern other areas such as research, new technologies, and innovations in the life sciences.

3.1 HIV/AIDS

One of the first infectious diseases to come to the attention of National Ethics Committees was HIV/AIDS. In the years after its discovery, science made rapid progress in understanding the disease, but there was still uncertainty in politics about what a responsible approach might look like, which public health measures are appropriate and effective, and where the limits of ethical justifiability might lie. These debates took place, for example, in the United States (Bayer 1988, 1990) as well as in Germany (Robert-Koch-Institut 2017). Among the open questions were, for example, whether individuals can be obliged to take tests, whether the infection status of some should be made known to others, whether and how the isolation of infected individuals would be permissible, and how clinical measures and health policy could be shaped under these circumstances. In other words, there was a need for ethical guidance in the face of new scientific and social challenges, here in medicine and public health, against the background of uncertainties about clinical and epidemiological aspects. It is noticeable in statements of ethics committees and working groups in this period that there were relevant, available ethical and legal frameworks, but it was unclear how exactly these could be applied to the specific aspects and consequences of the new disease. In an extensive statement from 1988, the French CCNE explains that the government has far-reaching options for action to contain epidemics from a legal point of view, but that their use should be necessary and proportionate (CCNE 1988, p. 8). Particularly relevant from an ethical perspective is the question of how to deal with information on the HIV status of individuals (CCNE 2009, pp. 9–16). The statement rejects a duty to report HIV infections and envisions compulsory testing only in the case of blood, organ, tissue, egg or sperm donations. For other scenarios, compulsory testing is either viewed critically or completely rejected since respect, freedom, and privacy of the individual are affected to an unacceptable extent. However, those who test positive should be informed of their HIV status. In addition, the public should be widely informed about the state of research. Other

National Ethics Committees such as the Luxembourgian Commission Nationale Consultative d'Ethique pour les Sciences de la Vie et de la Santé (CNE 1992) and the Portuguese Conselho Nacional de Ética para as Ciências da Vida (CNECV 1996) followed with substantially similar assessments. Statements like these illustratehow individual and collective risk-benefit considerations of different measures were an important point of concern on which National Ethics Committees provided guidance to decision-makers and the public. However, at the national levels such committees were much less common than they are today. More recent statements, for example from the Tunisian Comité National d'Ethique Médicale (CNEM 2009), deal with the prevention and treatment of HIV under the specific circumstances in the respective legal framework, health system and social context, for example ethically relevant aspects such as stigma, awareness-raising and access to health services.

3.2 SARS

The volume of publications from National Ethics Committees on the first major epidemic of the new millennium is more limited: although observers rated the SARS epidemic as a dramatic wake-up call that underscores the global interdependence of risks posed by new infectious diseases, requires global coordination, cooperation, and solidarity (Singer et al. 2003), and raises conflicts between public health, privacy, and freedom of movement (Gostin et al. 2003), we are not aware of SARS-focused position statements from National Ethics Committees. However, a widely received report on public health from the British Nuffield Council takes SARS as one of its case studies to illustrate ethical issues that arise in the prevention, transnational surveillance, and containment of disease outbreaks (Nuffield Council on Bioethics 2007, esp. pp. 70 ff.). Given the current pandemic caused by Sars-Cov-2, it might nevertheless be surprising that SARS was not discussed more systematically by National Ethics Committees. Part of this finding can be explained by the fact that National ethics Committees did not exist or had only recently been established in countries affected by SARS. Some of these Committees had other focus areas, e.g. the Bioethics Advisory Committee Singapore, which specializes in research ethics. Furthermore, the SARS epidemic, with a total of just over 8,000 confirmed infections worldwide (Chan-Yeung and Xu 2003), took a relatively benign course. Given that it was possible to control SARS relatively quickly, other diseases were the subject of at least some statements from National Ethics Committees in subsequent years. Regardless of which pathogen should trigger the next pandemic, SARS underlined that ethical questions would arise, *inter alia*, with regard to resource allocation, the rights and duties of health care workers, the permissible extent of restrictions on freedom, and international cooperation in public health emergencies.

3.3 *Pandemic Influenza*

The pandemic scenario considered most likely in the following years was an outbreak of influenza caused by new zoonotic pathogens, i.e. viruses transmitted from animals to humans, in particular avian influenza A/H5N1. WHO highlighted a range of ethical challenges posed by influenza pandemics (World Health Organization 2007, 2008; Schröder-Bäck et al. 2008). National Ethics Committees published relevant guidance documents. For example, the New Zealand National Ethics Advisory Committee—Kāhui Matatika o te Motu emphasizes the need for prior planning and preparedness (NEAC 2007). In order to support this process, the Committee defines procedural and material ethical values which it considers action-guiding for managing epidemic outbreaks in New Zealand. This value framework is applied in a detailed discussion of two case studies and explains how values such as respect (manaakitanga), neighborhood (whānaungatanga) and unity (kotahitanga) can be implemented, e.g. by combining measures that preserve privacy and freedom as much as possible and by providing support to vulnerable groups.

A statement by the French CCNE (2009) also reads familiar from today's perspective. It anticipates the time pressure caused by rapidly increasing case numbers in the event of a pandemic, initial epistemic uncertainties about new epidemiological characteristics of the disease, the delay until new vaccines are available (assumed to be several weeks) and gaps in knowledge with regard to the effectiveness of different strategies for containment. According to the CCNE, it is precisely in the light of such expectations that prior reflection, clarification, and transparent communication are needed as to how, in the event of a pandemic, conflicting values should be balanced in order to be able to act in a timely and principle-oriented manner.

3.4 *Ebola*

The role of National Ethics Committees focusing on research ethics can be illustrated using the example of the Ebola epidemic in West Africa, which began in 2014. The combination of infection risk, high mortality, fragile health systems, and the lack of tested or effective therapeutics created a particular sense of urgency. One of the burning questions was whether and how experimental interventions can be used in an attempt to save lives and to contain the epidemic as much as possible (Fauci 2014; Joffe 2014). One example is the antibody mix "zMapp", which showed promising results in animal experiments (Qiu et al. 2014), but was scarce, expensive, and not systematically tested in humans. In principle, it seemed conceivable to take certain risks in an emergency like the Ebola epidemic (Rid and Emanuel 2014). Still, a number of open ethical questions needed to be addressed. For example, it was not immediately clear how the rapid clinical application of experimental interventions could be carried out responsibly, how patients could be helped and knowledge could be generated systematically at the same time, how approval processes could be streamlined, and how sustainable benefits could be generated for local populations. National Committees such as the Nigerian National Health Research Ethics Committee (NHREC 2014) decided in this context that the use of experimental interventions that are reasonably likely to be beneficial to patients can be carried out without prior consultation with a state research agency. Care should be taken to document the experimental use carefully and to conduct clinical studies as soon as possible. The export of biomaterials should also be allowed without a Material Transfer Agreement in order to speed up international research. Statements like these illustrate how National Ethics Committees apply research ethics standards during acute outbreaks in light of risk-benefit and fairness considerations for individual patients and the population as a whole. Committees of the countries most affected by Ebola in 2014, i.e., Guinea, Ivory Coast and Liberia, were practically confronted with a flood of clinical studies overnight. In Guinea, for example, the number of studies to be assessed increased from an average of less than ten per year to over 100 in 2014 and 2015 (Oumou Bah Sow, personal communication). Given the enormous time pressure and various attempts at influence both at national and international levels, it was not always easy to make an independent decision. These challenges and other ethical aspects of research processes in health emergencies are dealt with in a report published by the British Nuffield Council shortly before the start of the Covid pandemic (Nuffield Council on Bioethics 2020a).

Finally, reference is made to the previously mentioned role of National Ethics Committees in stimulating and strengthening public discourse on bioethical issues. This claim is taken up in a comprehensive statement on the Ebola epidemic by the US Presidential Commission for the Study of Bioethical Issues (2015). The Commission not only emphasized the need for prevention and preparedness, informed by both medical-technical competence and expertise from public health ethics. A recurring theme in the statement is of a procedural nature: the demand for mechanisms of democratic deliberation. In the event of unavoidable differences of opinion on the ethical desirability of certain courses of action, such mechanisms should facilitate a proactive, open, transparent, and evidence-based discourse on decision-making. This would not only ameliorate the effectiveness and legitimacy of measures taken, but would also improve preparations for future epidemics (cf. also Fenton et al. 2015).

4 National Ethics Committees and Covid-19

Covid-19 has once again underlined how epidemics and pandemics raise difficult ethical challenges. Since the beginning of the Covid-19 pandemic, the number of requests to National Ethics Committees has increased sharply in many countries, and a large number of statements have been published in a relatively short time. The World Health Organization, which as mentioned acts as the secretariat of the Global Summit of National Ethics Committees, promoted exchange among National Ethics Committees at global and regional levels and organized several online conferences on various ethical issues raised by Covid-19. Tables 1 and 2 provide an overview of some of the recurring ethical concepts and thematic priorities in Covid-19-related publications by National Ethics Committees. To a certain extent, both levels show continuity with previous work as outlined in Sect. 3, but new aspects and issues also come into focus.

It is striking that almost all statements by National Ethics Committees refer to solidarity in their positions, discussions and deliberations (see also the contribution by Kieslich and Prainsack in Chap. 3 of this book). On the one hand, this concerns the link between the welfare of individuals and the general public. On the other hand, solidarity is discussed with regard to the relationship between the welfare of individual countries and the global community, for example with regard to access to and distribution of diagnostics, therapeutics and vaccines (e.g. Belgian Consultative Committee on Bioethics 2020a; Department of Health, Ireland 2020; Nuffield Council on Bioethics 2020b). Several statements also draw a connection between solidarity and responsibility (e.g. CCNE 2020; CNB 2020; Deutscher Ethikrat 2020b): in a pandemic, responsible action, including properly understood individual responsibility, requires solidarity. Restrictions and other efforts are not only in the self-interest of individuals, but are also required to support society as such and in particular groups of people with elevated risk profiles. Other frequently mentioned values include respect for moral status and minimization of harm (see Tab. 1).

In response to rising case numbers, numerous countries have implemented large-scale restrictions on individual freedom of movement or social interaction. In the past, the ethical aspects of such measures were certainly on the agenda, but reflection on their use remained either hypothetical or prospective (NEAC 2007; Nuffield Council on Bioethics 2007) or did not apply to entire populations, but to individual individuals or patients, e.g. in the case of multidrug-resistant or extremely drug-resistant tuberculosis (Belgian Consultative Committee on Bioethics 2013). In the Covid-19 pandemic, National Ethics Committees are now discussing ethical frameworks for the nationwide, temporary restriction of freedom of movement.

There are at least two recurring themes in Committees' publications on this topic. First, they demand that awareness should be raised for the collateral damage of these necessary measures that must be taken seriously. Second, "opening up perspectives" (German Ethics Council 2020b, p. 6) are needed and restrictions are to be lifted again once their freedom-restricting aspects are no longer proportionate to their epidemiological effects. The latter demand is basically an application of the so-called "intervention ladder", a concept coined by the British Nuffield Council in its above-mentioned public health statement (Nuffield Council on Bioethics 2007, p. 41). According to the intervention ladder, which is also taken up repeatedly by other countries and organizations, the restriction of freedom and individual responsibility by state intervention is acceptable only to the extent that

Table 1 Selection of ethical concepts in the statements of National Ethics Committees during the Covid-19 pandemic

Concept	Addressed e.g. by	Quote
Solidarity	France, Comité Consultatif National d'Ethique pour les sciences de la vie et de la santé, "Enjeux éthiques face à une pandémie. Réponse à la saisine du ministre en charge de la santé et de la solidarité", 13.03.2020	"A just balance must be found between the need for collective solidarity, in particular towards vulnerable people, and the affirmation of autonomy" (p. 3; our translation). "It is essential to recall that a decision affecting an individual restriction of freedom has as its primary goal to protect the entire population in a spirit of solidarity" (p. 6; our translation).
Responsibility	Republic of Korea, National Bioethics Committee, "Statement on the COVID-19 pandemic from the Chair of Korean National Bioethics Committee", undated	"The public must endeavor to ensure the wellbeing of our society by adhering to social distancing and infection prevention measures with a sense of responsibility as community members" (p. 3).
Minimization of harm	Sweden, Swedish Council on Medical Ethics, "Ethical choices in a pandemic", 12.05.2020	Harm is unavoidable during a pandemic. The overarching objective in a pandemic should be to minimise harm and save lives" (p. 11).
Rights, e.g. human rights, fundamental rights	Mexico, Comisión Nacional de Bioética, "Bioethics in the face of the COVID-19 pandemic", 12.03.2020	"During infectious disease outbreaks, countries must respect their obligations under international human rights agreements, such as the *Siracusa Principles on Limitation and Repeal Provisions of the International Covenant on Civil and Political Rights*" (p. 3).
Human dignity	Germany, German Ethics Council, "Solidarity and responsibility in the Corona crisis", 27.03.2020	"The guarantee of human dignity requires an egalitarian basic equality and thus a corresponding basic protection from discrimination for all" (p. 3; our translation).
Vulnerability	Belarus, Committee on Bioethics, "Statement of the Committee on Bioethics of the Republic of Belarus", 08.04.2020	"We believe that the priority attention today should be paid to the problems of vulnerable population – first of all, persons with disabilities, elderly people, refugees, people infected with Covid-19 or suffering from other serious diseases, and other categories of citizens."
Freedom	Ireland, Department of Health, "Ethical framework for decision-making in a pandemic", 27.03.2020	"Restrictive measures, such as limiting freedom of movement of individuals and/or introducing social distancing measures, may be necessary in the management of a pandemic. This could include closing schools, cancelling public gatherings and sporting events, limiting travel, and imposing quarantine and isolation measures. Such measures illustrate the potential tension between individual rights and the collective good, and require consideration of how justifiable it is to restrict individual rights and freedoms in order to achieve certain public health goals" (p. 13).

(continued)

Table 1 (continued)

Concept	Addressed e.g. by	Quote
Justice	Belgium, Beratender Ausschuss für Bioethik, "Avis n° 75 du 11 décembre 2020 relatif aux repères éthiques en vue du déploiement de la vaccination anti-COVID-19 au bénéfice de la population belge", 11.12.2020	"Justice and equity are not just issues that are relevant at the national or local level. Initiatives such as the one set up with the COVAX alliance are essential and should be actively encouraged" (p. 31; our translation)
Respect	United Kingdom, Nuffield Council on Bioethics, "Ethical considerations in responding to the COVID-19 pandemic", 17.03.2020	"While it may in some circumstances be proportionate to restrict people's liberties (even in quite draconian ways, such as through extended quarantine), this must be done in a way that shows respect for them as individuals—of equal moral worth with all others" (p. 4).
Transparency	Canada, Public Health Ethics Committee, Commission on Ethics in Science and Technology, "Framework for reflection on ethical issues related to the COVID-19 pandemic", 03.04.2020	"The value of transparency specifically relates to information and its communication. It requires that the information transmitted to the concerned public be available in a timely, easily understandable and useful manner. Transparency therefore does not require that all the information possessed by decision-makers be transmitted: dissemination must be calibrated in order to allow recipients to use it in an informed manner" (p. 4; our translation).
Trust	Portugal, National Council of Ethics for the Life Sciences, "Public Health Emergency Situation due to the Covid-19 Pandemic", April 2020	"Actions and different steps taken in the context of healthcare emergencies must be timely and clearly explained and their technical and scientific support should reach all population by the use of an adequate discourse. Only then can trust, awareness and responsibility of citizens be reinforced towards a social commitment to comply to public health strategies (confinement, social distancing, hand hygiene, personal protection)" (p. 9).
Evidence-based decision-making	Italy, National Committee for Bioethics, "COVID-19: Public health, individual freedom, social solidarity", 28.05.2020	"Especially if it is deemed necessary to adopt the most restrictive measures, these should be justified by evidence of their effectiveness. However, in relation to this last requirement, the limits must be underlined at this stage, in consideration of the still insufficient knowledge on the virus and its methods of spreading" (p. 11).

it is necessary and proportionate. As the German Ethics Council states in view of Covid-19, balancing benefits and harms of such measures is "only legitimate insofar as they do not permanently undermine or even destroy basic and human

Table 2 Selection of thematic priorities of national ethics committees during the Covid-19 pandemic

Topic	Addressed e.g. by	Quote
Restrictions on freedom of movement	Italy, National Committee for Bioethics, "COVID-19: Public health, individual freedom, social solidarity", 28.05.2020	"The ICB takes note of the exceptional nature of the threat posed by COVID-19 to the health of individuals and the community, which calls for renewed reflection a) on health, in its multiple dimensions (physical, psychological, social), b) on the relationship between individual health and public health, c) on the relationship between the principle of freedom and autonomy of the individual in managing his or her own health and the principle of solidarity. In considering the dialectic between these principles, the ICB considers it essential to distinguish between 'extraordinary' interventions (lockdown and limitation of citizens' freedom), adopted in the most acute phase of the pandemic and justified by the seriousness of the threat to public health 'ordinary' interventions, in line with current health policies" (p. 3).
Intensive medicine and triage	Austria, Bioethics Commission, "On the use of scarce resources in healthcare in the context of the Covid-19 pandemic", 31.03.2020	"With regard to decision-making in dilemmatic triage situations, international recommendations include the use of all possible support services, such as collegial consultations or clinical ethics consultation services, in order to distribute the decision-making burden across multiple shoulders and relieve the pressure of moral stress. Any triage, regardless of the constellation, still remains a dilemma because the decision to forego or discontinue a life-saving treatment indicated for one person in favor of another person cannot be justified in the context of ethical values and legal norms, especially since one life cannot be weighed against another in terms of its quality" (p. 13; our translation).
Digital contact tracing	Switzerland, National Ethics Commission in the field of Human Medicine NEK, "Contact Tracing as a tool for combating pandemics. Central aspects from the perspective of ethics", 06.04.2020	"In view of the foregoing considerations, the NEK-CNE concludes that ethical considerations do not fundamentally speak against the use of digital contact tracing. However, digital contact tracing can affect important interests and rights of the individual, in particular their privacy. Accordingly, digital contact tracing must be linked to the following conditions, which result in particular from the principle of proportionality" (p. 20; our translation).

(continued)

Table 2 (continued)

Topic	Addressed e.g. by	Quote
Vaccination strategies	Belgium, Comité Consultatif de Bioéthique de Belgique, "Opinion No. 75 of December 11, 2020 on ethical guidelines for the deployment of anti-COVID-19 vaccination for the benefit of the Belgian population", 11.12.2020	"The scale of prioritization that it [the Committee] proposes is a scale that takes into account the following values: the protection of the most vulnerable and social justice (in that it also includes a duty of reciprocity towards those who take a risk for the benefit of society). […] Justice and equity are not just issues that are relevant at the national or local level. Initiatives such as the one set up with the COVAX alliance are essential and should be actively encouraged" (p. 31; our translation).
Immunity certificates	Sweden, Swedish Council on Medical Ethics, "Ethical choices in a pandemic", 12.05.2020	"[I]ssuing immunity certificates raises a number of practical, medical, legal and ethical questions. One fundamental issue relates to how strong immunological protection against re-infection is, and how long it lasts. To date, there is no evidence for achieving short- or long-term immunity by having had the virus" (p. 54).
Communication	Canada, Public Health Ethics Committee, Commission on Ethics in Science and Technology, "Framework for reflection on the ethical issues related to the COVID-19 pandemic", 03.04.2020	"The prevention and protection measures (distancing, isolation, quarantine) put in place by the authorities must be communicated transparently in order to elicit the adherence of the greatest number. It has been shown that in the context of a pandemic, public health actions must be extremely well articulated in order not to jeopardize the population's trust in its government and in science, the latter being one of the foundations of public policy" (p. 8; our translation).
Ethics review	India, Indian Council of Medical Research, "National Guidelines for Ethics Committees Reviewing Biomedical & Health Research During COVID-19 Pandemic", April 2020	"In the ongoing COVID-19 pandemic situation, research has to take the front stage in order to tackle the novel challenges that have come to the fore in an unprecedented manner. There is need for extensive research to explore therapeutic options, deal with clinical challenges related to patient management and care, undertake epidemiological studies, fast track development of new diagnostic tools, identifying and tackling challenges impacting socio behavioural well-being, ways of reducing stigmatisation, need for quick research without compromising scientific integrity, sharing the samples, data transfer etc while protecting the rights, safety and well-being of research participants" (p. ii).

(continued)

Table 2 (continued)

Topic	Addressed e.g. by	Quote
Research	Saudi Arabia, The National Committee of Bioethics, "Guidelines for Research on Living Creatures in Epidemics/Pandemics and Emergencies", 12.04.2020	"The preparedness system [of research institutions] should include Standard Operating Procedures (SOPs) that can be efficiently adopted in current and future epidemics/pandemics and emergencies. […] Procedures for communication between research institutions (and their respective IRB/LECs [institutional review boards/local ethics committees]) and relevant national authorities (MOH, Weqaya or other organizations in health care) should be specified in the SOPs" (p. 6).
Care sector	Germany, German Ethics Council, "Minimum Social Contacts in Long-Term Care during the Covid-19 Pandemic", 18.12.2020	"The basic idea of § 28a para. 2 sentence 2 of the Infection Protection Act, according to which a minimum level of social contacts must be maintained, must be consistently observed and implemented in all forms of restrictions on visits and contacts in long-term care facilities. […] The minimum level of social contacts should not be abstract and general, but rather determined from the individual perspective of the respective resident and their life situation" (p. 3; our translation).
Deliberative Mechanisms	United Kingdom, Nuffield Council on Bioethics, "COVID-19 and the basics of democratic governance", 25.04.2020	"We have set out in earlier blogs […] our concerns about obscurity and lack of engagement in decision-making; about how important transparency is for trust and trustworthiness. Let us now be completely clear about what we think this means for the UK Government. It should: • Show us (the public) what it is doing and thinking across the range of issues of concern • Set out the ethical considerations that inform(ed) its judgements • Explain how it has arrived at decisions (including taking advice from e.g. SAGE, MEAG), and not that it is just 'following the science' • Invite a broad range of perspectives into the room, including wider public representation • Think ahead—consult and engage other civic interests. These exhortations arise from the basic principles of democratic governance."

rights or other fundamental values. Even the required protection of human life is not absolute. The rights of freedom and participation as well as economic, social, and cultural rights should notbe unconditionally subordinated to it" (Deutscher Ethikrat 2020b, p. 5).

In the case of Covid-19, these measures have a special urgency: as argued for example by the Austrian Bioethics Commission (2020, p. 8), they are carried out out of a social responsibility to avoid dilemma situations in clinical care as much as possible. The reports from Wuhan and Bergamo have shown to the world that Covid-19 could lead to resource scarcity in intensive care, which might necessitate triage. In the past, National Ethics Committees have worked on resource allocation, scarcity, and possible rationing at the level of health systems and their financing (e.g. NHMRC 1993; CNB 1998; Deutscher Ethikrat 2011), but less often with an explicit focus on specific clinical decision-making scenarios. An exception is the National Bioethics Committee of the Republic of San Marino (CSB 2017), which deals with triage in a statement on the ethics of disaster medicine. In addition to the requirement that every human life must be respected regardless of age, gender, ethnicity, social status or abilities, this statement does not formulate any further substantive criteria, but focuses on the demand for clearly defined procedures, their consistent application in the event of a disaster, and the corresponding training of medical personnel. With regard to Covid-19, criteria tend to be formulated by medical and health-care professional organizations in the form of guidelines for clinical practice (Joebges and Biller-Andorno 2020). In line with the function of National Ethics Committees to pool expertise, Committee statements also point to these existing instruments as well as to the need to apply and balance criteria such as equality, saving as many lives or live years as possible, and prioritizing certain groups (Emanuel et al. 2020). The German Ethics Council (Deutscher Ethikrat 2020b, pp. 3–4) refers to the criteria formulated in the guidelines of professional societies, but points out that human dignity and the principle of equality do not allow state-level balancing on the basis of parameters such as age and prognosed life expectancy; thus, the active termination of an indicated treatment of one patient in favour of another "is not objectively legal" (Deutscher Ethikrat 2020b, p.4). Overall, this is a position for which the Council also received criticism (Ehni et al. 2020, pp. 483 f.). The Belgian Consultative Committee on Bioethics (2020b, p. 14) shares some specific evaluations, e.g. the inadmissibility of making medical care dependent on age or individual risk behaviour. But above all, the Committee recognises that these criteria themselves, their concretisation, and balancing are the subject of debate and controversy. Against this background, it calls for recognition of the fact that there is no unanimity on these questions, and that relevant discourses and deliberations must thus be continued and fostered proactively.

National Ethics Committees also provide guidance on further Covid-19-related issues such as digital contact tracing and the distribution of vaccines (see Tab. 2) by systematising current knowledge and providing expertise in connection with the context-sensitive assessment of different options. With regard to the immunity certificates mentioned at the outset, the German Ethics Council eventually advised against their introduction in autumn 2020 in view of uncertainties about immunity, infectiousness, and the informativeness of antibody tests (Deutscher Ethikrat 2020c). The Council announced that it was divided on the question of whether immunity certificates would be justifiable "if the scientific and medical prerequisites develop favourably" (Deutscher Ethikrat 2020d). This once again underlines how National Ethics Committees, in addition to formulating concrete recommendations, can mark ambiguity and open questions and encourage further debate.

5 Summary and Outlook

National Ethics Committees provide expertise at the interface of ethics, research, and policy-making. They issue ethical guidance on the identification, evaluation, and weighing of different options. In view of the complexity, urgency, and significance of decision-making processes in times of pandemics, Covid-19 has further increased public awareness of the work of these bodies. Many decision-makers in countries with existing National Ethics Committees have consulted the expertise and advice of their Committees in this exceptional situation. It remains to be seen whether countries without a National Ethics Committee will receive an additional impetus for their establishment as a result of the Covid-19 pandemic.

National Ethics Committees differ in their structures and functions (Sec. 2). Many of the Committees advise policy-makers, review and accompany research activities, and strengthen public discourse on bioethical issues. The statements of National Ethics Committees have traditionally focused on research ethics and new technologies in medicine and the clinic, but have also repeatedly addressed infectious diseases such as HIV, influenza, and Ebola (Sec. 3). Covid-19 demonstrates how outbreaks of infectious diseases raise and intensify ethical challenges. National Ethics Committees have been involved in policy and public discourse from the beginning of the pandemic and have offered ethical orientation on issues which certainly had received attention by bioethicists in the past, but which rarely had to be translated into concrete decisions at the national and global levels with such urgency and significance (Sec. 4). Among other things, National Ethics Committees have highlighted the importance of solidarity in the face of mutual dependencies, the implications of such dependencies for responsible action, and the importance of necessity and proportionality when assessing public health measures. Not all judgments are as clear-cut as in the case of immunity certificates, on which the German Ethics Council ultimately issued a negative advice to the Minister of Health in view of remaining scientific questions about immunity and antibody tests. Indeed, statements often point to open questions and tensions. Based on this, they outline corridors for further political and public discourse and decision-making.

As mentioned in Sec. 2, National Ethics Committees, their statements, and their influence are not automatically legitimate and authoritative, but can certainly be measured and criticized by reference to different standards, e.g. independence and transparency. Even if no detailed discussion or evaluation of such standards—or the work of National Ethics Committees in light of these standards—is carried out within the context of this text, it should nevertheless be pointed out that it can and should be continuously debated to what extent National Ethics Committees succeed in making heard the voices and perspectives of the various stakeholders. Various further issues deserve continued attention: whether and when advice, expertise, and orientation take on a directive character or even compete with parliamentary processes, whether and when proximity to political decision-making processes possibly undermines independence, whether Committees always deal sensitively enough with indeterminacy and pluralism, and/or whether *National* Ethics Committees have paid sufficient attention to *global* issues. This is merely a selection of questions about the roles of National Ethics Committees that can and should be debated during and beyond the Covid-19 pandemic—a discourse to which the National Ethics Committees themselves would and should encourage us.

Acknowledgements For helpful feedback on an earlier version of this text, we are very grateful to Peter Dabrock, Serena Bischoff, David Samhammer and the editors of this volume.

References

Annas GJ (1994) Will the real bioethics (commission) please stand up? Hast Cent Rep 24:19–21. https://doi.org/10.2307/3562381. Accessed 31 Jan 2021

Archard D, Dabrock P, Delfraissy J-F (2020) Human-genome editing: ethics councils call to governments worldwide. Nature 579:29. https://doi.org/10.1038/d41586-020-00614-3. Accessed 31 Jan 2021

Ärzte-Zeitung (2020) Ethikrat soll Stellung zu Corona-Immunitätsausweis nehmen (3. Mai 2020). AerzteZeitung.de. https://www.aerztezeitung.de/Politik/Ethikrat-soll-Stellung-zu-Corona-Immunitaetsausweis-nehmen-409096.html. Accessed 31 Jan 2021

Bagheri A, Moreno JD, Semplici S (eds) (2016) Global bioethics: the impact of the UNESCO international bioethics committee. Springer, Cham

Bayer R (1988) AIDS and the ethics of public health: challenges posed by a maturing epidemic. AIDS 2:S217–S222

Bayer R (1990) AIDS and the future of reproductive freedom. Milbank Q 68:179–204

Becker KB, Schmoll H (2020) Corona: Warum der Immunitätsausweis vorerst gescheitert ist. FAZ.NET. https://www.faz.net/1.6755649. Accessed 31 Jan 2021

Belgischer Beratender Ausschuss für Bioethik (2013) Gutachten Nr. 55 vom 13. Mai 2013 über die Behandlung von Patienten mit multiresistenter Tuberkulose vom Standpunkt des Schutzes der öffentlichen Gesundheit aus. Brussels

Belgischer Beratender Ausschuss für Bioethik (2020a) Avis n° 75 du 11 décembre 2020 relatif aux repères éthiques en vue du déploiement de la vaccination anti-COVID-19 au bénéfice de la population belge. Brussels

Belgischer Beratender Ausschuss für Bioethik (2020b) Aspects éthiques relatifs à la priorisation des soins en période de COVID-19. Brussels

Bioethikkommission Österreich (2020) Zum Umgang mit knappen Ressourcen in der Gesundheitsversorgung im Kontext der Covid-19-Pandemie. Wien

Bouësseau M-C, Reis AA, Ho WC (2011) Global Summit of National Ethics Committees: an essential tool for international dialogue and consensus-building. Indian J Med Ethics 8:154–157. https://doi.org/10.20529/IJME.2011.062. Accessed 31 Jan 2021

Capron AM (2017) Building the next bioethics commission. Hastings Cent Rep 47:S4–S9. https://doi.org/10.1002/hast.710. Accessed 31 Jan 2021

CCNE (1988) Avis sur les problèmes éthiques posés par la lutte contre la diffusion de l'infection par le virus de l'immuno-déficience humaine (VIH). Rapport. Comité Consultatif National d'Ethique pour les sciences de la vie et de la santé [Frankreich], Paris

CCNE (1993) La coopération dans le domaine de la recherche biomédicale entreéquipes françaises et équipes de pays en voie de développementéconomique. Rapport. Comité Consultatif National d'Ethique pour les sciences de la vie et de la santé [Frankreich], Paris

CCNE (2009) Questions éthiques soulevées par une possible pandémie grippale. Comité Consultatif National d'Ethique pour les sciences de la vie et de la santé [Frankreich], Paris

CCNE (2020) Enjeux éthiques face à une pandémie. Réponse à la saisine du ministre en charge de la santé et de la solidarité. Comité Consultatif National d'Ethique pour les sciences de la vie et de la santé [Frankreich], Paris

Chan-Yeung M, Xu R-H (2003) SARS: epidemiology. Respirology 8:S9–S14. https://doi.org/10.1046/j.1440-1843.2003.00518.x. Accessed 31 Jan 2021

CNB (1998) Etica, sistema sanitario e risorse. Comitato Nazionale per la Bioetica (Italien)

CNB (2020) Covid-19: public health, individual freedom, social solidarity. Comitato Nazionale per la Bioetica [Italien], Rom

CNE (1992) Avis au sujet de tests de dépistage obligatoires de l'infectionpar le virus HIV. Commission Nationale Consultative d'Ethique pour les Sciences de la Vie et de la Santé, Luxemburg

CNECV (1996) Parecer sobre a Obrigatoriedade dos Testes da Sida (16/CNECV/96). Conselho Nacional de Ética para as Ciências da Vida [Portugal], Lissabon

CNEM (2009) Le VIH-SIDA, problèmes éthiques et juridiques. Comité National d'éthique médicale [Tunesien], Tunis

CSB (2017) Bioethics of disasters. National Bioethics Committee of Republic of San Marino

Department of Health (2020) Ethical framework for decision-making in a pandemic. Irland

Deutscher Ethikrat (2011) Nutzen und Kosten im Gesundheitswesen – Zur normativen Funktion ihrer Bewertung Stellungnahme. Deutscher Ethikrat, Berlin

Deutscher Ethikrat (2018) Global health, global ethics, global justice. In: 11th global summit of national ethics/bioethics committees, Berlin/Germany, 16–18 March 2016. Deutscher Ethikrat, Berlin

Deutscher Ethikrat (2020a) Infobrief 01/20. https://www.ethikrat.org/fileadmin/Publikationen/Infobrief/infobrief-01-20-web.pdf. Accessed 31 Jan 2021

Deutscher Ethikrat (2020b) Solidarity and responsibility during the Coronavirus crisis. Deutscher Ethikrat, Berlin

Deutscher Ethikrat (2020c) Immunitätsbescheinigungen in der Covid-19-Pandiemie. Deutscher Ethikrat, Berlin

Deutscher Ethikrat (2020d) Press release 07/2020: German Ethics Council currently advises against Covid-19 immunity certificates. /https://www.ethikrat.org/en/press-releases/press-releases/2020/german-ethics-council-currently-advises-against-covid-19-immunity-certificates/. Accessed 31 Jan 2021

Deutsches Ärzteblatt (2020) SARS-CoV-2: Spahn bittet Ethikrat um Stellungnahme zu Immunitätsausweis (4. Mai 2020). https://www.aerzteblatt.de/nachrichten/112538/SARS-CoV-2-Spahn-bittet-Ethikrat-um-Stellungnahme-zu-Immunitaetsausweis. Accessed 31 Jan 2021

Dodds S, Thomson C (2006) Bioethics and democracy: competing roles of national bioethics organisations. Bioethics 20:326–338. https://doi.org/10.1111/j.1467-8519.2006.00511.x. Accessed 31 Jan 2021

Effa P, Massougbodji A, Ntoumi F et al (2007) Ethics committees in Western and Central Africa: concrete foundations. Dev World Bioeth 7:136–142. https://doi.org/10.1111/dewb_172.x. Accessed 31 Jan 2021

Ehni H-J, Wiesing U, Ranisch R (2020) Entscheidungen unter akutem Ressourcenmangel: Europäische Triage-Empfehlungen in der COVID-19-Pandemie. Zeitschrift für medizinische Ethik:475–488. https://doi.org/10.14623/zfme.2020.4.475-488. Accessed 31 Jan 2021

Emanuel EJ, Persad G, Upshur R et al (2020) Fair allocation of scarce medical resources in the time of Covid-19. N Engl J Med. https://doi.org/10.1056/NEJMsb2005114. Accessed 31 Jan 2021

Ethikratgesetz vom 16. Juli 2007 (BGBl. I S. 1385)

Fauci AS (2014) Ebola – underscoring the global disparities in health care resources. https://doi.org/10.1056/NEJMp1409494. Accessed 31 Jan 2021

Fenton E, Chillag K, Michael NL (2015) Ethics preparedness for public health emergencies: recommendations from the presidential bioethics commission. Am J Bioeth 15:77–79. https://doi.org/10.1080/15265161.2015.1054162. Accessed 31 Jan 2021

Friele MB (2003) Do committees ru(i)n the bio-political culture? On the democratic legitimacy of bioethics committees. Bioethics 17:301–318. https://doi.org/10.1111/1467-8519.00347. Accessed 31 Jan 2021

Fuchs M (2005) Nationale Ethikräte. Hintergründe, Funktionen und Arbeitsweisen im Vergleich. Nationaler Ethikrat, Berlin

Gefenas E, Lukaseviciene V (2017) International capacity-building initiatives for national bioethics committees. Hastings Cent Rep 47:S10–S13. https://doi.org/10.1002/hast.711. Accessed 31 Jan 2021

Global Summit of National Ethics Committees (2018) Call for action: bioethics, sustainable development and societies. In: 12th Global Summit of National Ethics Committees. Dakar

Gostin LO, Bayer R, Fairchild AL (2003) Ethical and legal challenges posed by severe acute respiratory syndromeimplications for the control of severe infectious disease threats. JAMA 290:3229–3237. https://doi.org/10.1001/jama.290.24.3229 Accessed 31 Jan 2021

Hummel P, Adam T, Reis AA, Littler K (2021) Taking stock of the availability and functions of National Ethics Committees worldwide. BMC Med Ethics 22:56. https://doi.org/10.1186/s12910-021-00614-6

Joebges S, Biller-Andorno N (2020) Ethics guidelines on COVID-19 triage—an emerging international consensus. Crit Care 24:201. https://doi.org/10.1186/s13054-020-02927-1. Accessed 31 Jan 2021

Joffe S (2014) Evaluating novel therapies during the ebola epidemic. JAMA 312:1299–1300. https://doi.org/10.1001/jama.2014.12867. Accessed 31 Jan 2021

Kirigia JM, Wambebe C, Baba-Moussa A (2005) Status of national research bioethics committees in the WHO African region. BMC Med Ethics 6:10. https://doi.org/10.1186/1472-6939-6-10. Accessed 31 Jan 2021

Köhler J, Reis AA, Saxena A (2021) A survey of national ethics and bioethics committees. Bull World Health Organ 99:138–147. https://doi.org/10.2471/BLT.19.243907 Accessed 31 Jan 2021

Langlois A (2014) The UNESCO bioethics programme. New Bioeth 20:3–11. https://doi.org/10.1179/2050287714Z.00000000040. Accessed 31 Jan 2021

Leinhos M (2005) The US National Bioethics Advisory Commission as a boundary organization. Sci Public Policy 32:423–433. https://doi.org/10.3152/147154305781779308. Accessed 31 Jan 2021

Mali F, Pustovrh T, Groboljsek B, Coenen C (2012) National ethics advisory bodies in the emerging landscape of responsible research and innovation. NanoEthics 6:167–184. https://doi.org/10.1007/s11569-012-0157-z. Accessed 31 Jan 2021

Montgomery J (2017) The virtues of national ethics committees. Hastings Cent Rep 47:S24–S27. https://doi.org/10.1002/hast.715. Accessed 31 Jan 2021
NEAC (2007) Getting through together. Ethical values for a pandemic. National Ethics Advisory Committee—Kāhui Matatika o te Motu [Neuseeland], Wellington
NHMRC (1993) Ethical considerations relating to health care resource allocation decisions. National Health and Medical Research Council [Australien]
NHREC (2014) Statement on the use of innovative or non-validated medical treatment in Nigeria. National Health Research Ethics Committee of Nigeria, Abuja
Nuffield Council on Bioethics (2007) Public health: ethical issues. Nuffield Council on Bioethics, London
Nuffield Council on Bioethics (2020a) Research in global health emergencies: ethical issues. Nuffield Council on Bioethics, London
Nuffield Council on Bioethics (2020b) Fair and equitable access to COVID-19 treatments and vaccines. Nuffield Council on Bioethics, London
Presidential Commission for the Study of Bioethical Issues (2015) Ethics and Ebola. Public health planning and response. Washington, DC
Qiu X, Wong G, Audet J et al (2014) Reversion of advanced Ebola virus disease in nonhuman primates with ZMapp. Nature 514:47–53. https://doi.org/10.1038/nature13777. Accessed 31 Jan 2021
Rid A, Emanuel EJ (2014) Ethical considerations of experimental interventions in the Ebola outbreak. Lancet 384:1896–1899. https://doi.org/10.1016/S0140-6736(14)61315-5. Accessed 31 Jan 2021
Robert-Koch-Institut (2017) 1981 bis 1990: AIDS—die politische Dimension in den 1980er-Jahren. https://www.rki.de/DE/Content/Institut/Geschichte/Bildband_Salon/1981-1990.html. Accessed 31 Jan 2021
Ruiz de Chávez Guerrero MH, Pina RJ (eds) (2015) 10th Global Summit of National Ethics/Bioethics Committees—finding paths through the world: June 22–24, Mexico City 2014. Comisión Nacional de Bioética, Mexico City
Schmidt H, Schwartz JL (2016) The missions of national commissions: mapping the forms and functions of bioethics advisory bodies. Kennedy Inst Ethics J 26:431–456. https://doi.org/10.1353/ken.2016.0037. Accessed 31 Jan 2021
Schröder-Bäck P, Sass H-M, Brand H, Winter SF (2008) Ethische Aspekte eines Influenzapandemiemanagements und Schlussfolgerungen für die Gesundheitspolitik: Ein Überblick. Bundesgesundheitsbl 51:191–199. https://doi.org/10.1007/s00103-008-0449-1. Accessed 31 Jan 2021
Schüklenk U, Lott JP (2005) Bioethics and (public) policy advice. In: Thiele F, Ashcroft RE, Wütscher F (eds) Bioethics in a small world. Springer, Berlin, pp 129–138
Selgelid MJ (2005) Ethics and infectious disease. Bioethics 19:272–289. https://doi.org/10.1111/j.1467-8519.2005.00441.x. Accessed 31 Jan 2021
Siewert S, Dabrock P (2020) Pluralität achten—Nachdenklichkeit erzeugen—Orientierung anbieten: Der Deutsche Ethikrat als Spiegel und Katalysator gesellschaftlicher Debatten. In: Manzeschke A, Niederlag W (eds) Ethische Perspektiven auf Biomedizinische Technologie. de Gruyter, Berlin, pp 246–261
Singer PA, Benatar SR, Bernstein M et al (2003) Ethics and SARS: lessons from Toronto. BMJ 327:1342–1344. https://doi.org/10.1136/bmj.327.7427.1342. Accessed 31 Jan 2021
The Council for International Organizations of Medical Sciences (CIOMS) (2016) International ethical guidelines for biomedical research involving human subjects. Council for International Organizations of Medical Sciences (CIOMS), Geneva
UNESCO (2010) National bioethics committees in action. United Nations Educational, Scientific and Cultural Organization, Paris
World Health Organization (2007) Ethical considerations in developing a public health response to pandemic influenza. World Health Organization, Geneva

World Health Organization (2008) Addressing ethical issues in pandemic influenza planning. Discussion papers. World Health Organization, Geneva

World Health Organization Regional Office for the Eastern Mediterranean (2017) Eastern Mediterranean/Arab states regional summit of national ethics and bioethics committees. http://www.emro.who.int/rpc/rpc-events/regional-summit-of-national-ethics-and-bioethics-committees.html. Accessed 31 Jan 2021

World Health Organization Regional Office for the Western Pacific (2019) Second Asia-Pacific Regional Meeting for National Ethics/Bioethics Committees. Meeting report. https://apps.who.int/iris/handle/10665/330848. Accessed 31 Jan 2021

Clinical Ethics Consultation in the Covid-19 Pandemic. Practical Challenges for Safety and Quality

Andreas Frewer

Contents

1 Introduction . . . 303
2 Digital and Telephone Consultation for Safety from Infection . . . 305
3 Video Conferences for Protected Consultation in the Event of Covid-19 . . . 308
4 "Distancing" in Design and as an Object of Consultation . . . 309
5 Consequences of Covid-19 as a Topic of Ethics Consultation in the Clinic . . . 310
6 Consultation on Quality Assurance for Research and Clinical Trials . . . 312
7 Bedside Allocation? Ethics Advice on Triage and Justice . . . 313
8 Summary—Consultation for Quality Assurance in Medicine . . . 315
References . . . 319

1 Introduction

The Covid-19 pandemic is a great challenge and of high relevance for ethics and ethical counseling at all levels. Here, several areas of institutionalized ethics expertise need to be distinguished: ethics councils, ethics commissions and ethics committees.[1] The German Ethics Council (DER) advises the federal government's policy, coordinates with the Robert Koch Institute (RKI), the Standing Committee on Vaccination (STIKO) and the National Academy of Sciences (Leopoldina) the

[1] For the German-speaking area, it must be seen that the terminology in Switzerland uses the terms ethics commissions and ethics committees reversed. The example of the Federal Republic of Germany is used below. Of course, there are also other institutions in addition to the three mentioned bodies, such as the Central Ethics Commission at the German Medical Association (ZEKO) and others.

A. Frewer (✉)
Professorship for Ethics in Medicine, Erlangen-Nürnberg University, Erlangen, Germany
e-mail: andreas.frewer@fau.de

© The Author(s), under exclusive license to Springer-Verlag GmbH, DE, part of Springer Nature 2023

A. Reis et al. (eds.), *Pandemics and Ethics*,
https://doi.org/10.1007/978-3-662-66872-6_18

fight against epidemics and strategies between quarantine and lockdown, hygiene measures and vaccination priorities (see also the article by Hummel and Reis in this volume). Ethics commissions at the level of the federal states and medical associations as well as at the medical faculties are responsible for the evaluation of research applications and have to deal with the pandemic with the increased workload of faster and more comprehensive processing of studies for the scientific analysis of the various questions of dealing with this new disease and resulting follow-up problems. At the level of care in hospitals, clinical ethics committees are challenged by the resulting problems and questions in the context of Covid treatment measures as well as by the difficult conditions for the direct counseling of the affected persons. The latter level is the subject of the present contribution, which focuses on the practice of work in clinical ethics counseling and, based on counseling cases that have arisen, sheds light on requirements in everyday life.

For clinical ethics consultation at a university hospital of maximum care (Frewer and Hack 2019; Kaschube et al. 2019; Krull et al. 2019) there are special challenges in the pandemic, which are outlined in this overview article.[2] The aim is to present the structural peculiarities of consultation situations under Covid-19 conditions and to pass on experiences to other ethicists through the treatment or solution options we found. In this way, problems should be pointed out and hints given for coping as quickly as possible and even during the pandemic or upcoming new waves of infection (Bielefeldt et al. 2020; Frewer et al. 2020b). The focus of this chapter is the ethical reflection of dealing with the insecurity caused by the special pandemic conditions on all levels. For the background of ethics consultation, reference is made to the German literature, which has been growing steadily for more than one decade (Frewer et al. 2008; Groß et al. 2008; Dörries et al. 2010; Fröhlich 2014; Frewer 2019; ZEKO 2019).[3]

This article examines the different forms of (in)security (see also Frewer et al. 2020a as well as Peter and Funcke 2013) in clinical practice in relation to the type of ethical consultation carried out (2 and 3), problems relevant to safety measures (4) and "clinical side effects" of the pandemic (5). In addition, the aim is to discuss quality assurance for clinical trials and research (6) as well as the moral questions of distributive justice at the sickbed (7). Finally, summary considerations on safety and insecurity under the current conditions of the Covid-19 crisis and possible perspectives for the future (8) are presented.

[2] This article is a revised and expanded version of the article Frewer (2020). I would like to thank both publishers for their permission to use modified and updated sections of the article from the "Jahrbuch Ethik in der Klinik" (Königshausen & Neumann).

[3] For ethics consultation specifically at the University Hospital Erlangen, see, for example, Kaschube et al. (2019), Krull et al. (2019) and Frewer (2019) as well as for theory in particular Frewer and Hack (2019). For basics Frewer et al. (2012) and in general the Jahrbuch series (JEK).

2 Digital and Telephone Consultation for Safety from Infection

The tried and tested form of clinical ethics consultation, which is characterized by a direct conversation with all persons involved and which also integrates other affected parties in a discourse-ethical manner, can only be carried out to a limited extent or not at all due to the pandemic situation. In this respect, all requests since the beginning of 2020 have had direct and indirect references to the Covid-19 situation. The Clinical Ethics Committee at the University Hospital Erlangen[4] was initially faced with the task of finding alternative formats for consultations. For example, a case consultation requested ad hoc in mid-March 2020 was then carried out by three people from the office of the Clinical Ethics Committee by telephone under the circumstances; this variant of the usual consultation corresponded to the explicit wishes of the person making the request and the consensus of all parties involved. The following is a sketch of the content of the consultation, which serves to introduce the usual procedures in the work of Clinical Ethics Committees and Ethics Consultation Services. The focus was on the situation of a patient over 90 years of age who was treated in an intensive care unit. The general condition deteriorated after an operation. This was followed by a severe lung infection with sepsis, which was on the verge of multi-organ failure. At the time of the ethics consultation, the patient was neither arousable nor contactable; he was ventilated with an oxygen mask. The dosage of the drugs for stabilizing the circulation had reached considerable heights; a progressive decline in kidney function was observed. In addition, there was a comprehensive medical history, including heart attacks, the removal of a kidney due to a malignant tumor, and speech problems two years ago when there was suspicion of the onset of a dementia-related illness. In the overall view, the sick person was not competent to decide. The specific medical ethical question arose from the following constellation: The relatives of the sick person demanded “maximum therapy”. However, in view of the various symptoms and the unstable appearance, the question arose from the medical and nursing perspective of how—with special consideration of the patient’s well-being—the further course of therapy should be designed. It remained open to what extent the statutory guardians, the son and daughter of the patient, adequately took into account the patient’s presumed will when making the demand for a maximally further-reaching therapy. In view of the very poor prognosis, the treatment team was faced with the question of whether intubation and ventilation would merely mean prolonging the dying process. It was necessary to evaluate and discuss the

[4] The University Hospital Erlangen is a house of maximum care with around 1,500 beds and 7,000 employees. The Clinical Ethics Committee was initiated at the beginning of 2000 and is thus one of the first committees in university medicine. The Chair of Ethics in Medicine at the University of Erlangen-Nuremberg runs the office of the Ethics Committee and several working groups (Frewer 2019).

appropriateness of a therapy goal that was only questionable curative with a focus on the patient's well-being and the patient's will as well as the further course of action with regard to the wishes of the relatives.

Discussing this multi-layered case with the treatment team by telephone turned out to be a new and at the same time not ideal situation. On the one hand, it became clear that although there was a living will, its validity was doubtful due to several contradictory statements. The specific content of the living will was neither known nor able to be checked in detail on site at the time of the ad hoc scheduled ethics consultation. On the other hand, according to the medical and nursing assessment, a curative prognosis could no longer be assumed. Based on this assessment, the son and daughter, as legally appointed guardians, were informed of possible complications and a suggested change in therapy goals. Despite comprehensive medical clarification, the relatives continued to demand maximal therapeutic action. They justified this with the conviction that there was generally a particularly high life expectancy in the family. It was discussed to what extent doubts existed as to whether the authorized relatives still had the patient's welfare in mind, and whether the guardianship situation should therefore be checked. However, according to the assessment of the participating ethics counselors, this was not (yet) indicated, but rather the conversation should be sought again. It was explicitly stated that neither the patient's age nor the current situation in the context of the Covid-19 pandemic with possibly expected bottlenecks in ventilation places on the intensive care unit in the future were decisive arguments for the clinical assessment. In the background, such fears seemed to be present in view of the higher age. The ethics consultation was able to offer an important accompaniment, especially in the clarification and determination of further action in the interests of the patient. Since in this special case of a telephone consultation neither the patient nor his medical records or living will could be seen directly at first (as is usually the case), which was due to the unusual conversation situation, this circumstance should be mentioned in addition to the unusual conversation situation as a special challenge for comprehensive advice and recommendation by the ethics consultation. There are always cases for consultation in order to clarify the will of a patient who is unable to give consent or make decisions in more detail. However, a new and specifically pandemic-related problem was the somewhat anonymous situation of the consultation only by telephone. At this point it should be mentioned that, of course, at the time of the consultation, other and probably more personal consultation models, for example by means of Zoom or Skype conferences with the six other participants, were conceivable, but that at this time no final decisions had been made by the institutions with regard to the assessment of data protection or data security, nor any specific licenses had been issued. Although in this case trust could certainly be built up and confirmed in the conversation, neither the usual joint meeting around a table nor the visit to the patient's bedside could be carried out—to protect the participants—which was perceived as suboptimal by the ethics committee. In this context, the interpretation of the advance directive as a special sub-problem of the ad hoc telephone consultation was particularly perceived.

While the very timely and flexible appointment finding was a clear advantage, the inability to critically review the constellation on site was a hurdle to ensuring the quality of the ethics consultation. For example, when the contents of the directive were discussed by telephone, the ethics consultation team was specifically dependent on the fact that the person concerned from the clinic truthfully and accurately reported the facts. There was no reason whatsoever to doubt the reliable representation of the legal and ethical framework in this case, but it was, nevertheless, concluded as a partial experience that even in telephone consultations at least a "four-eyes principle" should be implemented. In each consultation place of a multilateral discussion group, ideally at least two persons (as independent as possible) should participate under protective measures. In this way, the immediate review and confirmation of the contents of the advance directive and the patient's file by another person would be possible. Since the (short-term possible) forwarding by email or fax is not desired in the sense of data protection and the postal transfer in a big hospital can take (too) long in individual cases, the synchronized and validated representation of the exact contents of key documents is of particular importance. As a specific feature of the pandemic constellation, the anticipated mistrust of the (foreign) family was added, which apparently could easily imagine a restriction of therapies due to the patient's advanced age and possibly impending shortage of ventilator places could, however, had little knowledge of the general framework conditions of sensible treatment options with a reasonable perspective. Here, the precise clarification and the winning of trust were important developments in order to align the sometimes irrational-seeming or represented demands and expectations on the part of the relatives in the light of clinical-ethical expertise in terms of practice; this could be guaranteed. In addition, intubation and ventilation with a course of observation was carried out as a clinical measure with further counseling offers, but was not continued after about a week due to the rapidly deteriorating function of several organ systems. In coordinated palliative care and accompanied by relatives—of course also under the necessary infection protection measures—the patient finally died. There was no shortage of ventilator beds. Intercultural problems or projections of age discrimination could be eliminated: A reference to the higher age of the patient was never a criterion for the procedure. The poor overall clinical constellation was decisive, which unfortunately often leads to the reflex of wishes for maximum therapy by relatives who first have to arrange themselves with such a difficult acute situation. All in all, this case has developed relatively normally in the context of the Covid-19 outbreak, but according to our experience, telephone-based clinical ethics consultations can only be recommended to a limited extent. Although the described consultation was evaluated by the treatment team as quite helpful, but the non-verbal communication and especially the direct conversation level were felt to be missing. Although a telephone consultation has the advantages of a quick and low-threshold offer, a video conference—which we will talk about right afterwards—can be seen as a better alternative.

3 Video Conferences for Protected Consultation in the Event of Covid-19

After the legal and practical framework conditions had been clarified, the format for "video conferences" acquired by the university under license was used (the trade name is omitted here for reasons of neutrality). At this point, it should be pointed out with a view to the European Data Protection Basic Regulation that 100% security is probably not achievable in all conference systems, but that previous important data gaps have been closed. The format of the video consultation concerned both the regular meetings of the consulting working group and the plenary sessions of the entire Ethics Committee as well as the individual case consultation in response to requests from the clinic. In this way, the video conference could establish itself as an important tool and as a good alternative to a telephone conversation. The addition of visual information makes the consultation situation more personal, although it is also associated with various other aspects for all participants: The wealth of impressions can be quite strenuous, and technical hurdles can arise again and again (picture, sound or general WLAN problems, etc.). In the best case, in this format, in addition to the distance rules, important tasks, familiar processes and a roughly comparable communication can be guaranteed by virtually achieving proximity and presence in a time of social or physical distancing. The gained eye contact is particularly relevant for the preference for video consultation over telephone consultation; by being able to see each other, not only trust is built up, but communication is also significantly improved. However, these positive effects were accompanied by challenges, such as the sometimes occurring difficulty of ensuring access to suitable devices with a camera for all participants; since in some cases the necessary equipment was not yet available on computers in the clinical area, new hurdles arose for a common and uniform consultation situation. Although an ethics consultation by video conference has long been the established and usual form, there are still further specificities. The exchange over longer periods of time is experienced by some people as problematic; more extensive consultation processes become more difficult in this way. Technical restrictions can temporarily impair access or the smooth running, but after an introduction by the office of the Ethics Committee, all participants have quickly got used to the framework conditions. While on the one hand the restriction of personal-direct contacts is still experienced as a certain deficit, on the other hand the flexibility and accuracy of the video consultations are also perceived as positive. The sequence of hand movements in discussion processes can be technically mapped just as well as the carrying out of—anonymous—voting processes by means of prepared forms.

Overall, the use of video conferencing in the clinical ethics consultation setting appears to be a valuable and helpful tool. Important for the success of a video consultation is both a priori work on technical issues as well as the establishment of a certain sensible etiquette, which for example includes muting and discussion discipline. In addition, it was found that the previously agreed moderation is an important pillar for the success of video conferences on ethics. In this way, the distribution of roles is improved and the concentration on content-related debates is facilitated during the implementation. Accordingly, the "remote consultation" offers an important possibility to secure expertise in difficult situations—independently of the infection risk. An online video consultation is suitable for ethicists both for discussions on burdensome and difficult cases in clinical care and for internal consultation.

4 "Distancing" in Design and as an Object of Consultation

Since the beginning of the Covid-19 pandemic, not only telephone or video conferences have been held, but also other ways have been suggested or expressly favored by inquiring clinics: One department, which initiates advisory cases quite often with the competent working group (AG) of the Ethics Committee, has also requested direct consultations in the current phase. These ethical consultations were then carried out in a large room, partly even in the lecture hall of the clinic, and with the corresponding protective clothing. In this way, for example, the relatives of the patients could be integrated and a direct-personal advisory constellation could be achieved more easily in difficult cases. However, consultations in protective clothing and with a mask are demanding and strenuous on several levels: Glasses may actually offer an additional safety component according to recent studies, but they fog up and therefore only allow limited visibility at times. The fact that all participants have to wear masks makes it difficult to perceive the speakers as good as usual: For example, a large part of the facial expression and thus the non-verbal communication remains hidden under the protection. Direct contact and the exact monitoring or (co-)perception of the emotional situation of the counterpart are made more difficult or even impossible in very emotional cases such as in neonatology and pediatric clinics or in intensive care units. Nevertheless, sitting in a larger room with ventilation also has clear advantages. The shared presence in one place allows all participants to share the atmosphere of a (conversation) situation in which they consult with each other about very personal questions and sometimes dramatic course of diseases. This can contribute fundamentally to alleviating a feeling of insecurity or even powerlessness as a sensation. The personal struggle for the best possible procedure with high personnel and time expenditure is also seen and appreciated by relatives. Of course, these are only individual cases and pioneer consultations, a systematic survey of the experience of relatives or a comparative analysis of two different settings has not been possible or adequate so far. Parents of children in particularly difficult neonatal or intensive medical situations are under great stress; the required conditions under Covid-19 make visits to the clinic more difficult on all levels. Here there were very different constellations in the consultations; it seems to be the right approach to adjust flexibly to the needs of all participants in a case-specific manner and not to insist on personal-direct ethical consultations per se, but to make the offer of an online consultation quite possible. The close cooperation with the chaplaincy as well as the social service has proven to be very successful in the consultations.

In addition, clinical ethics consultations were also requested in cases related to the actual necessary safety distance as content. This was about safe working conditions and the moral assessment of (non-)compliance with safety precautions at the individual level. At the beginning of March 2020, the Ethics Committee was informed that the safety distance and behavior rules would no longer be adhered to in a canteen where free provision of food for staff working during the Covid-19 pandemic was introduced. The secretariat of the Ethics Committee was therefore asked for support in discussing further action or informing the clinic management. As a result, it was initially possible to recommend that responsible persons from the affected areas were involved. Subsequent contact with the management of the supply center revealed that they too had already tried to discuss and remedy deficiencies, but had the impression that they had not been heard adequately. Non-harm and benefit for all those involved were central questions for ethical mediation here.

The communication between different institutions such as clinic management, crisis team and ethics committee was also discussed several times as part of the meetings of the Ethics Committee and the Working Goup Ethics Consultation. Here, of course, the complexity of the crisis and the difficulty of coping with it on different levels and with various people have to be stated. Since all those involved have not yet been able to play through comparable catastrophe cases on a clinic level, the problem of timely adaptation to necessary behavioral measures is an understandable difficulty, but also in the microcosm of a larger organization, amazing, unreflective and unsolidary behavior is shown (for example, the refusal to wear masks despite immunocompromised employees in institutes). The ethics consultation can thus also receive a quite ambivalent role in the sense of a tightrope walk between the alleged "know-it-all" or "moral apostle", but must pay attention to the strict observance of hygiene rules in the sense of the principle of non-maleficence in counseling as well as in general.

5 Consequences of Covid-19 as a Topic of Ethics Consultation in the Clinic

In mid-April 2020, there was another request (by telephone) for ethical advice from the relative of a patient in a specialist clinic. Relevant aspects in the context of the pandemic were: The seriously ill father had been in hospital for more than two weeks and the planned discharge into home care after another treatment cycle was not possible due to the unstable general condition. The ban on visits meant that the father felt very alone. It was also unclear when, if at all, the patient would die due to his deteriorating condition. The patient's daughter was a nurse, so home care with support from an outpatient palliative care team was originally planned.

The pandemic situation created a particularly great deal of uncertainty and helplessness in the family. The relative also told the Ethics Committee that they could not understand why the doctors and nursing staff on the ward could not spare any additional time for the father. Since a relative of the son's partner also had some experience with counselling services, contact was made to ask whether the ethics committee was responsible and whether someone from the counselling team could be there for the patient for half an hour on a regular basis. This showed the increased need for personal contact in the clinic and the great strain on the staff on site (personnel from the affected clinic had also been withdrawn to support other Covid-related wards). The son was informed that, of course, the increased need was understood, but that the same restrictions on direct contact applied to the ethics committee and that, in addition, the clinic chaplaincy and psycho-oncology on site were responsible. The relatives then wanted to contact the ward to discuss the patient's wish for pastoral and psychological support. The relative also wanted to know from the Ethics Committee what options there would be in the event of an imminent death of the father with regard to a relaxation of the ban on visits. The staff of the clinic had repeatedly pointed out the current ban on visits to him on repeated enquiries; he did not want to bother the staff any further. The behaviour of the relatives should not be seen by the clinic as too demanding. When asked whether it had been discussed when the patient would be transferred to the palliative care ward in the event of further deterioration, the son reported the described planning of home palliative care. However, no mention had been made of a transfer to the palliative care ward—the family wanted to clarify this. With regard to the visiting regulations for the accompaniment of dying patients, it was pointed out that the palliative care ward was particularly working on ways and means of accompanying patients through relatives in the light of the visiting regulations. If a transfer to the palliative care ward was pending, the current options could be enquired about again (see DGP 2020). Uncertainty about these existential questions initiated ethical advisory needs. Information and communication aspects were in the foreground here, which are often also guaranteed very competently by the patient representatives as members in the Ethics Committee. In the phase of dying, visits must be possible.

In addition, it played a role to what extent the telephone support of relatives by psychosomatics would also be open to relatives of non-Covid-19 patients. This option of consulting the telephone service of psychosomatics for other relatives could be guaranteed (equality and justice). Internally, it was clarified with an inquiry to palliative care how the current visiting regulations or the possibility of adding by image would look in detail.[5] For this purpose, two tablets were purchased and the use of video conferences was also set up. On other wards, similar considerations were made and, as a result, special regulations were found for dying patients, even if this was not the case throughout the clinic. This case

[5] On the palliative care unit, at that time two visitors could be selected and specified for dying patients within the framework of the Corona conditions.

was subsequently the occasion for the systematic linking of the support and hotline services by the Working Group Ethics Consultation in a moderated expert discussion. In this context, not only an exchange of content was guaranteed, but also the accessibility for all concerns of patients was aimed at in the context of the pandemic (here, in particular, the Department of Psychosomatics and the clinic chaplaincy were involved). The office of the Ethics Committee assumed the coordinating function for the agreement on the psychosocial care of patients, employees and relatives. At this point it became clear that the needs of the employees were very different, it being assumed that psychosocial care is of particular importance in all phases of the pandemic. In addition to the hotlines set up by the Department of Psychosomatics for all employees of the clinic and relatives of patients, the clinic also implemented measures to promote direct contact in such a way that employees of psychosomatics were assigned to wards where Covid-19 patients are located in order to provide direct accompaniment. The focus of this support offer was the effort to relieve conversations in this demanding Covid time. In addition, a hotline was also set up by the chaplaincy. Such efforts to network individual offers, initiated by the office of the Clinical Ethics Committee and its interdisciplinary members, proved to be very helpful for the respective departments in this time. This not only created an overview of the different offers, but—if necessary—also the possibility of forwarding to the appropriate places.

6 Consultations on Quality Assurance for Research and Clinical Trials

Two specific consequences of the Covid-19 pandemic appear to be the increase in applications to the Research Ethics Commission (REC) and the Clinical Ethics Committee (CEC) and the direct requests for individual clinical trials to the CEC. While ethics commissions at faculties, as described above, review applications for scientific research, clinical ethics committees are responsible for moral issues in the context of bedside treatment. Most ethics committees at university hospitals probably know the problem of misdirected requests when study protocols or Serious Adverse Events (SAEs) are sent to the CEC instead of to the Research Ethics Commission. All causes and variants up to "committee hopping" to avoid more complex and cost-relevant application procedures are conceivable. However, it can only be speculated whether the motivation is rather to consult a committee with the term "ethics" in the title at all than none, especially in order to be able to inform scientific journals at a later stage that an "Ethics Committee/Board" has received, reviewed or approved the application in advance. That international journals rarely know the German differentiation between Research Ethics Commission and Clinical Ethics Committee exactly and may also be satisfied with the date of a supposedly official (short) "application", shows the complexity of the consultation forms and procedures (for research ethics and the specifics of human experiments, see in particular Schmidt et al. 2020 and Faust et al. in this volume as well as, inter alia, Jamrozik et al. 2015). In the context of Covid-19 developments, such cases have become more frequent while at the same time more consequential: the absolute need to find an effective therapy against the virus has quickly increased the number of Covid-19 research projects. Perhaps also due to the ignorance of some scientists, but structurally also for the above-mentioned reasons, cases have landed in clinical ethics consultation that actually belonged to the ethics *commission* must be addressed. There is a certain grey area in the form of the so-called "individual treatment trials". While the terminological classification is hardly possible nationally and internationally (e.g. "compassionate use", "individual trials" etc.), the responsibility for the respective assessment of this form of treatment is also not clearly regulated. Partly because of research backgrounds, but still because of an individual case which is not to be regarded as a serial procedure (study) and therefore also (not yet) falls within the competence of the ethics committees. Clinical ethics committees are probably asked with the best of intentions here, because although consultation is not mandatory and also does not change the responsibility of the participating medical researchers, the differentiated consultation procedures have apparently proved to be so informative and positive for several scientists that there are even repeated requests for very complicated clinical-scientific casuistries in this sector. There have also been consultation cases in the context of the Covid-19 pandemic which have even caused a very special Covid dynamics in individual cases, for example when patients from abroad are flown in for meaningful and approved treatment trials, but special pandemic protection measures and the conditions for risk areas also have to be observed very closely. Of course, Covid-19 also delays the development of clinical studies and thus leads to more individual treatment trials requiring advice. Travel is so restricted in times of Covid-19 that flying for helpful or even life-saving therapy is considerably more complicated. The globalised world does indeed benefit from the worldwide research efforts, but for the individual patient concerned, this can cause considerable difficulties in pandemic times—including ethical follow-up problems (cf. also Luo and Qin 2020; Zhang et al. 2020).

7 Bedside Allocation? Ethics Advice on Triage and Justice

The probably most difficult counseling requests and consultations carried out concerned the potential distribution of scarce resources such as places in intensive care units or on ventilators. There was already a critical discourse on the tasks and limits of the role of ethics counseling before Covid-19 (cf. AMA 2009; Hurst et al. 2008; Ventilator Document Workgroup et al. 2011; Evans et al. 2015; Magelssen et al. 2017; Magelssen and Bærøe 2019). In the phase when the problems of resource scarcity in the context of the Covid-19 pandemic became most apparent in Italy (Bergamo), Spain (Madrid) or the USA (New York), the Clinical Ethics

Consultation at the University Hospital Erlangen was also consulted several times. In this context, the Working Group Ethics Consultation was of the opinion that the CEC was, in the broadest sense, responsible for working on ethical problems that arise in the planning and implementation of triage, at least at the theoretical level. Central was the involvement in the development and formulation of criteria with the aim of enabling good decision-making and work under triage conditions (cf. in particular Tolchin et al. 2020). At that time, cooperation between the CEC and the clinic's crisis staff appeared to be quite useful and important, provided it was desired by the latter. Additional uncertainty arose due to a lack of official mandate and lack of information, but this is of course inherent in crises themselves. The CEC could have worked with the clinic's crisis staff on a clinic-wide uniform guideline for the procedure in triage situations. However, the question also arose on which levels the CEC's or the Working Group Ethics Consultation's involvement is most effective: in the development of ethical criteria for (the avoidance of) triage decisions, as members of a triage team or in individual counseling of teams on site who have to implement a triage decision? Here, the crisis staff deployed was certainly acutely challenged on too many levels and occupied with clarifying numerous individual questions, so that coordination with a monthly meeting body such as the Ethics Committee may have appeared impractical and/or too little knowledge of the counseling structures existed among selected leaders. Since in addition, an acute shortage situation did not arise at the University Hospital, but even some free intensive care beds could be used for patients from abroad (e.g., Italy), the acute consultation together with the Working Group Ethics Consultation of the CEC was also not so urgent and not a priority in terms of time.

During the different meetings to develop and implement clinic-wide uniform and binding triage criteria, the attending physicians at consultant and chief physician level initially spoke out against the desired standardization. In their opinion, decisions should still be made individually by the persons on duty on site at that time. The use of special point scores or the classification of patients into categories—according to these values—was not initially planned. Central—and certainly worthy of reflection—were in addition the criteria for pre-clinical decisions or assessment of prospects for success, as these should already decide on the further treatment options in advance. As elsewhere, the targeted collection of the patient's will or the presumed will should also be decisive for the further distribution of the available resources.[6] From the Working Group Ethics Consultation, the clearing of bed capacities (justice) or the early involvement of comorbidities in triage decisions on the basis of international literature was critically assessed. In addition, the involvement of ethical counseling in case of disagreement seems both sensible and

[6] Here, the guideline paper developed by DIVI, AEM and other professional societies as well as private individuals should be mentioned in particular (DIVI et al. 2020). The author of this article was involved in this process. A multi-layered discussion is taking place, for example with regard to the rights of people with disabilities. See also Marckmann's contribution in this volume.

supportive for the staff on site (reduction of "moral stress", strengthening of resilience). It was recommended to set up clinic-wide uniform and binding procedures that are also documented. Only in this way can individual decisions be made transparently and consistently in accordance with ethical assessment and the principle and sub-questions of justice can be sufficiently taken into account.

As a particularly compelling experience of clinical ethics consultation, a request from intensive care medicine presented itself in this context. On the one hand, there was a consultation forum with senior physicians of the department via video conference, on the other hand, the ward team wished to contribute ethical expertise to a "Triage Simulation" carried out on site. Here, the intensive care unit wanted to test how to react in individual cases to acute shortages of ventilation places along the "Decisions on the allocation of intensive care resources in the context of the COVID-19 pandemic" of the DIVI guidelines. The ethical sensitization for the difficulties of a bed-side rationing as well as the emphasis on the equality of all intensive care patients—with or without Covid-19—were important aspects of a differentiated accompaniment. In the course of this, further questions arose in the hypothetical planning of a—at least—"six-eye principle" for capacity questions. Could or should our Clinical Ethics Consultation participate in this? Would a 24-hour staffing of this position be guaranteed? Wouldn't there be any other (more) intelligent instrument to strive for a *pre-clinical* selection and distribution of intensive care places? Here, the pandemic situation and ethics consultation have developed to such an extent that there was no acute need to develop concepts in detail, because the capacities for ventilation places could be increased significantly in parallel and bottlenecks—at least so far—could be avoided successfully. However, important discussion processes could be initiated in the Working Group Ethics Consultation as well as in the Clinical Ethics Committee, which led to a sensitization for the complexity and pitfalls of these topics. In addition, the topic was further discussed on the intensive care unit in the context of low-threshold "ethics visits" and background information was discussed in the CEC plenum and in the "Ethics Café" in continuing education courses.

8 Summary—Consultation for Quality Assurance in Medicine

The Covid-19 pandemic has been posing unprecedented challenges to the healthcare system. Uncertainty was the dominant feeling in many phases, as well as a decisive dimension that can be found structurally[7] at

[7] The differences between "subjective" and "objective" perceptions of security cannot be discussed in depth here, even though these things are not only individually, but also structurally of great importance, for example in terms of strategies for securing in the sense of defensive medicine (with follow-up problems of overdiagnosis to futility, etc.).

all levels.[8] This practice report from everyday clinical life on selected cases with a Covid-related background shows quite different areas in which problems of uncertainty are particularly relevant: The way in which ethics consultations are carried out has changed abruptly in order to ensure the safety of the persons concerned. Here, measures for adaptation and quality assurance are necessary to better adjust to the new situation. Due to the pandemic conditions, there are primary and secondary uncertainties and effects in the clinics: While, for example, hardly any problems arose from postponed operations in our area for ethics consultation, nevertheless, side effects of the restrictions on patients in particularly vulnerable phases were reported and also became the subject of consultation. Here, the challenge of the Covid-19 time is to relieve resulting problems and to cope with contact and visit restrictions, which the ethics consultation can accompany and flank, but the individual wards or sub-clinics must find adequate and creative solutions, for example in the care of seriously and terminally ill people. The weighing up between "social distancing" (see also Schloemann 2020) for the safety of all persons involved and practicable forms of contact in existential life and death phases is often a fine line that the Clinical Ethics Committee had to find ways between sensible reason and not completely excluded risks.

Clinical ethics consultation is particularly challenged when it comes to allocating ventilators and intensive care beds. Here, in key questions of distributive justice, the special moral urgency as well as the fluid transition to problems of public health or even global health ethics becomes visible. The possibilities and limits of consultation must be seen very precisely, individual overloads avoided and practicable solutions found through networking. Clinical ethics committees and consultants are confronted with requests and expectations that are both unfamiliar in their implementation and in the requirements, such as in allocation questions or even triage decisions or test exercises. "Bedside triage" is certainly not the royal road, but a preclinical and procedural avoidance of overloading the individual decision-makers—on the intensive care unit as well as in the management area. The utilitarian rescue of the "greatest number" should not be the task of micro-allocation, human dignity could become the "calculable value" (Dufner and Schöne-Seifert 2019; Marckmann 2020; Schockenhoff 2020; Taupitz 2020; see also Barnett et al. 2010). Even better coordination with the relevant crisis teams as well as further development in the field of health care ethics committees at the meso level would be important options. The intensified scientific exchange, for example with professional societies as well as health authorities in the region, is a sensible option for networking and distributing responsibility in decision-making uncertainty.

[8] The personal level of planning security cannot be discussed here, but it should only be mentioned that even in the team of the office of the Ethics Committee, greater uncertainties have arisen in some Covid phases, for example through the possible upcoming division for pandemic deployment in intensive care medicine or also necessary quarantine phases abroad, etc.—pandemics are prime examples of the development of uncertainties at all levels.

Despite all this, there are still enough moral challenges that will continue to cause discussion in the field of Covid-19. While the role and work of clinical ethics consultation remained nominally the same, but has become increasingly digitalized on the one hand, it was confronted on the other hand with important new questions of prioritization and possibly necessary rationing. Not only changes, but also tasks and limits of the competence of clinical ethics consultation and practical implementability in individual situations could be shown. To professional support, the Academy for Ethics in Medicine (AEM) held a discourse to cope with the challenges associated with the pandemic.[9] It was emphasized here that the processing of allocative ethical problems in triage situations differs considerably from the usual activity of clinical ethics consultation and has not been indicated as a core competence of an ethics consultation curriculum so far. Alternatively, the consultation could be taken over by—so far too few—public health specialists, but practice shows that there is a structural gap here: The local clinical staff obtains information directly from the clinical ethics consultation on site and requests orientation or support. In addition to a lack of scientific debate, the need for processing these questions was made visible by the current situation. Ethics consultation in the Covid-19 pandemic shows the great uncertainty and the particularly high need for consultation on many different levels: Clinical ethics in the inpatient individual case, organizational ethics for the entire hospital, public health ethics in the sense of networking within a region and at the same time the reference points to global health ethics in the fields of international exchange in terms of content as well as with a view to the admission of patients from crisis regions (Bundesärztekammer 2020; Wild et al. 2020). This cannot eliminate unavoidable uncertainties, but it can help to reduce them to some extent. The requirements for practical planning were and are high, the economic consequences—key words creation of intensive care beds, capacity release, postponement of operations etc.—especially for a university hospital of maximum care are enormous. Hospitals and clinical ethics experience great challenges with immense difficulties in the usual consultation processes, but perhaps also opportunities, for example in digitalization and a stronger integration into clinical facilities, despite the serious conditions. It is certainly also sensible to further improve the networking of ethics consultation services in the individual regions[10] as well as (inter)national comparative studies in order to draw constructive conclusions from the experiences

[9] The head of the KEK office and author of the present article was initially involved here as well as in individual forums of the AEM. In addition, he was one of the experts in the short-term assessment of the AEM-DIVI guideline, see DIVI et al. (2020) as well as in prioritization in the regional vaccination center.

[10] In the present case there were contacts to another large hospital in the city with an exchange of experiences at the level of chairpersons and office managers. At this stage, a newspaper article in the local press "Serious allegations …" had been raised and the daughter of a deceased Covid-19 patient suspected negligence in clinical care (Erlanger Nachrichten from May 5, 2020); this was discussed in a working group.

elsewhere for an even better quality assurance.[11] The question raised by practical philosophy as to whether we need more ethics, more than ethics or more ethicists in the Covid-19 crisis (Hack 2020) can only be answered with a clear "yes". We need more ethical competence and education in science and society, from the micro level at the sickbed to the macro dimension for national and global political areas (see, inter alia, Etzioni 2020; Heinemann et al. 2020; Howe 2020). With regard to "lateral thinkers", vaccine critics or conspiracy theorists, the Covid-19 crisis is also a catastrophe of practical reason, which is why a strengthening of philosophy and moral theory can only be helpful. The continuous review of the proportionality of all Covid-19 measures is also an important task in which ethics and law play key roles (see, inter alia, Birklbauer 2020; Kröll et al. 2020; Leitlein 2020; Lübbe 2020; Wolbert 2020). And that medical ethics also reveals the various forms of false securities and fundamental as well as specific uncertainties in clinical practice should be useful in order to avoid inappropriate reactions such as futility and "defensive medicine" during and after the pandemic (see Dinges 2020 and the contributions in Frewer et al. 2020a,b).

Even if the formula "More ethicists bring more ethics" (or morality) in terms of practical good action is certainly very simplified, it nevertheless applies to essential areas of science and society that a deeper reflection should also help to improve practice (see, inter alia, Jungert et al. 2020; Marckmann et al. 2020). Of course, "much more than ethics" is also needed, because, for example, deficiencies in the areas of nursing and digitalization have become even more apparent through the pandemic. Ethics can and must by no means replace nursing and medical expertise, but together we can act reflectively and resource-efficiently in the right direction with a view to the individual patient's well-being and the common good. Clinical ethics and public health ethics do not have to contradict each other, they are—and this with a long tradition of "valetudo" and "salus publica" on the front and back of a Roman coin, see, for example, the title image in Schäfer et al. 2008—also two sides of the same coin. What is important here for the future of ethics is that there are indeed fundamental debates on the foundations of moral philosophy between teleological and deontological concepts, but no ideological trench warfare on human dignity versus utilitarianism. As the examples from clinical practice show, from the perspective of clinicians and those affected, the moral-theoretical foundations are less often called into question, but rather common decision-making for the guarantee of the dignity of the sick in practice. Here, clinical ethics consultation has its special role; possible trends towards an even stronger focus on the primacy of the collective in the context of a pandemic must be very carefully observed. Often the distance between practical ethics in individual cases and political theory is quite far. One possible structural measure here

[11] Here, critical exchange in public discourse is very important. In addition to publications in the journal Ethik in der Klinik, the Clinical Ethics Committee and the AG Ethikberatung have also stimulated further publications, see, for example, Jäger and Gründel (2020) with explicit thanks to the Ethics Committee.

could be the formation of "committees for ethics in healthcare" ("KEG"), inter alia with the aim of contributing to better networking with health authorities and health policy and creating supra-regional instruments for the necessary professionalization of ethics in healthcare. This could be particularly important in federal countries such as the German-speaking countries with individual cantons, federal states or free states within a nation. Another central instrument for quality and safety are comparative case studies from the "Inter-CEC" perspective: Structural questions of ethics consultation can be significantly advanced by comparative analyses (e.g. Frewer and Bruns 2011; Frewer 2019). Also the initiatives of the Academy for Ethics in Medicine, to offer regular forums for the discussion of ethical issues in the context of the Covid-19 pandemic and thus to deepen the debates, are important steps towards quality and safety (Academy for Ethics in Medicine e. V. 2020a,b).[12]

Acknowledgements I would like to thank the staff of the office of the Clinical Ethics Committee (CEC) as well as the committed members of the Working Group Ethics Consultation of the CEC at the University Hospital Erlangen (UKER) for their support.

References

Akademie für Ethik in der Medizin e. V. (2020a) Möglichkeiten und Grenzen von Ethikberatung im Rahmen der COVID-19-Pandemie (31.03.2020). Ein Diskussionspapier der Akademie für Ethik in der Medizin. In: Ethik in der Medizin (published online April 29, 2020). https://doi.org/10.1007/s00481-020-00580-4

Akademie für Ethik in der Medizin e. V. (2020b) Protokoll zum Online-Meeting klinische*r Ethiker*innen zu COVID-19 23.04.2020. https://www.aem-online.de/fileadmin/user_upload/Protokoll_zum_Online-Meeting_2020-04-23.pdf. Accessed May 6, 2020

American Medical Association (AMA) (2009) Opinion 9.067. Physician obligation in disaster preparedness and response. Code of medical ethics. Chicago

Barnett DJ, Levine R, Thompson CB, Wijetunge GU, Oliver AL, Bentley MA, Neubert PD, Pirrallo RG, Links JM, Balicer RD (2010) Gauging U.S. emergency medical services workers' willingness to respond to pandemic influenza using a threat- and efficacy-based assessment framework. PLoS One 5(3):e9856

Bielefeldt H, Klotz S, Herrler C, Frewer A (2020) Vorwort: die Rechte Älterer und "Corona". In: Frewer A, Klotz S, Herrler C, Bielefeldt H (eds) Gute Behandlung im Alter? Menschenrechte und Ethik zwischen Ideal und Realität, Menschenrechte in der Medizin/Human Rights in Healthcare 8. transcript, Bielefeld, pp 7–16

Birklbauer A (2020) Die Verhältnismäßigkeit der Covid-19-Maßnahmen aus strafrechtlicher Sicht. In: Kröll W, Platzer J, Ruckenbauer HW, Schaupp W (eds) Die Corona-Pandemie. Ethische, gesellschaftliche und theologische Reflexionen einer Krise. Nomos, Baden-Baden, pp 137–152

[12] See also German Ethics Council (DER) (2020), Fischkoff et al. (2020), Knox (2017), National Academy of Sciences Leopoldina (2020), Reis (2016), Swiss Academy of Medical Sciences (SAMW) (2020), The Hastings Center (2020) and Working Group Ethics/AG Ethik (2020).

Bundesärztekammer (BÄK) (2020) Orientierungshilfe der Bundesärztekammer zur Allokation medizinischer Ressourcen am Beispiel der SARS-CoV-2-Pandemie im Falle eines Kapazitätsmangels. Berlin. https://www.bundesaerztekammer.de/fileadmin/user_upload/downloads/pdf-Ordner/Stellungnahmen/BAEK_Allokationspapier_05052020.pdf. Accessed January 31, 2021

Deutsche Gesellschaft für Palliativmedizin (DGP) (2020) Handlungsempfehlung zur Therapie von Patient*innen mit COVID-19 aus palliativmedizinischer Perspektive 2.0. https://www.awmf.org/uploads/tx_szleitlinien/128-002l_S1_palliative_Therapie_bei_COVID-19_2020-04_1.pdf. Accessed October 7, 2020

Deutsche Interdisziplinäre Vereinigung für Intensiv- und Notfallmedizin (DIVI), Deutsche Gesellschaft für Interdisziplinäre Notfall- und Akutmedizin, Deutsche Gesellschaft für Anästhesiologie und Intensivmedizin, Deutsche Gesellschaft für Internistische Intensivmedizin und Notfallmedizin, Deutsche Gesellschaft für Pneumologie und Beatmungsmedizin, Deutsche Gesellschaft für Palliativmedizin, Akademie für Ethik in der Medizin (2020) Entscheidungen über die Zuteilung von Ressourcen in der Notfall- und der Intensivmedizin im Kontext der COVID-19-Pandemie, Version 2: Klinisch-ethische Empfehlungen. 2., überarbeitete Fassung vom 17.04.2020. https://www.divi.de/joomlatools-files/docman-files/publikationen/covid-19-dokumente/200416-divi-covid-19-ethik-empfehlung-version-2.pdf. Accessed January 31, 2021

Deutscher Ethikrat (DER) (2020) Solidarität und Verantwortung in der Corona-Krise. Ad-hoc-Empfehlung. https://www.ethikrat.org/fileadmin/Publikationen/Ad-hoc-Empfehlungen/deutsch/ad-hoc-empfehlung-corona-krise.pdf. Accessed January 31, 2021

Dinges S (2020) Sichere Patient*innen – verunsichertes Team? Zwei Fallbeispiele aus Psychiatrie und Covid-19-Krise. Jahrbuch Ethik in der Klinik 13:273–282

Dörries A, Neitzke G, Simon A, Vollmann J (2010) Klinische Ethikberatung. Ein Praxisbuch für Krankenhäuser und Einrichtungen der Altenpflege, 2nd edn. Kohlhammer, Stuttgart

Dufner A, Schöne-Seifert B (2019) Die Rettung der größeren Anzahl: eine Debatte um Grundbausteine ethischer Normenbegründung. Zeitschrift für Praktische Philosophie 6(2):15–42. https://doi.org/10.22613/zfpp/6.2.1

Etzioni A (2020) Micro and macro ethical considerations of COVID-19. J Clin Ethics 31(4):318–325

Evans DK, Goldstein M, Popova A (2015) Health-care worker mortality and the legacy of the Ebola epidemic. Lancet Glob Health 3(8):e439–e440

Fischkoff K, Neuberg G, Dastidar J, Williams EP, Prager KM, Dugdale L (2020) Clinical ethics consultations during the COVID-19 pandemic surge at a New York City Medical Center. J Clin Ethics 31(3):212–218

Frewer A (2019) Wieviel Emotion braucht und verträgt die Ethikberatung? Fallstudien aus der „Inter-KEK"-Perspektive. In: Frewer A (ed) Fallstudien zur Ethik in der Medizin. Beratungsbeispiele aus Ethikkomitees. Königshausen & Neumann, Würzburg, pp 79–84

Frewer A (2020) Unsicherheit durch die Covid-19-Pandemie. Klinische Probleme im Spiegel der Ethikberatung. Jahrb Ethik Klin 13:253–269

Frewer A, Bruns F (2011) "Inter-KEK". Strukturfragen der Ethikberatung in komparativer Analyse. Jahrb Ethik Klin 4:225–228

Frewer A, Hack C (2019) Ethikberatung am UK Erlangen. In: Frewer A (eds) Fallstudien zur Ethik in der Medizin. Beratungsbeispiele aus Ethikkomitees. Königshausen & Neumann, Würzburg, pp 319–332

Frewer A, Fahr U, Rascher W (eds) (2008) Klinische Ethikkomitees. Chancen, Risiken und Nebenwirkungen. Jahrbuch Ethik in der Klinik (JEK), vol. 1. Königshausen & Neumann, Würzburg

Frewer A, Bruns F, May A (eds) (2012) Ethikberatung in der Medizin. Springer, Heidelberg

Frewer A, Bergemann L, Langmann E (eds) (2020a) Unsicherheit in der Medizin. Zum Umgang mit Ungewissheit im Gesundheitswesen, Jahrbuch Ethik in der Klinik 13. Königshausen & Neumann, Würzburg

Frewer A, Klotz S, Herrler C, Bielefeldt H (eds) (2020b) Gute Behandlung im Alter? Menschenrechte und Ethik zwischen Ideal und Realität, Menschenrechte in der Medizin/ Human Rights in Healthcare 8. transcript, Bielefeld

Fröhlich G (2014) Theorie der Ethischen Beratung im Klinischen Kontext. Philosophische Grundlegung eines anwendungsbezogenen Modells zur Falldiskussion und Lösung wertbasierter Konflikte. Königshausen & Neumann, Würzburg

Groß D, May AT, Simon A (eds) (2008) Beiträge zur Klinischen Ethikberatung an Universitätskliniken. Lit, Berlin

Hack C (2020) Ethikberatung und Covid-19: Brauchen wir mehr Ethik, mehr als Ethik oder mehr Ethiker? Z Prakt Philos 7(2):279–306

Heinemann T, Proft I, Sahm S, Schockenhoff E (2020) Covid-19. Ethische Empfehlungen über Beginn und Fortführung einer intensivmedizinischen Behandlung bei nicht ausreichenden Behandlungskapazitäten. Books on Demand, Norderstedt

Howe EG (2020) What we should learn from the COVID-19 pandemic. J Clin Ethics 31(3):197–208

Hurst SA, Reiter-Theil S, Slowther A-M, Pegoraro R, Forde R, Danis M (2008) Should ethics consultants help clinicians face scarcity in their practice? J Med Ethics 34(4):241–246. https://doi.org/10.1136/jme.2006.019828

Jäger C, Gründel J (2020) Zur Notwendigkeit einer Neuorientierung bei der Beurteilung der rechtfertigenden Pflichtenkollision im Angesicht der Corona-Triage. Zeitschrift für Internationale Strafrechtsdogmatik 4:151–163

Jamrozik E, de la Fuente-Núñez V, Reis A, Ringwald P, Selgelid MJ (2015) Ethical aspects of malaria control and research. Malar J 14:518

Jungert M, Frewer A, Mayr E (eds) (2020) Wissenschaftsreflexion. Interdisziplinäre Perspektiven zwischen Philosophie und Praxis. Mentis, Paderborn

Kaschube M, Eibauer C, Frewer A (2019) Ethikberatungen am UK Erlangen. Eine Übersicht zur Falldokumentation (2002–2017). In: Frewer A (2019), Fallstudien zur Ethik in der Medizin. Beratungsbeispiele aus Ethikkomitees. Königshausen & Neumann, Würzburg, pp 293–308

Knox JBL (2017) Ethical competence training for members on clinical ethics committees (CEC): experiences from Denmark. Int J Ethics Educ 2(2):203–213. https://doi.org/10.1007/s40889-017-0040-4

Kröll W, Platzer J, Ruckenbauer HW, Schaupp W (eds) (2020) Die Corona-Pandemie. Ethische, gesellschaftliche und theologische Reflexionen einer Krise. Nomos, Baden-Baden

Krull L, Aigner S, Frewer A (2019) Entschleunigung als Funktion von Ethikkomitees? Ergebnisse einer Studie zur Beratung am UK Erlangen. In: Frewer A (ed) Fallstudien zur Ethik in der Medizin. Beratungsbeispiele aus Ethikkomitees. Königshausen & Neumann, Würzburg, pp 309–318

Leitlein H (2020) Behandlung von Corona-Patienten: „Wir dürfen die Ärzte nicht alleinlassen“. Zeit Online. https://www.zeit.de/gesellschaft/2020-04/behandlung-coronavirus-patienten-krankenhaeuser-triage-notfallmedizin-aerzte-annette-dufner. Accessed January 31, 2021

Lübbe W (2020) Orientierung in der Corona-Krise? Nicht mit Doppelbotschaften. Medizinrecht 38:434–439. https://doi.org/10.1007/s00350-020-5557-4

Luo Q, Qin T (2020) Managing clinical trials for covid-19. The importance of ethics committees. Br Med J 369:m1369. https://doi.org/10.1136/bmj.m1369

Magelssen M, Bærøe K (2019) Can clinical ethics committees be legitimate actors in bed-side rationing? BMC Med Ethics 20(1):97. https://doi.org/10.1186/s12910-019-0438-y

Magelssen M, Miljeteig I, Pedersen R, Førde R (2017) Roles and responsibilities of clinical ethics committees in priority setting. BMC Med Ethics 18(1):68. https://doi.org/10.1186/s12910-017-0226-5

Marckmann G (2020) Coronavirus and ethics: ‘act so that most people survive’. Interview, Deutsche Welle. https://www.dw.com/en/coronavirus-and-ethics-act-so-that-most-people-survive/a-52895179. Accessed May 6, 2020

Marckmann G, Neitzke G, Riedel A et al (2020) Möglichkeiten und Grenzen von Ethikberatung im Rahmen der COVID-19-Pandemie. Ethik in der Medizin 32:195–199
Nationale Akademie der Wissenschaften Leopoldina (2020) Ad-hoc-Stellungnahmen zur Coronavirus-Pandemie. https://www.leopoldina.org/uploads/tx_leopublication/2020_08_05_Leopoldina-Stellungnahmen_Coronavirus.pdf. Accessed January 31, 2021
Peter C, Funcke D (eds) (2013) Wissen an der Grenze. Zum Umgang mit Ungewissheit und Unsicherheit in der modernen Medizin. Campus, Frankfurt/Main
Reis A (2016) Ethische Fragen bei der Erforschung, Prävention und Behandlung von Infektionskrankheiten. Analysen im Kontext der Weltgesundheitsorganisation. Habilitationsschrift, Erlangen
Schäfer D, Frewer A, Schockenhoff E, Wetzstein V (eds) (2008) Gesundheitskonzepte im Wandel. Geschichte, Ethik und Gesellschaft, Geschichte und Philosophie der Medizin, vol 6. Franz Steiner Verlag, Stuttgart
Schloemann J (2020) Der Ausdruck soziale Distanz ist ein Unding. Süddeutsche Zeitung 118:19
Schmidt U, Frewer A, Sprumont D (Eds) (2020) Ethical Research. The Declaration of Helsinki, and the Past, Present and Future of Human Experimentation. Oxford University Press, Oxford
Schockenhoff E (2020) Die Ad-hoc-Empfehlungen des Deutschen Ethikrats zur Corona-Pandemie. In: Kröll W, Platzer J, Ruckenbauer H W, Schaupp W (eds) Die Corona-Pandemie. Ethische, gesellschaftliche und theologische Reflexionen einer Krise. Nomos, Baden-Baden, pp 25–35
Schweizerische Akademie der Medizinischen Wissenschaften (SAMW) (2020) Covid-19-Pandemie: triage von intensivmedizinischen Behandlungen bei Ressourcenknappheit (Version 3.1, December 17, 2020). Bern
Taupitz J (2020) Verteilung medizinischer Ressourcen in der Corona-Krise. Wer darf überleben? Medizinrecht 38:440–450
The Hastings Center (2020) Ethical framework for health care institutions responding to novel coronavirus SARS-CoV-2 (COVID-19). Guidelines for institutional ethics services responding to COVID-19. https://www.thehastingscenter.org/wp-content/uploads/HastingsCenterCovidFramework2020.pdf. Accessed December 31, 2020
Tolchin B, Latham SR, Bruce L, Ferrante LE, Kraschel K, Jubanyik K, Hull SC, Herbst JL, Kapo J, Moritz ED, Hughes J, Siegel Mark D, Mercurio MR (2020) Developing a triage protocol for the COVID-19 pandemic: allocating scarce medical resources in a public health emergency. J Clin Ethics 31(4):303–317
Ventilator Document Workgroup/Ethics Subcommittee of the Advisory Committee to the Director/Centers for Disease Control and Prevention (2011) Ethical considerations for decision making regarding allocation of mechanical ventilators during a severe influenza pandemic or other public health emergency. https://www.cdc.gov/about/advisory/pdf/VentDocument_Release.pdf. Accessed May 6, 2020
Wild V, Buyx A, Hurst S, Munthe C, Rid A, Schröder-Bäck P, Strech D, Thompson A (2020) Covid-19: eine Ad hoc Public-Health-Ethikberatung. Gesundheitswesen 82:507–513. Stuttgart und New York: Thieme. https://doi.org/10.1055/a-1174-0086. Accessed January 31, 2021
Wolbert W (2020) Kantianismus, Utilitarismus und die Menschenwürde. In: Kröll W, Platzer J, Ruckenbauer H W, Schaupp W (eds) Die Corona-Pandemie. Ethische, gesellschaftliche und theologische Reflexionen einer Krise. Nomos, Baden-Baden, pp 119–136
Working Group Ethics/AG Ethik (2020) Public health ethics and Covid-19. The ethical dimensions of public health decision-making during a pandemic. https://www.aem-online.de/fileadmin/user_upload/Policy_Brief_Pandemic_Ethics_GeneralF.pdf. Accessed May 6, 2020

Zentrale Ethikkommission (ZEKO) (2019) Stellungnahme "Außerklinische Ethikberatung". Deutsches Ärzteblatt 117(12):A1–A8. https://doi.org/10.3238/baek_sn_aeb_2019. Accessed January 31, 2021

Zhang H, Shao F, Gu J, Li L, Wang Y (2020) Ethics committee reviews of applications for research studies at 1 hospital in China during the 2019 novel coronavirus epidemic. JAMA. https://doi.org/10.1001/jama.2020.4362. pmid:32202608

Religion, Pandemics and Ethics. A Diaconal-Ethical Perspective on the Covid-19 Pandemic

Ulrich H.J. Körtner

Contents

1 The Covid-19 Pandemic as an Ethical Challenge and Test of Endurance 325
2 Religion in Times of Covid-19 326
3 Christian Ethics 330
4 Human Dignity, Freedom and Responsibility 331
5 Allocation Questions 333
6 Ethical Culture and Dealing with Border Experiences and Guilt 334
7 Dying in Times of Covid-19 335
8 Outlook 336
References 337

1 The Covid-19 Pandemic as an Ethical Challenge and Test of Endurance

The crisis resulting from the corona pandemic is not just a medical, political, social and economic crisis, but also an ethical challenge and test of endurance. It not only concerns questions of medical ethics, nursing ethics and ethics in healthcare in general. The corona crisis touches on social ethical, but also individual ethical, personal ethical and environmental ethical aspects in a very comprehensive way.

The corona crisis is a focal point and at the same time a catalyst and trigger of global, but also regional, social and political developments. It highlights the strengths and weaknesses of social sub-systems, for example in the healthcare

Expanded and revised version of my contribution: Körtner 2020a.

U.H.J. Körtner (✉)
University of Vienna, Vienna, Austria
e-mail: ulrich.koertner@univie.ac.at

© The Author(s), under exclusive license to Springer-Verlag GmbH, DE, part of Springer Nature 2023

A. Reis et al. (eds.), *Pandemics and Ethics*,
https://doi.org/10.1007/978-3-662-66872-6_19

system and nursing, especially in the care for and assistance of the elderly and people with disabilities.

It has often been said that the corona pandemic is almost a democratic phenomenon because the Covid-19 virus indiscriminately affected all people on all continents, rich and poor, old and young. In fact, however, the risk of contracting and dying from Covid-19 is not only distributed unequally worldwide, but also within Europe and even within individual European countries. The health risk is not only dependent on age or pre-existing conditions, but also on social factors such as income, professional position, living conditions, etc. The economic consequences—for example, short-time work and unemployment- and the consequences of the health policy strategy to contain the pandemic in the education sector (kindergartens, schools, universities) are also distributed very differently in society. In addition, the gender aspect is significant. Sociologists, for example, speak of a "re-traditionalization" of gender-related role models in the corona crisis (Allmendinger 2020). The corona crisis raises questions of justice in many ways. And it exacerbates the situation of particularly vulnerable and marginalized population groups. These are challenges that the Diakonie and Caritas have always faced. Their principles and self-understanding are now being put to the test in a special way (cf. Moser 2020). What is the relation between the aspirations and the reality of diaconal work? To what extent do diaconal institutions and companies succeed in bringing their Christian principles of social work to life even in extreme circumstances such as the corona pandemic?

2 Religion in Times of Covid-19

The corona crisis has also become a stress test and a test of endurance for religious communities, churches and university theology. In a state of emergency, society and politics discovered how important not only doctors and nursing staff, but also police officers, soldiers and sales clerks are. They were publicly applauded. There was no mention of pastors. There were no exceptions for churches and other religious communities during the first lockdown and the next (partial) lockdown. According to the teachings of the past few months, religion is not "system-relevant" in secular society. Churches, synagogues and mosques were closed, public worship and Friday prayers were prohibited, while hardware stores and garden centers remained open or were allowed to reopen after Easter. Religious family celebrations had to be largely omitted, weddings and baptisms postponed. Funerals were only allowed to take place in the immediate family, and hospital chaplains were often barred from inpatient facilities, unless they were a permanent part of the treatment team. Some on-call chaplains, however, also had to experience the painful realization that they were not called by relatives at all.

The sociologist Rudolf Stichweh predicts that "the system of religion could turn out to be the true loser of the Corona crisis" (Stichweh 2020), since religious attempts to interpret the crisis caused by Covid-19 played no significant role outside of church milieus. The managing director of the German Association of Towns and Municipalities, Gerd Landsberg, takes a different view. The churches are "in the truest sense of the word system-relevant", after all they—together with the municipalities—stand at the forefront of efforts to contain the pandemic and its consequences (cf. Evangelisch.de 2020). However, one must make a distinction: the social welfare and health care work of the church as part of the welfare state and health care system are indeed still system-relevant—one only has to think of hospitals and nursing homes in church or diaconal ownership. Apparently, this is no longer the case to the same extent for the churches themselves. And what the Christian or church aspect of today's diaconal work consists of is controversial right up to employment law. The belief that no state can exist without the churches, because by itself it cannot guarantee its moral and ideological preconditions, which are based on a Christian civil-religious foundation, proves to be fragile.

What role religion plays in the context of pandemics such as the Covid-19 pandemic is a multi-layered question. The following aspects must be distinguished: (1) Religion as a resource for interpretation and meaning. (2) Religion as a resource for ethical action and for combating pandemics. (3) Religion as a possible source of danger.

1. Religion as a resource for meaning can help people to cope with the personal and collective crises caused by a pandemic. Religious faith can strengthen the will to live. It can mobilize forces to resist personal illness and collective distress. But it can also give the strength to endure unavoidable suffering, to accept the finiteness of life and death. Thus, accompanying dying and grieving people is a kind of religious assistance. More abstractly formulated, religion acts as a form of coping with contingency by means of a cultivated reference to transcendence.

A historically widespread view interprets diseases and natural disasters as divine punishments. Historical examples are the plague epidemics in Europe during the Middle Ages and modern era or the Lisbon earthquake of 1755. However, the interpretation of this as a divine judgment has also found considerable opposition in the philosophy of the Enlightenment, which persists in Albert Camus' novel "The Plague". Already in Greek mythology, divine arrows of plague were considered the cause of the disease. But with the progress of modern medicine, the penal theological interpretation of the plague was pushed back. An interpretation of the Corona pandemic as a punishment of God is rejected by the Christian churches to a large extent. One Christian argument is that Jesus of Nazareth healed people and did not kill them. The God incarnate in him does not want the misfortune but the salvation of people. To what extent this argumentative figure contributes to giving a convincing answer to the theodicy problem is not the subject of the present article, as further theological-dogmatic questions are also left out. Occasionally, however, there are also voices in Christian circles that interpret the infection as a punishment for human misconduct, for secular society's apostasy from God and a misguided way of life. Similar patterns are known to us from the heyday of the AIDS pandemic, which broke out in the early 1980s. In a weakened form, one can speak of the disease as a test, as a trial of endurance or as a learning ground for a fundamental transformation of the globalized economy and mobility towards more sustainability, climate and environmental protection. Punitive motives also occur in secular form, when instead of God, nature is spoken of as a subject that resists human exploitation and strikes back in the form of diseases. The cause-and-effect relationship known from religious contexts also seems to apply where the spread of the virus is attributed to human misconduct, for example to the keeping and consumption of wild animals and the high mobility of modern world society and its air traffic.

As Rudolf Stichweh rightly observes, such religious or quasi-religious interpretive patterns have not played a predominant role in the public presentation of the Corona crisis. They are certainly not guiding principles in politics and the health system. The question is to what extent a secular society still expects religious guidance from the churches. Church leaders and their leading representatives have been accused in some cases of having remained silent during the lockdown and of not having accompanied the seriously ill and the dying sufficiently (cf. Finger 2020; Lilie and Lieberknecht 2020). Declaring "distance" as a new form of neighborly love was a fatal mistake (cf. Prantl 2020). Church representatives have defended themselves against such general criticism. They also like to point out how high the demand for church services on television, radio and the Internet has been. However, how far the demand extends beyond the church's core still needs to be investigated more closely.

2. Religion as an ethical resource was first evident in the cooperation between state authorities and religious communities. In this context, churches, mosques and synagogues have justified the waiver of church services and other religious gatherings not only with reference to state regulations. They have also understood the closure of their places of worship as a practical contribution to containing the pandemic, which is justified by the religious commandment of love of neighbor. Only one percent of the usual number of believers were allowed to travel to Mecca for the annual pilgrimage to Mecca in 2020.

Even in times of plague, the care of the sick could be justified by the commandment of love of neighbor. The plague pamphlets of Martin Luther, who called for not abandoning the plague-stricken to themselves, but to stand by them in trust in Christ (cf. Körtner 1998, pp. 88 ff.), are particularly impressive. When the plague broke out in Wittenberg in 1527, many residents of the city fled the disease. Even the university, professors as well as students, moved to Jena. But Luther remained in Wittenberg with Bugenhagen and two chaplains, continued to give lectures and sermons, and provided services to those in need as a pastor (cf. Junghans 1983, 19). Although the motif of the disease as punishment can also be found in Luther's writings, it is primarily seen as a test of faith in Christ. At the same time, Luther interprets medicine as a good gift from God that should be used. In this sense, contemporary theologians also emphasize that to trust in medicine and science is an expression of Christian faith in God the Creator. Therefore, the primacy of science in the Corona crisis is to be welcomed from a Christian point of view. The apocalyptic idea that the world could be abandoned by God, on the other hand, must be rejected as absurd (cf. Kaufmann 2020).

3. Religion can not only be a resource, but also *a source of danger* in pandemic times. On several occasions in the past months, religious services have contributed to the spread of the Corona virus because the required hygiene regulations were not observed. In South Korea, churches have proven to be true superspreader hotspots. However, it is important to distinguish between the reasons why safety regulations have been ignored. This can be due to carelessness or inadequate information due to insufficient language skills in migrant communities of any religion. But the reasons can also lie in religious or other ideological convictions. In all religions there are groups (evangelical, Catholic, Jewish-Orthodox, Islamic) that oppose an enlightened biopolitical regime. For example, some Christian communities have a magical understanding of the sacrament, according to which the Lord's Supper or the Eucharist protects against infection with Covid-19. Shiite pilgrims who, despite restrictions on movement, flock to the Kadhimiya shrine in Baghdad in large numbers, believe that they are protected by the blood of their martyrs. In Israel, some ultra-Orthodox hoped that the Messiah would end the Corona pandemic before the Passover festival (cf. Harrer 2020). In general, the initial infection rates were particularly high among Orthodox Jews in Israel and certain communities in New York (cf. Henschke 2020).

Sometimes, explicitly religious ideas can overlap with other worldviews, as with anti-vaccination activists or followers of different conspiracy theories. The boundaries between religion and esotericism are fluid in the field of alternative medicine, where religious and worldview attitudes can also form an amalgam with political convictions (e.g. "Esoteric Nazism"). Just as there is the belief in "faith healings"—that is, the belief that the sick can be healed by prayer and laying on of hands without university medicine—there are those who believe that a strong faith protects against diseases. In secular guise, it is the trust in the power of positive thinking. But religious convictions can be combined with the belief that the danger of the Corona virus is exaggerated by state authorities and medical experts to the point that the existence of the Covid-19 virus is denied altogether. It is particularly problematic when preachers reinforce such convictions and incite their believers to resist the state and its orders. One example is the Sarang-Jeil Church in South Korea. More than one third of the new infections with Covid-19 that occurred in August 2020 took place in the context of this sect (cf. Erdmann 2020). Religion becomes a danger when it fuels the search for scapegoats. In Europe, medieval plague epidemics have on several occasions given rise to Jewish pogroms (cf. Graus 1994; cf. Scholl 2019, pp. 112 ff.). The Jews were accused of poisoning wells and thus causing mass death. Pogroms took place in southern France and the Holy Roman Empire in 1348/49. These were the worst persecutions of Jews until the Holocaust. Most of the Jewish communities were destroyed. The perpetrators were not only peasants, craftsmen and townspeople; in some cities, the collective murder of Jews was ordered from above. The murderous activities were tolerated by the Church, even though Pope Clement VI tried to refute the anti-Jewish conspiracy theory with rational arguments. Centuries later, the reformer Martin Luther blamed the Jews for the spread of the plague. When today parallels are drawn between the Corona pandemic and the times of the plague, one must also remember this dark side of the history of Christianity.

One of the ethical questions in connection with the Corona pandemic is the question of where the limits of freedom of religion lie. The fact that in the case of the Sarang-Jeil Church all church buildings were temporarily closed by the authorities is understandable for people who do not subscribe to the conspiracy theories of their main pastor. In Korea, there have even been some calls, to ban the sect. However, this would be a far-reaching interference with freedom of religion, which belongs to the universal human rights. We should also not forget that in Germany too, moderate Christians and journalists have discussed whether the closure of all churches on Good Friday and Easter was justified. According to the critics, at least in large churches and cathedrals, services could have taken place under strict safety regulations, because religious practice is not to be regarded as a potential source of danger, but also as a resource for coping with crises, for strengthening resilience and for social cohesion. However, during the lockdown, numerous churches were also open for individual prayer.

The following focuses on a diaconal-ethical perspective, since diaconal institutions, hospitals and nursing homes, but also mobile nursing services in diaconal ownership are a central part of the health system in Germany or Austria. In 2018 alone, almost 600,000 people were employed in diaconal institutions in Germany. With just under 700,000 employees, the German Caritas Association is the largest private sector employer association nationwide. Under the governance of church or diaconal health facilities, all health professions are represented. This is worth mentioning because medical questions in dealing with a pandemic like Covid-19 cannot be considered in isolation, but always in a larger systemic and social ethical context.

3 Christian Ethics

Faith is not a must. But even in a "secular age" (Charles Taylor) it remains an option (cf. Taylor 2009, pp. 843 ff.; cf. Joas 2012). The Church and the Diakonie consider it their task to bear witness to the gospel and God's unconditional turning towards people and his creation through their proclamation as well as their practical action in the world. The gospel is a source of faith, love and hope, not only of resilience, but also of solidarity and commitment to people in need of our help. The biblical message in times of Corona can be boiled down to a sentence from the second letter to Timothy: "God has not given us a spirit of fear, but of power and of love and of sound mind" (2 Timothy 1:7).

Every Christian ethic draws from this spirit. Christian ethics is an ethics of responsibility ("Verantwortungsethik") guided by the spirit of love (cf. Körtner 2019, pp. 85 ff. and pp. 112 ff.). The evangelical view of responsibility is directly related to the faith in the justification of the sinner by faith alone. On this basis, the distinction between person and work is made, which frees us from the compulsion of self-justification and thus enables us to assume responsibility. The perception and assumption of responsibility does not only take place in the knowledge that people can fail, but also in the confidence that we will be forgiven. Responsibility ethics in the Christian sense is not a casuistic legal ethic, but relies on the personal responsibility of those who find themselves in their freedom before God. People are not only capable of error and fallible, they can also become guilty despite all good will.

In addition to love and responsibility, freedom stands as a basic concept of evangelical ethics. The core of the biblical gospel is a message of freedom. "For freedom Christ has set us free!" Paul writes in Galatians 5:1 and warns against squandering the always endangered freedom of faith with a new legalism. Christianity is the religion of freedom, and all churches as well as diaconal institutions are to be measured by how far they are an institution of freedom. To have newly brought this to bear in theory and practice is the lasting importance of the Reformation.

In 1520 Luther published his treatise "On the Freedom of a Christian" (WA 7:3–38). It begins with a seemingly paradoxical double thesis: "A Christian is a free lord over all things and subject to no one. A Christian is a dutiful servant of all things and subject to everyone." (WA 7:21) Freedom in the biblical and reformatory sense is not to be confused with unlimited individualism and the supposed right of the stronger, but it is always paired with responsibility to God and our fellow human beings and can only be lived in the spirit of God's love and love of neighbor.

4 Human Dignity, Freedom and Responsibility

In the further course of the Corona pandemic, it will be very important to bring freedom and responsibility into a balanced relationship. The freedom to live and the dignity of the human being, which may not be offset against other goods, include the freedom to die, that is, the freedom to self-responsibly assumed health risks. If life and health are declared to be the highest good in an abstract way, the inevitable consequence is paternalism, which leads to the supervision and disempowerment of people. The commendable principle of protecting particularly vulnerable groups of people from Covid-19 must not lead to the supervision of patients and residents, who are ultimately protected to death from themselves, because people's survival is bought with a social death—the disproportionate restriction of visiting and freedom rights.

The measures taken to combat the Corona pandemic have not only saved lives, but have also come at the cost of health disadvantages and even damages. Think of patients who, in case of a suspected heart attack, did not go to the doctor or to the clinic, of postponed operations or of the psychological consequences of weeks of isolation, a worsening of confusion in people with dementia or the deterioration of the general condition of residents of nursing homes as a result of infection control measures.

According to a Christian understanding, every human being has the same dignity, which forbids to weigh human lives against each other. The utilitarian approach of the greatest possible benefit for the greatest number of people is in contradiction to this. Nevertheless, there can always be conflicts of interest in life, for example, when life is pitted against life.

In an interview, the German Bundestag President Wolfgang Schäuble, a confessing evangelical Christian, explained: "But when I hear that everything else has to give way to the protection of life, then I have to say: This is not correct in this absolute manner. Basic rights are mutually limiting. If there is a value that is absolute in our Basic Law at all, then it is the dignity of the human being. This is inviolable. But it does not preclude that we have to die." (Tagesspiegel.de 2020) And he added: "The state must ensure the best possible health care for everyone. But people will continue to die of Corona." (Tagesspiegel.de 2020) These sentences are not to be understood in a utilitarian sense. But they rightly point to a basic aporia of modern medicine and state health care.

After the end of the first lockdown and also during the second (partial) lockdown, the political dispute over the right way to fight the pandemic and the proportionality of restrictions on freedom has gained in intensity. Compared to the initial willingness to show solidarity among broad sections of the population, a shift has taken place. Personal responsibility is seen primarily in relation to one's own life and no longer to the same extent in relation to the community and the common good. One could say that it lies in one's own best interest to also show solidarity.[1]

The limits of individual freedom and the individual's right to take risks and possibly act in a self-destructive manner are reached when one's own behaviour endangers other people. It should also be borne in mind that in today's society we are precisely dependent on a strong welfare state and a functioning healthcare system in order to lead our lives in freedom. In order to maintain a functioning healthcare system and thus keep individual hospitals and care facilities functioning, restrictions on individual freedom are not only permissible in law but also ethically. However, the proportionality of such restrictions must be checked and corrected depending on the course of the pandemic.

Human dignity and the right to life go hand in hand. While the right to life was originally conceived as a defensive right ("Abwehrrecht"), it has increasingly become a participatory right ("Teilhaberecht") as a result of medical progress. The right to life now also means the individual's claim to the best possible healthcare. Health is an individual right and an individual good. But in the case of disease

[1] This aspect also plays a role in the debate on contact tracing and the question of whether suitable apps should be used on a voluntary basis or, as in some Asian countries, prescribed by law. See Schweizer Nationale Ethikkommission im Bereich Humanmedizin 2020a, Contact Tracing als Instrument der Pandemiebekämpfung.

control, it is also understood as a good that is supra-individual. To what extent can health be defined as a collective good in legal and ethical terms? As individual defensive rights, fundamental rights such as the right to life and the right to privacy not only protect against attacks or abuse by third parties, but also against the state itself. But how far does the right to protection *by* the state extend against a collective threat or even against the reckless, harmful behaviour of third parties? Example: Compulsory vaccination for measles. Would a vaccination obligation also be conceivable in the case of Covid-19? In general, or for certain groups of people (e.g. members of the health professions)?

5 Allocation Questions

Health is certainly not everything in life, but without a functioning healthcare system, hospitals and care facilities, the economy cannot exist. Without a thriving economy, of course, the existing health system cannot be maintained. Its preservation also includes maintaining the economic viability of hospitals and care facilities. The focus on bed capacity for Corona patients and the temporary closure of wards has led to significant revenue losses in clinics.

In the first phase of the pandemic, possible triage decisions were also discussed (cf. Körtner 2020b, pp. 12 ff.). Expert associations have developed guidelines for triage decisions in the context of the Corona pandemic. The German Ethics Council (2020) and the Austrian Bioethics Commission (2020) have also taken a position on this issue. Prioritization and triage are examples of the general allocation required in healthcare, i.e. the allocation of scarce resources to potential users. Allocation issues in healthcare arise not only in connection with the Corona pandemic (cf. Schöne-Seifert et al. 2006; cf. Gethmann-Siefert and Thiele 2008; cf. German Ethics Council 2011). Their transparent discussion is a democratic task in which the Church and Diakonie also have a role to play.

There are three levels of allocation:

- Macro level
- Meso level
- Micro level

Considered from a medical ethic point of view, allocation decisions should be made as far away from the individual patient as possible. This also applies to the care situation in the Covid-19 pandemic. First of all, it is necessary to alleviate the situation of scarce resources through appropriate allocation measures, such as the transfer of patients who do not require intensive care to an Intermediate Care Unit or to a Normal Ward. In principle, allocation requires not only *rationalization,* but also *rationing.* It should be noted that there are not only phenomena of under-supply, but also of over-supply and of wrong-supply, which can have a negative effect not only on the overall system from a medical-economic point of view, but also on the individual patient's well-being.

Basic principles for prioritization decisions are (1) the principle of justice (fairness) as well as the principles of (2) patient autonomy—i.e. as far as known, the patient's will—and the (3) human dignity. Another criterion is (4) the chances of survival and the prospect of clinical success.

The recommendations of the German Interdisciplinary Association for Intensive and Emergency Medicine (DIVI) and the Academy for Ethics in Medicine based in Göttingen, with regard to ethical criteria for prioritization and triage decisions state: "Accoding to the principle of equality prioritization is not justifiable only within the group of Covid-19 patients and *not* permissible *solely* on the basis of chronological age or social criteria." (German Interdisciplinary Association for Intensive and Emergency Medicine (DIVI) 2020, p. 4) In other words: On the one hand, there must be no age discrimination. The likely life expectancy after recovery is irrelevant for admission to an intensive care unit. On the other hand, even in the event of a disaster, intensive care beds are needed for other patients, for example for accident victims, heart attack and stroke patients or patients who have just undergone major surgery. Thus, in the event of a disaster, patients who are not infected with Covid-19 can also be affected by triage.

Particular attention must also be paid to the situation and development in stationary nursing homes (cf. Schweizer Nationale Ethikkommission im Bereich Humanmedizin 2020b; cf. Akademie für Ethik in der Medizin 2020). There is a danger that residents infected with Covid-19 will be transferred to hospitals too quickly. Here, a pre-triage is required in which, as part of the *Advanced Care Planning,* it is checked whether a patient can remain in the nursing home and, if necessary, also die there with palliative care. However, such decisions require careful weighing and justification, otherwise the age would be an exclusion criterion for nursing home residents. This, however, would violate the alleged ban on age discrimination. In this case too, multidisciplinary clinical ethics consultation is desirable, which can not only support individual decisions, but can also help to develop internal guidelines.

6 Ethical Culture and Dealing with Border Experiences and Guilt

Politicians like doctors and nurses, but also leaders in hospitals and social service organizations, have to make difficult decisions, even at the risk of getting it wrong. In April 2020, German Health Minister Jens Spahn said: "We will probably have to forgive each other a lot in a few months." (quoted after: SPIEGEL 2020) Christian ethics is aware of the limits of ethics, the fallibility of humankind, of guilt, but also of forgiveness. I wish for an ethical culture in hospitals with a church or social service background that is shaped by this awareness and by the spirit of strength, love and of a sound mind.

This should be reflected in a culture of ethical counseling, which is still in need of improvement in many places. The hospital staff needs psychosocial and pastoral support, also to deal with possible feelings of guilt. Hospital chaplaincy can play an important role here. Doctors and nursing staff need not only ethical counseling, but also comfort and support.

The pandemic makes people aware of their vulnerability and finiteness, also the vulnerability of a highly complex society and its social systems. People are looking for not only practical help, but also for support and comfort. Many people – perhaps without always saying it so directly—are now confronted with the question of what their only comfort in life and in death is (Heidelberg Catechism, Question 1). This is not only asked by sick or dying people and their relatives, but also by the relatives of health care workers who are exposed to special stress in times of Corona.

7 Dying in Times of Covid-19

In the periods of the lockdowns, the peculiarities and deficiencies of today's culture of death and dying become particularly clear. Already decades ago, the sociologist Norbert Elias described the loneliness of the dying in modern society (cf. Elias 1991). If the epidemiological view dictates the actions taken in the Corona crisis, the loneliness of the dying increases in intensive care units and in nursing homes. In the fight against the pandemic, it is sometimes overlooked that we all have to die, with or without Corona.

Dealing with death is highly paradoxical. It is present, but at the same time it is concealed. On the one hand, it is beyond question that everyone has to die. Medicine may have made great progress, but in the end the death rate is always 100%. However, death at the wrong time is to be avoided. Natural death, however, is in fact a utopia. The idea prevails that, if possible, people should reach a ripe old age and only die after a long, fulfilled life. One wishes for death as a peaceful extinction, which then no longer touches society. The French historian Philippe Ariès has characterized this idea as a "feral death" and a questionable attempt to "reconcile death with happiness" (Ariès 1980, p. 789; see Körtner 1996, pp. 11 ff.). In the Corona crisis, however, death was staged as an enemy and threat: "Soon," said then Austrian Chancellor Kurz, "each of us will know someone who has died of Corona." (Quoted from Kleine Zeitung 2020).

Doctors and nursing staff who have seen many people die of Covid-19 in recent weeks are more than ever emotionally burdened. If our mortality is suppressed, every death must be experienced as a failure. This leads to moral stress among clinical staff (see Eisele 2017). Only a medicine that allows death and does not treat it merely as a numerical value in the daily Corona statistics is a humane medicine.

Saying farewell to the deceased belongs to a human way of dealing with death. Religious mourning rites are part of the freedom of religion, which has been severely restricted in the containment phase. Interference with fundamental rights, including the right to visit and the pastoral care for the sick and dying, can be justified in the acute phase of a pandemic. However, their proportionality must be continuously checked.

Excessive measures that undermine the right to end-of-life care and a dignified farewell are not justifiable. According to the Robert Koch Institute, the risk of infection risk from those who have died from or with Covid-19 is no greater than of those who have died of influenza, as the virus is mainly transmitted by droplets (see Robert Koch Institute 2020). Dead people don't breathe. If usual hygiene standards are observed, there is apparently no reason why relatives should not say goodbye to the dead of Corona in person—also with pastoral care accompaniment. However, when religious rites are concerned, it must be ensured that the possible infection risk is taken into account. Doctors recommend avoiding contact with the body or ritual washing, or at least providing adequate protective equipment.

8 Outlook

Maintaining the health system has become more than ever a joint collective effort. How well it works, which therapies can be financed and how patients are cared for has become a very great challenge during economically hard times due to corona. For example, it is possible to quickly reach a consensus on the demand for greater appreciation of nursing staff. And of course, it is true that recognition must be expressed not only by public applause, but also by better pay. As long as it remains unclear who will bear the additional costs for higher wages, decisions of the legislature to raise salaries are questionable. Structural problems in inpatient and outpatient care and in particular in the field of old-age care cannot be solved solely by salary increases. Above all, what is needed is more staff and duty rosters that provide more time for the care and treatment of each individual patient. This takes us back to the allocation questions mentioned above.

In the end, all citizens will have to pay for the costs of the lockdown and the further fight against the Corona pandemic with their tax money. It is to be hoped that the discourse on key decisions will be conducted not only by a few experts, but again publicly and transparently. Here, too, the Diakonie and Caritas are called upon as stakeholders in the health care system and social policy actors. After the end of the lockdown, it is not only the time of the executive, nor is it the time of the parliaments alone, but now civil society is needed. A vibrant and free democracy cannot exist without civil society. Without it, the Corona crisis will not be manageable. The participation of religious experts is also required. Discussions between governments and representatives of religious communities with the aim of informing them about the measures decided by the state and seeking their consent and support cannot suffice in the long run. The Covid-19 virus will not disappear like a temporary storm. It has come to stay. We will have to learn to live with it, even if there are effective medications and a vaccine against Covid-19 in the foreseeable future. This requires not only medical or statistical expertise, but also sociological, psychological and cultural as well as theological expertise.

What role churches and Christian theology play in political crisis management and how they participate in the debates about the causes, consequences and possible solutions to the Corona crisis are not only questions of religious sociology and social ethics, but also of public theology (cf. Körtner 2020c; cf. Körtner et al. 2020). The religious communities are and remain an important part of civil society, even in a secular society like ours. I do not see their task solely in shaping the religious life of their members and advocating for their interests. It is not only about defending the freedom of religion—which also includes the right to freedom from religion—and the right to individual and collective religious practice in times of Corona. Rather, the religious communities also have the task of actively participating in the social and political discourse about dealing with the Corona pandemic. After all, this is part of the self-understanding of the Christian churches.

References

Akademie für Ethik in der Medizin (2020) Pflegeethische Reflexion der Maßnahmen zur Eindämmung von Covid-19. https://www.aem-online.de/fileadmin/user_upload/2020_05_12_Pflegeethische_Reflexion_Papier.pdf. Accessed 18 June 2020

Allmendinger J (2020) Die Frauen verlieren ihre Würde. https://www.zeit.de/gesellschaft/zeitgeschehen/2020-05/familie-corona-krise-frauen-rollenverteilung-rueckentwicklung. Accessed 18 June 2020

Ariès P (1980) Geschichte des Todes. dtv, München

DER SPIEGEL (2020) Spahn wirbt um Verständnis. https://www.spiegel.de/politik/deutschland/coronavirus-gesundheitsminister-jens-spahn-wirbt-um-verstaendnis-a-8b8cd313-2ea6-4a33-8683-c83ba3be7c3e. 22.04.2020. Accessed 28 Nov 2020

Deutsche interdisziplinäre Vereinigung für Intensiv- und Notfallmedizin (DIVI) (2020) Entscheidungen über die Zuteilung von Ressourcen in der Notfall- und der Intensivmedizin im Kontext der COVID-19-Pandemie. Klinisch-ethische Empfehlungen. https://www.divi.de/joomlatools-files/docman-files/publikationen/covid-19-dokumente/200325-covid-19-ethik-empfehlung-v1.pdf. Accessed 8 June 2021

Deutscher Ethikrat (2011) Nutzen und Kosten im Gesundheitswesen—Zur normativen Funktion ihrer Bewertung. Stellungnahme. https://www.ethikrat.org/fileadmin/Publikationen/Stellungnahmen/deutsch/DER_StnAllo-Aufl2_Online.pdf. Accessed 18 June 2020

Deutscher Ethikrat (2020) Solidarität und Verantwortung in der Krise. Ad-hoc-Empfehlung. https://www.ethikrat.org/fileadmin/Publikationen/Ad-hoc-Empfehlungen/deutsch/ad-hoc-empfehlung-corona-krise.pdf. Accessed 8 June 2021

Eisele C (Ed) (2017) Moralischer Stress in der Pflege—Auseinandersetzung mit ethischen Dilemmasituationen. Facultas, Wien

Elias N (1991) Über die Einsamkeit der Sterbenden in unseren Tagen, 7th edn. Suhrkamp, Frankfurt am Main

Erdmann K (2020) Kirchengemeinde wird erneut zum Corona-Hotspot. https://www.deutschlandfunk.de/suedkorea-kirchengemeinde-wird-erneut-zum-corona-hotspot.886.de.html?dram:article_id=482608. Accessed 2 Sept 2020

Evangelisch.de (2020) Landsberg: Hätte mir Öffnung der Kirchen früher gewünscht. https://www.evangelisch.de/inhalte/170315/19-05-2020/landsberg-haette-mir-oeffnung-der-kirchen-frueher-gewuenscht. Accessed 18 June 2020

Finger E (2020) Lasst die Seelsorger rein! https://www.zeit.de/2020/17/krankenpflege-altenpflege-seelsorge-pflegeheime-isolation-einsamkeit. Accessed 2 Sept 2020

Gethmann-Siefert A, Thiele F (ed) (2008) Ökonomie und Medizinethik. Fink, München

Graus F (1994) Pest – Geißler – Judenmorde. Das 14. Jahrhundert als Krisenzeit, 3rd edn. Vandenhoeck & Ruprecht, Göttingen

Harrer G (2020) Klopft Gott bei uns an? Der Standard. https://www.derstandard.at/story/2000116740623/klopft-gott-bei-uns-an. Accessed 2 Sept 2020

Henschke S (2020) Risikogruppe Ultraorthodoxe. Die Zeit. https://www.zeit.de/entdecken/2020-04/coronavirus-orthodoxe-juden-israel-pandemie-covid-19/komplettansicht. Accessed 28 Nov 2020

Joas H (2012) Glaube als Option. Zukunftsmöglichkeiten des Christentums. Herder, Freiburg

Junghans H (1983) Luther in Wittenberg. In: Junghans H (Hrsg) Leben und Werk Martin Luthers von 1526 bis 1546. Festgabe zu seinem 500. Geburtstag, vol 1. Vandenhoeck & Ruprecht, Göttingen, pp 11–37

Kaufmann T (2020) Pest und Cholerona. Wie Seuchen und Pandemien die europäische Geschichte prägten. https://zeitzeichen.net/node/8277. Accessed 2 Sept 2020

Kleine Zeitung (30. Mar 2020) Bundeskanzler Sebastian Kurz: "Bald wird jeder von uns jemanden kennen, der an Corona gestorben ist". Kleine Zeitung. https://www.kleinezeitung.at/politik/innenpolitik/5793215/Bundeskanzler-Sebastian-Kurz_Bald-wird-jeder-von-uns-jemanden. Accessed 28 Nov 2020

Körtner UHJ (1996) Bedenken, daß wir sterben müssen. Sterben und Tod in Theologie und medizinischer Ethik. Beck, München

Körtner UHJ (1998) Wie lange noch, wie lange? Über das Böse, Leid und Tod. Neukirchener, Neukirchen-Vluyn

Körtner UHJ (2019) Evangelische Sozialethik. Grundlagen und Themenfelder (= UTB 2107), 4. utb, Göttingen

Körtner UHJ (2020a) Ethik in Zeiten von Corona. Eine diakonisch-theologische Perspektive. In: Kröll W, Platzer J, Ruckenbauer HW, Schaupp W (eds) Die Corona-Pandemie. Ethische, gesellschaftliche und theologische Reflexionen einer Krise, Bioethik in Wissenschaft und Gesellschaft, vol 10. Nomos, Baden-Baden, pp 341–356

Körtner UHJ (2020b) Ethische Leitlinien für die Triage im Kontext von COVID-19. Ärzte Woche 34/17:12–14

Körtner UHJ (2020c) Religion und Corona. Eine erste Zwischenbilanz aus evangelisch-theologischer Sicht. https://konfessionskundliches-institut.com/allgemein/religion-und-corona/. Accessed 18 June 2020

Körtner UHJ, Anselm R, Albrecht C (eds) (2020) Konzepte und Räume Öffentlicher Theologie. Wissenschaft—Kirche—Diakonie, (= Öffentliche Theologie 39. Evangelische Verlagsanstalt, Leipzig

Lilie U, Lieberknecht C (2020) War die Kirche für die Alten da? https://www.zeit.de/2020/28/corona-krise-kirche-bischoefe-fuersorge-pflegeheime. Accessed 2 Sept 2020

Moser M (2020) Ethische Konflikte in Zeiten von Corona (Argumentarium Nr. 7 des Instituts für öffentliche Theologie und Ethik der Diakonie, Wien). https://diakonie.at/sites/default/files/diakonie_oesterreich/ethik/argumentarium_corona-200525.pdf#page=1&-zoom=auto,-82,848. Accessed 18 June 2020

Österreichische Bioethikkommission (2020) Zum Umgang mit knappen Ressourcen in der Gesundheitsversorgung im Kontext der Covid-19-Pandemie. https://www.bundeskanzleramt.gv.at/dam/jcr:772d37b0-3db9-4c8b-b4fe-e6dca7b1b8d3/200402_Covid_Bioethik.pdf. Accessed 18 June 2020

Prantl H (2020) Was war mit Glaube, Liebe, Hoffnung? https://www.sueddeutsche.de/politik/kirche-corona-kolumne-prantl-1.4992658?reduced=true. Accessed 2 Sept 2020-

Robert Koch Institut (2020) Empfehlungen zum Umgang mit SARS-CoV-2-infizierten Verstorbenen. https://www.rki.de/DE/Content/InfAZ/N/Neuartiges_Coronavirus/Verstorbene.html. Accessed 18 June 2020

Scholl C (2019) Die Judenverfolgungen zur Zeit des Schwarzen Todes am Beispiel der oberdeutschen Reichsstädte Ulm, Augsburg und Straßburg. In: Pest! Eine Spurensuche. Ausstellungskatalog zur Sonderausstellung "Pest!". LWL-Museum für Archäologie Herne (Hrsg), Darmstadt, pp 112–121

Schöne-Seifert B, Buyx A, Ach JS (eds) (2006) Gerecht behandelt? Rationierung und Priorisierung im Gesundheitswesen. Mentis, Paderborn

Schweizer Nationale Ethikkommission im Bereich Humanmedizin (2020a) Contact Tracing als Instrument der Pandemiebekämpfung. https://www.nek-cne.admin.ch/inhalte/Themen/Stellungnahmen/NEK-stellungnahme-Contact_Tracing.pdf. Accessed 18 June 2020

Schweizer Nationale Ethikkommission im Bereich Humanmedizin (2020b) Schutz der Persönlichkeit in Institutionen der Langzeitpflege. Ethische Erwägungen im Kontext der Corona-Pandemie. https://www.nek-cne.admin.ch/inhalte/Themen/Stellungnahmen/NEK_Stellungnahme_Schutz_der_Persoenlichkeit_in_Institutionen_der_Langzeitpflege_-_final.pdf. Accessed 18 June 2020

Stichweh R (2020) An diesem Imperativ kann die Politik scheitern. https://www.faz.net/aktuell/feuilleton/debatten/an-diesem-imperativ-kann-die-politik-scheitern-16714610.html?premium=0xb23580cb82b0ebc56a9c91cb03f39bcb. Accessed 18 June 2020

Tagesspiegel.de (2020) Schäuble will dem Schutz des Lebens nicht alles unterordnen. https://www.tagesspiegel.de/politik/bundestagspraesident-zur-corona-krise-schaeuble-will-dem-schutz-des-lebens-nicht-alles-unterordnen/25770466.html. 26.04.2020. Accessed 1 Dec 2020

Taylor C (2009) Ein säkulares Zeitalter. Suhrkamp, Frankfurt am Main

Pandemics, Medicine and Ethics. An Outlook

Andreas Reis, Martina Schmidhuber and Andreas Frewer

Contents

References 346

Already in ancient Egypt and Greece, epidemics such as smallpox, leprosy, diphtheria and tuberculosis were described (Nelson and Williams 2014). Relevant legal and (medical) ethical questions were also discussed in the times of the Codex Hammurabi (Winckler 1902) and Sun Simiao (Unschuld 2005). But only since the beginning of the 21st century are pandemic-relevant prevention and treatment measures and programs subjected to a systematic ethical analysis by the relatively young discipline of "public health ethics".

HIV, tuberculosis, SARS, pandemic influenza, MERS-CoV, Zika, Ebola and now Covid-19: all these epidemics and pandemics have caused major crises in recent decades, often with far-reaching individual, social and economic consequences at national and international level. Pandemics and crises force us to make decisions, and differential justifications grounded in ethics and action theory are a central criterion of good planning and action. This is already contained in the linguistic root of the word "crisis" from the Greek verb "krinein" for "decide".

A. Reis (✉)
Health Ethics and Governance Unit, Department of Research for Health, World Health Organization, Geneva, Switzerland
e-mail: reisa@who.int

M. Schmidhuber
Professorship for Health Care Ethics, Karl Franzens University Graz, Graz, Austria
e-mail: martina.schmidhuber@uni-graz.at

A. Frewer
Professorship for Ethics in Medicine, Erlangen-Nürnberg University, Erlangen, Germany
e-mail: andreas.frewer@fau.de

© The Author(s), under exclusive license to Springer-Verlag GmbH, DE, part of Springer Nature 2023

A. Reis et al. (eds.), *Pandemics and Ethics*,
https://doi.org/10.1007/978-3-662-66872-6_20

While some ethical questions have already been dealt with in individual articles in the context of pandemics, the present volume tries to provide a more comprehensive overview of the most important topics. Despite the diversity of contributions in this volume, there are of course still other relevant topics; therefore, some of them should be mentioned here. One group of people who, according to recent studies, suffered particularly from the conditions of the Covid-19 pandemic, were those of children and adolescents. They were not allowed to go to school for many months, therefore they did not meet their friends anymore and were, to a large extent, "at the mercy" of their stressed parents who had to work from home. In smaller apartments with several children, this situation was particularly burdensome. While the lockdown in spring 2020 was still tolerable because one could at least stay outside more and was also allowed to do so without contacts for compensation, the situation in autumn and winter 2020 was more difficult over the cold months. In seasons when one usually finds staying home cozy, if this becomes a duty, it can lead to great tension, violence and even abuse in families. According to a study that was carried out at the beginning of the pandemic, mental disorders in children and adolescents increased from 18 to 31%. Hyperactivity, emotional problems and behavioral disorders were mentioned most often (Deutsches Ärzteblatt 2020). In addition, the elimination of child care can also impair important current intangible interests in the well-being of infants. The minimized contacts to the outside and the often for children tangible stress of their parents—such as exhaustion and existential fears—can burden children very much. The easygoingness and the play with peers are lost (cf. Ahadzada 2020 and Platz 2020).

People with a migrant background are also among those who face great challenges in a pandemic, because they are the ones who are particularly affected by unemployment. But precarious employment relationships and the associated precarious living conditions also increase the risk of infection (Giesing and Hofbauer 2020); just think of the accommodation for harvest workers or low-wage workers in factories. In times of a pandemic, racism also increases. Intersectionality plays a special role here, as the example of women with a migrant background shows. The many challenges during a pandemic that people of different social and cultural backgrounds have to cope with can lead to poverty. In this context, it is essential to distinguish between different concepts of poverty that can play a role in the crisis (for the following see Döring 2003). First of all, it should be noted that poverty is a lack of goods, both intangible and monetary. (1) The basic distinction is between absolute and relative poverty: Absolute poverty means that a subsistence minimum is undershot and as a result basic physical needs, such as food, clothing, and housing, can no longer be covered. Relative poverty, on the other hand, is defined in relation to the social conditions of persons. Limited participation opportunities in social life are in the focus here, e.g. when it is not possible to afford the theatre visit with friends. (2) Another distinction is made between material and immaterial poverty. Material poverty refers to the lack of goods and services such as food, clothing and shelter. Immaterial poverty is also called social poverty because it is about social, ethnic, religious, cultural and political aspects of the human being and to what extent one can participate in social life. (3) The distinction between objective and subjective poverty refers to the perception of the affected person or outsider. So objective poverty can be seen from the outside, it is measurable and also provides information about the claim for social assistance. Subjective poverty, on the other hand, refers to the view of the affected persons themselves. It is about the feeling of insecurity in everyday life, lack of perspective, powerlessness and exclusion. Subjective poverty is often not recognizable from the outside because it is based solely on personal experience. (4) Furthermore, fought and hidden poverty are differentiated. People who claim social assistance fight their poverty by securing their subsistence minimum. If people do not claim their social assistance, whether out of ignorance or shame, it is hidden or latent poverty. These people then try to get by with means below the subsistence minimum. (5) Finally, temporary and persistent poverty must be distinguished. If there is temporary poverty, e.g. during the time of studies, one speaks of temporary poverty because students have to get by with little money over a certain period of time, but there is a general perspective for the future. They can normally (!) assume that they will get a good job after completing their studies. The situation is different with permanent poverty: Here the perspective of a better future is lacking, for example if someone receives a very low income continuously. Based on these five distinctions, it becomes very clear that poverty is multidimensional and that many people are affected by one form of poverty or even several during a crisis. Since social life can be greatly reduced, single people in particular may feel particularly affected by immaterial poverty. Students can no longer be sure that they will escape temporary poverty despite a good degree as a result of the crisis, which has also hit the labour market full force. Subjective poverty can affect people who have never had money problems before, but suddenly have existential fears because their job has become insecure.

Ebola and Covid-19 have shown that, in addition to investments in the discipline of health ethics for better global "pandemic preparedness", significantly greater international cooperation in the sense of global solidarity is also needed (see chapters Kieslich and Prainsack). On the one hand, it is urgently necessary to intensify the efforts of the international community to develop vaccines, diagnostics and therapeutics for potentially pandemic-causing pathogens. Over seven years ago, WHO and its partners established the "WHO R&D Blueprint" to promote research into a number of diseases associated with a high risk of epidemics (WHO 2016). Examples include MERS-CoV, Ebola, Lassa, Zika and Marburg fever. While the Covid-19 pandemic has shown that it is possible to develop several effective vaccines within a year by means of massive investment, this could take much longer for other diseases (see, for example, HIV). Nevertheless, despite some progress in this area, the efforts must be considerably intensified in the next few years if the international community wants to reduce the risk of the next pandemic.

On the other hand, the Covid-19 pandemic—like pandemic influenza in 2009—has once again clearly pointed to the inadequate or non-existent international solidarity, in particular in the area of fair access to vaccines. Supported by several lower and middle income countries, Indonesia, for example, refused in 2007 to hand over bird flu virus samples for the development of vaccines to the international community, with the argument that the country would not have access to these vaccines until years later (and thus too late!) (Fidler 2008). This finally led to the "Pandemic Influenza Preparedness (PIP) Framework" after more than two years of tough negotiations (see https://www.who.int/influenza/pip/en/). The aim of this framework agreement was to strengthen the exchange of influenza virus samples and at the same time to guarantee fair access to influenza vaccines resulting from research for lower and middle income countries. Unfortunately, since 2011, the international community has failed to develop a similar framework agreement for all potentially pandemic-causing pathogens beyond influenza.

The Covid-19 pandemic made these shortcomings glaringly apparent. A coalition had to be hastily forged in order to achieve at least a minimum of fair access to Covid-19 vaccines for lower and middle income countries: The "Covid-19 Vaccines Global Access (COVAX)" initiative, led by WHO, the World Bank, the EU, GAVI, CEPI and other organizations, set the goal of initially vaccinating 20% of the population of all countries (WHO 2020). However, most industrialized countries secured the lion's share of vaccine production for 2021 through pre-contracts with the pharmaceutical industry, often to cover their populations 200% with vaccinations. The later increasing willingness to also let poorer countries share in the blessings of the vaccines was probably less due to international solidarity than to the realization that virus mutations in lower and middle income countries can very quickly produce new, possibly vaccine-resistant strains of viruses and spread them worldwide. For this reason, calls were made to restrict patent protections for Covid-19 vaccines (and in future pandemics in general) and possibly even to oblige the industry to a kind of "compulsory production". South Africa and India submitted such a request to the World Trade Organization (Danaiya Usher 2020); however, the effectiveness of such measures in increasing vaccine production is highly controversial among experts. The establishment of local production capacities in lower and middle income countries certainly plays a decisive role.

However, close international cooperation appears to be important at all levels. Once again, the COVID-19 pandemic showed alarmingly immature patterns of national resentment. If, for example, a Covid-19 repeatedly underestimating former US president spoke pejoratively and blamefully of the "China Virus", this is just as unspecific as an expression of the use of populist enemy images. This continued on several other levels: In Great Britain, for example, only the "Turkish" developers of the BioNTech vaccine were mentioned at times and the location of Germany was omitted, while in return the vaccine developed in England by AstraZeneca also gave rise to specific reservations in other European countries—triggered by the difficult constellation in the hot phase of Brexit and English-European export differences (see, for example, "vaccine wars" in the yellow press). Here, the international community of states fell back into immature, unscientific and ultimately unproductive clichés of nationalist stereotypes or patterns of discrimination. Global cooperation and practical solidarity in coping with the Covid-19 crisis are central ethical desiderata that ultimately lead to success in implementation.

The epidemics and pandemics of recent years, in particular pandemic influenza, Ebola and Covid-19, have underlined what a crucial role the discipline of health ethics/public health ethics can play in policy advice and development as well as the implementation of socially acceptable options for action. At the same time, however, they have also shown that a certain further development of the discipline is necessary, accompanied by increased investments on the side of politics and academic institutions, in order to be better prepared for future crises. On the micro level, for example, the nationwide establishment of Clinical Ethics Committees (CECs) in all hospitals is an important desideratum, as well as the setting up of Committees for Ethics in Healthcare (CEHs) at the meso level (cf. Frewer chapter). At the national level, there are currently around 100 ethics committees worldwide, but for various reasons—e.g. mandate, expertise, resources etc.—by far not all of them are able to provide effective policy advice in times of crisis. Here, in many countries, further investments are still needed to strengthen existing or newly establish national ethics committees (cf. Hummel and Reis chapter). Since many urgent ethical questions—e.g. vaccine distribution and travel restrictions—cannot be solved at the national level alone, the international cooperation of national ethics committees must be further strengthened, both regionally and globally. International networks, such as the regional and global summit meetings, as well as the "Public Health Emergency Preparedness and Response Ethics Network" should play a central role in the future. In addition, ethics must be much more integrated into pandemic preparedness measures, and the existence of an "ethics infrastructure", i.e. CECs, CEHs, research ethics committees and national ethics committees, should be included in monitoring and evaluation (M&E) instruments, as an essential indicator for good pandemic planning, in a similar way to the availability of laboratory and surveillance capacities. Risks posed by new mutations, fairness in vaccine distribution, differential protection measures for vulnerable groups and many other questions: nationally and globally, the world is facing major challenges. A culture of ethical reflection in crisis management and decision-making is needed at all levels. In the present volume, expertise from seven countries on several continents has been brought together in the shortest possible time—international cooperation and solidarity will also be key in coping with the enormous current problems as well as future pandemics.

THE ENGLISH VERSION: The German version of this book, "Pandemien und Ethik", was published in 2021. Since the finalization of the various chapters of the book in mid-2021, the world experienced several further waves of the Covid-19 pandemic and related debates about ethical issues. As the herd immunity increased and the Covid-19 related mortality decreased, some of the basic parameters for the discussions—e.g. on mandatory vaccinations—were considerably altered. In addition, on July 23, 2022, the WHO Director-General declared the escalating global monkeypox outbreak a Public Health Emergency of International Concern, and more recently, both Ebola and Marburg virus outbreaks have taken place. So the editors of this book fully recognize that while some of the chapters are timeless, some other chapters, in particular those dealing with Covid-19 specifically, would have benefited from updates and new aspects could certainly have been added. Moreover, for an international version, a broader authorship with perspectives from all around the world would be desirable. However, the present English book is an AI-based translation of the German original version of 2021, with only very minor updates. We are still convinced that this translated version can serve to provide an international audience with useful insights. The publisher is considering a major update for a potential new edition of the book in 2024/2025.

References

Ahadzada A (2020) Coronapandemie: Psychische Gesundheit von Kindern verschlechtert. Deutsches Ärzteblatt 8:340

Boylan M (Ed.) (2022) Ethical Public Health Policy Within Pandemics.Theory and Practice in Ethical Pandemic Administration. Springer, Berlin

Danaiya Usher A (2020) South Africa and India push for COVID-19 patents ban. Lancet 396:1790–1791. https://doi.org/10.1016/S0140-6736(20)32581-2. Accessed 4 Mar 2021

Döring D (2003) Armut: Begriffliche Unterscheidungen. In: Böhm R, Buggler R, Mautner J (eds) Arbeit am Begriff der Armut. Working papers. Salzburg, pp 26–30

Fidler D (2008) Influenza virus samples, international law, and global health diplomacy. Emerg Infect Dis 14(1):88–94. https://doi.org/10.3201/eid1401.070700. Accessed 4 Mar 2021

Giesing Y, Hofbauer M (2020) Wie wirkt sich Covid-19 auf Migration und Integration aus? In: ifo Schnelldienst, ifo Institut—Leibniz-Institut für Wirtschaftsforschung an der Universität München 73/07, pp 41–46

Jäggi CJ (2021) Die Corona-Pandemie und ihre Folgen.Ökonomische, gesellschaftliche und psychologische Auswirkungen. Springer Gabler, Berlin

Lohse AW (Hrsg.) (2021) Infektionen und Gesellschaft.COVID-19, frühere und zukünftige Herausforderungen durch Pandemien.Springer, Berlin

Nelson K, Masters Williams C (2014) Early history of infectious disease: epidemiology and control of infectious diseases. In: dies (eds) Infectious disease epidemiology. Theory and practice. Jones & Bartlett, Burlington, pp 3–18

Platz M (2020) Wohlergehensverluste bei Kleinkindern durch den coronabedingten Wegfall der außerhäuslichen Betreuung. Eine kritische kinderethische Analyse der Betreuungsverbote und -einschränkungen. Z Prakt Philos 7/2:359–384

Shaw R, Gurtoo A (Eds.) (2022) Global Pandemic and Human Security. Technology and Development Perspective. Springer, Berlin

Ulrich CM, Grady C (Eds.) (2022) Nurses and COVID-19: Ethical Considerations in Pandemic Care. Springer, Berlin

Unschuld P (2005) Sun Simiao. In: Gerabek W, Haage B, Keil G, Wegner W (eds) Enzyklopädie Medizingeschichte. de Gruyter, Berlin

WHO (2016) An R&D blueprint for action to prevent epidemics. World Health Organization, Geneva

WHO (2020) WHO concept for fair access and equitable allocation of COVID-19 health products. Final working version 9 September 2020. World Health Organization, Geneva

Winckler H (1902) Die Gesetze Hammurabis, Königs von Babylon, um 2250 v. Chr. Das älteste Gesetzbuch der Welt. J. C. Hinrichs, Leipzig

FSC
www.fsc.org
MIX
Papier aus verantwortungsvollen Quellen
Paper from responsible sources
FSC® C105338

If you have any concerns about our products,
you can contact us on
ProductSafety@springernature.com

In case Publisher is established outside the EU,
the EU authorized representative is:
Springer Nature Customer Service Center GmbH
Europaplatz 3, 69115 Heidelberg, Germany

Printed by Libri Plureos GmbH
in Hamburg, Germany